Sustainable Urban Plannin

the design of building the City doth go on apace; and by
description, it will be mighty handsome, and to the satisfaction
of people. But I pray God it will come out not too late.

Samuel Pepys, Sunday, 25 November 1666,
two months after the Great Fire of London

Sustainable Urban Planning

Tipping the Balance

Robert Riddell

350 Main Street, Malden, MA 02148-5020, USA
108 Cowley Road, Oxford OX4 1JF, UK
550 Swanston Street, Carlton, Victoria 3053, Australia

First published 2004 by Blackwell Publishing Ltd

Library of Congress Cataloging-in-Publication Data

Riddell, Robert, 1934–
  Sustainable urban planning : tipping the balance / Robert Riddell.
    p. cm
  Includes bibliographical references and index.
  ISBN 1–4051–0289–6 (alk. paper)—ISBN 1–4051–0290–X (pbk. : alk. paper)
  1. Urban ecology.   2. City planning—Environmental aspects.   3. Sustainable development.
I. Title.
HT241.R53 2003
307.76—dc21   2003051819

A catalogue record for this title is available from the British Library.

Set in 10 on 12.5 pt Palatino
by SNP Best-set Typesetter Ltd., Hong Kong
Printed and bound in the United Kingdom
by MPG Books Ltd, Bodmin, Cornwall

Illustrations by Bruce Weir

For further information on
Blackwell Publishing, visit our website:
http://www.blackwellpublishing.com

Contents

List of Boxes

List of Figures

Acknowledgements

At base the design features incorporated into this book emanate from practice. I gratefully acknowledge the experience also gained and lessons learned from my own and James Lunday's studio classes at Auckland University; student-planner design efforts for tract after tract, setting out to free up community space, provide mixed-use neighbourhoods, and doubling – often quadrupling – the formula density. An outstanding illustrator from these classes was Bruce Weir who cheerfully took on the job of preparing most of the line drawings featured as urban detail in chapter 5 (Urban Growth Management).

There are colleagues and friends to acknowledge; bringing back pleasurable ever-fresh memories. At the University of Newcastle-upon-Tyne 1964–72 Paul Brenikov and Cameron Blackhall. From Cambridge 1972–84 David Williams (Wolfson College President, later Vice-Chancellor), and the late Paul Howell also of Wolfson College. At Auckland University (1984–2000) I was influenced by, and remain grateful to past and present faculty colleagues, who will I hope warm to passages where they discern vestiges of their influence: Jim Dart, Derek Hall, Michael Pritchard, Morris Taylor, Harry Turbott, Tricia Austin, Dan Barry, Jeanette Fitzsimons, Robert Hotten, Megan Howell, Mark Tollemache, Tony Watkins, Elizabeth Aitken-Rose, Hirini Matunga, Catherine Edmeades, Bill Berrett, Marjorie van Roon, Robert Collin and Mark Bellingham. I am also grateful to Phil McDermott, latterly Professor of Planning at Massey University, for his insight and support.

Following retirement from Auckland University I was fortunate to be invited to assist at Auckland's UNITEC campus where I teach a little, use the excellent library service, and profit from the stimulus of new design insights, for all of which my particular thanks go to Jacqueline Margetts, Katrina Simon and Rod Barnett; and also to my stimulating and helpful new colleagues in the School of Landscape and Plant Science.

New Zealand affords a capsule context for studying the New World regional urban and suburban situation, and the sustainability phenomenon, with research support for an individual academic in proportion to the nation's population! This I have cause to regard as an advantage in the wider context of open scholarship and freedom of expression. So, armed with institutional support from the University of Auckland, and with the benefit of sabbatical visits to the other Anglo-styled settler societies and their groves of academe, I set about this project.

I remain ever-grateful to my spouse Heather for her long-suffering patience, loving support, and tolerant understanding of this project. My daughters Kate Taylor and her husband Louis, and Anna Brown and her husband Steve, have been ever helpful: best of all matching my work-rate with the production of magical grandchildren – Phoebe, Bonny, Grace and Oliver – who, along with the frank and guileless little ones at Helensville Montessori, are a constant reminder of the need for sustainable and secure urban places.

Glossary

[Monetary references throughout are in US dollars]

Aboriginal   First native peoples of New World nations generally; and
                    specifically of Australia.

Aboriginal autonomy Formal recognition of the special standing of 'first native
                    peoples' in New World Nations; legally recognizing their
                    resource attachments, their policy basis for resource
                    development, and their structure of representation within
                    State Administrations.

affordable housing Being 'housing that can be afforded by households with
                    incomes of 80 percent or less of metropolitan area median
                    income, paying [financed from] no more than 30 percent
                    of the gross [household] income for housing' (Connerly
                    and Muller 1993).

Agenda 21   Outcomes for the twenty-first century from the 1992
                    United Nations Conference on Environment and
                    Development, at Rio de Janeiro. (See also Local Agenda
                    21s.)

agricultural unit   An economically viable unit of agricultural production –
                    capable of providing an income from farm production
                    sufficient to meet all business out-goings *and* sustain a
                    family living on the site, without recourse to supplemen-
                    tary incomes.

AMCORD   Australian Model Code for Residential Development.

APEC   A negotiating protocol for institutionalizing (1997) an
                    Asia Pacific Cooperation Forum

Australasian   Pertaining to Australia *and* New Zealand. Also *antipodean*.

capacity building	The enablement and empowerment of stakeholders to participate effectively in development and conservation: i.e. to effect an improving impact on the environment and habitat through effective participation.
CER	A protocol for Closer Economic Relations between Australia and New Zealand.
CNU	Congress for New Urbanism; a US-based coalition of urban professionals promoting diversity of design and population in pedestrian-scaled ecologically sound urban environments.
conservation	In environmental terms, and from many social aspects, a retention of acceptable (usually 'native') flora and fauna, together with soil water and air purity; sustainably and indefinitely. Conservation sets out to deliver 'the greatest good to the greatest number for the longest time possible' (Gifford Pinchot, cited in Stewart, Drew and Wexler 1999).
CBD	Central Business District
CZM	Coastal Zone Management
development	Progressive advancement of an overall sense of material improvement over time. *Sustainable Development* expands and enhances the quality of human life without debasing the ecological capital.
EEZ	Economic Exclusion Zone
Ex-urban	The prefix 'ex' relative to the noun 'urban' denotes landscapes which are physically beyond the urban edge, although not wholly within the rural heartland. Ex-urban landscapes can be thought of as uneven bands around settlements, often lying within the influence and attraction of one or more settlements. Ex-urban localities offer opportunities to reside (the *dominant* activity), in close proximity to some farming (the *regressing* activity).
eminent domain	The doctrine which decrees that individual rights yield to collective interests; thus the right of a state government to take private property for public purposes.

empowerment   A term which can be regarded as similar to but less
                    politically centrist than 'enablement'.

enablement   The inculcation of skills and education for enabling indi-
                    viduals and communities to comprehend their situational
                    circumstances responsibly, enabling them to take eco-
                    logically acceptable action and to make progressive social
                    change. Self-esteem and mutual trust are outcomes of
                    enablement.

GATT   General Agreement on Tariffs and Trade.

GIS   Geographic Information System

hh   Households (per acre/hectare)

inclusionary   Controls aimed at specifying a category of uses and users
                    for inclusion in a specified area. Inclusionary 'rural'
                    zoning is aimed at including rural activities, land uses
                    and farming occupiers – and by inference, excluding the
                    likes of urban activities and urban-worker residents.

Landcare   Rural land-use programmes engaging a bottom-up
                    philosophy wherein landowners are guided to identify
                    their own problems and provide their own sustainable
                    solutions.

Local Agenda 21s   A phrasing coined from the 1992 'Rio Declaration' (United
                    Nations Conference on Environment and Development)
                    published as *Agenda 21* – an agenda for environment and
                    development in the twenty-first Century. A 'Local Agenda
                    21' is a policy-and-plan document which embodies the
                    Rio Declaration principles in a local manner and style. See
                    Appendix to chapter 5.

MAI   Multilateral Agreement on Investment, an 'on hold'
                    global protocol for free trade without tariffs.

metric equivalents *Distances*: One metre is 3.28 feet (1 foot is 0.305 m); 1
                    kilometer is 1000 m: approximately 0.62 mile: one mile is
                    1.61 km.
                    Areas: Hectare 10,000 m^2 – and approx 2.5 acres: one acre
                    is 43,560 sq. ft. – and aprox 0.4 ha. 1 m^2 equals 10.75 sq. ft.

NAFTA	North America Free Trade Agreement

neomodernism — In the context of this writing, both a condition and an attitude whereby monetized growth, industrial production, and consumer expansion (all modernist) are redirected toward social and resource *sustainability*, wherein utility of the resource base to support future populations is not compromised. 'Modernism' is of the consume-and-discard *present*. 'Neomodernism' invokes a future which extols societal fairness, environmentally balanced resource utilization, and economic harmonization. In this text neomodernism equates with sustainability. Most writing on neo(post)modernism is complex, and is seldom centred on sustainable pragmatics.

New World — For the purpose of this book, the reoccupied and resettled former frontier lands; with a particular association to the transpacific English-languaged Anglo-cultured settler society nations of the United States, Australia, Canada and New Zealand, cited in the text as the Anglo settler societies.

Northern Nations — The 'Rich Northern Nations' club which includes Canada, United States, Australia and New Zealand, for whom the Organization for Economic Cooperation and Development (OECD) predicates economic growth and employment and an ever rising standard of living.

planning — Public forethought and conscious involvement preceding the pursuit of community-determined action; achieving social goals for the common good in both the public and private domain. Carter (1993) holds 'the core definition of planning [to be an] ability to manipulate form and place'.

pp — Persons per (acre/hectare)

preservation — Additional to 'conservation': mothballing natural and heritage resources on account of their perceived societal significance.

settler societies — The mostly Euro-settled societies of the Anglo New World, incorporating the indigenous first peoples of those lands along with other subsequent incomers from Africa and Asia. Generally characterized by the use of English as the official language, with the Protestant ethic and Anglo-triumphalism prevailing. In a grouping: the United States, Canada, Australia, New Zealand – cited in these pages as the Anglo settler societies.

Southern Nations

The poorer 'Third World' nations comprising 70 per cent of the world total population, arising generally (Australasia excepted) in the 'southern' global sector. Also known as developing nations, and sometimes as under-developed nations. The per capita average annual incomes of Southern Nations do not exceed US$1,500 – but the harsh reality for over half the world population is that per capita average annual income is less than US$300.

subsidiarity

The political process whereby decision-taking is devolved to the lowest workable political level.

sustainability

A systemic people-controlled process combining conservation *with* development which sets out to meet consumer needs at socially and environmentally acceptable costs, and without degrading natural resource flows or depleting resource capital. The central tenet is consensus for a durable permanence. It is also held to be 'trans-generational' – in short *socially responsible, environmentally harmonious, and economically equitable*. Sustainability combines with neomodernism to fashion a future unimpaired by current practices. Distinction is made sometimes between 'weak' (local) sustainability and 'strong' (planetary) sustainability.

Terra Psyche

Appreciating the ownership and trusteeship of the earth as an extension from the soul of an individual; the qualitative affinity which humanity has with the land. (See box 1.1.)

think big projects

Macro, politically inspired, well-intentioned but economically, socially and environmentally discordant projects.

transpacific

For this text specifically: Canada, the United States, Australia, New Zealand.

triple bottom line	Engaging in and accounting for an economic-social-environmental balance between development and conservation. The 'environmental' context includes resources, and the 'social' context includes cultural and political factors.
urban	The *fractal* components within human settlements which link or cohere to provide a cityscape. In spatial terms most of the geographically occupied urban space is *suburban* – given over to human habitation in automobile-accessed households. In functional terms urban places mostly *import* foodstuffs and fibres, minerals and energy, and *export* heat, gaseous wastes, sewage, stormwater, and solid wastes. Urban communities evoke conceptually complex loyalties and loathings (Jackson's *Maps of Meaning*, 1989).
WTO	World Trade Organization. An outgrowth from Bretton Woods, the Uruguay Round, and GATT attempting the almost impossible: non-tariffed trade between poor and wealthy (and democratic and not-so-democratic) nations, protecting the environment, and safeguarding differentiated worker rights.

Introduction

The within-nation planning practices critically appraised in this book are grounded in the United States, Canada, Australia, New Zealand and also Britain, societies differing one from another, yet tethered to each other linguistically, culturally, *urbanistically*, and through their openly democratic styles of government.

A social conscience and a conservation ethic exists in every community. Concerns for the consequences of environmentally damaging and resource-depleting actions sit uneasily alongside individual desires to also achieve material prosperity. One consequence is that these Anglo-heritage nations have not proactively pursued the *Agenda 21* protocol (1992 Rio: *UN Conference on Environment and Development*). The major difficulty is that government and commerce regard profit gearing as a religiosity, binding politicians from both the 'left' and 'right' of centre into a growth-on-growth mantra. It is little wonder that most politicians, and some planning operatives, put their conservativism before conservation, property exclusion ahead of community preference, and allow resource plunder in denial of future generations. Much growth is substantially 'good', yet for settler societies it has not been 'good enough' in terms of overall socio-environmental outcomes.

Concern over the global future of course varies from nation to nation. Some poor nations, some small wealthy nations, and parts of some large rich nations find paths away from the 'growth at any cost' and 'urban sprawl' models. A socially balanced construct for economic growth, incorporating social wellbeing and environmental equilibrium, is established as the logical future course to follow – essentially a matter of doing well while doing good. The challenge is to identify useful and fulfilling styles of development which include a socially acceptable conservancy component. Aspiring to full harmony is a pipe-dream; yet a free-for-all commodification of resources is untenable. Attention to the overall *quality* of living, rural and urban, is the sensible way ahead for the North American and Australasian settler societies.

'Development' (progressive improvement in human living circumstances) is related to and dominates 'planning' (putting consciously predetermined public policy in place effectively). Self-evidently this is true for the New World – particularly the settler societies of Australasia and North America – where the planning function attracts much blame for the failures which litter those landscapes. What I have come to understand about regional growth patterning and urban planning practice is how permanent become policy changes blithely induced; and how in a decision-flash they can be a lasting influence for either 'good' or bad'. Get urban and rural policies wrong, and things mostly stay wrong; get them right, and development and conservancy practioners know that they have performed a beneficial and lasting service. These thoughts are based on an awareness of the socio-environmental significance of 'development' instilled during practice and research with mining, agriculture, tourism and urbanism in the service of less-developed (Third World) economies. That economic-social-environmental *bound-up together emphasis* is carried over to these pages.

During the 1970s I encountered a disappointing mismatch between the ecodevelopment policies put out by Tanzania, Jamaica and Papua New Guinea, and the actual on-site outcomes. And today, for OECD nations, there is many a mismatch between web-site and on-site. Contemporary student envoys, comparing official 'Local Agenda 21s' with actual situations on the ground, return disillusioned. This point is made to show how possible it is to be deluded into the writing of policy-making and design-formulation in a context removed from real on-the-job conservancy and development practice. Hence my emphasis on local people, local politics, local action, local habitat, local wellbeing and locally beneficial outcomes. Not 'everything', nor of course 'nothing', but *something* progressive and agreeable, achieved by 'tipping the balance'.

Ten years after 'Stockholm' I produced *Ecodevelopment*, addressing the Third World situation (1981). Now, ten years and more after 'Rio', the North American-Australasian context inclines toward an economic-social-environmental emphasis on 'sustainability' *with economic growth the policy lead*. Validating this growth-led emphasis in a populist way, it is worth reflecting for a moment about the automobile, pilloried as the root of much environmental evil. But what an amazingly useful invention, and what a dynamic accessory to individual freedom and choice it has proved to be. People can be encouraged to walk, bus, cycle, but should not be threatened with an absolute automobile ban. The path to neomodern sustainability is ever-improving progress based on good social and environmental science, *not* a leap of blind faith.

This book is about adaptations of a beneficial kind, most emphatically for sustaining a balanced quality of life which is realistic and realizable for the middle-income majority. The line of reasoning advanced is founded in historical reality, resource fact, the received landscape ecology and social understanding. The challenge for this new century is to retain and build on the vitality inherent in every community. Pragmatic sustainable performance of the kind sought is a function of the delivery of effective administrative power to the point of action. Get the delivery of power and policy wrong – likely with contra-indicated projects, confused sectoral administrations, and conflicting legal instruments – and the outcome is economic imbalance, entrenched social discord, and environmental degradation.

When the delivery of policy is effective – in a phrasing, cleverly steered toward balanced growth – the achieved result can be *economic growth advantage, social betterment and habitat enhancement* – a synergistic uplift to the overall quality of life. This can be metaphorically portrayed as a neomodern 'tapestry'. The 'belief warp' is democratic government, intoned by John Ralston Saul (1997) as 'the most powerful force possessed by the individual, her own government' – a neatly balanced quip which nests comfortably with the 'strategic weft' from Jane Jacobs's (1961) 'communities working with their social capital'. And it is on the basis of these and other exemplars, principally from North America, that this project sets out to reason for improvements to the urban habitat – the dominant way of life for Anglo New World citizens.

In terms of structure I have worked from the 'whole' (global ecological-economic problematics, and socio-environmental issues), to the 'part' (regions, cities, towns, suburbs). At its core the book addresses the use of *power*: will-power, household power, community power, regional power, and the political power of the state. What is targeted for explication is how socio-environmental improvements can be merged with consumer growth for the Anglo New World urban context where, confronted with a choice between 'sustainability' and 'consumerism' those societies have reacted, as Oscar Wilde would have advised, by choosing both! Engaging twentieth-century environmental science, the need is apparent to fashion a value-based methodology for bundling development policies together with conservation practice; to now walk the talk within openly democratic administrations which provide property security, fiscal stability, and contractual certainty.

The title for this book can be understood keyword by keyword by referring separately to 'sustainable', 'urban' and 'planning' in the Glossary: applying the contemporary take on 'sustainability' as a generalism in popular non-dictionary use. As a phrase *Sustainable Urban Planning* connotes process, something practised and delivered. The subtitle 'Tipping the Balance' needs no elaboration.

The lesser Principles block (chapters 1 and 2) addresses classical sources, attends to lessons from experience, and observes longer-cycle trends from what was to what is; and is definitional. The major Practice block leads with the elaboration of a 'Charter' (chapter 3), then turns to 'Growth Pattern Management' (chapter 4), and then attends to the specifics of 'Urban Growth Management' (chapter 5).

My through-line has been, and remains, one of getting sustainable-in-intent *conservation* connected to profitable-in-intent *development*.

Part I

Principles

All nations access and exploit the rural and some of their wilderness realms. Cities expand, mostly unconstrained, and incoherent suburban pods fatten-up.

For the top-third life is good. For the bottom-third the situation is ugly. The catch call is for the middle-third, the majority-commanding group, to heed this plight and target the sensible way ahead.

1

Sustainable and Ethical

Chapters 1 and 2 lay foundations: express definitions, establish theory, explore philosophical understandings. These are precursors to the practical guidelines given in later chapters: the 'Charter' (chapter 3), 'Growth Pattern Management' (chapter 4), and 'Urban Growth Management' (chapter 5). The reader versed in planning theory principles and philosophy, or bent on getting to grips with planning practice, can make direct access to the Practice section.

What impresses the newcomer to the Anglo settler society nations of Northern America and Australasia is how resource discovery, scientific and technological invention, and political force have so powerfully and rapidly imprinted a 'rightness' over the last two hundred years (pastoralism and agriculture as well as plantation forestry, along with urban settlement) and a conjoint 'wrongness' (flora, wildlife and soil evisceration, along with much misery for the indigenous 'first' peoples). What is easily overlooked is that in earlier centuries the Old World was also subjected to resource discovery, inventions and political forces which vastly modified the landscapes of those times – sometimes to a state of disutility.

Hindsight, into the working relationship of the inhabitants of Anglo settler societies – North American and Australasian – is the context for this book. It is a project which derives its rationale from a situation where most developers in OECD settler societies acknowledge environmental issues in the breach, and pursue projects for profit – a circumstance where the outcome for both profit taking and environmental conservation clearly could be more mutually supportive.

This scene-setting chapter focuses attention upon key issues explored in three passages: *first* there is some delving into 'development', 'planning' and 'sustainability'; *second* there is an attempt to deconstruct the meanings of 'property', 'interests' and 'neomodernity'; and the *third* passage provides a foundation understanding of sustainability in the neomodern context of the 'triple bottom line' paradigm – which is an amalgam of growth, community, ethical and environmental factors.

The historical connection between development and planning – that is between pragmatic development and politically led planning – is not a conundrum of the 'chicken or egg' kind, for clearly the development thrust for investment return

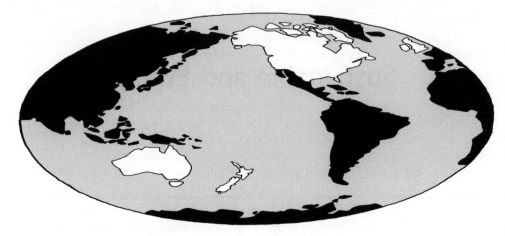

Figure 1.1 Anglo settler society nations. 'New Zealand, Australia, and Canada, all with strong frontier traditions, small [low density] populations, and a British-induced cultural dislike of cities, share the American [suburban] experience' (Kenneth Jackson, *Crabgrass Frontier*, 1985).

'Since the mid-eighteenth century, more of nature has been destroyed than in all of prior history.'
Hawken, Lovins, Lovins, *Natural Capitalism*, 1999

has always been dominant. Land-use patterning originated with community conflicts which arose when landowners set out to exercise their property rights unfettered, excluding all outside influence, even in some instances resisting zoning, that most normative of interventions.

At *best*, land policy determinations were arrived at previously with some assembly of data and analytical input as the precursor to either a 'letting out of the belt' or a 'filling in the gaps' pattern based on an expansive 10- to 20-year look ahead, inducing low densities for at least the first ten years. At *worst*, land-use practice was based on expansionist greed, originating with landowners and developers working with 'booster' local government leadership, largely ignoring or overriding planning advice and input. As evidence, the Anglo-settled North American and Australasian nations are adorned with plaques commemorating the frontier intrepidity of surveyors, the project prowess of engineers and architects, and the visionary inspiration of politicians – with few plaques in place or public service medals handed out to commemorate the work of urban planners.

Disclosed on the web by Andres Duany (1999) sourcing Jane Jacobs. 'The pseudoscience of planning seems almost neurotic in its determination to imitate empiric failure and ignore empiric success.'

The reality is that planning, and planners, fell in with exploitation-led and consumer-driven developer trends. Lacking a conservancy ethic, community leaders encouraged the production and use of formula rule books and plans, promoting the commodification of rural land assets into urban sprawl where, as evocatively related in Campoli, Humstone and MacLean's *Above and Beyond* (2002: 197) 'Like a dog chasing its tail we pursue the dream of unlimited space, unrestricted movement and total control (in situations where) What we want is is an unspoiled rural landscape, but in pursuing it, what we get is sprawl.' The way that suburbia exhibits these sprawl characteristics, for different North American and

Australasian situations, is well explained in *Visions of Suburbia* edited by Roger Silverstone (1997).[1]

One contemporary complication is the awesome efficacy of modern technology, another is the insatiable money-doubling expectation of investors. Some benefits can be identified for citizens, like the legal *certainty* enshrined by crude yet clear property rights zoning. There has also been, for property developers, the benefits to them of *departures* (sometimes known as dispensations) from the strictures of zoning and the rule book. There is also the *freedoms* for occupiers to consume and discard. All these 'certainties, departures and freedoms' are at odds with emergent community preferences to establish more socially acceptable environmental behaviour: and in pursuit of that ideal 'zoning based systems' have occasionally morphed into *Flexible Zoning* (Porter, Phillips and Lasser 1991) with pejorative results.

> 'The Human psyche can tolerate a great deal of prospective misery, but it cannot bear the thought that the future is beyond all power of anticipation.'
> Robert Heilbroner, 'Reflections', 1991

The money-based energy-fired and technologically inspired 'resource exploitation' and 'consumer discard' syndrome (explored more fully in chapter 3) has drawn political leaders and the populations of wealthier societies into a growth-on-growth maze, from which they can find neither the 'central meaning' nor a 'way out'. A socially driven planning function is one instrument of intervention available to communities for coercing, advising and regulating these development forces and consumer preferences. But it is now obvious that the outcomes (the output) are often failing society in terms of the quality and sustainability of the results being delivered up. This is a matter which calls for consumers to ensure that they win out against destructive producer preferences, pursuing, in a phrase, conservation with development.

> 'People became so obsessed by a hatred of government that they forgot it is meant to be their government, and is the only powerful public force they have purchase on.'
> J. R. Saul, *Unconscious Civilisation*, 1997

Acknowledging the need for conservation with development is not only a matter of seizing the moment, of shifting moral ground. It is also a battle to link business and the profit ethos to the development with conservancy ethic.

With the demise of glasnost and despotic governments most nation-states and their citizens work within the only remaining proven system, democracy. That style of governance cleaves, as it always has, to a business-for-profit and a growth-on-growth ethic, with corporate environmental responsibility now inserted into a wider Corporate Social Responsibility.

In a postscript to their recent *Environmental Discourse and Practice*, Benton and Short (1999) put the view that there is 'one common belief: society must change its attitudes about its use of the earth'. This 'belief' I fully endorse – it is on my wish list. But 'must change'? And 'society'? My own take on the socio-environmental compact is that movements in the direction of corporate social responsibility, which include corporate environmental responsibility, can partly be induced by championing the socio-environmental cause, can be more fully enforced through the use of regulatory instruments, but can only be really effective

> 'Economic growth has become the bogey of the ecologically anxious'
> Felipe Fernandez-Armesto, *Millennium*, 1995

> 'For most ecologists, big cities are off limits'
> Mari Jensen, *Ecology Moves Downtown*, 1999

when socio-environmental responsibility becomes part of profitable business practice.

I discern three business-style 'certainties' to new-age life in settler societies. The *first* is that new-age technology is certain – the solar-powered car will be followed by the hydrogen-powered car – and these new technologies will be as profitable to new-age business as the steam engine was to George Stephenson and the combustion engine was to Henry Ford. The *second* is that the bottom-line purpose of business will remain business for profit. The *third* is that new-age democratic governments will decree, variously, against energy use profligacy, the exploitative hollowing out of finite resources, the dumping of reusable waste, and the exposure of toxic residues to the biosphere.

'The complex environmental problems that challenge our future are the direct result of human, political, social and economic judgments exercised by nature *and on other people* during the preceding industrial age.'
Robert Collin and Robin Morris Collin, 'Sustainability and Environmental Justice', 2001 (Italics added)

Incorporating Fernando-Armesto's epilogic collation (*Millennium* 1995) adds in these additional 'certainties'. *Four*: population growth will be contained. *Five*: totalitarianism will return. *Six*: big states will continue to fragment.[2] *Seven*: cities will wither (!). *Eight*: initiatives will continue to shift.

And here are two more 'certainties' rounding up the set to ten. *Nine:* that domestic investing and government taxation will always outweigh the economic significance of international investments. *Ten:* that settler society governments will always be more powerful than corporations.

LIVING HEAVILY
Economic growth the objective
Dysfunctional suburbanism
Environmentally exploitative
Energy profligate
Waste disposing
Toxic dumping

LIVING LIGHTLY
Social harmony a priority
Balanced growth an ideal
Conservation with development
Energy efficient
Waste reused, reduced, recycled
Toxins closed-off from biosphere
Even-handed standards

My point, the point, is that the means to achieve environmental responsibility and social responsibility – better lifestyles – amounts to considerably more than moral browbeating and polemic grandstanding; what it calls for is a getting from 'here – living heavily' to 'there – living lightly'.[3]

Different administrations of varying complexion have diverse objectives. Different nations, and different regions within larger nations, have varying standards. Business, though, has one objective and one standard – stakeholder profits – and the generation of stakeholder profits conditions their make-up, now and in the future, within every open democracy. Governments can tax and legislate business as they variously see fit – but they will always ensure that legitimate enterprise is never put out of business. Indeed it is the job of government to fashion situations in which business can operate and profit. Business-based laws can be also passed to prohibit the dumping of toxins, to limit rates of non-renewable resource extraction, to achieve efficiencies in the use of renewable resources, and to observe the socio-environmental benchmarks and achieve socio-economic outcomes.

But a dilemma confronts. First there is the morality angle about which we hear a great deal; and then there is the matter of ethics (and philosophy) which has a covert objective, to ensure that the mistakes of a free-for-all past, and the desire for a harmoniously balanced future, do not get confused. Setting out to reconcile this dilemma enables us to get our heads around the fact that living off the environment, living together in communities, and living from the product of our work, are intertwined activities. It is no longer viable to separately compartmentalize human beings and nature, for it is now clear that if people keep on thinking that same old way they will keep on making the same mistakes. One clear objective is the formulation of 'conservation *with* development' to accompany 'business *with* profit'.

A lesson learnt is that when you pause to think about the consumer maze, frustration is encountered. If you already possess every material utility and have reached what could be supposed to be the 'centre', you will find that in fact nothing of real substance is there. The only satisfaction comes from either 'going back' or 'getting out'; it certainly does not lie with 'going on' as before.

The challenge, which is particularly a consume-and-discard *control* challenge, is for communities to safeguard and regulate the governance of their own habitat, in a phrase, for communities to be locally empowered. This is at base a matter of turning away from the as-of-right attitude to consumer growth and pollution discard which has been the mode of urban expansion since Fordist mass production of the automobile, and to turn away because the pattern is dysfunctional, namely *un*sustainable and ultimately *un*tenable. In short, without discarding established technological benefits from benign processes, the call is to recognize, respect and fit in with cyclical, seasonal, birth–life–death patterns of empowerment, conservation, development and human capacity.

'In the western mind scarcity is an aberration correctable by the appropriate application of capital, technology and labour. The response to scarcity is to apply more of these factors of production.'
Virginia Abernathy,
Population Politics, 1993

Is this a seeking of the impossible, particularly for settler societies which tend to play down the interventionist role of the state and play up an opportunist role for the market? The challenge is serious, massive and complex, *and* although a World Agency 'mandate' exists in terms of the *Agenda 21* initiatives (Appendix to chapter 5) neither growth-on-growth nor consumerist addictions and discard practices are easily forsworn or overthrown.

'two forms of confederation . . . the Portland [constrained-conservative] form, and the Orange County [freeflow-liberal] form, will compete for ascendancy. . . . the Orange County model will, on the whole, dominate.'
Robert Kaplan, *Empire Wilderness*, 1998

The consequences of *not* picking up the sustainability trace induces anxiety in many of those educated in economics, and deeper angst for those educated in the social sciences and the earth sciences. The late twenty-first-century situation for nations which retain access to the sustainable development option – and most nations certainly do retain this option – is that they can either square up to sustainability or gradually decline both materially and morally.

At the Rio Summit, 1992.
'The American way of life is not up for negotiation.'
George Bush [Senior],
US President

Development, Planning and Sustainability

For the wider purpose of this book the definition of growth goes beyond that which is natural and benign. It includes the synthetic (nuclear proliferations and toxic accumulations), the synergistic (multi-millionaires created from opportunism), and the hedonistic (resource depletions and discard accumulations) – all 'growth'! Understood as 'capitalism' the outcome is neatly summarized by David Landes's (1989) favourite cynicism 'that capitalism is the privatisation of gains and the socialisation of losses'.

A capsule definition for **development** is that it is a process which sets out to achieve progressive advancement to the human condition, involving taking action and attaining material growth and social fulfilment over time. Myerson and Rydin (1996) hold that 'development is only "real" if it improves the quality of life', which tends to establish that some development is 'bad' and, indeed, that 'good' development is only that which achieves progressive advancement to the human condition. What is under consideration here is the way the development-through-growth emphasis results in the commodification of land and landed resources, *along with* the generation of solid gaseous and liquid wastes, and an accumulation of irreducible toxins. A complication arises in that in 'new age' terms the process is now also expected to be 'sustainable' in the style of conservation with development – a coupling which has historically been characterized as mutually excluding.

An important point to make is that this matter of sustainability will not be socially acceptable or societally workable if it harps on about less consumption, a reduced economy and reduced profits, and, or also, an economic slowdown. From a Canadian perspective (Lucie Sauvré 2002) there is for sustainability a 'sort of "newspeak" that is spreading throughout the world, superimposed on each culture and reducing the ability to think differently about realities'. The trick is to enhance investment and growth within a sustainability framework. This involves the exercise of a strategic choice – to achieve conservation and development outcomes concomitantly, and consciously to set about creating and maintaining landscapes worth cherishing.

A selection from myriad definitions of **planning** is public forethought (the setting of objectives) and conscious involvement (the empowerment) before taking community-determined public-interest action to effect improved change. Thereby arises a compound definition for planning: a democratic advancement of the overall human condition; connecting public prescience (setting objectives); and conscious involvement (community discourse and empowerment) before action is taken to bring about improved change. This emphasis fits into a larger framework of understanding arising from a North American (Myers and others 1997) set of 'Anchor Points for Planning's Identification' which I summarize, add to, and rerank.

In these terms planning

- Links knowledge and action: connectedness
- Improves the humanized and natural environments
- Holds out for useful interconnections
- Focuses on the future

- Honours cycles: seasons, life patterns, highs and lows
- Designs artfully and redesigns thoughtfully
- Balances socio-economic-environmental outcomes
- Engages in a participatory style of decision-making
- Works for diversity and variety of outcome
- 'Works around' rather than 'pushing through'.

Aside from semantic quibbles, this compound list-phrasing portrays something democratic, spatially applied, and potentially flexible, in the public domain; a public-interest prescriptive matter which, following consultation and discussion, is *done and delivered*. Planning is the actual bringing about of desirable changes for an improved overall future through the medium of predetermined human action. It also involves the interpositioning of design, particularly growth pattern (regional) design and urban physical design.

Within democracies these desirable changes implicate a vast complexity, which can be viewed as part balance with, and part trade-off between, the 'pursuit of material growth', the 'attainment of social wellbeing' and the 'maintenance of an environmental harmony'. Another way to make this point is that *sustainable* planning embroils an all-resources (human, fiscal, physical) management. That context, in accordance with contemporary idiom, is where this writing 'is coming from': reformist in democratic intent within an enabling socio-economic-environmental context; in character 'neomodern' and in emphasis 'sustainable'.

'Sustainable development (and conservation?) meets the needs of present generations without compromising the ability of future generations to meet their own needs.'
World Commission on Environment and Development, 1987

Contrasting with depictions of 'development' and 'planning' no consistent capsule definition of **sustainability** can be produced, with each nation and every sector staking out different claims, all normal dictionaries becoming useless in a play where the goalposts are frequently moved. The general notion and discourse about sustainability is not misunderstood, even if it largely figures in tokenist statements and is observed 'in the breach' by most governments, many local communities and most individuals. It is in the urban context that the main blind spot occurs, the settlements where 80 to 90 per cent of the Anglo settler society populations live.[4] Here the population is unreservedly consumerist, and generally considered to be beyond sustainable recovery.[5] Urban places consume resources from without, and discard wastes to the beyond, to a degree which is in fact *un*sustainable!

Of course urban inhabitants could – and many do – live in a more sustainable way by reducing consumption and waste disposal. Over the longer term that kind of progressive outcome might be socially engineered, bringing into being a congruence of social policy and environmental justice – albeit *uneven* social policy and *rough* environmental justice. Along this path 'sustainability', a former 'specialism', is now becoming a core philosophical 'generalism' for urban and regional planning and planning school curricula. Power for the sustainable ideal arises from the fact that nobody now argues openly against it; indeed a problem has arisen for committed 'green' enthusiasts through a hijacking of their environmentalist lexicon by the likes of genetic engineers and fossil-fuel providers!

An aspect that is frequently misunderstood is that the pursuit of sustainable policies can factually mean more, not less, economic activity – a 'win-win' factor not lost on the automobile industry and some fuel and energy providers. Sustainable planning practice – essentially conservation *with* development – engages more people, takes up benign yet quite complex technologies, and results in more money being spent on both conservation and development.

Principle 8
'To achieve sustainable development and a higher quality of life for all people, States should reduce and eliminate unsustainable patterns of production and consumption and promote appropriate demographic policies.'
The Rio Declaration, 1992

There is a remaining question: how, against the hedonic OECD–GATT–WTO consumer trend, did a worldwide prognosis arise in the style of the *Agenda 21* Rio Declaration (United Nations Conference on Environment and Development 1992: see Appendix to chapter 5) for the imprint of an international protocol? This, from a sceptical standpoint, is something of a contradictory new-age hoax, for 'sustainable conservancy' and 'material development' are for the most part separate and exclusive of each other. *Agenda 21* attempts a radicality: 'sustainable development', vaguely defined. This comes across as blurred imagery because of the diplomatic necessity at the Rio Conference to accommodate the vagaries of the rich and poor nations being courted. The pragmatic challenge, in the phrasing of Robert Fri (1991) is 'to put our practice on a par with our principles'. Quite so: but signatories to the 1992 Rio Earth Summit protocol had not produced their 'Agenda Statements' by the agreed 1997 deadline simply because the decision-taking processes involved were *neither* fully understood *nor* partially fashioned by that date.

'Sustainable development is not a fixed state of harmony, but rather a process of change in which the exploitation of resources, the direction of investments, the orientation of technological development, and institutional change are made consistent with future as well as present needs. We do not pretend that the process is easy or straightforward. Painful choices have to be made. Thus, in the final analysis, sustainable development must rest on political will.'
Bruntland, *Our Common Future*, 1987

The contemporary sustainable basis of reasoning had its genesis within the Brundtland Report (1987) prepared for the World Commission on Environment and Development as *Our Common Future*. That document defined 'sustainability', somewhat tautologically, as comprising three goals:

- *To ensure* that all societies' needs are met.
- *To ensure* that all members of societies' have their needs met.
- *To ensure* that all development and conservation is sustainable over time in a social, economic and environmental sense.

A characteristic of the sustainability narrative is the persistence of emphasis on unimpaired environmental quality over time, with no loss of material wellbeing, yet exhibiting some social gain. This adds up to the impracticality of attempting to both 'have and eat the same environmental cake'! Operationally, that is in the procedural context of neomodern conservancy *with* development, there arises a moral challenge to retain an *ethical* focus, along with a practical challenge to assess and resolve all manner of unacceptable *risk*. This is not merely a matter of obviating the monetary risk to big-game players. It involves heralding composite risk, social, economic, environmental, for all sectors and individuals within communities of concern – for households, for neighbourhoods, for settlements and for regions.

An intensive and well-balanced attempt at 'Defining a Sustainable Society' is available from a Robinson, Francis, Legge and Lerner (1990) presentation. Their expression reaches beyond sustainable development into cultural neomodernity for a 'sustainable society'. In their collegiate context these four set out to establish 'that there is no single version of a sustainable society'. They 'rule out environmental autocracy' and establish the useful notion that for organized human society, 'sustainability can never be said to be completely achieved'. The neomodern paradigm stemming from their contention gives rise to the view that 'we can usually say more about what is not sustainable than what is sustainable', a position that is not only correct, it is also one that strives to explain what sustainable urban planning entails as well as being a stimulus to bringing it about.

There is also Crosson's (1994) more pragmatic and targeted definition: that a 'sustainable agricultural system (his example) is one that *indefinitely* (American usage) meets demands for agricultural output at socially acceptable economic and environmental costs'. Clearly 'cyclicity' – birth–life–death, climatic seasons, water cycles, and the carbon cycle – is central to the human pursuit of sustainability. Extending from this, it is possible to fashion a parallel neomodern definition of 'sustainable *urbanization*' as that democratic style of urban provisioning which *indefinitely* meets the need for access to employment, education, entertainment and recreation at a socially acceptable environmental cost.[6]

Emphasis will be placed later, in chapter 3 (Charter) on the awkwardness of the 'sustainable management' notion in the sense of its 'environmental only' application, The main point is that the forces of market drift, consumer desires and developer inclination are significant, and have generated compulsions within settler societies, particularly affecting the peoples excluded from, and culturally ambivalent about, the Western development ethos.

It is also important to recognize the place and role of the appeal-hearing agencies (courts or tribunals in some jurisdictions) because of their placement for the delivery of progressive, useful, politically correct and ethically acceptable rulings. These tribunals are custodially and legally significant because, in their absence, the entrenched position of local government has been one of 'leave it to us' (the elected local officials), to the 'landowners' (the holders of development rights), to 'developers' (who presume to provide what they believe citizens want); and above

> 'Sustainable development recognises that sound economic and social development is not possible without a healthy environment; and conversely that a healthy environment is threatened by development that is not sound.'
> Megan Howell, Auckland University, 2002

> Legal Principal Three 'States shall maintain ecosystems and ecological processes essential for the functioning of the biosphere, and shall preserve biological diversity, and shall observe the principle of optimal sustainable yield in the use of living natural resources and ecosystems.'
> Bruntland, *Our Common Future*, 1987

> Sustainable Development has been defined as 'Using, conserving and enhancing the community's resources so that ecological processes, on which life depends, are maintained, and the total quality of life now and in the future can be increased.'
> Australian Government, 1992

all else, leave everything to that imperfect accessory to societal wellbeing, the 'market force'.[7] The greatest challenge to neomodern – thus of the twenty-first century – settler society is to retain the ability to achieve capacity empowerment and social wellbeing in a manner which avoids environmentally damaging growth.

Property, Interests and Neomodernity

Development planning and conservancy practice requires, for each individual jurisdiction of concern, a local working knowledge of legal, administrative and regulatory procedures, along with a capability to negotiate ever-improving outcomes.[8] An important situational context for this passage is that settler society citizenry has not been greatly moved in the past to organize changes to the way freehold land is occupied or used at the urban edge. This is a situation in marked contrast to much of the Old World, most notably Britain, where even during the prolonged period of right-wing Thatcherism the urban-rural line of distinction was held.

'Property', 'Interests' and 'Neomodernity' connect also with the Growth Pattern pragmatics examined in chapter 4 (the Ownerships and Rights passage).

Property

As an introduction, and to portray the significance to individuals of 'property interests', appraise Kevin Wong Toi's construct, presented in box 1.1 **Terra psyche: the land settlement continuum.**[9]

Of integral significance to an understanding of the origins of settler patterns is adherence to *landed* property ownership – so much so that the power of eminent domain on the part of central and local government to intervene in a landholder's title is viewed with widespread mistrust. This cleaving to land and resource ownership rights underlines a basic urge for individuals to attain a sense of security in an uncertain world through an absolute possession of some corner of it. This security-blanket attitude extends to a reluctance to endorse any public rights, to favour the allowance of *private* development works on privately owned land, and to inhibit *public* developments on freehold lands. For those who train in *planning* (community forethought before common-good action) and would *plan* for an improved future, managing the use of freehold lands has been piecemeal and patchy. That pattern has become entrenched because of a fortress attitude to private property rights *and* a community adoption of 'status quo zoning' which, in many ways, is public planning forsaken.

A metaphor for 'land possessed as women' has been identified in Australian and North American literature highlighting the masculine dominance, productive gain and exploitation associated with rural property ownership.

Schaeffer, 1988, Kolodny, 1975, Byrnes, 1993

For a wider perspective consult Joni Seager's *Earth Follies* (1993).

In the New World, demarcation and land-title registration systems, although legally robust, have been applied orthogonally, and in the process failed to adapt to the landscape diversity

Box 1.1   Terra psyche: the land settlement continuum

To better understand human attachment to the land, a qualitative construct, the *terra psyche*, is postulated and cultivated within a developmental frame of reference. In historical terms the continuum of development theory advances from the collective mana of first peoples through to the individual 'rights' of freehold property ownership, and beyond. Ultimately it is 'the beyond' continuum to which planning should be committed. Within the idiom of development theory this is designated as a 'post' or 'neo' modern phase. This phase denotes the transition from a modern to a neomodern mode of development and conservation.

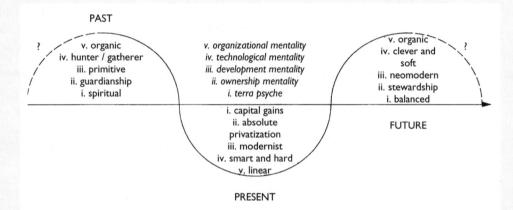

Terra psyche suggests an appreciation for the earth from within the soul of the individual. When considering terra psyche from an etymological perspective, 'terra' embodies the physical and tangible component of land, while 'psyche' represents the abstract perception that every individual possesses. Hence terra psyche is an expression which can be applied as a conceptual medium to embrace the relative qualitative affinity which humanity has with the land.

When applying the terra psyche construct to the development and conservancy experience, it is the prevalent attitude towards the land which is being articulated. The first collective attitude to be depicted is that of indigenous peoples, whose psyche and attachment manifested itself at two levels. One level can be described as a basic material terra psyche, where land is a resource supplying the life-giving needs to humanity. Another level is that of a spiritual terra psyche, evidenced by the infrangible bond between indigens and their homeland. The spiritual terra psyche placed limits on development that advanced beyond the attainment of basic needs, and resulted in a non-teleological 'primitive' phase. Following the pre-European era the New World lands were subjected to the arrival of colonial settlers. Their attitude portrayed an exploitative terra psyche, as land was treated as an economic commodity with land speculation rife. Consolidation of the exploitative terra psyche has occurred up to the present day. The recent circumstance can be defined as a modernist period of development, characterized by capital gains. The present transits into the future phase of neomodern development with conservancy, which promotes a balanced terra psyche propelled by a responsible identity with the land.

This cursory survey of the terra psyche not only reflects intrinsic attitudes towards the land, but also reinforces the priority assigned to particular organizational outcomes. Development rights are aligned with the capital gains psyche, while 'public' rights are associated with the as yet unrealized 'balanced' psyche. There is a conspicuous philosophical rationale in the design of this terra psyche construct. For example, the rectilinear quantification of land, symptomatic of an exploitative attitude, reveals a reductionist disposition in pursuit of its short-term objectives through expedient means; whereas a balanced terra psyche adopts a holistic awareness of land and its dynamic qualities. Land is and will continue to be an indispensable resource for human existence. The terrestrial aspect of human organization has been subject to an evolving state of quantification. Through the cognition of a terra psyche, the qualitative dimension of land can be promoted as an integral constituent of neomodern development.

Source: construct and argument devised by Kevin Wong Toi.

encountered. The system of recording landownership in the manner of a stock-holding facilitated the bartering of land. If boundaries were to be guaranteed (and thereby surveyed) it was found expedient and cheaper to assign large rectilinear (often 'quarter-square' blocks in North America, 1,000-acre blocks in New Zealand, larger for inland Australia) with seldom an allowance for, or fitting in with, the varied land form and its salient topographical features.

The United Kingdom is also a 'property'-owning democracy. How often North Americans and Australasians returning from a visit to Britain, probably to cement their cultural heritage, comment on the rural landscape's visual order. This experience stands in contrast to the confused shading of suburbia into ex-urbia in the New World. The point is that the British, despite a relatively high density of population for their landscape, have kept apart the urban and rural predicaments.

No effort was made in the Anglo settler societies to set aside the field paths and rural byways of Arcadian Britain and some other parts of Europe. It was a case of geometry beating topography, described in an Australian context (Lines 1991) as identifying surveyors as the principle agents of change, who 'opened the land to invasion, enabling the history of conquest to begin, and transformed the amorphous face (of what was considered to be an unhumanised landscape) into an imperial possession'. The land surveys and the follow-up registration of title facilitated land transaction, but in so doing imposed an unyielding privatization and passed to freeholders the right to exploit landscapes without any further contribution to the public domain. The general public retained no constitutional privilege of general access over the fully 'enclosed' lands. In settler societies, there was an abandonment of the Old World situation where much of the privately owned landscape is a publicly accessible part of the national estate (the situation in Scotland), and neglect of the rights of pedestrian traverse (the footpath system of rural England).

The land capture process is illustrated for the Antipodean context by the Wakefield company settlements, which began with Adelaide in Australia (1836) and moved on to New Zealand, beginning with Wellington in 1840. These early company-formula towns were instrumental in establishing an orthogonal 'militaristic' pattern for urban settlement. The Vertical Social Section approach excluded the indigenous first people and other non-European settlers. Company settlement was systematic colonization, consisting of two important organizational principles: effective regulative power over the on-sale of land at fixed prices *and* subsequent municipal control. Brilliantly entrepreneurial though they were, the Wakefield's social conditioning meant that they could only conceive a stratified social order. Professional 'men' and 'gentlemen' of means were seen to be important in the establishment of a governing gender and a dominating class. In theory, there was to be a hierarchy: professionals, artisans, labourers and native labour on arrival, conveying European notions of breeding and class to the New World. But the settlers were soon realigned into an egalitarian situation, albeit within communities which gave vent to 'racism' and 'settlerism'. It was a melting pot where many an avaricious small-time speculator soon made it rich, simply because the land-stock taken from the indigenous people was obtained virtually free of payment. From Benton and Short (1999) 'The main spoils of imperial expansion into the North American continent was land . . . The basic problem for the (US) Republic was what to do with the Indians.' Settlers of substance and wealth became an upper-crust citizenry, and a significant propertied sub-set maintained their positions of power privilege and dominance. These 'jump-started' families are present today throughout settler societies in the well-established law firms, business conglomerates, and as patrons of the arts and sport. To many North Americans and Australasians those early settler communities are now glamorized as searching out an actualization of utopian ideals, alluded to by Hunter (1987) as suburban pastoralism, achieving a European sense of urban fulfilment, along with sets of European place names.[10]

Relevant to the wealthier democratic nation context, McAuslan (1980: 2) identifies the presence in Western societies of three commanding property-ownership maxims, much at odds with each other.

- *Firstly*, 'that the law exists and should be used to protect private property and its institutions . . . the traditional common law approach to the role of (land governing) law'.
- *Secondly*, there is law 'used to advance the public interest, if necessary against the interest of private property; this . . . is the orthodox public administration and planning approach to the role of law (in the public interest)'.
- *Thirdly*, certain 'law exists . . . to advance the cause of public participation . . . the radical or populist approach to the role of law.'[11] used for the likes of borrowing to finance 'land banking'.

Nations of the transpacific settler society kind have elevated the *first*-order laws which protect 'freehold' property rights to a constitutional level where tenural sanctity remains secure and stable against outside claims. This 'bundle of rights' concept shakes out into four strands, in two binary pairs: the 'hold and dispose' entitlements commanded by freeholders; and the 'use and enjoy' entitlements which are to varying degrees influenced by the wider community, there being only one external distraction – 'eminent domain' the governmental right of compulsory acquisition for public use purposes. McAuslan's *second*-order interventionist law, broadly described as administrative law, has an uphill battle against the freehold-rights philosophy. This leaves little opportunity for an application of his *third*-order principle for public participation to secure wider public interests; and/or also my suggestion of a *fourth*-order consideration of the recognition of less tangible community 'interests' (spiritual aesthetic) in private landscapes. Because property rights are legal rights, they confront public values in an exclusionary way, inducing the separation of private property interests from public good interests.

From the United States *Constitution* – 'Fifth Amendment'

'nor shall private property be taken without just compensation.'

Guilt for land theft from native first peoples, and attempts to assuage that guilt, are reflected historically throughout settler societies by the creation of wilderness areas and National Parks on tracts initially considered useless and worthless. That shame also underwrites the credibility of contemporary Green politics and bolsters the bank accounts of environmental organizations.

From John De Grove (1984: 396)

'The issue of city (urban) development and redevelopment (can) be seen as the reverse side of the protection of important agricultural, forest and open space land.'

Interests

The more one thinks about the dominance of private property ownership the harder appears to be the battle to turn landowners toward sustainable urban planning, unless this can be fashioned profitably. Shifting from property fixation to the identification of individual and community interests – an interests gaze being a neomodern way of connecting the sustainability concept with the entrepreneurial psyche – the possibility arises that public 'interests' in a wider environmental context could replace narrowly defined 'ownerships' as the basis of planning.

William Fischel in his *Economics of Zoning Laws* (1985) examines the property rights dimension of zoning-as-planning.

The question often raised is 'who pays' and 'who benefits' from plan making? The symmetrical beauty of an 'interest-based methodology' renders it theoretically possible to have only winners, with some winning more than others, and *no* losers. This happy outcome would derive from an interest-based bargaining process which fairly balanced out the proportions of benefit to all stakeholders.

Community plan-making can be identified as a process for selecting equitably between conflicting and cooperative claims, mediating misunderstandings, and ameliorating the adverse circumstances of the least advantaged – in short, the brokerage of progressive common-interest changes. With her 1997 title, *Collaborative Planning*, Healey edges toward endorsement of an interests-based approach. Interest brokerage identifies a clear role for the planner as assessor and mediator, and passes to the fair-minded and even-handed practitioner the 'power of proposal' *and* a role to play in the important 'power of arbitration'. Looking in objectively, an 'interest' basis to planning would create opportunities for the engagement of owner, community, commercial, conservationist and other attachments to an alliance, enabling beneficial change to be negotiated and mediated.

THE CONCEPT OF
INTEREST: PROPRIETARY
STAKEHOLDERS
Owners
Tenants
Developers
Infrastructure
providers
Statutory undertakers
First people inheritors
Firms
Institutions

NON-PROPRIETARY
STAKEHOLDERS
Natural heritage
conservationists
Cultural heritage
preservationists
'Third party'
stakeholders
Political advocates
Bureaucratic
organizations
Professional practice
stakeholders

Neomodernity

A neomodern future is interpreted here as one where the acknowledged excesses of unsustainable modern lifestyles are exchanged for lifestyles which are economically, socially and environmentally balanced – hence the sustainable-in-spirit reasoning. A principal complication throughout Australasia and North America is that the inherited attitude to physical resources is dominantly economic, with little effective consideration for the wider environment or indeed for upholding societal values of a conservationist kind. And a further contemporary difficulty, despite contra-signals from some sections of society and from a 'hurting' environment at large, is the way governments stream their administrative conscience into an enabling-now rather than an outcome-later public policy format. The developmental thrust of successive governments in the New World has centred around exploitation of the natural resource capital, and an obsession with fiscal growth-on-growth based largely on an ever-expanding money supply and technological change. As monetized growth has increased in compound fashion to compromise the environment, this generates what is usually described as an 'economic crisis' which, in fact, is also a 'social values' crisis and an 'environmental' crisis. The rallying call is for administrations to pursue life-and-nation practical goals which set out to establish social wellbeing and environmental harmony *as well as* achieving economic growth.

This book takes up the challenge to set out pragmatic development and conservation objectives – *national, regional, community and household*. The policy issues are outlined in chapter 3, where they are collated in box 3.7 as a **Matrix** for conservation with development. The appeal made there is to identify the essential economic-social-environmental public policies in win-win-win terms for growth-community-environment moving from received patterns of 'smart' modernity, to thinking in a 'clever' neomodern way.

> Settler society populations remain mostly ambivalent about environmental protection. People recycle papers and bottles, but will not trade in their automobile for some bicycles; or forgo a jet-plane vacation for a regionally available widerness respite.

This emphasis on within-nation growth management also follows the lead of seven of the United States – Oregon in particular – in the pursuit of a reasonable ambition: that as resource-plundering and ex-urbanization profiles alarmingly, the mandate for urban and rural growth management control should be strengthened and locked on. The thrust lies squarely with socially appropriate conservation with development on a within-nation basis: within regions, within communities and of course within households. The societal preference at the larger scale is for dual-democracy administrations to move toward an opening-up of local government to wider 'powers of general competence' or to the lesser 'subsidiarity' basis of operation. The sustainable concomitant is the application of growth pattern powers which establish firm urban and rural delineations, backed up with incentive-based encouragements and occasional enforcements (use of the 'carrot' and 'stick' approach).

The neomodern emphasis is too important to leave to the vagaries of the open market simply because the market response leads to a 'cash-profit resource-deficit' outcome. Additionally, and importantly, markets 'optimize' by working to a demand immediacy, whereas the longer-term future of every community is dependent on *perpetual* wisdom with regard to the utilization of resources. Communities need to seek out a more clever, value-based future, one which includes custodial regard for the whole of a nation-state as a resource common. It falls to the voters in open democracies to define the clever new 'public interest' and establish goals for the 'common good'.

> 'Landscape guilt' – the setting aside of pristine wilderness areas, the camouflage of environmental damage, and the pocket creation of natural heritage – is a theme explored by Robert Thayer in *Grey World Green Heart*, 1994.

Box 1.2 New-age pragmatics

The issues, objectively, with what is modernist and neo-modernist are complexly epistemological (refer to Urmson and Ree 1989 throughout; see also David Harvey 1989, and Anthony Giddens 1990); yet there is little pragmatic difficulty for settler society citizens with what is modern and, inferentially, with what is neomodern. To be 'modern' is to be scientific and improved: accepting almost as a 'truth' that the present is better than whatever went before. Philosophically such modernity has proved disappointing; and the citizens of settler societies are now aware that it creates generational and ethnic disparities and a form of consumerism which is neither improving nor uplifting, and an ever-increasing resource degradation where demand exceeds the potential to supply, and a level of pollution where dumping exceeds the environment's absorptive capacity.

Postmodernism by one interpretation is modernism only worse. Planning is the recipient of a much more positive literary tack on postmodernism as it connects to sustainable development – Milroy (1991), Beauregard (1989), Huyssen (1986). Huyssen depicts the web of postmodernism, as a 'shift in sensibility, practices and discourse formations'. This was interpreted by Milroy three ways: (1) 'as adjustments to compensate for failings'; (2) 'as a new stage in the relationship between culture and capital'; and (3) 'as not a replacement [for modernism] as it is both/and'.

The last of these three notions allows a connection between traditional (modernist) techniques and radical (neomodernist) sensitivities, although it is not acceptable to assume that if neomodernism is *in* then modernism is *out*. Pronouncing for planners, Milroy contends that a further theme (4) 'is promoting reflective rather than objectifying theory . . . so as to not feel anything about [an object of study] or to want to manipulate it in anyway, but only to discover the truth about it'. Even more to the planning point, Tett and Wolfe (1991: 199) contend that 'planners increasingly ground their legitimacy on a commitment to encouraging many voices to speak. [And] If planners are to realise their potential the discourse of plans must be understood on all its levels'. The 'traditional' and 'radical' contexts of planning practice are reviewed more fully in chapter 2.

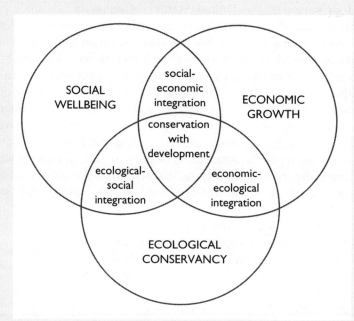

A structural depiction of the sustainability connection within neomodernity acknowledging a 1992 UNESCO–UNEP construct in *Connect*, vol. 18.

Box 1.2   *Continued*

To act in a pragmatic neomodernist manner in the New World context is to behave sensitively and cleverly in relation to ecology, economy and society. This is about cultural survival exercised through political choice. So it is very much a 'political' matter. The call in the twenty-first century is to integrate this preference with practice. Cross-referencing with the expansive Box 3.7 Matrix given in chapter 3, consider the following pragmatic array:

'Was' twentieth-century 'SMART'	'Could Be' twenty-first century 'CLEVER'
Power: Dominion over nature	Wisdom: harmony with nature
Top-down command structures	Bottom-up: knowledge sharing
Material growth	Human fulfilment
Mono-culturalism	Multi-culturalism
Interdisciplinary	Trans-disciplinary
International	Regional and local
External dependency	Within-nation reliance
National intervention	Local action and delivery
Bulk exporting	Niche exporting
Military posturing	Demilitary positioning
Paradigmatic science	Biospheric science
Environmental restoration	Environmental defence
Hard technology	Soft technology
Exploiting resource 'capital'	Living off resource 'interest'
Fordist production	Flexi-production
Land-use zoning	Sustainable planning
Driving a car	Walk–cycle–bus–train
Dump and forget	Repair–recycle–reuse
Trauma entertainment	Role-model entertainment
Urban expansion	Urban revitalization
Sprawl	Consolidation
Rebuilding	Retrofitting
Push through	Work around
Workplace employment	Homeplace employment
Network television	Local radio
Online telephoning	Cellular telephoning
Postal services	FAXing and emailing
Impact assessment	Impact avoidance
Disposable packaging	Reusable packaging

Above all else, acting correctly in a neo-traditional (neomodern) way, invokes humanity and humility. A key pragmatic necessity can be identified as employment. Modernist employment policies engage 'smart' people who can operate sophisticated technologies, leaving vast numbers unemployed. Neomodern employment policies would seek also to 'cleverly' engage a wider spectrum of lesser-skilled workers to operate real-work technologies. The pragmatic litany given above is not directly relevant to low-income nations, which require a specific-to-them construct.

The fact that the Anglo settler societies confront multiple confusions vindicates the introduction of broad-spectrum policies for achieving balance and empowerment. The structural nature of this neomodern spectrum is indicated within box 1.2 in the style of **New-age pragmatics** with an emphasis on sustainable performance (see also the Charter **Matrix** detailed in chapter 3, box 3.7).

In order to test the pervasiveness of modern technology rank this list of alphabetically ordered twentieth-century technological step-changes in order of importance – listing those you could least do without 'first', and those you'd be most ready to give up on 'last'.

Antibiotics
Airplane travel
Automobiles
Birth pill
Computers
Electricity
Food preservation
Genetic engineering
Motion pictures
Nuclear capability
Plastics
Plumbing in the home
Radio
Reinforced concrete
Space travel
Tapwater supply
Telephone
Television
Sewerage disposal
Vacationing

See where, on the list, you would draw a cut-off line if it were imperative to do so!

The basis for conservation practice and development planning was defined during and after World War II in four main ways: in consideration of *environmental, gender, ethical and first-people* verities. It is almost as though the values of nature (for whose sake? does nature have a soul?) have now been added in to the anthropocentric equation. To the 'four ways' listing Beatley (1994) identifies those faced with ethical judgements about land use: namely, landowners, homeowners and landholders, public lands users, custodians of community interests, elected and appointed managers, the land management professionals and their institutions. A deconstruction of their conflicting and often mutually excluding motives informs sustainable urban planning.

There is also a need to understand the motivational forces and the moral and bio-ethical basis for development, conservancy and planning interventions; to identify (Hillier 1993) 'whether any form of discursive democracy is actually achievable' and or also whether community empowerment, particularly urban community empowerment, is deliverable? What we know is that governments – left and right – have clutched at difficult times to social wellbeing; then at other more affluent times to environmental harmony; and most consistently to development and growth. Despite adverse social and environmental consequences, one theme has always been around, namely material monetized growth by every means available. This includes the delusion of consuming tomorrow's goods today, mostly using tomorrow's capital! As a consequence planners have had to face the reality that individual profits and material immediacy has come before community needs and preferences, particularly in the conscience of elected political representatives working hard to keep their political place.

So confusing and discordant has the growth objective been in relation to the ideals for social wellbeing and environmental harmony that it spawned a school of planning 'thought' offered up in the early post-war decade as the *Science of Muddling Through* (Lindblom 1959) involving 'incremental politics and partisan mutual adjustment'.[12] This was a long way from look-ahead socially

reformist planning theory, now also compromised by the contemporary just-in-time mode being adopted for the production of
consumer durables and consumables.

The underlying values, vested interests and motivating factors
of neomodern development planning and conservancy practice
can be identified as *social secureness with lifestyle diversity and
variety, material wellbeing, and a healthy habitat.* Considered widely
(at the level of federal government) a significant emphasis for
local conservation and development involves attention to the needs of those not
yet employed, unwillingly unemployed, chronically unemployable, and to those
retired prematurely from employment.

An evocative way to come to a view about the extent to which a society or its
leadership accepts or declines official intervention in the 'market process' (strictly
not a consciously understood process in and of itself) involves a categorizing of
official leavenings of public policy on a 'doing nothing' basis (approximating to
the 'muddling through' approach), a 'doing something' basis (the 'traditional' *conservative* approach), or on a 'doing everything' basis (the 'comprehensive' *socialis-
tic* approach). The 'traditional' and 'radical' construct given as box 2.1 in chapter
2 elaborates this reasoning.

While difficult to pinpoint, it is at least pragmatically acceptable to accord the
recognition in contemporary governments and elected political representatives of
their alignment mostly to the centre-right-or-left; and to identify a 'leftish' liberal
conscience which supports, somewhat separately, 'development', 'conservation'
and 'planning'. Issues of equity, balance and fairness confusedly trip over issues
of competitiveness and profiteering, with 'rightist' administrations allowing
market rationality to hold sway. My view is that nations of an overdeveloped yet
democratic persuasion, which have established the hard-fought privilege of being
able to elect federal parliamentarians, are entitled to depend on them to uphold
societal mores; and they are also entitled to look to them to articulate community
values and hold to the national ethos.

Parliamentarians and lesser political champions, while they hold elected office,
are expected to think and utter in accordance with a societal, rather than a personal, conscience – in short to engage their representational minds before opening
their mortal mouths. A guiding theme, in the phrasing of Service (1975: xii) is that
'leadership clearly seems to have a causal priority'. Yet unfortunately, as politicians evolve into 'state persons' they tend to become detached from societal goals.
They are then prone, through 'leadership dominance' (Service 1975) and 'consumer contentment' (Galbraith 1992) to be drawn to vote *against* social reforms,
even against environmental integrity, and most of all *against* distributive justice in
accordance with their slide toward a 'democracy of the contented and the comfortable'. This is endorsed by Friedmann (1987: 326) in these terms: 'I have found
that young, educated urban Americans have difficulty accepting the household as
the central institution of civil society. Many have succumbed to the ideology of
individualism to such an extent that they see themselves as history-less atoms.'
Individuals can, and will continue of course, to think and act for themselves 'indi-

vidually' for their material welfare, although within democratic systems they can also be conditioned to act for the wellbeing of society at large, and for a conservation of the natural environment.

A separation of development and conservation outcomes from spatial theory, in the direction of political theory, was the subject of much academic-professional discourse in the closing decade of the twentieth century. What is important in the context of the 'knowledge-power-outcome' sub-plot (chapter 2) is that theory does not remain an 'otherwise' factor, and is recognized to be the core to planning practice.

The pragmatic achievements of the past, such as they are, have been grounded in spatial theories now well understood. Here, for example, is a perspective, with which I concur, from Low (1991: 279):

> Land-use planning was instituted as a result of the perceived inadequacy of the market, not only to produce a socially acceptable physical environment but also to resolve conflicts among landowners. Property in land could not be defined simply in terms of absolute ownership rights over territorial parcels, because the value of a particular parcel of land was tied in with the value of all neighbouring land. Professionalism and bureaucracy eventually came to be employed in conjunction with the land market to form a new hybrid institution for the mediation of interests and the resolution of conflict.

During the closing decades of the twentieth century the conventional link between development theory and spatial theory gave way, in societally receptive contexts, to a connection of planning practice to political theory. In this Low (1991: 257) is 'attached to the shared interest in human emancipation that is the project of all modern societies: modern that is, as opposed to traditional and not to postmodern'. This contention connects politically with the neomodernist reasoning posited here for sustainable urban planning.

Conservancy and Development Ethics

If planned development and conservation is to aspire to a homologous trinity – *equitable material growth, harmonious social wellbeing, environmental balance* – then we can surely search planning theory to garner the societal and individual points of philosophical attachment to that trinity. What emerges is strong evidence in support of Friedmann's (1987: 87) contention that 'profound social reform in the public interest' may be called the central tradition. Does social reform, then, lie at the heart of decisions to intervene, and provide growth management, as part of a government's responsibility? If the answer is in the affirmative, and it surely ought to be, then we should be able to identify the focus of that attention. For the present purposes an assemblage, omitting Marxist perspectives, has been compiled and depicted in box 1.3 as **Connecting philosophy to planning**.

The philosophical basis and ethical nub to intervention in conservancy and development comes down to whether practice translates ideals into worthy out-

Box 1.3   Connecting philosophy to planning

There has never been a clear philosophical basis to planning. Different preferences fell into place in different historical contexts over time. A three-component 'traditional' and three-component 'radical' polarity has been selected for this representation, the principal sources being Thomas Harper and Stanley Stein's 'Centrality of Normative Ethical Theory to Contemporary Planning Theory' (1992), John Friedmann's *Planning in the Public Domain* (1987), and John Udy's *Typology of Urban and Rural Planners* (1991).

Traditional 1   Utilitarian (positivist) theory (consult Smart 1972)

Although remaining in place as the most dominant and readily identified 'philosophical' basis to local development planning throughout the Anglo-influenced world there are many critics and a lesser proportion of defenders of this hedonic style of practice, which sets out to accommodate what landowners, developers and politicians perceive to be good, as good for everybody. Although Utilitarian Theory has its devotees, in community terms it is now viewed by the majority of planning practitioners as reactionary. Yet from Hobbes and Locke to J. S. Mill and Herbert Spencer, those of an empiricist mindset have believed that development policy can be determined and driven according to rules which endorse dollar-style measures of worthiness. This approach still aligns with populist sub-national planning reasoning in peripheral Australasia and North America, on the basis that development outcomes should not be faulted (so the reasoning runs) if an identifiable balance of 'goodness or happiness' is secured. As the twenty-first-century opens out there are few practising defenders of Utilitarian Theory. To my mind there is no great difference in intended outcome between Utilitarian Planning Theory and the popular (imputed to Adam Smith) neo-classicist Libertarian Development Theory, where it is acceptable that individuals simply and directly make what they are conditioned to perceive to be their own choices, solely to optimize what they perceive to be their own wellbeing.

Traditional 2   Negative rights theory (consult Nozick 1974)

Western philosophy 'negative rights' theory identifies with the *ultra vires* doctrine which delineates the community bounds, up to which individuals may do as they wish with their owned property provided this is within the limits of prescribed laws. Negative Rights Theory is aligned to 'utilitarian theory', the essential difference being that the former attaches to individuals, whilst the latter attaches to community. In upholding these 'natural rights of entitlement' the cut-and-dried Negative Rights hypothesis finds favour with most administrators, the established professions, and a high proportion of physical planning practitioners.

Traditional 3   Communitarian theory (consult Sandel 1982)

This approach nests within the 'traditionalist' pattern on the presumption that policy positions 'should' arise via individual discovery of community attachments, legitimated for each separate community of concern, separately. It exhibits liberal attachments, but in practical outcome comes down to endorsing a systematic pact between profiteering developers and property-enhancing political representatives. A tenuous lineage for the underlying principles, from Plato and Kant, has been identified; the North American perspective of Harper and Stein (1993) being that 'while the communitarian view is often associated with liberal political views, it seems (to them) to have very conservative implications'. In other words, it is 'good' as far as it goes, but it is hardly 'good enough' for modern complex societies larded through with minority, marginalized and non-property-owning subcommunities.

Radical 'A'   Conscience-raising theory (Habermas 1979, 1984, 1986)

The Habermasian emphasis on 'communicative action' in association with 'instrumental action' (the Frankfurt School 1951: Adorno and others) is concerned with connecting improved and undistorted communication ('ideal speech') to better social science. This, for planning, means a raising of the level of social conscience for planners, their political mentors, and the participating public. This positions planners, in particular, to operate as both mediators and critics. In the context of the Jungian mantra 'thinking feeling sensing intuiting' to raise the level of participatory conscience (social listening) and to recognize unconscious distortions and mis-communications. A planning (non-philosopher) connection can be traced to the 'advocacy' writings of Davidoff (1965) and Healey (1996).

Box 1.3   *Continued*

Radical 'B'   **Liberty–equality theory (consult Rawls 1971)**

This is the most 'ethical' of the philosophies which transect with planning, because it incorporates the dominant moral ideals of 'liberty and justice' with transdisciplinary ideals for social opportunity, fairness and equality. Harper and Stein (1993) hold to the view that Rawls 'offers the most promising procedural NET (normative ethical theory) for planners' which practitioners in Australasia should be cautioned to appraise 'regionally' relative to this theory's derivative association with a wider basis of recognition of inequality in the USA. Urmson and Ree (1989) identify a philosophical trace from Locke, Rousseau and Kant through to Rawls.

Radical 'C'   **Social transaction theory (consult Popper 1974)**

To planners on both sides of the Atlantic (Friedmann, USA, 1987; Reade, UK, 1987) a Popparian transect with 'best practice' for local planning can be identified. Popper's approach is dialectical, involving 'piecemeal social engineering' as a transactive process. And although planners will discern much in common between Habermas, Rawls and Popper, all three found it necessary to disagree, as philosophers are wont. A difficulty presented by Popper's dialectical approach for active planning practitioners is his clear abhorrence of proactive embodiment in preference to an individualized discursiveness 'out of the collective loop'.

---

comes for the communities impacted upon. It clearly benefits society to establish such a topology, to forge the ethical and philosophical verities on which actions emanating from the planning, development and conservation statutes are derived and elaborated.

> David Harvey notes a 'significant tranche of support [for environmental rationality] from the heartland of contemporary political-economic power. The rising tide of affluence ... [has] ... increased middle class interest in environmental qualities.'
> 'The Environment of Justice', 1995

A source of background support for social reform as the central tradition upholding the ideal of planning for conservation with development is Perry's prescient passage on 'Conscience and Ethics' (1954) which identifies the need for government intervention to achieve perceived social good. Another North American source, profiling a European style of reasoning, is Timothy Beatley's *Ethical Land Use* (1994), expressing the hope that groups of people – communities of concern – will organize themselves to advance social improvement in society, to 'will' it upon governments that they get their say, and uphold their point of view.

Practice ethics

Individuals are of course different one from another, and they can and do vary in the balance of their attachment to community ideals. This also depends on their loyalty make-up, the atmosphere within their household, their employment role and individual ranking, and their levels of contentment and envy. So planning operatives, the 'designers and deliverers' along with the bureaucrats and other technocrats *cannot* be relied upon to attach themselves consistently to acceptable beliefs (community, aesthetics, sustainability). In these terms developers, conservationists and planners, among others, contribute to community decisions; and

'BENIGN'	'WICKED'
Love	Mistrust
Truth	Deceit
Tolerance	Ruthlessness
Service	Exploitation
Justice	Anarchy
Perfection	Disorder
Aestheticism	Brutalism
Meaningful	Chaotic
Safe	Dangerous
Belonging	Footloose
Esteem	Hate
We	Me

The 'benign' column is based largely on Maslow's 'Hierarchy of Needs' (1968, *Toward a Psychology of Being*). For an insight into the 'wicked' hypothesis, consult Rittel and Webber's 'Dilemmas in a General Theory of Planning' (1973, *Policy Sciences*, 4 (2)). Refer also to Bolan (1983) Figure 1 'Range of Moral Communities of Obligation *Journal of Planning Education and Research*, 3, 1983.

Figure 1.2 Characteristics of individuals.

on account of the community implications of their decisions they are subject to rather more public scrutiny and criticism than most other contributors.

A prescient review, 'Planning Power and Ethics' (Gerecke and Reid 1991), noted that 'Planning has no equivalent of the grouping styled as Doctors for Social Responsibility [and] . . . planners have been less willing to look at alternatives in a serious way' or indeed to follow through their decision-making with a view to ascertaining how well it works. Planning is a self-conscious service, aligning closely with the conservative, commodifying and consumerist mores of those being planned for.

A relative complication is illustrated in figure 1.2, **Characteristics of individuals**; the left column shows the individual emanations of a saintly 'benign' kind, juxtaposed with those on the right of a Hobbesian 'wicked' kind. One does not have to be all that cynical to accept that some people lead 'benign' lives, others lead 'wicked' lives, and some others live moderately 'Jekyll *and* Hyde' benign *and* wicked lives! The outcome (Reade 1985: 95) 'depends entirely on what we wish to achieve, and these actions, clearly, can be answered in terms of our values, which may change'. Three observations can be made relative to the contemporary *ethical* situation.

First: that 'worthiness, goodness, rightness and liberty' (Rawls 1971) are not necessarily or inherently the kinds of outpouring to be expected from any person wishing to maximize their freedoms and increase the variety of their lifestyle. Individuals within Galbraith's (1992) 'culturally content' situation, the one-dollar-one-vote system of delusional democracy, cannot be relied upon to guide

For reasons of difference between developers, public persons, professional practitioners and politicians it is useful for students of planning, development and conservation to de-construct individual motives and preferences.

development down societally virtuous paths – to embrace conservancy and communitarian values. Some individuals have always stood out against tax-gathering (evasion and avoidance). Others stand against control over plunder-freedoms, and there are others who hold out against the likes of resource quotas (free-range ocean fishing and the exploitation of indigenous forests). Some others opportunistically cruise the commercial cyberspace – namely, the economic buccaneers who plunder societal resources through the use of imperfectly regulated instruments (stock exchange hits, futures leveraging, commodity buyouts, franchise dealings, capital shunting, tax avoidances). Of course many others live a 'to them' higher code, although even they mostly extract from, and fail to restore and regenerate, the resource base they consume.

Second: the family, the household and the individual are best positioned to focus on development and conservation values because it is at these levels that it is pos-sible to identify a connection to social and economic wellbeing, the environmen-tal heritage, and their attachment to the cultural heritage.

Third: the embodiment of socially appropriate development and conservancy principles into the law of the land, as part of a new liberal corporatism, gives rise to the 'sustainability' mode for establishing rules for community involvement and associations of a neomodern kind.

It is the parliamentarians and lesser political figures who provide the legal and operational breath of life for neomodern sustainable conservancy and develop-ment, for at base operations of these kinds have a political genesis. One challenge is to wean ourselves away from a populist 'if you cannot beat them join them' conservatism. This is Beatley's (1994: 202) perspective on that matter.

> Frequently officials make decisions about controversial land-use issues by counting and comparing the number of people speaking for and against a proposal. What emerges often in these decisions is a kind of utilitarian logic with public officials seeking, in the crudest of ways, to support the interests of the majority . . . Politics in land-use matters is not inherently bad. Indeed it is essential – no public decisions can be made that are not political, but the ethical content and focus of these policies are inadequate . . . What is desperately needed is to expand the land-use debate, to begin to recognise that ethical and moral obligations extend beyond narrow economic or utilitarian views.

Communities end up with whatever policies politicians form and the guidelines they promote – all a consequence of their example while holding onto their elec-toral mandate – mindful that the ballot box always awaits them!

Conservation with development practice has at its core one dominant and several accessory value sets. The core is 'social value' which is, of course, diverse and complex, comprising national-level social goals, regional and local community goals, indigenous peoples' pre-ownership values and rights, settler-freeholder landowner values, developer ambitions, conservancy aspirations, minority and special-interest values and rights, political ambitions, religious beliefs, and cultural values – among others. In the current libertarian, but nevertheless corporatist political climate, governments toy with environmental morality and discuss what is 'right' and what is 'wrong', when the dominant and prevailing value system all along is economic growth. This situation even prevails at a time of change when governments seek out more in the way of social equity and environmental harmony.

Despite the dominance of economic growth-on-growth, it is 'social values' which make up the 'neomodern value system' comprising material growth, the attainment of social wellbeing, and the emplacement of an environmental harmony. This is where skills, technology and resources line up in parallel to create societal benefits. Conservation with development is, simply, an interconnected process comprising a 'balanced trade-out', exhibited by a practical sum:

$$\sum \text{ACTIVITY}^1(a^1,b^1,c^1...) \quad \text{RESOURCES}^1(m^1,n^1,o^1...)$$
$$\text{EFFECTS}^1(u^1,v^1,w^1...) \quad \text{ACTIVITY}^2(a^2,b^2,c^2...)etc$$

an ever-continuing outcome in the larger sense, between central regional and local objectives.

It remains, in this review of the ethical basis to sustainable urban planning, to run an 'ethical measure' over practising planning specialists and to establish a 'canon'. This is considered important by David Harvey (1985) because of the 'planners commitment to the ideology of social harmony ... [which] ... puts them in the role of righter of wrongs, corrector of imbalance, and defender of the public interest'. These are exuberantly put presumptions which position planners, for sure, to acknowledge that they are custodians for some collective interests on behalf of the community they serve, backed up by their local and central government system. The call is to ensure that the battle between environmental ethics and the growth mantra – which, anyway, environmentalists cannot win without an economics connection – does not sideline the social purpose of planning.

One set of North American findings (Howe and Kaufman 1979) indicates that, as would probably also be the case for the rest of the transpacific New World, public planning specialists have a low tolerance for bribery and abhor the distortion of information.[13] But the findings also illustrate that such practitioners are not averse to using trade-offs, or to engage in symbolic appeals

Individuals have moral relationships with other individuals, with families, and with their communities – but not realistically, in these contractual times, with the institutions and corporations for whom they work – characterized in former times as a mutually supportive employer – employee undertaking. The relationship of an individual to an institution or corporation is now, more than ever before, merely a service contract.

My aim within this passage on ethics is to avoid ascribing a lofty 'professional' quality to planning practitioners, preferring to impute that rating to priests, lawyers and doctors, whom George Bernard Shaw depicted as a 'conspiracy against the laity' – completely *not* the social service ideal for planners!

Jane Jacobs in her *Death and Life of Great American Cities* (1961), and Ivan Illich in his *Disabling Professions* (1977) are critical of professionalism masquerading as creativity.

In *Everyday Ethics for Planners* Carol Barrett (2002) profiles the practical, personal, agency and guild ethics which constitute issues of confusion within real-context situations.

to gain acceptance of 'their' proposals, or to leak information to outside groups who are fighting 'their' agency. Another set of base findings about these situation ethics, and from the same source, indicates that practitioners in public service differ markedly one with another in their level of agency loyalty, in their propensity to express personal values in their work, and also in their willingness to promote political preferences in their job context. Howe and Kaufman (1979) establish that 'aside from a fairly constant ten percent who were undecided' and the somewhat equal 'conservative' and 'liberal' respondents (totalling around 20 per cent) there was a surprisingly high 70 per cent of hybrids 'combining both the technical and political dimensions of role' which outnumbered the conservative and liberal categories.

The tension this finding indicates for North American local government service has its parallels elsewhere in the New World. I can identify, for example, that the Australasian practitioner is as confused by what Howe and Kaufman describe as official 'role orientation' on the one hand and 'personal preferences' on the other, as are their North American counterparts.[14] This ambivalence may be ascribed to deficient education, the absence of an appropriate professional canon, ambiguous employer guidelines, and/or also to a lack of sound political leadership. The largely unintended result is a high proportion of public servants in local government who can be presumed to espouse 'developer' and 'landowner' preferences *personally*, and to express these in their work to the likely disadvantage of the communities they are paid to serve.

A British exploration of the attitudes and self-image of planners (Knox and Cullen 1981) also establishes rapport with the New World circumstance in that 'The average higher-echelon planner is very much a middle-class animal'. This study explores and finds wanting the extent to which planners have the 'public good' at heart. Even more telling, the Knox and Cullen study concludes that British planners 'may be seen as the functionaries of a political apparatus which exercises its power to create a physical landscape in its own ideological image, and to sustain a social environment conducive to its own preservation'.

These American and British indications open out onto a wider plane of ethical concern and education, pointing up concerns about the ideological baggage and the need for urban-rural and regional planners to have a set of guiding ethics.

Ethics is grounded in moral philosophy, and so the conservancy specialist and also the development planner can dip into works as separate over time as Socrates and Foucault. More to the contemporary point, the writings of Popper, Habermas and Rawls (box 1.3) have now been connected into the neomodernist sustainable urban planning ethos. This linkage has been pursued within several subject-specific writings (Thomas and Healey 1991; Howe 1990; Beatley 1984 and 1994) making the connection between philosophy, sociology and planning. In this way, additional to the largely utilitarian thrust of development, it is possible for both students and practitioners alike to fashion a link with deontological (moral duty-based) concerns, relating actions to effects and outcomes. The point to such a leavening is that those students and practitioners who engage in moral reflection are encouraged thereby to reveal and address their personal shortcomings and ethical limitations. This serves to avert or thwart an inclination to behave incorrectly, dishonestly or corruptly.

Those prepared to translate 'normative-traditional' planning practice into new-way 'radical-ethical' planning practice will find themselves ascending an ever-steepening learning curve, signposted confusingly as 'moral responsibility' *and* 'multiple belief'. This is uphill going, with rewarding perspectives continually unfolding. It is a process of *re*-education and *self*-awareness which Kaufman (1993) describes as a provisioning arrangement that furnishes planning practitioners with an 'ethical compass' at the ambivalent intersection of planning theory and planning practice. Yet the enhancements are not uniquely moral. They come to the practical aid of planning operatives at each and every level of day-to-day operational encounter. Such an ethical compass is also significant within the formalized 11-Step plan-making progression detailed in chapter 2 (figures 2.6 and 2.7) particularly so at the 'formulation of aims and objectives' the 'data evaluation and diagnosis' the 'formulation of proposals' and the 'test' stages of plan-making.

In the terms now established, the planning operative is supplied some moral-philosophical considerations to range and review against, ethically. This positions the practitioners of conservancy and development to weigh up the 'lessons of historical reason' against the 'voice of experiential conscience'. They are then able to appraise and come to a view on such day-to-day philosophical yet practical concerns as 'loyalty to whom?', 'worth and worthiness for what purpose?' and 'should I manipulate this data to attain an uncontentious compromise, fulfil personal belief, or to achieve simple peace of mind?'[15]

In a provocative piece *'To boldly go where no planners have ever . . .'* Hillier (1993) sketches a setting wherein:

> Without substantial political power of their own, planners may feel threatened by political pressures. Politicians may engage in vote-catching to ensure re-election; developers may attempt to push projects through without detailed examination; neighbourhood leaders and identity groups may vociferously make life uncomfortable. As such, planners may succumb to pressure and recommend the policy outcomes which they perceive as the least bothersome for themselves, whilst still appearing to hide behind a neutral, technical facade of rationality.

Each of us differs individually in our make-up, from being 'softies or hustlers', or 'radicals or conservatives'. The neophyte probationer and the hardened practitioner alike needs considerably more than Practice Guidelines in order to fight a fair fight for the development *with* conservancy ideal, the community they serve, and also to guide their own conscience. The overall objective is to be, according to the phrasing of Wachs (1985) 'systems challenging' rather than 'systems maintaining'. Six ethical precepts are offered in box 1.4 as a set of ethical edicts, an **Ethical canon for community transactions**.

Box 1.4   Ethical canon for community transactions

- *First* is the primary need for an 'allegiance to the public interest' and for public participation, independent of the background capital investment, on the grounds that for planning specialists the principal client is the future community, recognizing first-people's rights, gender concerns, environmental needs and religious-cultural diversity. Planning operatives must have the 'space' to dissent and negotiate independently over line-of-command capital and political expediencies when this is found to be necessary, and to seek always to enhance 'variety' and 'choice'.
- *Second* and deferential to the above is the standard 'integrity to client' values which ensure that the employing interests are understood and held in confidence where this is called for, and are not thwarted by the personal values and beliefs of the planner. Adherence to this obligation can become confused in the mind of practitioners in private practice, who often switch daily from individual landowning clients to local government agency clients. That confusion can be overcome by holding to the preceding 'public allegiance' edict.
- *Third* is a societal imperative that the appropriate 'professional' guild must ensure that the persons licensed to practise planning have the skills to do the job on two planes: structurally in that they have the 'functional skills' to attain planned outcomes which exhibit economic social and environmental integrity, and the equally important 'organizational skills' to reconcile ethical values with statutory requirements and agency guidelines. All practising planners should be able to pledge to a 'Planners For Social Responsibility' ethic.
- *Fourth* is an extension of the previous item, obligating practitioners who evolve skills to do their job, to pass on these skills in their workplace to those who are entering their vocation; to disclose their results and promote their findings as research; and to keep up with Continuing Vocational Development.
- *Fifth* is the need to align with the statutory requirements; not necessarily to be 'driven' by those requirements, but to 'keep in line' with them. An ethical corollary also establishes that the planner specialist truthfully ensures disclosure at public hearings, which may implicate disclosure of pre-hearing partisan information when there is a call for this to be part of the public record.

- *Sixth* is the normative and enforceable obligation to adhere to Codes of Conduct prescribed by the behaviour-controlling practitioner association. For more recently emergent vocational governing bodies (as is the case with planning) the evolving nature of their practice renders this easier to establish than is the case for other well-entrenched professionals (priesthood, law, medicine) reliant upon outdated and often protectionist principles.

The *similarities* between Anglo settler societies give way to *differences* when considering ethical standards; noticeably so with regard to variations in the recognition of 'human care' and 'utilitarian rights' for alternate jurisdictions. A widely cast overview is provided in the lead-in to Barrett's *Everyday Ethics for Practicing Planners* (2002) supplemented throughout the body of the text by worked examples (affordable housing, favours, confidentiality *etc.*) as advice to planners on holding out for the observance of ethical principles, and including an interesting pen-picture of the Ethical Planner.

Intervention in market forces for the common good is never value-free at any level of involvement, for even the 'planner as mediator' is also embroiled in 'action for change'. Indeed, the planning practitioner at the meeting-point of individual, community and political contributions to the development and conservancy process is the operative most expected to indicate, on balance, the optimal path to pursue. This is a huge challenge, evidenced by practice at the control agency level on the basis of Nozickian 'negative rights' precepts which only evaluate proposals and objections in terms of the extent to which individual rights are upheld or violated.

Two writings on the obligations of planners (Wachs 1985, and Marcuse 1976) fuel my compilation of the six-point canon (box 1.4). These authors offer ethical guidelines for planners; moral precepts, which although they are not legally enforceable seek, in the phrasing of Hendler to establish that planners 'speak of ethics while walking the fine line between respecting others in all shapes, sizes and ethical orientations on the one hand, and retaining the right to contribute to the discussion on the other'. All of this is complemented by the sixth item in the canon, a 'thou shall not lie steal or cheat' code of conduct which can, if necessary, be enforced by the behaviour-controlling practitioner guild.

Sue Hendler's *Planning Ethics: A Reader* (1995) contains most of the North American sources quoted throughout this passage.

The top-down 'ethical compass' detailed in box 1.4 incorporates and legitimates the normative moral dynamics and expectations of society. From time to time the need will arise for a professional body to improve and recast its code of conduct, to facilitate access to continuing professional education, to enshrine a planners for social responsibility ethic; and occasionally to also punish bad behaviour.

Another complex moral consideration is that conservancy and development specialists, those who strive to induce improvements for the future of their employer community, are part of the professional manager class in society. These practitioners are of a sector identified by higher educational attainment and higher-level incomes, Over recent decades this professional manager class as a whole has become more self-serving, less liberal, and much more income-focused. Most professional manager personnel are keyed into the income expectations, the lifestyle ambitions, and the consumption values of their class. This serves to embroil them in a 'conspiracy bias' in favour of 'developer client' interests, often against the intrinsic needs and objectives of the 'community' they ostensibly serve. This is *not* acceptable; yet in reality, ethical guidelines are frequently observed 'in the breach' and are often treated by practitioners as an irrelevancy.

Recruiting into training establishments for conservation and development planning practitioners fails society when there is a skew away from the indigenous first-people's rights; or when there is an over-representation of one gender, or some other admissions bias within the vocational body.[16] It is also preferable that the recruiting base for planning operatives is not so much 'like from like' (planning recruits drawn from managerial-professional family backgrounds), as trainees emerging into the service from non-professional and non-planning family backgrounds. In this context it is gratifying to observe the well-balanced ranking structure of conservancy specialists and development planners throughout North America and Australasia, and balanced male-to-female and older-to-younger enrolments in training establishments. Some difficulty arises from the fact that planning attracts to its graduate-training programmes a high proportion of general arts and science people, many of whom get by in planning as 'transactors', but experience difficulty in the pursuit of planned 'transformer' outcomes.[17] A four-kind typology for planners – reformers, systemizers, administrators, synthesizers – is advanced by Udy (1994) as underlying the planning profession's vulnerability.

The emphasis in this book lies with neomodern development – a sustainable context often depicted here and elsewhere as the 'triple bottom line' (social economic environmental). Chapter 3 (*Charter*) sets down sustainability principles; then comes *Growth Pattern Management* (chapter 4); and *Urban Growth Management* (chapter 5).

Figure 1.3 My first plan-making effort (*c.*1960) was for the village of Helensville (a *locus classicus* with port, rail station and highway convergence) an hour from Auckland. This student effort was based on the then usual 20-year 'look ahead' notion. I produced an uninspired zoning-in of the status quo and the gaps between, resulting in four times the length of shop frontage needed for a town of 2,000 persons (3,000 now); with industry gracing the main road entry and exit.

The professional manager values identified by Ehrenreich (1989: 14) as 'home ownership in a neighbourhood inhabited by other members of their class, college (university) education for their children, and such enriching experiences as vacation trips . . . and the consumption of culture in various forms' can be also identified as inducing planners toward a status wherein they become progressively more out of touch with lower-income community values as they mature and gain job seniority. The sub-politics of envy also induces a frustration, in that the likes of practising planners seldom get to wield *real* political power or direct the *actual* investment decisions of the moneyed classes.

To the extent that conservancy and development specialists (typically planners in local government service) are role-facilitators for those who intervene and provide alternative strategic directions, they have not, to any significant degree, been identified with the effective initiation of social reform or economic equilibrium. I concur with Beauregard (1989) that 'practitioners and theorists must rededicate themselves to the built environment as the object of action and enquiry' and that they 'must open planning to a variety of constituencies'. Given a lack of previous understanding about what must be done for the future, a lot therefore confronts planning practitioners in the new 'sustainability' era. In effect there is really only one direction for planning practitioners to go: to become more politically embroiled (in a sustainable and ethical manner) and to become wired in to all manner of community constituencies.

Planners can and should take credit and take heart, for again from Ehrenreich (1989: 260; emphasis added) we can identify, in the work of planners, among others, the 'good and pleasurable and decent work . . . the *pride of the professions* that define the middle class'. This suggests that planning operatives can consider themselves well placed and fortunate, as part of an elite group, those who Ehrenreich identifies as the 'caring, healing, building, teaching and planning professionals'. Planners, then, are among the creative, society-serving specialists privileged to work for broad-church community improvements. But much as socialists, ardent in their youth, tend to fade toward conservatism as they age, development practitioners and conservancy specialists as they 'mature' have to make an extra effort to appreciate minority, disadvantaged and lower-income needs, to be aware that whatever their income-class origins they will be drawn toward managerial class desires and cohort values. This underscores the case made out earlier for mandatory 'continuing professional development' and the need to join a Planners for Social Responsibility grouping in pursuit of the 'triple bottom line' – equitable growth, social wellbeing and environmental harmony.

With Sustainable and Ethical Intent

New styles of libertarian administration *at worst* cleave to well-intentioned but wrong-footed practices of the past and, *at best* fall in line with the six-point 'community transaction' canon outlined earlier – pursuing triple-balanced outcomes.

This approach justifies various policy removals (political deviousness, legal obfuscation, fiscal chicanery); policy remedies (real jobs, benign technologies, territorial connectedness, identity clarification); policy additions (management by objectives, political cooperation), and social connectedness (enablement, empowerment and capacity fulfilment). In those terms the crucial issue is to get clever – not always to attempt *smart* ways of 'talking' or 'buying' a way through, but to 'think' 'perform' and 'negotiate' a cleverly informed way around.

Hold to the following:

- Planning for urban and rural settings, and regional purposes, provides a forum for operating strategically within a spatial setting (bounded reality) and in a political realm which has the public interest as its community purpose. It seeks to infuse an improved future quality and diversity of life, and thereby embodies conservation with development, and is trans-generational.
- Planning manages human effects upon the natural environment, and sets out to conserve the natural heritage, to restore impaired ecosystems, to maintain material wellbeing, to preserve the cultural heritage, and to represent and moderate the needs of all interest groups.
- In capsule terms conservation *with* development aspires to a homologous trio: equitable material growth, social wellbeing, environmental harmony – the 'triple bottom line'. It is learned and provided as both a 'transactor' and a 'transformer' activity: a future-shaping delivery process that seeks 'sustainably and indefinitely' to fashion worthy humanized environments and conserve the natural and cultural heritage.
- Development planning and conservation practice are social services which strive to improve the quality of life, respect first people's treaties and international protocols, uphold cultural values and gender emancipation, and to maintain uncorrupted and ethically correct positions.

> Conservation with development seeks a triple-balanced harmony–
> - material growth
> - social wellbeing
> - healthy habitat.

The foregoing involves the concomitant identification and endorsement of socially responsible (enabling-empowering), and environmentally acceptable (sustainable-protective) projects. Yet at any future date a new technology (cheap mass hydrogen production, effective superconductivity), or a new ideology (liberal theology, capacity building, WTO breakthrough) can overturn previous certainty. Integrated value-based progress must include tangible physiological security and aim for psychological wellbeing; and these factors always prove ultimately more important than a few extra dollars in the pocketbook. The nub of the conservation *with* development issue comes down to one of close-the-gap politics in favour of 'sustainability' pursued 'indefinitely'. The outcomes are, essentially, grounded and transacted as transformation practice. Goals of the grounded-in-reality sustainable kind outlined in this chapter, and in chapter 3, seek incorporation via the planning service into development projects and conservancy practice.

2

Knowledge Power Outcomes
The Theory Fundamentals

As a novice practitioner I mostly worked on the assumption that 'real planners do not do theory', a sentiment identified in Breheny and Hooper's *Rationality in Planning* (1985) positing that theoreticians 'retreat from practice' and 'are opposed in principle to the idea of prescribing for practice, but are equally unhappy about what appears to be a consequence of not doing so'. This situation calls for an identification of foundation principles and practice specifics. Readers with an understanding of lineal and multiplex planning theory and practice could move directly to the Charter, and the Regional and Urban pragmatics outlined in chapters 3 through to 6.

This chapter, about 'knowledge power and outcomes' examines the principles and constructional theories of planning practice.[1] It is presented relative to such transformative factors as enablement, empowerment and fulfilment. It is also concerned with the procedures engaged to bring into effect progressive planned outcomes within a multiple belief society. With deference to both design and practice, this passage examines traditional lineal methodology and offers a reconstruction of radical planning theory on a multiplex (sustainable) basis, for Anglo settler societies where development practice and conservancy management is being continuously repoliticized, recombined and recalibrated.

> 'The future presents itself as an impenetrable medium, an unyielding wall. And when our attempts to see through it are repulsed, we become aware of the necessity of wilfully choosing our course.'
> *Ideology and Utopia*,
> Karl Mannheim, 1929

Incursion into other statutory and professional stakeholdings induces proprietary confusion over disciplinary boundaries, imparted in planning schools, for planning, as a 'franchise' understanding.

Characteristically plan-making activities and planning processes have always been around in these pragmatic contexts:

- *International security* (army, navy, air force: operations research, customs and immigration)
- *Within-nation security* (police, fire service, terrorist surveillance: inter-service networks)
- *Economic development* (trade policy, future studies, GATT, WTO, NAFTA, APEC, CER)
- *Social welfare* (education, health, welfare; and the likes of drug abuse and prison programmes)

- *Conservation* (protecting and conserving the natural and cultural heritage)
- *Regional agencies* (supply and disposal services: conservancy and resource management)
- *Local government agencies* (land-use controls and bulk and location formulations)
- *Statutory undertakings* (utility provisioning: electricity, gas, water, sewerage. Public transport companies, and the like)
- *Private sector* (industry, commerce, services: production, marketing, waste disposal)

'a better quality of life from a planning system and a planning culture which provides both institutional and ideological space for the assertion and accommodation of a wide range of interests.'
Healey, McNamara, Elson and Doak 1988

What is sought here, for definition, is the operational mode for an essentially *social* provisioning and transformation practice within the urban-rural and regional contexts, the 'what' and 'how' of development *with* conservation. It mainly explores procedural and delivery theories formatted through an interdisciplinary lens. This Healey (1996: 253 original 1992) contemplates and expresses neatly as a nuanced way of 'making sense together while living differently'.

A difficulty is that whereas development theory connects explicitly to political economy, the conservation function and planning practice has little credible connection with orthodox economics. Sustainability has had to establish a science-based signature of its own, born of the relatively recent socio-environmental polemic which orbits about and radiates away from Carson (1962), Meadows (1972), and Schumacher (1974).

The profiteering ethic, throughout the nineteenth and twentieth centuries, was predicated upon resource plunder, continuous growth, and capital accumulation; all in the name of efficiency – economic efficiency.

The regional-rural-urban planning activity has traditional connections to the nineteenth-century 'city beautiful' movement. The truth, in fact, is less romantic and less idealistic. The unhealthy cities which the Industrial Revolution created were threatening the growth and output of profits, and something had to be done about that. To the extent that rational adjustments were called for, the 'planners' who carried this public health reform into effect were legitimized. In this way planning can be identified, from the end of the nineteenth century, as the handmaiden to capitalism. The concerns for the first half of the twentieth century were for 'seemliness, security and sanitation' with well-understood connections to political economy as an accessory to the compelling growth-for-profit mantra. Here is David Harvey's reasoning on this matter, from an article 'On Planning the Ideology of Planning' (1985):

Perhaps the most imposing and effective mystification of all lies in the presupposition of harmony at the still point of the turning capitalist world. Perhaps there lies at the fulcrum of capitalist history not harmony but a social relation of domination of capital over labour. And if we pursue this possibility we might come to understand why the planner seems doomed to a life of perpetual frustration, why the high-sounding ideals of planning theory are so frequently translated into grubby patches on the ground.

The systemic order planning was expected to deliver to Anglo society settlers has historically worked through as under-achievement to both the planners and those planned for. Christine Boyer's *Dreaming the Rational City: The Myth of American Planning* (1983) traces group failure and incoherent identity for traditional planning in consonance with Harvey's reasoning.

During the 1980s planning was out on a credibility limb, only tentatively connected into the political economy establishment, and largely at odds with the growth-on-growth mantra. Since that time the sustainable ethic and science-based evidence has brought twenty-first-century planning in from the procedural wilderness, and provided an ethic, some good science, and an economic rationale in place of earlier ineffective idealism.

> The tenuous attachment of urban and regional planning to development theory may be the reason why so much attention is paid to connecting those processes to administrative law. Even if somewhat bereft of a philosophical keystone, planning has become enshrined into the law of most OECD nations as legal fact. A knock-on problem which then arises is that planning, according to legal dicta, is denied a proactive role, and is frequently turned into a reactive enforcer of legal conformity.

At the level of the detached average person, planning is, simply, what planners 'do'. It is an 'elsewhere' issue which is presumed to produce worthy outcomes, characterized by failure at worst, ineffectiveness at best. It is instructive, then, to identify what the beneficial outcomes of pragmatic planning are, or were intended to be. Taking a cue from John Friedmann (1987: 28) figure 2.1 presents the **Overall uses of within-nation planning** as a summary of the extent to which it, planning, can permeate individual and community interests.

The uses detailed in figure 2.1 do not comprise a list to adopt uncritically. Indeed in these so-named libertarian times of deregulation and a leave-alone emphasis, validating the likes of item 5, 'Redistributing income', as official reform is questionable, indeed improbable. On the other hand item 4, 'Protecting property', can be identified as a realistic component of most local and regional planning practice. It is the vertical-horizontal range, scope and potential content of the

> PLANNING GOALS
> Social (common social good)
> Physical (sustainable 'indefinitely')
> Economic (wellbeing via equitable growth)

applications to which planning can be put in the service of development with conservation, which is useful to establish. The density of the array in figure 2.1 discourages close inspection. Yet such inspection is rewarding. Development planning and conservancy practice can be observed as applied processes for *achieving social goals for the common good in the public domain* through the causative influence of community service. Contrast this with the comprehension of planning on the part of the 'average' individual, staying close to item 4, 'Property protecting provisioning', associated with territorial zoning. In these introductory terms it can be seen that a wide gap exists between the municipal perception of planners as 'hold-the-line functionaries' and the wider societal expectations of planners as 'enablers and achievers'. This is in line with Faludi's depiction (1985: 30) of planning within local government as the 'process of responsible decision-making concerning future courses of action'.

Four illustrative cameos, two Australasian, the others from Great Britain and the United States, reveal the philosophical self-consciousness and apparent lack of

1   Providing public services to meet the general needs of the population (national defence, education, health).

2   Investing in areas of community provisioning that are of little attraction to private capital because of low rates of return, diffused benefits and the large size of the investment required (mass transit, hydroelectric facilities, public housing, state-owned enterprises).

3   Subsidizing corporate interests to encourage specific actions (sectoral growth, redevelopment, infant industries, farm acreage reductions, relocation of industry, employment of handicapped) workers.

4   Protecting property owners and local business interests against the ravages of unrestrained market rationality (land-use planning, zoning, anti-pollution controls).

5   Redistributing income to achieve a more equitable and just social order.

6   Applying comprehensive and coordinated planning approaches to problem resolution and the development of potentials (multipurpose river basin development, comprehensive rural development, growth management).

7   Restraining market rationality in the name of social interests (coastal planning, job protection, wilderness preservation).

8   Transferring income to the victims of market rationality (unemployment payouts and worker compensation).

9   Ameliorating other dysfunctional consequences of market rationality (social and spatial inequalities, business cycle aberrations, resource conservation).

Figure 2.1   Overall uses of within-nation planning

attachment to cogent belief for those who would plan. They also illustrate the extent to which local and regional planning has held a marginal position within the policy framework of settler society governments.

Ann Forsyth gives a five-group listing of proponents for competing 'visions of good city form . . . [as] . . . expansionists, developers, scientific environmentalists, local environmentalists, consolidationists'. Rouse Hill as first envisaged by developers and planners has been scaled back, modified and constrained.

The first Australasian context is from Williams's (1985: 51) data-based assessment of how well the local government planning system was working for New Zealand in the mid-1980s. The local agencies he approached were asked at that time to describe, along with a host of other questions on local government matters, the main purpose of their statutorily required District Planning Schemes. Only a handful of the 231 local authorities consulted – all of whom replied – were able to furnish a response on this item relating to 'purpose', a lack of response which predicated a lack of planning belief. The second example arises from Ann Forsyth's 1999 study of the massive Rouse Hill project in Sydney (*Constructing Suburbs: Competing Voices in a Debate Over Urban Growth*) further 'exposing the rhetorical nature of planning' pushed and pulled by market forces and the environmental and governmental participants she styles as 'middle-level, middle-class professionals and activists'.

From Britain (Reade 1987: 84) there is an observation that 'the consequences of planning . . . seem to be very much out of line with those intended, and to be to a large extent even the opposite of those intended'. Given the widely presumed efficacy of planning in England, Scotland and Wales, this is both revealing and disappointing – highlighting in this case a lack of resonance between grounded beliefs and received theories.

The illustrative context from the United States is more colloquially expressed. Friedmann (1987: 311) in a mid-text passage, *Where Do We Stand*, concludes: 'And Now a Secret Must Out. Talk to planners, and nine out of ten will describe their work as a "failure" or of "little use". They will say "we no longer know what to do. Our solutions don't work. Knowledge and action have come apart. The link is broken."' Again, disappointment highlighting a mismatch between idealism and realism.

It could be that those who would plan delude themselves into attempting the well-nigh impossible. From Klosterman's perspective 'Arguments for and Against Planning' (1985):

> Planners' concern with the physical city was viewed as overly restrictive; their perceptions of the urban development process seen as politically naive; their technical solutions found to reflect their Protestant middle-class view of city life; their attempts to promote a collective public interest revealed to serve primarily the needs of civic and business elites; and [their] democratic comprehensive coordination of public and private development proven to be organisationally and politically impossible.

'The only thing we can be certain of is the protean character of cities, their resistance to top-down planning or prediction.'
Ken Warpole and Liz Greenhalgh 1999

In terms of these observations it is not contextually surprising that zoning is about as successful as planned prescription (mainly for suburbs) has got in Anglo settler societies because of its singular emphasis on property value protection (item 4 in figure 2.1).

The land-based and water-covered platform resources furnish the spatial context for cyclical human activities and enjoyments. Within-nation planning sets out to achieve propinquity between four constituent parts of that territorial habitat. It reaches beyond fixed land-water spatial limits, embracing: *first* and generally, the biospheric domain and all its terrestrial components; *second* and specifically, it is applied instrumentally to the humanized rural and urban landscape parts; *third* it provides the working, schooling and recreational places and provision for movement between those places; and *fourth* it identifies and conserves the cultural values, institutional beliefs and nature-based inheritances of communities. In all of these there are indications of 'cyclicity' and 'connectedness'.

Information and documentation about the pursuit of planning within these four constituent contexts is variously available, although the professional skill to embody this into *complete plans* is frequently lacking. As a consequence of 'less than complete plans' and a constrained physical format, by the late 1980s the planning movement became becalmed. Local government advis-

1984. Doing a round of professional and developer courtesy calls in downtown Auckland brings to mind one property investor claiming that he had no interest in the City Plan. When a concept for a project came up he went straight to City Hall to 'kick it around' with some officials he felt he could work with, and to then hand it over to his lawyer to cut a deal with the city fathers!

ers were overawed by landowner, developer and political collusion. They ended up with nothing more in place than neutral trend zoning as the only acceptable pan-community public imposition upon private lands, achieved mainly because of that general protection which zoning gave to property values.

Planning can be identified as *not* working when it is uncon-

Negotiating Environmental Agreements: How to Avoid Escalating Confrontation. Lawrence Susskind with others 2000.

nected to community preferences and day-to-day processes, and directly exploits and tacitly excludes minority and weak-voiced sections of society (Collin and Collin 2001). Planning operatives find it difficult to figure out and keep up with the increased rate of technological and social change which affect communities.

This has led to anti-planning formations and an operational orientation to straw-activities (policy planning, forward planning, process planning) which appear to be relevant activities even though they fail collectively to define the plan, the planner, or planning. The certainties of step-by-step gradualist change undertaken by divide-and-rule formulaic planning in the past has given way to multiplex understandings and processes. This has brought officials and political leaders to 'talk past each other', generating confusion, anger and misunderstanding. Some cyclicity and connectedness might emanate from their annual reports, but these are seldom clearly profiled, let alone adhered to.

How discourse is handled within a multiple belief society emerges as a matter of significance to the enabling-empowering practice of planning. It is essential for practitioners to find a way to 'listen' to the community they serve. They need to heed those who 'speak' – including the 'voices' which come to them from nature, and to 'hear' the narrative of places – *and* to strain conscientiously to relate back to the community they serve. In a phrase, planners need to sustain a dialogue; from the reasoning of Tett and Wolfe (1991: 199) to contemplate the following:

'to create a more transcendent and universal politics.... to find a discourse that unites the emancipatory quest for social justice with a strong recognition that social justice is impossible without environmental justice.'

David Harvey, 'Environment of Justice', 1995

Do we speak or are we being spoken? Can we be both modernist in our desire to create a future of choice, and [neo]modernist in our recognition of the multiple discourses that shape that choice? Further, can we as planners produce a discourse that is both accountable and inclusive?

What this indicates is that those who would practice 'sustainable' development *with* conservation in the service of their client community need to be sensitive to the obtrusiveness of their own language and reasoning. Again from Tett and Wolfe (1991: 196) to guard against:

- Passive non-transactive grammatical constructions.
- Suggestions that change is agent-less.
- The use of legality to fabricate a legitimacy.
- Simulacrous references to dialogue with the public.

In these terms developers, conservationists and planners are gatekeepers and stakeholders positioned to influence community outcomes. To wield power they must be on their guard against tautology, fabrication, meaninglessness and distortion, showing a willingness to fashion what Schneekloth and Shibley (1995: 7) depict as a dialogic space 'focussing attention on what is part of the dialogue and what stands outside'.

Aside from the attainment of social goals in the fishbowl of public interests, faith has to be also placed in both 'new technology' and 'old market' principles side by side. This is rather like decreeing that the solution to fiscal woes is *both* to raise internal interest rates with a view to attracting outside investment, *and* to lower interest rates with a view to encouraging local investment! Both are desirable, but neither can be brought into line with the other at the same time. With sustainable urban planning, there cannot be absolution by further technological advances coupled to the free market. Nor of course can technology and the market be expected to work together, unfettered, for a balanced future. The required path implicates the empowerment of a neomodern style of planning in the public domain, performing a social service for the common good in the public interest. In those terms it is mission-directed, and in a sense this passage is a mission statement, setting out to identify capabilities for mediating the connection between an empowered humankind and a mostly unprotected ecology. In accordance with democratic beliefs, it reasons through rules for enabling the emergence of a new enlightenment. This calls into being a multi-lineal discourse which meets social needs, is in harmony with nature, and is neomodern in that it exhibits 'connectability', 'sustainability' and 'cyclicity'.

Planners, either or both as conservationist or development specialists, have drawn on the theories of others in commercial, military, academic and industrial disciplines to underpin their philosophical attitude and theoretical approach. So much so that there now exists a confusion of received theories, meanings and processes, of which only a token few can be identified as having helpful operational influence for practising urban and regional planners. Figure 2.2, given as **The planning franchise: a listing**, is a dual categorization of most of the development-led and socially focused approaches. Some other theory listings are appended as fringe oddities difficult to categorize.

For an overview there is Barclay Hudson's (1979) scoping of American normative planning theories under the SITAR rubric 'Synoptic, Incremental, Transactive, Advocacy and Radical'; refer also to Susan Fainstein and Scott Campbell's *Readings in Urban Theory* (1996).

Adding to the confusion of a world embroiled in technological change is the number of confusing theories on development and conservation. That is not all, for the world also experienced an anti-planning lurch during the 1980s (with a 1990s counter-check); and the OECD hegemony has seen off the communist ideology and created a discourse which now includes environmentalism and sustainability. Thus the matter of operational principle begs a major question – in accordance with what theory-logic? Certainly not by means of a review of the 40-odd units of theory knowledge listed in figure 2.2! A sort-out of understanding is called for.

Traditional theories	Radical theories
Development-led	Community-concerned
Target (selective)	Comprehensive
Master-lineal (blueprint)	Multiplex (hi-med-lo options)
Determinist	← Corporate
Programmed →	Utopian
Orthogonal (technocratic)	Organic (reformist)
Safety net	Innovative
Conservative	Revolutionary
Resource strategic →	Socially transforming
Iterative →	Parallel
Physical science	Social science
Policy analysis →	Cybernetics
Land-use planning	Social provision
Local →	← Regional
One option (fixed)	Variety (flexible)

Fringe theories

Action theory	Negotiation theories
Adversary theory	Underground theories
Advocacy theory	Mediation theory
Incrementalist theory	Mixed scanning theory

(The placement of an arrow → or ← is indicative of a theory inclining toward the other 'radical' or 'traditional' category.)

Figure 2.2   The planning franchise: a listing

The construct given in box 2.1, **Traditional and radical operational formats** exhibits notional outcomes for both 'traditional-lineal planning' and 'radical-multiplex planning' practice. The four-option construct depicts the same kilometre square (approximating the North American quarter-square) of humanized rural landscape which has, as a consequence of land title allocations, been settled (as shown in the lead-in depiction) by a forester, an orchardist and a horticulturalist, each separately holding an equal-*value* land parcel.

The 'traditional' *re*arrangement shown as 'B' in the construct is an adjustment of land usage which has forestry, orcharding and horticulture zoned in north to south for the appropriate Class I, Class III, and Class V soil-type tracts in a 'scientifically' ordained way. In this format the zoning depicted is clearly related to the intended outcome, even though the orchardist does not know how to cultivate a horticultural patch, or to manage a forestry tract. And, of course, the horticulturalist and the forester are similarly bemused because of their lack of those other enabling skills. It is in these terms that the 'traditional (means – ends lineal zoning) plan' although rationally correct, does not work out in practice.

Turning to the 'radical' (or reform) work-around solutions we see that in Option 'C' the owners – the horticulture, orchard and forester families – have pooled their equal-valued landholdings with a view to achieving the enablement

Box 2.1 Traditional and radical formats: an explication of theory

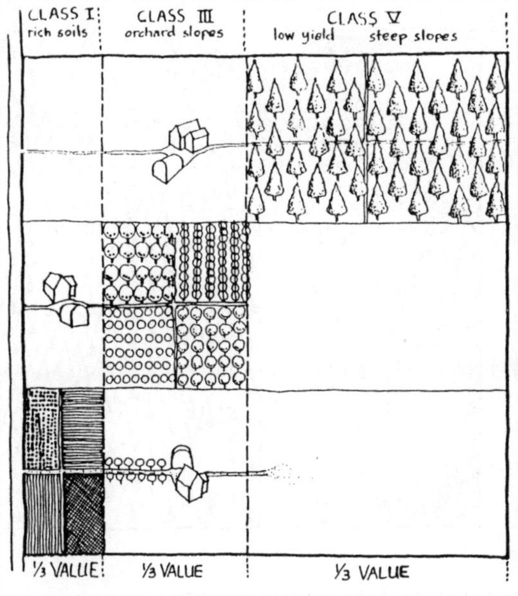

'A' Rural kilometre square

The given situation and problem involves a kilometre square of rural land exhibiting three grades of soil quality (Classes I, III and V). The rural square is divided and retained in three equal area ownerships – from the top-down: the forester's, the orchardist's and the horticulturalist's. Each 'properly manages', 'under-utilizes' and 'neglects' the different soils on their landholding, according to their ability to work the one-third part of the landholding suited to their individual skill.

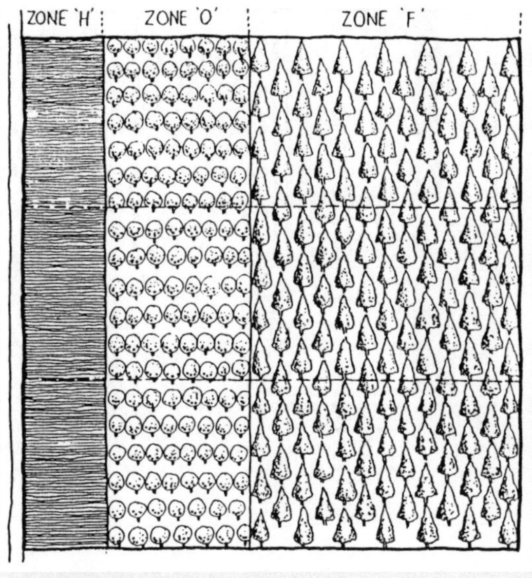

'B' Traditional (zoning) resolution

The land usage rearrangement shown here – according to soil type – has no time limitation for completion. That is left to the inclinations of the current landowners and market forces; a 'traditional' zoning approach for adjusting out of a problematic land-usage situation. To be effective, zoning must be coupled to enforcement. Such powers are very seldom invoked solely to achieve the correction of a supposedly inappropriate land usage.

Box 2.1 *Continued*

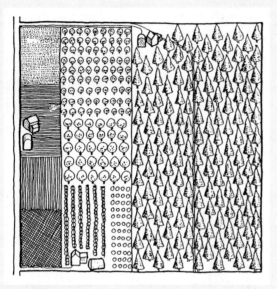

'C'   Radical (reformist) resolution

One 'radical' solution to wasteful land utilization involves the three landowners, each sensitive to the landscape's variety and their neighbour's skills, pooling their talents and resources in a multiplex joint venture.

A model for such larger-scale 'radical' correction to the poor land-usage syndrome is available via the collective *producer cooperative* mode (Campbell and others describing the Mondragon experience, 1977). Of lesser utility would be the state ownership of development rights (the Henry George approach) managed through development licences. Then there is the recently tried and found wanting *collectivist* centrally directed alternative.

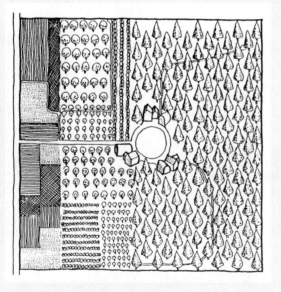

'D'   Radical-traditional resolution

This most carefully thought-through land-use resolution combines 'traditional' zoning with a 'radical' recognition of skills in a reapportionment process whereby each specialist landowner would obtain a refashioned land title appropriate to their landworking capability. It would be essential with such an approach to ensure that reapportionment ran with the title of the land and not with the life of the landowners.

and empowerment of a jointly owned trinity, operated on a profit-sharing basis. Yet because this was, let us assume, an action of the heart rather than the head, the three landowners have not prepared a legally effective contract, and it transpires that their imaginative arrangement gets undermined because of wrangles over unequal rates of participation. Even this outcome, compared with the 'traditional' approach 'B', does not quite match up with theoretical 'radicality', although it sets out to be sympathetic to the landscape.

> In the paraphrased opinion of Brian Quinn (quoted in Mintzberg 1994) 'planning [as zoning: styled 'B' in the construct] is like a ritual rain dance ... for ... it has no effect on the weather that follows – but those who engage in it think it does.'

A solution which would be awkward to implement, but bound to work, is given in the construct as option 'D', a radical-traditional resolution. For this format each landowner, according to their skill, is assigned the class of land appropriate to that skill. This retitling and reapportionment (known on the continent of Europe as *remembrement*) has not, thus far, struck a chord with North American and Australasian landowners, although it loosely accords with the adaptability ascribed to 'flexible zoning' (Porter, Phillips, Lassar 1991).

Such are the options and hopes for planners working for their 'communities of concern' in multiple belief circumstances where morally conscious and ethically driven private and public institutions set out to contribute to the future of their communities. Conservation with development is recommended, in this context, for urban, rural and regional landscapes in order to bring about a progressive three-point 'ranked' outcome. *First* there is the quest to generate ever-improving across-the-board material comfort and wellbeing; *Second* is the aim to provide security for individuals and to empower communities through their social structures; and *Third* there is harmonization in the use of resources and enjoyment of the environment within the overall landscape 'indefinitely'. This trinity or 'triple bottom line' is a rather at odds combination particularly difficult to achieve on all three fronts in these tumultuous times of technological advance, entrenched freehold ownership, political flux and liberalization of global trade.

How Planning Works

Development, conservation and planning all exist in combination as part of a public corporatist agenda for pre-figuring the general good of communities within society, and for the benefit of individuals. The intervention of 'planning' within otherwise 'natural' change patterns – urbanization, mining, forestry, fishing and agribusiness – is justified on the presumption that such intervention will make a useful difference – producing profit surpluses, inducing growth, providing variety, allowing diversity, and nowadays being sustainable.

Technical achievements of the modern world, in and of themselves, amount to nothing *except* in their service to society. Planning fails society when it establishes a land use in the wrong place (housing on flood plains, useless suburban backland reserves), or installs a community service that is not adequately connected

Varietal complexity in planning can be represented as

$$CD \Sigma f[P.A.T.M.I.]$$

where there occurs a Consequence of Development (CD) which is a function of the sum of:

P (population)
A (affluence),
T (technology)
M (management)
I (ideology)

with, of course, some synergies!

The parameters of socio-economic-physical development are varied. . . .

• Temporally (past-present-future)
• Spatially (three dimensional)
• Functional-to-aesthetic
• Selective-to-comprehensive
• Secretive-to-open
• Formal-to-flexible
• Conformist-to-enabalist

or used (token consultations, unused pocket parks). Conversely, sustainable urban planning serves society very well when it enriches life through the provision of enhanced places, sense of security, and when it establishes an improvement in the overall landscape ecology (habitat). These are all broadly social outcomes achieved through sound policies and thoughtful design. Of course consumer enhancement comes into the picture, but not as a stand-alone factor. The challenge this social emphasis passes on involves a multiplicity (variety, security, diversity, connectedness, enjoyment, capacity fulfilment) in contexts where the previous notable outcomes were constructions of solely physical utilities (roads, bridges, suburbs, sewerage plants).

Plan-making *invokes the future, involves change, and implicates causation;* in other words it engages human knowledge, consciously, to reach improving decisions which lead to worthy outcomes. A flaw in this reasoning is that it is perceived as serving a client or clients, who or which frequently elude identification – not least because many are inarticulate about these matters. Important in this are the consulting, designing and delivery processes leading to planned change.

The operational complexities of sustainable urban planning are challenging because of the number of 'actors' and 'agendas' implicated. Contrast this with corporate business which primarily takes decisions for a profit-making purpose, where the bottom line is explicit – a sentiment expressed by William Fischell (1985) in these terms: 'The profit motive of landowners forces them to consider many alternative uses and to compare each use with the others. No planner has a similarly powerful motive to gather information for each parcel in the city.' Also in business there are the PPBS (planning programming budgeting system), and the MBO (management by objectives) procedures. In contrast, planning decisions of the neomodern sustainable urban kind are continuing, cyclical, *non*-routine, and seldom profit-focused.

Two other complexities can be identified: *first* that contemporary and future development with conservancy decisions are of the 'wickedly difficult' variety; *second* that the 'economic social environmental' decision-taking process is not merely multiple, but 'radical' in terms of the discourse, mediation and work-around approach and ethic it calls into being. This highlights the further need for 'creativity' 'design' and 'concomitance'.

It is important that planning practitioners comprehend the theory which underpins the service they provide, because if there is no theory-logic, then their service will be judged wholly technical. The 'traditional' and 'radical' connotations (box 2.1) are now revisited in figure 2.3 as an ethical-attitudinal **Configuration of traditional and radical theories**.

	Traditional operational practice	Radical operational practice
OUTCOMES ANTICIPATED	Low variety	Complex (variety)
	Logical (step-by-step)	Creative (multi-phase)
	Technological	Humanist
	Will be done	Agreed to do
	About decisions	About values
	Target-led	Goal-led
	Attainments	Alternatives
	Lineal	Multiplex
	Structural	Procedural
	'What' to think	'How' to think
DESCRIPTIVE CHARACTERISTICS	Rational (one answer)	Radical (several answers)
	Top-down	Bottom-up and top-down
	Received	Grounded
	Coarse-grained	Fine-grained
	Extrapolates	Invents and improvises
	Pessimistic	Optimistic
	Normative	Varietal
	Deterministic	Probalistic
	Specific and rigid	Considers alternatives
	Computes answers	Thinks alternatives
	Reductionist	Responsive
	For 'me'	For 'us'
	Specific	Generalist
	Conventional	Interactive
	'Masculine'	'Feminine'
TECHNOLOGIES INVOLVED	Problem-solving	Potential-realizing
	Sieve technique	Heuristic discovery
	One way through	Several ways around
	Component analysis	Factor analysis
	Computor analysis	Cerebral prognosis
	Programmed	Non-lineal
	Mechanical	Creative
	Remove-replace	Mitigate-ameliorate
	Sorting	Sensing
	Extrapolating	Improvising
	Consultation	Negotiation

Figure 2.3   Configuration of traditional and radical theories

Development-focused providers have got into the habit of plunging into project assignments on an 'action' basis: writing down, if called upon, their attitudinal approach *after* the general form and context of their proposals have been agreed! Such a wrapping of 'theory' around reports and position papers *after* the key decisions have been settled is improper, hardly reflecting reliability accountability and legitimacy. It would be reasonable also to assert that most experienced local government practitioners handle much of their day-to-day workload with personal job-enhancing concerns uppermost in mind, a first objective (not helpful, yet understandable) being to promote themselves in their organization's and or also their profession's pecking order.

Clearly, it is an advantage to have an understanding of the means for attaining the 'targets' and 'goals' profiled in a mission statement, expressed in terms of the operational theory involved. Conversely a lack of understanding of mission goals induces the sense of frustration, aimlessness and under-achievement which, sadly, is the hallmark of many planners' work experience. The consideration here is with the delivery components of neomodern work-around practice. Healey et al. (1995 paraphrasing Faludi) have it that 'The purpose of plans is to provide, in one way or another, a store of decision rules to guide a subsequent stream of regulatory and investment decisions' and figure 2.3 lists the 'outcomes', 'characteristics' and 'tech-nological' bases of both traditional and radical planning. This connects with two items presented earlier in this chapter: the complexity and confusion of the 30-plus listing of theory nomenclature (figure 2.2); and the box 2.1 format depicting how the horticulturalist, the orchardist and the forester usually have the problem of improper land usage sorted out for them via best-use zoning, yet could have obtained improved production and enjoyment from their landholdings by engaging either the 'cooperative' or the 'reapportioning' options (C or D).

There are some approaches which fit neither the traditional-lineal nor the radical-multiplex reasoning. Here I have in mind the likes of the 'action', 'adversary', 'advocacy', 'target' and 'incrementalist' modes, each with its devotees and a liter-ature. The case against their lack of fit rests fundamentally with the litmus test of ability/inability for procedures of these kinds to nest recognizably within a multi-ple-belief system and or also to fit with the sustainable, conservation *with* devel-opment, reasoning. These distinctions are of particular importance in relation to operatives who wish to present themselves as 'radical' but who, if solely critical, vituperative or disruptive *for no achievable purpose*, are really 'out of the planning loop' and really not part of a multiple-belief neomodern operational system.

Figure 2.4 showing the **'SWOT' progression** illustrates sequential theory in a semi-scientific way (with 'prognosis' and 'implementation' laced in) combining the fundamental working components of *all* operationally effective traditional-lineal and radical-multiplex planning processes. An element of 'sleight of hand' is glossed over with the SWOT approach (sometimes styled SWOP – Strengths, Weaknesses, Opportunities, Problems) because of the glib way it proceeds 'magically' from potentials identification and problems detection to plans – a design-step mystery which will be addressed later.

Additional to the problem-solving and the potential-realizing distinctions within planning practice, there exists another significant operational distinction: between a formulaic legal-rules activity, and plan-led design actions. All people involved in mitigating, assessing, dealing, appealing, negotiating or ameliorating are, of course, implicated in planning issues; yet they may be remote from actu-ally 'doing or delivering' planned change. Operatives of a process-directed per-suasion find it easy to construe that, surely, their activity predicates the delivery of planning, even if daily practice has them in the environmental courts or at the

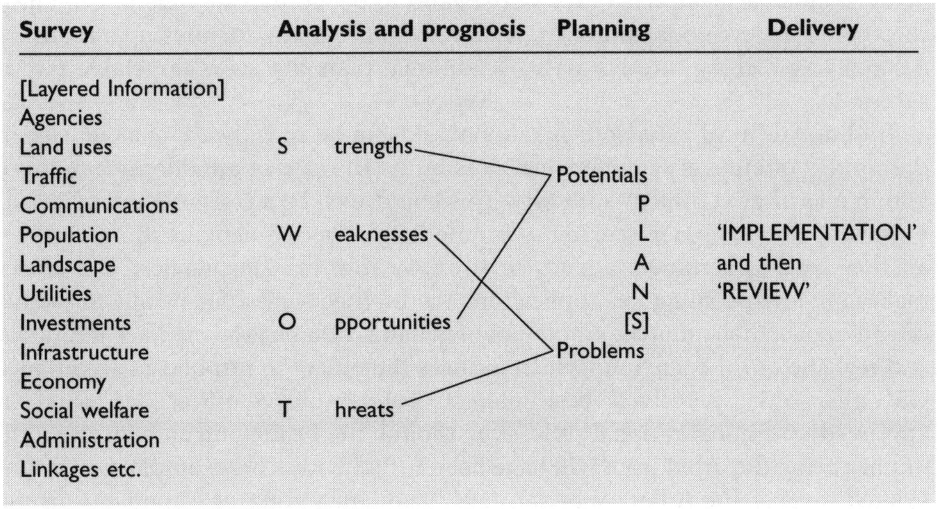

Survey	Analysis and prognosis	Planning	Delivery

[Layered Information]
Agencies
Land uses   S   trengths
Traffic   Potentials
Communications   P
Population   W   eaknesses   L   'IMPLEMENTATION'
Landscape   A   and then
Utilities   N   'REVIEW'
Investments   O   pportunities   [S]
Infrastructure   Problems
Economy
Social welfare   T   hreats
Administration
Linkages etc.

Figure 2.4 The 'SWOT' progression

negotiating table – supplicating, negotiating, ameliorating, applying, assessing and monitoring. These process-planning activities often constitute 'the tail that wags the whole dog' in modern planning: observed by Jean Perraton decades ago (1972) as an activity where 'problem solvers tend to play down the importance (or even deny the possibility of) innovation'. The point to now register within this revisitation is that the intended characteristic of the planning activity being addressed here is of a goal-led, plan-led multiplex character.

The plan or plans resulting from plan-making show indicated outcomes and preferred results: and the central concern for this chapter is to clarify understanding about the preparation of such plans within a multiple belief system – an openly democratic environment. That 'grounded' context is the focus of the next passage, which examines the working of traditional-lineal planning; *followed by* a passage which explores the radical-multiplex strictures for development with conservancy.

After a planned intention is made known, and differences of value emerge, *dispute resolution* comes into play. For guidance consult: Lawrence Susskind and Patrick Field, *Dealing with an Angry Public* (1996).

Before a planned intention is disclosed, *consensus building* can be harnessed to bridge between value differences. For guidance consult: *The Consensus Handbook*, Susskind, McKearnan, Thomas-Larmer 1999.

Traditional-Lineal Planning

The traditional planning procedure has provided, historically, a purposeful-targeted foundation to human domination over the biospheric envelope. At base this amounts to: What do we have? What do we want? What do we do to get it? It is predicated on the notion that communities actually 'know' what it is they 'want' and will be energized enough to attain it; and, or also, that planners have the requisite certainty of *knowledge* to be safely left with the *power* to apply their operational skills to achieve what they understand to be worthy *outcomes*! It is a lineal corporatist means–ends approach, which simplifies and structures operations on a make-way-coming-through basis. Traditional planning seeks targetable physical results.

Traditional-lineal behaviour is rational and can be considered, analogously, in the context of an everyday personal possibility: the case of a footloose employee within a local government authority. This could well be a conservation officer or a development planner seeking a promotional appointment in the service of another local government agency or to move into private practice. The officer makes out an appealing job application, is presented with a financially attractive offer to move, then quits the employment in hand. What has taken place is rational and realistic lineal behaviour which induces the officer to respond in accordance with their own perceived best interest. The employee-officer has acted in approved traditional-rational style, even though the future outcome for the community being departed from will have been trifled with. This example can be considered against the fuller Weberian (1947) understanding of 'rationality in the means-ends sense when (a person's) action is guided by considerations of ends, means and secondary consequences'. There is empathy here with Habermas's (1984) *Theory of Communicative Action*. At a stroke a failing with the 'traditional-lineal mode' is identified – that it is generally self-serving, and lacking in visionary breadth.

'Chunked' into being, settlements are hugely influenced by their rural roading and field boundary inheritances. At the time greenfields are swallowed into suburban tracts, the extant rural road pattern re-emerges as part of the new street pattern; and out of the extant field pattern emerges the new zonings. The plots assigned within the two-dimensional zonings then shape the buildings. This should work the other way around: building setting being the initiator rather than an end-point installation.

Traditional procedural development and conservancy planning of the 'cookbook' kind is still the dominant operational mode – the way through – for local and regional planning in settler societies, although once popular expressions such as 'master plan' and 'blueprint planning' are now *passé*. The practitioners of this approach are technicist: those who get things going and have works carried out – the engineers, surveyors, lawyers and architects who 'traditionally' rolled back the wilderness. They were orthogonal in their two-dimension operational mode, working to the precept that 'development equals good' and also that as 'development equals change' then 'change' was always 'good' as well! According to Reade (1987: 92) it was inevitable that 'in sociological terms, developers and planners will come to develop a shared sub-culture' with an emphasis on development which excluded conservation, and physical growth for developer profit with minimum attention to community concerns or needs. Little room, here, for mutual gains, the triple bottom line, connectedness and cyclicity.

The project-by-project traditional planning specialists got on with the pursuit of development in a manner which mostly excluded conservation and social outcomes. Not being overly concerned either for spiritual cultural or ecological values, mistakes were made. From Gerecke and Reid (1991) it has been identified that: 'The ethic of professionalism in the 20th Century has been science and management. This has produced a false and very narrow sort of instrumental rationality, and while no one wants to admit ethical shortsightedness and amnesia over the past century, the state of the earth speaks to our narrowness and neglect.' Out of World War II there followed the behavioural refinements of operations research, systems analysis and scientific management, mainly to cut down on time losses and fiscal costs. These techniques were followed in turn by the also empiricist 'social impact assessment' and 'environmental impact abatement' procedures. The carry-over to contemporary urban planning is a replica, repeating and reproducing what has gone before. This is apparent with procedures which endorse the status quo. What happens is that the indicator usage pattern is extrapolated and enlarged upon in urban plans, serving developer gains ahead of the interests of the communities they are intended for. Another example arises in the context of scheduling prime agricultural land for 'enclosure' into urban use on a 20-year look-ahead basis, serving local developer cash-up and move-on interests ahead of national needs. From these examples it can be seen that the nineteenth and twentieth centuries have been, and largely continue in the twenty-first century to be, identifiable with formula-growth models, the trend being set by developers and landowners rather than the identification of settlement roles and community needs.

An abbreviation and re-expression of the traditional plan-making process, based on Le Breton and Henning's classic (1961) *Planning Theory* is presented in figure 2.5 as the **Traditional planning sequence**. The core is the lineal progression: a step-after-step progression where theoretically, and usually in practice, each 'step' is completed in sequence.

In relation to the nineteenth- and twentieth-century work of the settler engineer, surveyor, and architect, the traditional planning sequence, whether consciously pursued or not, gave rise to such orthogonal examples as the *box* bridge, the settlement *grid*, and the office *block*. The 11 steps leading to finite project completion in figure 2.5 are processional, one event following the other in an ordered sequence, culminating with completion.

Data analysis and design can be refined and improved by revisiting the earlier steps (1–5) on a 'feedback' basis within the '11-step' sequence. These feedback refinements are of little improving effect if the blueprint itself is flawed, which is frequently the case. Two adverse outcomes via the blueprint approach can be anticipated: *first*, 'master urban' plans take unconscionably long periods of time to come to fruition when left to the machinations of the marketplace; *Second*, 'master urban' plans are put in a constitutional quandary because their fixed

A personal early lesson arising from the 'traditional planning' approach arose during the mid-1960s following my preparation of constitutionally correct first-time 'master plans' for Ba, Nadi and Sigatoka: river-crossing settlements on the westerly side of Viti Levu in Fiji. The hurricanes which hit the island a few years later swept away many of the railroad bridges, which underwrote these *loci standi*. The replacement bridges were sited 'elsewhere' at the then technically most appropriate positions, throwing the master plans into disarray. From this early experience was gained an insight into the limitations of 'traditional' master planning, and the role and utility of 'flexibility'.

Because so much down-time, money and emotional energy can be lost on fatuous information assembly, I re-express here the title headings to the Step 5 principles of data assembly as: *suitability, economy, efficiency, relative accuracy, sufficient to the cause, and simplicity;* keywords emphasized because information assembly is the stage where many planning practitioners become mesmerized by data collections and data comparisons – to the neglect of plan-making.

Step 1	Emergence of the need or desire for development or planning. Issue identification.
STEP 2	The formulation of aims and objectives, including their communication to the public. Task definition.
Step 3	Obtaining agreement or consent to proceed, and communicating this.
Step 4	Assembling a team, assigning responsibilities and outlining the procedure which is to be followed.
Step 5	Gathering data. Information assembly.
Step 6	Data evaluation (analysis and diagnosis) along the lines of the SWOT depiction given in figure 2.4. Leading to diagnosis (problem identification) and prognosis (potential defining).
STEP 7	The all-important design step. Formulation of the general policy direction; then the presentation of a proposal (or proposals) along with a statement relating to the commitment of resources this proposal will command. Creative synthesis.
Step 8	Testing of the proposals. Also, if necessary, a testing of the data quality and a data evaluation. Continuing critical review.
Step 9	Approval: usually including 'conditions of approval', along with a communication of this outcome to all interested parties.
STEP 10	Implementation, usually in accordance with the dictates of market forces and the vicissitudes of land owner and developer inclinations: otherwise, for projects in stages, via the application of appropriate Log Frame (chapter 4, box 4.7) monitoring evaluation and adjustment procedures. Tangible output occurs at Step 10.
Step 11	Overview, recasting and re-expression.

Figure 2.5 Traditional planning sequence

legal arrangements are difficult to undo and put together again in accordance with due legal process and constitutional correctness.

The downside to the traditional-lineal approach includes these summary observations: that this mode –

- Provides for the future on a normative (adjustment and extrapolation) basis, with little accommodation of 'the big picture' or 'what if' alternatives and ambitions.
- Avoids conflict via a reductionist pigeon-holing of activities into sub-components; straitjacketing politically 'wicked' multifaceted problems into technically benign, singular, procedures.
- Focuses on physical outcomes to the neglect of social issues – hence two-dimensional physical 'blueprint' and 'master' plan-making.

The 11-step 'Traditional sequence' given earlier in figure 2.5 is now represented in line-drawn format as figure 2.6, **Sequential progression for traditional planning**, which also shows the in-line 'feedback' feature.

Excepting the virtue of being readily understood, there seems to be little on the credit side to align with the trend-formula approach to traditional-lineal

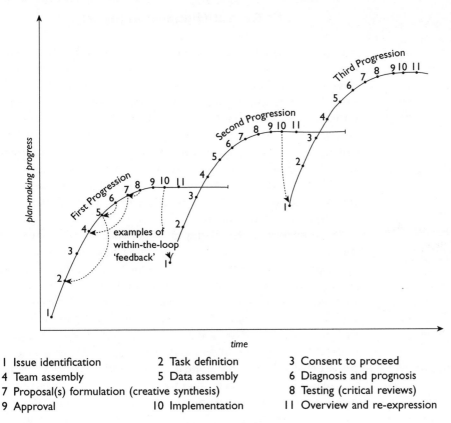

I Issue identification   2 Task definition   3 Consent to proceed
4 Team assembly   5 Data assembly   6 Diagnosis and prognosis
7 Proposal(s) formulation (creative synthesis)   8 Testing (critical reviews)
9 Approval   10 Implementation   11 Overview and re-expression

Figure 2.6   Sequential progression for traditional planning

practice, although conservancy fits the lineal progression reasonably well. Two positive leavenings for the traditional-lineal
approach can be identified. These include 'certainty to the
public', and a mostly assured 'review' opportunity. The 'certainty to the public' aspect needs no further explanation
because it is based on the predication that legal (usually
zoning) mandates, coupled to conservative appeal mechanisms, can wrap up the 'law of the land' and the 'choice of the
people' in one legally sure, simple property-protecting
package. The 'review' emphasis is an elaboration of the basic
utility for revisiting the sequence through 'feedback'. Identification of this 'improving' feature within the previous two illustrations (figures 2.5 and 2.6) is often perceived more in the
breach than in outcome. Traditional plan 'reviews' are mostly
notional and less than convincing; although few planning practitioners would gainsay the value of ever-improved data for
the re-identification and re-expression of goals, targets and
plans – even ordinary zoning plans.

It is a matter of
practical utility to keep
in view that all
complete plans have
five identifiable
components:

1 Title (the identifier).
2 Notation of the
   authorizing,
   compilation,
   approving and
   implementing
   agency.
3 Recording of the
   start-up, stage
   completion, and
   completion dates.

4   Statement of
    intentions and a
    programme for
    implementation.
5   Summation of the
    resources required
    to implement the
    plan.

NEW WORLD PARADIGM
        SHIFT
    Policy analysis
    Decolonization
Emancipation and civil
        rights
    Democratization
  Liberation theology
   Environmentalism
  Information-sharing
    Technological
      advances

The Radical-Multiplex Approach

The post-World War II emergence of a sensitive, discursive, open and above all democratic and grounded approach to development planning and conservancy practice can be linked, causally, with the decolonization, emancipation, and liberal education movements. It is also associated with the modernization and enlargement of local government, and with the linkage to world changes, world markets and world information. Behind all can be identified the vast additional amount of knowledge and understanding society now has obtained from the Marxist, feminist, libertarian theology, first peoples and environmental movements.

It is important to distinguish between two streams of 'radical' conscience: that which identifies with a largely spontaneous activism; and that which is neomodern and democratic. Radical conservancy *with* development enables planning operatives to stand back from being 'part of the problem' in a manner which ensures that they can be identified as a truly objective and facilitative 'part of the solution'.

Traditional, markedly physical planning in its various styles continues to be applied because it has the appealing 'positivist' virtue of being easily understood and readily operated across a broad public policy spectrum. It is, after all, the underlying format for urban planning-as-zoning activity. Radical planning is more substantive than traditional practice because it exhibits connective understandings and incorporates cyclical progressions; accepting that (from Schneekloth and Shibley 1995) 'we can no longer assume that . . . professionals "know" and others "don't-know"': to which simplification must be added a complexity; namely that there are considerable social risks and operational pressures associated with development planning and conservancy practice. In Low's phrasing (1991 emphasis added) 'the more open the debate the better, the more informed the debate the better, the more equal the opportunity to participate in the debate the better . . . [for] . . . justice is a matter of *fair outcomes* as well as fair process'. Clearly communication skills are of importance in the furthering of debate and discourse within any multiple-belief system.

RADICAL-MULTIPLEX 'KEY
OPERATOR PHRASINGS'
Empowering: sensitive:
    participatory
  What for? – What if?
    Neomodern:
    sustainable
    Mitigating:
    ameliorative
  Open: interactive:
      enabling
    Fair process:
  equitable outcomes
  Mutually beneficial
Facilitative: discursive
  Social-economic-
    environmental
  Variety and choice

Another commentator, Hillier (1993), delineates the problematic for what is depicted here as radical planning practice, as lying within a framework of 'discursive democracy', which

> Accepts the inevitability of conflict and obstacles to transparent decision making such as hierarchy, inequality in the ability to make and challenge arguments, political strategising, deception, the exercise of power, manipulation, entrenched ideas and

self-deception. Nevertheless, with the aid of an effective facil-
itator, consensus or negotiated compromises can be reached
based on mutual recognition of, and respect for legitimate, if
different, interests and discourses.

Radical development *is not* out of the planning loop in
some aimless pluralist way, as with the 'muddling through'
prognosis (Lindblom 1959). Radical planners can of course be
protesters. Exercises in freedom of expression, activation of
rights, and expressions of discontent are valid. But
the general run of strident protestation against officialdom
is *not* mainstream radical planning. Connectedness and
cyclicity are the key to radical planning practice, instituting a
'working around' rather than an 'imposed over' philosophical
approach.

Clarification of understanding about roles, between activists
who mostly do *not* get involved professionally in the development or conservancy processes, and the operationally effective
'radical mode' planner, is a significant issue. Sustainable-sensitive
planning operatives would be likely to accede to Popper's (1963: 358) contention
'that it is impossible to determine ends scientifically. There is no scientific way of
choosing between two ends . . . There is (always) a quarrel about ends.' This
degree of difficulty is well understood, calling into being the need for a management advocacy (Lawrence Susskind et al., *Negotiating Environmental Agreements*,
2000).

What, then, can be identified as the distinguishing mark of a radical-multiplex
approach to planning practice? Well, it is of course 'in the planning loop'. And it
is a *planning activity* because of the engagement of forethought before taking
improving action. It is directed toward community-enhancing outcomes. Additionally it is aligned with the neomodern ideals of sustainability (cyclicity) and
empowerment (connectedness). In the realm of values (Perry 1954) it suggests
working to endorse a framework for the municipalization of community ethics
and values. Politically, radical practice can be identified as coming from the mainstream 'right' (protecting individual property interests and upholding established
institutional entitlements); *and* from the mainstream 'left' (improving community
wellbeing and putting in place arrangements for safeguarding community
values). There is some concurrency with orthodox new-age groups, the 'greens'
and 'liberals', and those on-the-fringe minority interest lobbyists – an intersection
and an amalgam of multiple interests.

The social reformist and revolutionary movements are historically relevant to
radical planning. To Popper (1963: 358) the 'interventionist period of European
History' can be viewed as the seed-bed for the now neomodern style of radical
planning. The nineteenth-century 'company town' concept (Robert Owen in
England 1771–1858, and Charles Fourier in nineteenth-century France); the

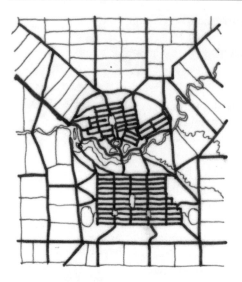

Adelaide: the initial layout

Here is Rexroth's droll
parody of nineteenth-
century communitarian
colonists who 'with flags
flying and music playing
to the wilderness . . .
began with a picnic . . .
[yet] within a few days
passions began to run
short, necessary skills
were found to be in
even shorter supply, and
tempers were shorter
yet. Soon competition
for what little was
available seemed worse
than in the world they
had left, and they began
to quarrel and accuse
each other.'

K. Rexroth,
Communalism, 1974

utopian philosophical link represented in Reps's (1965) writings on the *Making of Urban America*; and also the Australia and New Zealand company settlements (depicted in Williams 1966), are all historically relevant enterprises which interfaced public and private capital in the same utopian-radical venture. Then in the early twentieth century Clarence Perry (published 1929) identified the 'neighbourhood' as the defining, and again largely utopian, urban planning principle, being to his way of thinking a quarter-square (160 acres) with 5,000 to 6,000 population centred on an elementary (primary) school.

And for the present, is the pursuit of utopia identifiable? Are not the United States and Canada in North America, Britain, France, Germany in Europe, and New Zealand and Australia in the Antipodes, loose-fit 'utopias' from the perspective of the newly arriving Pakistan, Afghan, North African, Turkish, Pacific Island, East Asian and Mexican in-migrants? These movements are 'revolutionary' and 'social reformist' examples of people 'inventing an improved future' for themselves.

Authoritative support for the utopian movement comes from the ordered writing of Mumford (1961) and the broad polemic of Illich (1973) arguing for a communitarian approach. In terms of 'social reforms' there is no better advocate for this new-age 'utopia' than the oppressed, poor and uneducated moving toward their own perception of employment opportunities, personal security and advantage, constituting for themselves their own new-age ideal. Disparagement of 'revolutionary' ideals, simply because the inflexible and violent examples best known to us have failed, should not blind communities to the essentially social worth of purposefully achieved progressive utopian quests.

The reformists of Australasia and Northern America achieved 'quiet' twentieth-century democratic revolutions: the emancipation of women (particularly European women); and the recognition of rights for Native Americans, Maori and Aboriginal. But there has never been sufficient pain, oppression and brutalization to mobilize nationwide revolutionary revolt in the Anglo sectors of the New World. Within these settler societies spatial class segregation (through zoning) and the marginalization of people (through selective skills enhancement) gave rise to discord, and citizens grew to know that some discontent was there. The neomodern challenge is to communicate and channel this discontent from households and neighbourhoods into development and conservancy projects, in accordance with Harper and Stein's 'Wide Reflective Equilibrium' (1993).

The less-than-revolutionary yet identifiably radical sustainable urban planning paradigm is also bound into cyclicity and connectedness. The agents from below are principally the 'participants' and the 'technocrats' who work for community improvement. They often accept that their contribution is more an 'input of time' rather than the reward of an 'income'. Those who are purely angry, and lacking in creative and sustainable vision, are of little utility to the radical-multiplex process.

Radical planning implicates design. Furthermore it is always political. Patsey Healey (1995: 255) views 'The preparation and use of a plan [as] much more than a technical bureaucratic exercise. It is inherently an arena of political struggle.' If a purportedly planned activity does *not* so identify, then the activity being pursued is really little more than a 'technical fix' like status quo zoning. It also applies social and economic power with improving effect; bringing about structural changes through the linking of 'knowledge to power' and thence to 'control' and eventually to 'outcome'. This, for radical sustainable planning, is the directional 'what'. The remaining question is one of 'how' this substantive ideal can be rendered operational?

A start can be made by objectifying the components involved in neomodern sustainable and concomitant development with conservation practice. As with all planning, *power* is the lever; and power lies with those who have the *knowledge*; and those who have 'knowledge *and* power' can influence *outcomes*. Emphases already identified include connectiveness and cyclicity, to which can be added sensitivity, empowerment, variety and choice. The priority laid on 'knowledge being the key' underlines further the *designer* and the *mediator* basis to effective conservancy with development. This identifies a set of skills criteria, along with a set of performance criteria.

The skills set criteria are no different, in a listing, than the portrayal of talents required for 'traditional' planning; although the sensitivity of the facilitative skills identified for 'radical' planning are different in style and and complexity. These have been collated in box 2.2 as a **Radical-multiplex skills set**.

It is design capability which most enhances excellence of outcome. In these terms, relative to the Formulation of proposals (*Step 7* in figure 2.6, the '11-step sequential progression') an itemization of alternative approaches to the creative leap synthesis (which is the design step) would include the following:

- Brainstorming, a usually collegiate, creative-leap technique which suspends initial judgment in favour of a flow of policy and design suggestions; leading over the course of time to a mediated recommendation.

The generative 'brainstorming' reference is Osborn's (1954) *Applied Imagination*, which should be read in conjunction with the authoritative OECD output, Jantsch's *Technological Forecasting in Perspective* (1967). Brainstorming has proved useful for clearly focused projects; and less useful for resolving complex issues.

Box 2.2   Radical-multiplex skills set

The radical-multiplex planning skills set exhibits more promise than the traditional-lineal planning sequence because of its alignment with a continuously improving ethos for cyclical change in multiple belief systems. The 'RADICAL' PLANNING SKILLS SET INCLUDES –

- **Investigative skills** – the backgrounding and awareness aptitudes for determining 'how' the relevant 'matters' and 'issues' got to where they are, and 'why?' they got to be in the condition they are in.

- **Comprehension skills** – those 'what of' and 'what about?' understandings of governmental and non-governmental procedures and powers.

- **Data assembly competency** – 'sufficiently' accurate and 'analytical' (problem-solving) and 'diagnostic' (potential-realizing) aptitudes.

- **Prognostic skills** – the 'what if?' qualities of 'scientifically objective' planning; enabling operatives to evaluate and indicate policy outcomes and design directions.

- **Design skills** – entailing the 'what to do?' generation of creative-leap alternatives. The generation of innovative computer compilations and presentations, and above all else, a three-dimensional *and* a socio-economic design capability.

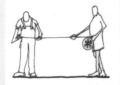

- **Technical skills** – available to evaluate policy issues, to argue marginalized positions and prepare spreadsheets and designs, as well as do the costing-out of proposals, withal getting involved in implementation.

- **Communication skills** – for both individual and group participation, empathy enhancement, negotiation and mediation. This also includes the engagement of 'win-win' discourse skills implicating the engagement of rhetoric in ways which ensures that reform arguments are always well presented.

- Presentation of 'high-medium-low' design possibilities, presentations which vary in their output-cost and input-management content.
- Engagement of 'trial and testing' procedures, the demonstration of design proposals modelled mathematically as 'virtual reality'.
- Use of the Delphi Technique, which devises a discourse programme for engaging in a succession of interrogations and information-feedback cycles which arrive at a socially optimal design recommendation.
- Reflecting on a listing of Key Words and their antonyms and synonyms as a stimulus for considering alternative recommendations (Riddell 1985: 28).
- Gaming and modelling simulation 'apodictic' (near reality) techniques varying from the abstractness of computer-modelling through to the realism of table-top modelling.
- Brokerage, bargaining and negotiation techniques for resolving design issues within the process of 'getting to yes': consult Susskind and Cruikshank, *Breaking the Impasse* (1987).
- Symbolic analogy formulation, the 'sensitizing' techniques which are an extension out of cybernetics which leads toward the identification of design parameters.

The workings of most of the above are well understood. The last item, 'Symbolic analogy formulations', derives from Lynch's (1960) *Image of the City*. This was enlarged, updated and pragmatized in *Responsive Environments* (Bentley, Alcock, Murrain, McGlynn and Smith 1985). These urban considerations are explored in greater detail in chapter 5.

The *Performance-Set Criteria* connects realism with idealism. The clear inference with figure 2.6, 'Sequential progression' is that step follows step with feedback improving data, improving analyses and improving designs. The main additional features within a radical planning pattern are the Habermasian (1984) 'negotiating and improving' and 'social communication' characteristics. The inventive 'brainstorming', 'trial and testing', 'gaming simulation', 'bargaining' and 'symbolic analogy' approaches to design, listed earlier, are also useful. This creative 'designer' pattern for achieving sustainable outcomes is important because it connects the process back to its philosophical roots in accordance with the notion 'that we learn from our mistakes'. By continuously making these revisionist connections, the radical planning operative becomes aligned to an understanding about what is going on, what is being sought, and above all else, 'why' and for 'whom' sustainable urban planning is being produced.

The procedural challenge and sensitivity which the radical planning approach calls into being, generates these social questions:

- What are the 'issues'?
  Social policy redirection? Minority rights and needs? Resource uptake options? Waste dumping and waste processing policies? Urban layout alternatives? Regional multiplier potentials? Natural and heritage conservancy?

'In heterogeneity is creation of the world.'
'Over time, the rules for change get changed themselves.'
'Equilibrium is death.'
  Kevin Kelly, *Out of Control*, 1994.

- What are the 'indicators'?
  Malnutrition? Truanting? Crime figures? Unemployment? Pollution? Physical illness? Mental illness? Commercial indicators? Lost industrial opportunities? Species decline?
- What are the 'options'?
  Acquiesce? Defer? Resist? Confront? Fight? Cooperate? Negotiate? Modify? Mediate? Centralize? Decentralize? Ameliorate? Mitigate?

These 'issues' 'indicators' and 'options' enable the neomodern planner to recognize that they serve a multiple-belief system; that they must learn to negotiate mutual gain in conjunction with competitive entrepreneurial forces as well as the generally conservative elements of central and local government administration. From Healey, McNamara, Elson and Doak (1988) there is the view that 'rather than simple questions of "who do we listen to?" more complex problems arise of "who do we ask, how do we ask them, and what do we ask them about"?' And it is from these attitude-with-vision and consensus-building criteria, indeed a *sustainable attitude and a clearer vision* incorporating the dimension of *creativity* (Weisberg 1993) that the neomodern planner gains insight into what is to be done.

'The need for planning [in Canada] arises from two general sources. One is the *need to solve problems* associated with a particular project or ongoing development situation . . . the other main need is the *desire to attain an improved situation* [to realize new potentials].'
Gerald Hodge and Ira Robinson, *Planning Canadian Regions*, 2001.

Of course *both* the radical-multiplex and the traditional-lineal processes engage the orthodox (figures 2.5 and 2.6) planning sequence, which is as ancient as the first teleologically conscious pattern of human intervention. *Both* attempt to achieve 'progressive change' within the logic of the planning sequence for 'designing' and 'implementing' an improved and enriched community future of greater variety. *Both* radical and traditional processes are founded on the general ideal of a public service which sets out to put in place societally beneficial outcomes for conservation and development. *Both* attempt to 'solve problems' and to 'realize potentials'. And *both* radical and traditional procedures are rooted in vested interests, public values, corporatism and national morality.

What particularly characterizes radical procedures are the variations of sensitivity, connectivity, cyclicity, multiplicity, mutual gain, empowerment and participation within the operational skills set and the performance-set criteria reviewed earlier and expanded upon in box 2.2.

There is a concern about cybernetics, SSM and GIGO electronics 'getting' to us and winning us over, before we get to address actual and immediate concerns and probable situations.

Additional to the previous underscoring of the commonality of outcome shared by many 'traditional' and 'radical' endeavours arise other computer-aided ways of handling instability and complexity. The 'soft systems methodology' (SSM) is an example of an approach which attempts the engagement of systems modelling to real world problem situations. This technique, we are led to expect, can provide a 'social audit' for such complex and ambivalent scenarios as: How to mitigate adverse environmental effects? How to integrate community boards effectively into local government? How to organize and integrate an indigenous first-peoples' meeting house into the wider urban community? *or*, more personally, Which university? Whom to befriend? When to marry? What job to apply for? When to move on?

With all these complex issues there is an easily understood empirical element; for example the *advantages* of impact mitigation, the *worth* of community boards, meeting houses, university training and overseas experience. Values-ordering in a systemic way predicates that the resolution of complex issues can produce multiple outcomes. Within the one and the same methodology a *traditional* consideration of the real world is attached to a *radical* consideration of 'rich pictures' and 'root definitions' leading to 'conceptual modelling' (Checkland 1987). The advocates for SSM perceive what takes place, operationally, as 'iterative', 'heroic' and 'immediate' – to which I would add 'dialogic' – putting SSM at the extreme end of the radical spectrum.

A serious complication with SSM concerns difficulties about incorporating the needs of persons who are marginalized or have minority standing. Persons of such compromised standing fear transactional and macro-institutional power, a particular problem for those too cowered, too domestically busy, too downright tired or sidelined by disability or age, or too under-educated to compete against the decisions and actions being dished out to them through their otherwise liberal democracy. The challenge for SSM is to incorporate the feelings and findings of such marginalized and repressed people. Sensitive and sophisticated the soft systems methodology may set out to be; yet it is mostly responsive and useful to people who know clearly what their problem is!

This passage on the radical-multiplex approach to planning, in association with the earlier passage on traditional-lineal planning has examined underlying theory in real-world situations. And that real-world is now, more than ever before, in touch with itself, better informed and educated, and is more prone to ask questions and expect results which are an improvement on the best-guesses which local government agencies previously dished out. Choosing a strategic way is both facilitated and impeded by an avalanche of information, analysis, diagnosis, prognosis and democratic participation.

Since WWII Anglo settler societies have been exposed to an exponential increase in resource exploitation and technological danger, which also gives rise to a host of advocates 'for' and 'against' each and every project. Radical development planning and conservancy practice is concerned to design and attain transformations which include growth and are socially improving within ongoing whole-community and whole-environment contexts.

'Immediacy' associates SSM with just-in-time consumer durable production, suggesting that a 'better fit' might be found for SSM with industrial-commercial planning in the private sector than with conservancy and development planning for the public sector.

'low income people, particularly parents, face great obstacles to participating in planning or other public processes. This situation is an obstacle to creating wider . . . communities . . . based on overlapping political interests. It is also a challenge for developing democracy.'
'Ethical Behavior is Extraordinary Behavior', Howell Baum, 1998

What is required is 'an alternative approach to "participation" that does not necessarily privilege the knowledgeable, the organised, the resourceful and the established interested parties'.
Land Use Planning and the Mediation of Urban Change, Healey, McNamara, Elson, Doak, 1988

Progressive Change

It is unfortunate that policy discourse has had so little influence on operational planning. In other words development outcomes still mainly reflect what landowners want, what developers perceive as most profitable, and what local government politicians match up with landowner and developer interests – in essence a 'booster trinity'.

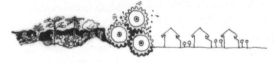

The 'booster trinity' at work

On the one hand there is John Friedmann (USA – 1987: 84) exhorting for planning that 'we cannot wish not to know, and we cannot escape the need to act'; and on the other Andrew Blowers (UK – 1980: 63) extolling that 'planning is a weak activity performing essentially a bureaucratic function'! One interpretation to place on this unlikely couplet would be to defend transpacific practice against the transatlantic! Yet looking at the two quotes in more detail, they can both be endorsed: Friedmann's because of his hope mirroring despair that so much of the available *theoretical* understanding is not being engaged, and Blowers because of his despair mirroring hope that so many available *technical* procedures are not applied.

A Nozickian minimal government attitude (box 1.3) to the planning process persists within local government, despite the post-World War II liberalization of administrative and business management. Here, in rounding off this theory-focused chapter, the level of dumbing-down discourse which poleaxes 'radical' endeavours is identified and noted. The hallmarks of negativity of this kind is colloquially expressed in figure 2.7 as a **Listing of 'new idea' killers** – but it is important to note the 'alternate' aside!

Life, including the greater part of conservancy managers' lives, is mostly *problems*-centred, whereas life for the developer specialist is focused towards the opening up of new *potentials* – which should work through as public ownership of good outcomes. The development and/or conservancy manager who understands clearly the current context, and past negative and passive experiences, is placed to see the direction ahead and how to make progress by engaging the flow-logic of sustainable planning. This mission direction is no one-day butterfly. The implemented results, for better or worse, are around 'indefinitely' and will impact significantly upon the next and succeeding generations. The main point here is that the radical way around is perceived as part of every multiple belief system, and in these terms can be identified as neomodern in style and character.

Making the creative leap or taking the design step is, as already noted, 'within the planning loop' for both the traditional-lineal and radical-multiplex modes. In my experience *the creative outcome of sustainable planning endeavour is the purest essence of planning pleasure and planning reward combined*. This gift of up-front creativity and long-lived certainty does not, to be sure, fall to development and conservancy practitioners evenly. Yet much can be done by individual practitioners to enhance their level of longer-term operational satisfaction. This is achieved

A good concept, but 'now' is not the right time.
It's too late to alter established procedure.
I just *know* it's *not* what the public want.
This has been tried and it 'failed'.
We are not big (wealthy) enough to alter our format.
This suggestion sounds fine in theory, but it simply won't work!
We cannot afford the extra research staff and lead-time.
Remember, profit is always the bottom line!
I 'think' this concept will be too expensive.
A good idea maybe, but you will never sell it.
It's always been done this way, why change now.
Later maybe, but not now, please.
We have no wish to be 'guinea pigs'.
Here, people like things the way they are.
Why change at all? Who *needs* change?
We do not wish to put off (landowners/ developers/ investors)
It may not be efficient, but technology will rescue us.
What do these (immigrant/ outsider) upstarts know about ... ?
I always reckoned she was too big for her boots!
Why change even if 'they' prove it is (cheaper/ safer/ better)?
How come, if this is a good idea, my father didn't think of it?
If it involves me, count me out.

Use community
networks
Supply information
Listen carefully
Notify early
Educate
See
Encourage
Develop skills
Be independent
Use informal channels
Be politically sensitive
J. Forester, 1980,
'Critical Theory and
Planning Practice'

Figure 2.7   Listing of 'new idea' killers

Based on a similar listing produced by the Work Psychology Department of the Danish Taastrup Technological Institute. Made available' by Professor Husingh of Erasmus University (1992).

through their engagement of improving techniques for 'creative reasoning' at the decision stage, by the use of heuristic styles of 'creative incubation' at the design stage, by adhering to an 'ethical canon' (box 1.4) and above all else by holding to the ideals of economic growth with social wellbeing and environmental harmony.

Robinson, Francis, Legge and Lerner, writing (1990) on the values and principles of 'sustainability', set out views about the make-up of participants for sustainable development, and or also, for the conservancy process:

To engage in good responsible design-making requires a minimum level of material and political equality and social justice, including equality of opportunity to realise one's full human potential, adequate material wealth, recourse to an open and just legal system, and freedom from political repression. It also depends on access to high quality education at all age levels, coupled with effective access to information. Other important characteristics are freedom of religion, speech and assembly.

Also consult:
• *Rebels Against the Future*, Kirkpatrick Sale, 1996.
• *Fear of Falling*, Barbara Ehrenreich, 1989.
• *The Corrosion of Character*, Richard Sennett, 1998.

While reasoning and incubation techniques can be learned (because they are experiential) they are difficult to impart, *to teach*. The earlier passages on brainstorming synectics and other forms of heuristic and symbolic reasoning are the key to creative and progressive practice, although they are perplexing to inculcate, except by working through examples. Also to be included, for the neomodernist new-age logic it heralds, is the holistic soft systems methodology and the likes of de Bono's *Parallel Thinking* (1994). These approaches look afresh at 'the real world' via an adaptation of the means available to us through systems-enhanced planning techniques, added to a conceptual prognosis which leads to improved design and better outcomes.

Of serious concern within radical planning practice is the confusion which arises between 'certainty' (as, for example, with means–ends zoning), and 'hunch' (such as the assumption that higher-density urban living is inherently better than lower-density urban living). Here I am not merely critical of 'action planning' proponents wrapping some theory and philosophy around proposals after the planned event. What is more deeply worrying is when, despite a consultative and inter-discursive search for fitness, the message-receivers are transmitting and working on hunch rather than proven, or at least tested, fact. For example, the claim that higher-density urban living (merely an illustrative example) is 'better' than life in suburbia, remains for me a personal persuasion, namely that well-designed higher-density living *is* preferable to tract suburbia. Yet it also has to be admitted that when one looks toward low-density suburbanity and some broad-acre living, a lot of good-quality patterning comes into view!

Something else: in a quasi-public role as whistle-blower of sorts, I have occasionally raised enough breath to produce a peep! Why only 'occasionally'? Well, for the reasons put clearly by Henry Mintzberg in his *Rise and Fall of Strategic Planning* (1994) which caricatures whistle-blower good intentions as being exacerbated by:

- *Entanglements;* getting discouraged and disillusioned by the procedural labyrinth.
- *Inefficiency;* the lack of utility of obfuscating data sets and questionnaire procedures.
- *Objectivity;* the removal of passion from planning – the acceptance of an operationally desultory situation.

Radical planning must avoid groping through the consultative and inter-discursive motions. It must 'talk-the-talk, and then walk-that-talk', fully testing alluring hunches, and above all avoiding the intrusion of smoke-and-mirror landowner and developer deceptions into the community discourse.

The point of an improved understanding of theory is that it indicates the *modus operandi* for aligning sustainable urban planning into corporatist civic life via the creative engagement of 'empowerment', 'capacity building', 'vertical and horizontal integration', 'participation', 'conflict management' and 'mediation'– and, overarching all, 'sustainability'. A core purpose underpinning the sustainable approach to urban planning, and indeed the point of this approach, is the actualization of national and community improvement, inducing greater variety and enriching lives through creative policy and design. The neomodern development and/or conservancy specialist can be positioned to attain those priceless personal satisfactions, which have previously eluded the majority of community serving manager-practioners, by providing well-planned triple-balanced outcomes.

Part II

Practice

The call is to look, smell, listen and think; to be against profligate resource use; and to be for conservation with development in the challenging context of urban growth management and job provisioning.

Part II

Practice

3

Charter for Conservation with Development

Out of the theory of change and a clarification of planning principles (previous chapters) emanates conservation *with* development, the accomplishment of quality-of-life goals in balance with economic growth. This is a 'thinking globally, acting locally' progression from established principles: collated in this chapter as the Soft Pathways, Kicking the Energy Habit and Matrix constructs, all precursors to the oncoming growth-pattern and urban-management reviews.

The objective for this chapter is to set out a rationale for conservation *with* development – first explored within the box 1.2 depiction of new-age pragmatics. That theme is enlarged here as a 'charter for conservation with development'; spelling out the core basics for a 'clean, green, caring yet also joyful and prosperous' community – stated simply as a matter of 'doing well while doing good'. This opening section offers up the ideal of neighbourhood-based sustainable urban planning, particularly as a social objective for middle-income households, in contrast to bluntly physical standard suburbia and urban sprawl. This reasoning derives from the socio-environmental paradigm established in chapters 1 and 2.

The advocacy is for a balanced style of fulfilled living, leveraged by an even-handed mode of administration which not only knows *what* policy it is they deliver, but also *why* they are delivering that policy. This rationale is beaten out by the neomodernist hammer of empowerment upon the anvil of irrefutable facts about closed-system ecologies. It is directed *against* lifestyles which are unsustainable – and is *for* those policies and actions which are prospectively and potentially sustainable. This attainable-sustainable reasoning is offered as realizable rather than utopian, repelling eco-cultism, yet not avoiding prescription if that is what it takes. What is called for are sustainable outcomes: working from *knowledge*, through *power*, to balanced socio-economic-environmental *outcomes*.

'a fivefold increase in economic output since 1950 has pushed human demands on the ecosystem beyond [that which] the planet is capable of sustaining.'
David F. Korten, 1995

At the Rio Summit, 1992: 'The American way of life is not up for negotiation.'
George Bush (Senior), US President

Backgrounding

Changes in the style of human habitat, social order and material wellbeing are part of the development and conservancy inheritance. And because the dynamics of knowledge-power, fiscal-power, resource-power and labour-power are all at work, this is perceived to be a 'process'. The challenge has always been to understand and manoeuvre that process over time to achieve *progress*. It is all teleological; relating causation and ends to final causes. The important perception to fix upon is one of 'qualitative improvement to the human condition over time'. This will usually be planned. Change which has previously resulted in economic decline, *and/or* degradation of the habitat, *and/or* social disorder, is of course 'regressive', spectacularly catalogued for the North American suburban and exurban context by Campoli, Humstone and MacLean in their photo-montages (*Above and Beyond*, 2002).

One example of the Campoli, Humstone, MacLean findings relates to a situation where the 39 species of animal life in a wilderness tract were reduced to ten remaining species after resizing the landscape into generous 'acreage' (lifestyle) blocks.

Whether or not a nation achieves economic and social progress can always be evaluated subjectively. Belief can, however, imbue a specious illusion of progress during periods of exploitation-led economic growth, with the eventual outcome, social discord and environmental degradation.

Our body of knowledge about the essentially transatlantic procedural arrangements for development and conservation is not compact, embracing the disparate writing of reports and in publications by thousands of ardent practitioners.[1] The present objective is to enlighten the teleological process (not merely to account for step-by-step volumetric growth); to provide a development critique, and then outline the practice of sustainability with particular reference to the middle-incomed urban majority.

'It is easy to have equality where land is abundant and where the population is small. This protected position, is sure to pass away. What will hasten the day when our [US 1890s] present advantage will wear out and when we shall come down to the condition of the older and densely populated nations? The answer is: debt, taxation, diplomacy, a grand government system, pomp, glory, a big army and navy, lavish expenditures, political jobbery.'
William Graham Somner, 1898. Quoted in *War and Other Essays*, Albert Keller, 1971

Adam Smith is the obvious luminary to begin with simply because he was of the early industrial era, and was the first to write authoritatively in English on political economy.[2] In his lifetime he witnessed the technological advances of canal building, spinning (Hargreaves), weaving (Crompton) and steam engineering (Watt), then followed the technological advances gained from the colonization experience throughout North America – the invention of barbed wire, sawmilling, long-distance railways, the telegraph. In all, a major technological and social changeover took place; from an Old World 'Age of Enlightenment' to a New World 'Era of Capitalism'.

The eighteenth-century upsurge of industrialism and 'free trade' throughout Western Europe gave rise to an imperialist mercantile axis English-Dutch-French, with a colonial periphery. From these beginnings, and the earlier Spanish-Portuguese conquest of Latin America, that industrial ethic expanded to include a dominantly 'northern' far-flung club; spanning from Europe westwards to

North America and east to Russia, and to later include Japan and Australasia along with a few oil-enriched outliers.

This 'industrial' revolution generated wealth from the exploitation of natural resources, and opened the way to a widespread 'civilizing' (mainly Christianizing and Westernizing) of indigenous peoples. Social injustices arose from the duping of first-nation peoples, along with environmentally prejudicial forms of selective trade expansion, now thoroughly documented.[3] The consumerism equated in turn with resource capture, resource exploitation, and the abandonment to nature of unprofitable wastes and toxins. In writing of this in *The Wealth of Nations* (1776) Smith laid the foundations of contemporary social, particularly economic, science. The focus was essentially British first, European second. Then came the New World where France and Britain were sorting out territorial claims in North America, whilst the likes of Captain Cook were reporting favourably on settlement prospects in New Zealand and Australia. There was, at the time, no conscious plan for industrialization; it was simply ordained.

> Adam Smith's philosophy in summary! 'In the beginning was Smith, and Smith told us not to worry about economic growth. Left alone people would sort things out, do what they do best, make appropriate choices to maximise return. The market would take care of the rest, rewarding reason and quickness and knowledge and punishing the opposite. All of this, moreover, would work to the general advantage, augmenting wealth and leading nations through a natural progression of stages from agriculture and industry to commerce. Long live the invisible hand.'
>
> David Landes, 'Rich Country, Poor Country', *New Republic*, 1989

In Smith's time – the late eighteenth century – the socio-cultural perspective of the then industrialized nations was derived principally from Judaic and Christian belief, perceiving human creatures as superior *to* rather than as an integral part *of* nature. This sense of moral superiority and righteous consumer lust was ordained by God, upheld as the Creator of Earth for humankind to occupy and make perfect; and on the surface of which, in accordance with the received view, He had in His beneficence placed the plant and animal species. Judaic-Christian humankind was guided by the Scriptures to use its God-given human skills to fashion 'civilization', a condition assumed, without much questioning, to be a proper improvement upon wild 'nature'.[4]

Thomas Malthus, stimulated by the findings of Adam Smith, Jeremy Bentham, and William Godwin (the utilitarians), published in 1798 a series of reactionary essays on population. The immense power and rapacity of the collective industrial 'machine' worried Malthus; and in *An Essay on Population* written when the North American mid-west 'breadbasket' had been barely explored, he envisaged the approach of an end to the further expansion of agricultural production. Population was forging ahead at compound rates of interest, at a time when it was believed that food production could only be increased by arithmetic additions; and to Malthus the known last frontiers for grain production as he understood the situation had already been put to the plough. Christian philosophers of that era had a vision of the earth's vitality falling away as time passed. What they did *not* reckon with was the geographical abundance of the New World, with not much more than a hint at that time of Australasia's pastoral potential; nor did they envisage the multiplier power of agricultural technologies yet to be discovered.

From the works of Smith and Malthus two further important pathways can be traced. One, through *social science* elaborated lastingly by Marx: the other, through *natural science* elucidated first, and again lastingly, by the mid-nineteenth-century output from Darwin, reinforced by the late nineteenth-century writing of the lesser appreciated Marsh.[5]

Charles Darwin, in his *Origin of Species* (1859) put the secular cat among the theistic pigeons. North America was won; Australasia, temperate Latin America and Southern Africa were being settled by Euro-Christian colonists; and every exertion of mind and muscle, coupled to technological invention and limitless resources, produced more and yet more food and energy for consumption.

The tropics and subtropics were mostly bypassed, for often these regions were already colonized (notably Latin America and India), or were *either* already densely peopled and well organized (China, Thailand, Japan), *or* were lands of little attraction for European exploitation or settlement (tropical Africa). Nevertheless wherever the tropical areas could produce resources or labour as grist to the European industrial maw, they too were opened up to exploitation.

DOWN-SIDE PARADIGM SHIFT
- Deforestation
- Noxious alien flora and fauna
- Topsoil erosion and silting
- Water-way and water-table pollution
- Air pollution, smog, acid rain
- Ambient temperature rise [greenhouse effect]
- Nuclear threats and disasters
- Production of unassimilable toxins [DDT, CFCs, nuclear wastes]
- Waste discard accumulations
- Resource depletions
- Reduced bio-diversity of life form
- Human disorders and diseases.

Darwin witnessed this in the course of the global journey recorded in his *Voyage of the Beagle* (1839). With the exception of some views on Brazilian slavery, and a sideswipe at what he discerned to be sloth in the Antipodes, his observation of human social conditions were not notable. On the other hand his scientific treatise *The Origin of Species* perceived the existence of what we would now identify as an ecological interdependence and adaptation. This raised a furore because it challenged the Judaic-Christian anti-mutation orthodoxy head on. Humankind, Darwin illustrated, was *not* ordained by a moral premiss of superiority to consume at will from the planetary resource base. Furthermore, in the New World, he observed how incoming animal and plant species soon modified primordial nature. His observations of plant and animal mutation and adaptation, the 'survival of the fittest' reasoning (also attributed to Herbert Spencer), and the dominance of some species (leading to an elaboration of social Darwinism) were all expressed as scientific certainties. Abuse nature, as he witnessed with cattle grazing on the Pampas and rabbit browsing in Australia, and several options became closed.

Then G. P. Marsh published *Man and Nature* (1864), a capsule title so imaginative and lively (although unconsciously sexist) that it remains as thematically significant now as it was when first produced. In it he wrote about the influence environment has on culture and, more significantly, the *effect of cultural processes* upon the environment. Marsh was recognized ultimately as the patron of ecology, an expression first used by Ernst Haeckel in 1868, which led to the 'new geography' studies of MacKinder (1887).

These late nineteenth-century works laid the foundations for a deluge of contemporary writings on human ecology.[6]

Marx was not concerned with a consumer-reducing policy so much as a more just system of resource distribution. He belittled Malthus, but as far as I have been able to ascertain, was not aware of Marsh. He did read and commend Darwin, because although *Das Kapital* and *The Communist Manifesto* did not emerge in English until the late nineteenth century, he was working on these at the time Darwin's publications were being put out. Marx also claimed that nature existed only for mankind, which aligned fortuitously with the received anthropocentric Judaic-Christian posture, which he perceived to be 'religious humbug'.

Marx absorbed social commentaries. He seldom worked away from literary sources. The 'revolution', his first practical suggestion and big mistake (based on what he perceived to be the relative success of the French Revolution), predicated the demise of capitalism, about which he was also mistaken. What he learned of social inequity, arising from the distributive injustice of 'class' he strove to set right, through the totalitarian reform of government; and in this he was also, again, far from successful. Nevertheless his advocacy for equity in human organization much influenced governments and policy reasoning throughout the world during the twentieth century.

Western leaders of the nineteenth century looked to their stores of library knowledge and the technological wonders erupting all about them, and came to two important conclusions. *First*, there was a perception that technological advances would improve the material wellbeing of both the 'settler' and the 'colonized' 'indigenous' peoples. *Second*, it happened often that the indigenous peoples and the useful resources and labour they owned could be exploited to serve European ends. This was the crude transatlantic model for socio-economic advance based on 'purloined' resources, 'stolen' lands and 'coerced' labour.

The transatlantic font of scholarship was the established Old World university schools of philosophy, politics and economics; not far removed from core subjects offered today as liberal art studies. Armed with their store of knowledge, technological superiority, and a Christian religiosity, it is plausible to comprehend the assuredness with which European settlers probed the global frontiers for resources and sought out the labour of non-Christian peoples. There was a presumption that the 'poor' at home in Europe, and the 'primitive' abroad, could be raised from hunting and fish gathering sub-cultures, via settled agriculture, to the meritocracy of a commercial-exchange culture. This was an Era of Reason and Enlightenment (*c.* 1650–1850) no less, where Eurocentric (later transatlantic) notions of self-interest and natural liberty were rampant. Of course these same human agencies could produce unintended consequences; but when all went well, the European poor

Darwin's determinism for the natural sciences has, over time, out-survived and out-flanked Marx's determinism for the social sciences. Darwin went alone into the scientific wildernesses and, against his Christian induction, carved out an understanding of inter-species dependency. Little wonder that Marx sifting through the received wisdom stored in the British Museum Library found Darwin's *Voyage* and *Origin of Species* so pure, assertive and undoubtedly correct as to wish to dedicate the first volume of *Das Kapital* to him. Darwin declined; a pity this, for although Darwin's ailing health would have prevented collaboration, the intellectual association would have tempered Marx's philosophical talent and personal ambition with an understanding of scientific limits, on which he, Marx, was adrift.

would become materially enriched and the native unbelievers would become 'enlightened'.

The significant early agents in this essentially economic conversion were not, solely, the imperial administrators; they included the evangelist from Britain and the entrepreneur from eastern North America. Not for them the logic of Adam Smith, the reasoning of Karl Marx, or the science of Charles Darwin; they were more in tune with the rectitude of John Locke (1690). His predication for the newly emerging settler societies within a 'labour theory of value', was that whatever land these incoming and God-fearing settler people secured *and worked* they were entitled to have and to hold in perpetuity. This was of course all very well for those who wanted to 'hear' what Locke had to say; but it was based on the unproven hypothesis that natural labour somehow adhered an incoming person to the land base on which that labour was performed, regardless of the landscape's historical pattern of indigenous ownership.

To paraphrase the transatlantic and later the transpacific perspective relative to the aboriginal peoples: take on the appropriate attitude, hand over your land (usually for nothing or for dross) and your circumstance will be transformed into an improved end state. By this logic was born a normative model for development which attracted religious zealots who brought in their wake a baggage of mostly poor opportunists, escapists and romanticists, a raffish admixture which laid foundations for the questing, individualistic, independent, and above all consumerist Anglo New World. Their paradigm grew from a transatlantic set of 'ordained' superiorities and 'civilizing' purposes, which included a settler overlordship of natural resources. This began an ever-quickening process, a chain of events in which the instruments for growth became stronger year by year. Science, during the late nineteenth century, was the handmaiden to evolutionary advance.[7]

The period of land capture in the Anglo New World coincided with the beginning of the modern carbon-fuel era, in relation to which Guha (1991) observed that 'for the first time in human history, societies were living not on the current income from nature but on nature's capital itself'. The settler people's rectitude led them to believe that they exhibited the 'right' attitudes – self-reliance and an adaptive frame of mind. The indigenous first peoples survived by a thread. Decimated by disease and subjugation, they declined in both numbers and identity. Over the same period the dominantly settler population became structurally mature in a demographic sense, more urban and urbane, gender-balanced, and progressively more bureaucratized.

An objective review of these mainly nineteenth-century values shows them to be flawed – hollow, avaricious, misguided and extortionate. The settler society of the Anglo New World evolved a conformist mantle of rectitude. In these terms settler endeavours can be judged as self-serving and pretentious, along with a recognition of some accidental excellence, Grand Plans in an era when their European contemporaries were making their Grand Tours, providing optimistic hope out of the Industrial Revolution, by good example Out West and Down Under.[8]

This appeal to history for an indication of the path ahead throws up indicators. That of a Smith–Rostow (1776 and 1960) character profiles the 'hidden hand' as working in compliance with market and entrepreneurial forces. Another path is suggested by the Marx–Meadows (1867 and 1972) analysis for an exploitative continuum, arising as a consequence of excess human consumption and a societal inability to effectively intervene.

A dilemma for modern society arose in terms of consumerist and protectionist traits. The Anglo New World nations, in particular, have been drawn to, and somewhat divided by, opposing mid-twentieth-century polemists: Hayek the free-marketeer and Polanyi the social protector. Of the two, Hayek has been the more persuasive and influential – open economies, tax cuts, trickle-down production benefits, less welfare, self-regulation, privatization – winning over the hearts and minds of conservative-voting North Americans and Australasians. Yet Polanyi, the would-be social protector and advocate for overall lifestyle quality, has also moved Democratic-Labour voting adherents, drawing attention to the ravages of resource exploitation, the need for security in old age, a fair start to life, and the scourge of unemployment. Governments remain anxious to appear pro-growth, pro-consumption and pro-market, yet also want to appease the elderly, the unemployed, and to be seen to be 'for' the environment! The problem here, as in much of life, is that the modern state cannot have Polyani's social protection *and* consume Hayek's free-market cake. The obvious mediation is to target a balance between and for 'growth community and the environment'.

> The Austrian polemicists: Friedrich Hayek, *The Road to Serfdom*, 1962.
>
> Karl Polyani, *The Great Transformation*, 1957.

Foregrounding

The entropy law, historically an undetected irrelevance, now enters upon this discourse, predicating that all natural systems tend toward a state of ever-reducing utility. Roughly expressed: the second law of thermodynamics (the 'entropic' law) asserts that all 'systems' (complex entities) tend toward end states of disorder and disutility. Accepting that the free-flow energy received from the sun can, for all practical purposes, be regarded as a continuing given, the entropy law then applies mainly to the degeneration and disaggregation of earthbound non-renewable (finite) resources, the fossil fuels and ecosystems. This we must acknowledge, particularly in relation to the previous two hundred years of previously unprecedented consumerism, when for the first time human beings began to live off their resource capital. This context is important because there lies the path which has led throughout the twentieth century to the disuse, decay and discard of earthbound resources, and the most rapid onset of species extinction during recorded human history.

> The ecosystem – which provides potable water, food- and fibre-producing soils, reoxegenated air, and handles all manner of wastes – does so at a mostly unpriced 'cost' to the ecosystem: *until now* with the advent in 2002 of an Australian CSIRO investigation into the fiscally priced 'worth' of natural systems, and the 'cost' of their degradation.

The entropy of biological and mineral resources is apparent to humankind as physical blight on the territorial landscapes and within the ocean bodies. Even high-income, resource-rich, low-density nations confront the *demographic fact* of mega-global population numbers, the *resource fact* of an end in sight for cheap fossil-fuel and fertilizer resources, and the *discard fact* of hazardous substances being embodied forever within a closed-system biosphere.

David Harvey's early prescience (1973): 'It is vital, when encountering a serious problem, not merely to try to solve the problem in itself but to confront and transform the processes that gave rise to the problem in the first place ... Alternative modes of production, consumption and distribution [and disposal] as well as alternative modes of environmental transformation have to be explored if the discursive spaces of the environmental justice movement and the theses of ecological modernisation are to be conjoined in a programme of radical political action.'

Again from David Harvey: 'one way to raise incomes of the poor is to pay them to absorb toxins ... [but] since most of the poor and the disempowered are people of colour, the impact is racially discriminatory ... are we not presuming that only trashy people can stomach trash? ... defilement, impurity and degradation become part of the political equation.'
'The Environment of Justice', 1995

These realizations, essentially of human society as an integral part of nature, were attested to by Gilbert White and Gro Brundtland at either end of the twentieth century. Yet now, more than ever before, the adverse breaches (flora and fauna blasted away, stockpiled toxins, altered weather patterns) are dramatic in impact. These impacts are now being felt *globally* as a reaction to previous resource plunder (undermining and overfishing), and toxic discharges (synthetics dumping, nuclear industry discards, and toxic waste disposal). They are also inflicted *locally* through the use of non-assimilable chemicals in agriculture and industry, the take-up of environmentally abrasive engine-powered technology, and the human dominance over nature. These outcomes and impacts led Lopez Portillo (United Nations, September 1982) to observe that for all countries the root cause is 'the enormous, volatile, and speculative mass of capital [which] goes all over the world in search of high interest rates, tax havens and supposed political exchange stability'. His prognosis foretells the causes and instructs the need for sustainability of intent, action and outcome. The challenge is for nations to be eager, their communities to be empowered, and for individuals to be committed, to combating socio-environmental injustices.

Returning to Portillo's 'enormous volatile and speculative' force of capital; by the eve of the recently concluded millennium there were an estimated 400 billionaires whose aggregate wealth equalled the combined incomes of half of all the world's people.[9] The sheer economic impact of that wealth on the earth-bound resource inheritance generates a counter-force, a counter-logic and a counter-leverage against the sustainability thesis. To be sure, the money-go-round is 'winning' the short play through geared profits, although for billionaires and peons alike the outcome of the end game, and the end result, is in the gift of nature.

The free trade protocols settled upon some nations in the last decade of the last century fell in with a Ricardian accommodation of comparative cost advantage. This is logical within a self-fulfilling context, establishing that just as resources, skills, climatic environments and capital are distributed unequally, some nations can provide goods and deliver services more efficiently than others. Along with this 'manufacturing imperialism' goes 'toxic imperialism', enabling wealthy nations to import goods from the cheapest supplier, and export their toxin-generating industries and wastes to lower-charging nations. But whereas Ricardo elaborated his thesis for a pre-modernist European region, contemporary free trade and free dumping now relates to a global context comprising billions of consumers with access to fast intercontinental shipments, instant credit and information sharing. This compels modern transnational companies to relocate, and if necessary relocate again to soft-on-labour jurisdictions, soft-on-minimum-wage labour laws, and soft-on-environmental-protection geographical regions. Specialization herds labour-intensive industry into labour-cheap areas, and concentrates resource exploitation 'up to the competitive margin' in resource-endowed regions.

The orthodoxy endorsed by the NAFTA (North America Free Trade), EEC (European Economic Community), APEC (Asia Pacific Economic Cooperation forum), and the Australasian CER (Closer Economic Relations) styles of agreement work against the production of within-nation goods and services supply and import-substitution. Instead, in the spirit of free trade and competitive marketing, these protocols encourage cheaper importation from marginally more favourable (usually lower labour-costing and fossil-fuel subsidized) production environments.[10] GATT and its offspring the World Trade Organization have, for example, displaced garment workers in economically more advanced 'northern' nations because of the comparative labour-cost advantages of garment assembly in densely populated lower-income 'southern' nations. Another example is free trade movements of the needless biscuits and confectionery kind, both ways between several producing countries. These sum-loss situations come about as a consequence of the overuse of fossil fuels – finite non-replaceable resources, no less – to facilitate trivial one-off profit-taking and transportations of no within-nation and little between-nation relevance.

Clearly, then, there is a downside as well as an upside to globalization and growth. Technical improvements in fibre and food production have always been welcome, yet gene transplanting, particularly between species, is perceived widely to be unnatural, even spooky. Similarly, imbalances of wealth between individuals has always been a tacitly accepted part of the human condition, even though it sometimes leaves the really poor and some first-nation people stuck with a Stone Age plight. Mastery over trade in accordance with a worldly mantra has, to some, a messianic attraction. But the reality is that all persons are individuals, all communities are different, all nations are distinct. A One World trade organization does not, and never will, fit all. Open trade unhindered by ideological protection is an ideal; but imposed from Geneva it is perceived by many as undermining internal hegemony, inhibiting national autonomy, and reducing cultural identity.

There is an ethical compass in individuals which amounts sometimes to a religiosity, for those who have a God a 'sanctity', and for those who do not have a God a 'certainty'. Those who hold to these sanctities and certainties accept and applaud the gains and benefits of science, appreciate the economy of advan-

James Lovelock, atmospheric scientist, contends that a [w]holistic regulation is at work, explaining the biospheric upheavals of the twentieth century. For some this mutual connectivity is a matter of simple conviction, for others science gives a better explanation. This is where Lovelock's Gaia finds accord with many of those who have a belief in God: as well as suiting many others who have no God. I consider it a mistake to rely on the mysticism of Gaia. The 'balance of nature' is wondrous, but do not push mystical explanations too far, for nature, of itself, lacks an anthropocentric conscience.

tage which arises from socially appropriate levels of trade liberalization, and accord approval to capitalism over communism. Yet clearly global science, global trade and global growth all have limits because they fall outside the scope, values, consciousness and beliefs – the ethical compass – of individual human beings and their local communities.

'We [late twentieth century] take only ten percent of our energy from directly renewable and non-polluting resources (sun wind and water) ... yet in a single year we burn some one million years' worth of non-renewable fossil fuels.'

Richard Rogers, *1995*
Reith Lectures

A gulf yawns between 'open society' trade and 'closed mind' protectionism. These are the extremes. For the proponents of both there is a need to fashion, locally, a ' tolerable path; conservation *with* development, served, conjointly, by sound science. A fresh perspective on this reconciliation comes to us from a capitalist-poacher turned societal-gamekeeper, George Soros. In his plain piece 'The Capitalist Threat' (1997: *passim*) he states bluntly that 'The main enemy of the open society is no longer the communist but the capitalist threat ... [because] ... too much competition and too little cooperation can cause intolerable inequities and instability ... [and because] ... Unsure of what they stand for, people increasingly rely on money as the criterion of value.' Soros is vexed about professions turned into businesses, the crude 'survival of the fittest' mantra, and the intense focus of individuals (like himself!) upon the capture of specific-to-themselves material gain. What also comes through from Soros (via Popper 1974) is that there can be no absolute truth – capitalist, neomodernist or socialist. Freely translated, this suggests support for an open society, open institutions and open minds as progressive accessories to sustainable conservancy *with* development.

Contrasting with the Third World survivalist imperative, by any means, Anglo settler society nations have the capacity to command resourcing which can underscore cyclical and continuing patterns of sustainable development *with* conservation.

The day-by-day outcome resulting from the opening up of nations to the forces of industrialization and commerce now registers largely as socio-environmental failure, for example, as ever-increasing water-body and atmospheric pollution and the ever-reducing diversity of living species. This is partly offset by occasional success: for example, impressive worldwide wilderness preservation as in Antarctica and National Parks, heritage conservation of historical antiquities, and an array of solar-biological projects. This, in the phrasing of Norgaard (1994) 'emphasises the complex maze of reciprocal causation between environment and culture', including, of course, capitalism.

Resource exploitation and pollution disposal is fired by a frustration, particularly within the lower-incomed Third World, at being separated from other nations in accordance with such vapid criteria as lower GNP per capita, less resource consumption per capita, and limited social services. Korten contends (*When Corporations Rule the World* 1995: 181) that 'World War II did not end the global domination of the weak by strong states. It simply cloaked colonialism in a less obvious, more beguiling form.' His advocacy is for a reversal of poorly secured bank lendings, creative tax manipulations, and a curtailment of GATT–WTO and the prospective MAI.

The tidal flow of what might be described as 'gross human contentment' in OECD nations is ebbing toward a condition of smugness. From the perspective of Galbraith (1992: 6): 'The fortunate and the favoured, it is more than evident, do not contemplate and respond to their own longer-run wellbeing. Rather, they respond, and powerfully, to immediate comfort and contentment. This is the controlling mood.' For most wealthy nations there is also an entrenched cadre of lifetime unemployed to contend with, along with resource ravages and waste discards. There is also the curdling Californian dream to contemplate, driven by an acerbic yet democratic legal process which predicates almost the reverse of this book's advocacy for a tolerable harmony. Individualization of life – an example being a rate of solo household formation in urban California which exceeds the rate of binary family household formation – is related for that State to the 1978 ballot initiative, *Proposition 13* for halving property taxes, later reflected in a reduced education vote. In this manner the Dream State lost its lustre. Worse, ballot box envy – or is it spite 'If I don't have children at school I'll vote against education taxes' – has fanned outwards across America, the Pacific and the Atlantic. The self-interestedness of individuals, pinpointed in the seventeenth century by Thomas Hobbs, lives on in the Californian heartland.

Passing power down to those who *deliver* the outcomes, subsidiarity, is very democratic. But putting the 'switches and levers' of power on the ballot box, away from prying eyes, is a nonsense because none of us has the capacity to see beyond our prejudices and pocketbooks or our personal sliver of formal education.[11] Clearly the ballot box is the place to elect 'representatives' and it is they – rather than the use of referenda – who must research, debate and decide, on balance, for their constituency. Simply put, if elected representatives get it too wrong too often, another election will roll around and out comes the ballot box again!

Levers and switches on the ballot box (and referenda) is clearly an unworthy way to decide specific action for any grouping in excess of a few thousand voters. Indeed because voting is anonymous via the ballot box and the secret slip, the voter is encouraged to avoid committing with their head or heart, and to vote with their wallet. On the other hand, with display voting at open meeting within smaller jurisdictions – New England Town Meetings and the Swiss *Landsgemeinde* – the democratic procedure is palpable; and the smaller the constituency the more heightened that palpability. Kirkpatrick Sale (1998) puts the matter this way: 'In smaller units people are more politically active, can understand the issues and personalities far more clearly, participate in all aspects of government and regard themselves as having some effective control over the decisions of their lives.' Subsidiarity, the passing down of decision-taking power, involves more than merely passing over the reins; it involves careful consideration of the plebisitary.

On a global scale, most of us feel comfortable about the United Nations, but less so with the World Trade Organization. And at the local scale personally (in

> A difficulty with the rational, modern and essentially democratic ballot-box process is that it exalts consumption without a thought for tomorrow or anybody else. Most of us, to varying degrees, rail against the purposeless depletion of non-renewable resources. What the Californian 'propositions' and Anglo 'referenda' show is the damage which atomized mobility, soft living and secret voting can track into our lives.

my small home town Helensville, population 2,700), I feel comfortable about town meetings, but am often dismayed with insensitive decisions emanating from the remote county centre over on the other coast.[12] Taking another personal example: academic meetings throughout my university time have often been tedious, yet opinions get aired and fair decisions are converged upon, even when the support funding is decided by a robotcracy. Of importance in all of this is the fact that not only is open democracy a function of smallness, but also that governance via subsidiarity is fair. Above all, the small nation-state works better for its populace than a superpower; the million population city works better than a metropolis; the valley region works better than the amalgam state – and so on down to the already established balance of the town meeting, community board or *Landsgemeinde* gathering. Small-scale governance will not save the world, but it does ensure that local sanity prevails, conserves the local environment, and can be made to work for the local economy.

The substance and hallmark of a sustainable lifestyle is *a slowly improving overall economic standing, increasing levels of employment, steady-state 'youthful' population, and a protected conservation estate*. Better a locally fashioned conservation *with* development goal than the inferno of lineally increasing resource capture and exponentially increasing levels of pollution.

For Anglo New World nations there are options to declare and decide upon: opposition to the rampant exploitation of finite resources, achieving a steady-state population, denying biological pollution of the biosphere, avoiding the chaos of unemployed in the workforce. In terms of the previous chapter, the wealthy peoples of the world now have the *knowledge*, from which they are positioned to wield the *power* and fashion the *control* – to produce a balanced environmental and socially harmonious *outcome*. What is needed is recognition of entropic fragility, and respect for genetic inheritance; for nations to be eager, communities to be empowered, and individuals to be committed to living cleverly and sustainably from their resource interest.

This need is traversed and reviewed in the six expressions of crisis given in box 3.1 as **The ever-changing scene** which suggests a haemorrhage of change. Mixing metaphors further, box 3.1 also suggests that the family silver is being sold off, and the roof is about to fall in! In fact material comfort, a well-established infrastructure, social connectedness, sound education, an awareness of lifestyle values and issues, and an environmental sanctity, all remain. Jane Jacobs highlighted this potential within a talking-heads dialogue, *Systems of Survival* (1992), as two moralities: *commercial* (trading) and *guardian* (territorial) syndromes which 'underpin viable working life'. People are mostly divided by these syndromes, yet they realize that there is a better way forward. Indeed they also *know* that

Box 3.1 The ever-changing scene

THE POLITICAL CRISIS noticeably apparent in the OECD during the 1960s is still evident. The issue here is not political conflict so much as the adverse knock-on effects of being ineffectively administered. There is always the hope, in every democratic society, that self-adjusting factors will apply, that 'bad' government will be replaced with 'good' and that sound new developments will compensate for previously malignant projects. Yet the available 'centrist' alternatives at election time usually come down to 'Pepsi or Coke' with some fringe attractions offered by minor diversionary parties. This is all much worse when the political prophets are proved wrong, their faith in growth scenarios misplaced, the outcomes calamitous and when they resort to a sell-out – less government mediation and more market freedom.

IDENTITY CRISIS has always been a feature of modern Anglo New World societies. Ceremonial incorporation of 'native' and 'settler' values is creditworthy, but a practical confusion between materialist and traditional values and practices abounds. For example, it is easily possible in New World communities to identify personalities surrounded by all the trappings of modern consumerism, who also tentatively align with conservation; conscientiously putting out bundles of old newspaper for recycling, and motoring up to the local bottle bank. In contrast many of those espousing traditional 'indigenous' values are *not* motivated to put out any newspapers for recycling or to drop off their empties! Balance, and the self-sufficiency ideal, reside uneasily within the New World competitive-consumerist psyche. A few individuals make an attempt to achieve a personal 'balance' between economics and ecology; most do not really try; and for the majority the issues and values involved are a confusion beyond their range of motivation to comprehend, analyse, or act upon.

CLASS CONFLICT is at base a crisis arising from the trinity of discord between the formal (taxpaying), dependent (benefit-receiving), and the informal (illicit economy), components of society. The results are tax avoidance and stock-jobbing swindles in the formal sector, beneficiary abuse from the dependent sector, and a vast amount of fiscal leakiness and community loss from an illicit sector cornered by a succession of desperate 'do we eat or heat?' situations. What started out during the pre-1960 era of fullish employment as distinctions based on levels of economic income, has grown into a class conflict between a smug moneyed class and a cowered underclass, with neither caring much about the other, and with both trying to increase their leverage on the economic system.

A TECHNOLOGICAL DILEMMA divides people across a wide philosophical spectrum. Some have a vision of a society which they believe ought to hunker down to food self-sufficiency, longer-term recycling, local materials house-building, and home entertainment; others welcome new energy-harnessing technologies, cheap and universal communications, and above all espouse a belief for the power of new ideas and technologies. In fact there is a role for 'both' selectively, and no need for a dilemma to exist.

A MANAGEMENT CONFLICT can be identified where the well-heeled blame the victims, the victims blame the well-heeled, and government veers off in the contradictory directions of saving and spending. The 'savings' arise from beneficiary-targeting, which is sometimes successful, and benefit-indexing, which is often unsuccessful; along with more efficient and thus more fair tax-gathering, which cannot of course be gainsaid. The 'spending' emphasis is, of the two, the more nightmarish: state management of state capital lacks adherence to private sector principles of 'utility maximization' because there is no fear, within governments, of the spectre of the low yields which haunt the managers of private capital.

A TERRITORIAL DILEMMA born of delusions about city-state grandeur has led to a discordance, which still exists, between central-local-regional levels (and, particularly, between central and regional levels) of public policy-making. This is particularly the case with centrally conceived 'think big' projects imposed upon discerning and perceptive communities without due consultation, and worse, without an open assessment of the likely social, environmental and economic downstream effects. But even more serious than debt from macro projects is the knee-capping of local and regional confidence, along with an erosion of community values. Simple resource plunder, at an uncaring national level, remains a significant territorial threat and policy obstacle to harmony.

there is a better, slower, way forward, and that the patterns and traces which produced triple-balanced harmony in the past have been neglected, and await refurbishment.

Laws I and II, the so-called 'Laws of Entropy', are a rendition and re-expression of the First and Second Laws of Thermodynamics, which can be characterized as the book-keeping principles of finite resource flows, particularly fossil fuels. *First* – and of marginal concern to this discourse – that energy (and for all practical purposes, matter) can neither be created or destroyed. *Secondly* – and of importance – that the transformation of energy (and for practical purposes all 'finite resources') results in resource disorder, degradation, and disutility.

The conservation *with* development issue comes down to one of close-the-gap politics applied as solutions to the six crises (political, identity, class, technological, management, territorial) detailed in box 3.1. The desired outcomes are essentially practical. The sustainable path is there to be taken, and the neomodern goals wait to be scored through sustainable stealth.

Resource Exploitation and Discard Dynamics

The interface of Jane Jacobs's *commercial* and *guardian* ethical criteria (*Systems of Survival*, 1992) illustrates human frailty; indicating the way people spawn entropic disorder, the mechanics of which can be put this way:

The Resource Commons Tragedy is based on Garrett Hardin's 'The Tragedy of the Commons'. First published in *Science*, 162, 1968

THE RESOURCE COMMONS TRAGEDY
Consider the ocean fish around the World's territorial shorelines. Competitive fishers for whom each haul adds to their store of capital, secure as much as possible of accessible stock in order to maximise their gain and thereby enhance their material lives. When an individual fisher brings in less than their vessel's capacity, and there is a seller's market, that person will lose out to other competitors who arrive at the market place to make up the shortfall. Thereby arises the compulsion to exploit stocks ahead of, and in greater quantity than, any other competitor; and to continue in this manner after it is realised that the natural replenishment of the stock is being jeopardised. This may result in an artificial intervention, the introduction of fishing quota, which is of course worthy but imperfect; identifying the exploitative and commercial instinct to maximise fish-catch gain by selectively retaining the highly sought-after species, even to the point of extinction.

Synergy can be identified beneficially, as well as negatively. The 'Synergistic Tragedy' portrayed here is adverse 'synergism' – the observable negative outcome of an interaction (e.g. in the atmosphere, between gaseous pollutants) in which the damage from the pollutants *inter-reacting* exceeds the sum of the adverse effects considered separately.

THE SYNERGISTIC TRAGEDY
Picture an agricultural entrepreneur. Following some commercial success, there is the allure of more advanced technology, disease controls, genetic modifications, chemically-assisted storage, assisted sales and a raft of other investment and diversification options, including farm aggregation. These all escalate simple success into an avalanche of profit-taking and induce a cash-enhanced lifestyle; leading to accelerated personal consumerism with, of course, an inevitable discharge of pollutants and toxins.[13] When local success feeds further success, entrepreneurs become role model attainers of 'desired goods'. Publicity enshrines such a synergy. Profit-taking, financial-gearing, market-manipulation and false-paper commodity trading follows; all with

scant appreciation of the consequent damage to the biosphere, the depletion of non-renewable resources, or the stress induced to the poorer members of society.

What is the driving force behind the Commons Tragedy and the Synergistic Tragedy? What causes individual human beings to put into jeopardy their collective wellbeing? Why do people exploit and run down *not only* the replenishable resource 'interest' available to them (fish stocks, indigenous timber, ground water and living soils), *but also* plunder the once-only non-renewable resource 'capital' – oil and gas reserves most particularly?

At base individual human greed, fired along by the commercial growth-on-growth imperative, can be identified. Putting this a little less bluntly: the cumulative social and environmental costs of the 'two tragedy' syndrome are a consequence of the unshackling of social co-dependency and co-responsibility. This contention leads to the next construct: a parody on the way in which 'order' trends toward 'disorder'. This assembly, coupled to the 'two tragedy' depiction, goes some way to explain exploitation and discard processes and their cumulative effect.[14]

❑ EXPLOITATION DYNAMICS

Excepting enforcements in accordance with national or global directives, all human individuals, local agencies and national entities *tend to act competitively and self-interestedly to maximize their consumption of profiting resources*, particularly those held in common domains to which they can secure access; and they do so urgently, up to the profiting margin, in response to the precept that should they delay any such opportunity, competitors will pre-empt them.[15]

❑ DISCARD DYNAMICS

Excepting enforcement of pollution protection in accordance with national or global directives, all human individuals, local agencies and national entities tend to act evasively and self-interestedly to avoid responsibility for disposal of their pollutants; and they do so in response to the precept that should they fail to externalize any such opportunity to discard their waste into the common domains, they stand to increase the ultimate cost to themselves, of discard disposal.

> 'From simply a human regard, there is a limit to the number of people who can be expected to know all the civic issues, all of the contending opinions.'
> Kirkpatrick Sale, 1998

> 'Property values are lower close to noxious facilities and that is where the poor and the disadvantaged are by and large forced by their impoverished circumstances to live.'
> David Harvey, 'The Environment of Justice', 1995

A context of resource uptake and pollution ejection, which illustrates *both* Exploitation Dynamics and Discard Dynamics, is available from the freeholder utilization of geothermal energy, as was once the case for urban Rotorua in the North Island of New Zealand.[16] In this situation, particularly because uptake of the geothermal energy was spread territorially over a residential neighbourhood, the landholder right to drill into the earth and install bores to take up the hot water for general heating was in conflict with the utilization of geothermal energy as an extensive public-property 'common', which happened also to energize the local Thermal Wonderland. Prior to recent (1991) controls and 'regional rules' each landowner was, literally, in competition to exploit the 'free' hot-water energy resource – the exercise of Exploitation Dynamics arousing a *tendency to act competitively and self-interestedly to maximize each individual landholder's geothermal energy consumption.* Furthermore, as the heat-intensity of the competitively abstracted water reduced, an increased volume was raised to the surface, exacerbating the run-off disposal problem from individual landholdings onto neighbouring private and public property – the Discard Dynamic thus arousing a *tendency to act evasively and self-interestedly to avoid individual responsibility for waste water disposal.* This example illustrates the way in which exploitation and discard dynamics interconnect for, as Norgaard puts the matter (1994: 93 – emphasis added): 'clearly we are part of the system we are trying to understand, hence what we do *affects the system* we are trying to understand.'

Exploitation dynamics has an association in the New World with the colonizing land grab. These actions, and the mind-set they engendered, laid foundations for the contemporary pattern of exploitation and discard dynamics. Indeed modern resource-winning operators (mining, fishing, logging) go to considerable lengths to burnish their frontier '*man* against the elements' image. This 'for myself' exploitation of 'free' resources is probably neither as serious (being amenable to control) nor as widespread (being localized activities) as are the waste discard dynamics, implicating a much more populous urban band of society, and affecting the extensive land-water and atmospheric 'footprint'.[17] The policy pillars of a charter for conservation *with* development come down to an inclusion of principles for reducing 'exploitation' *and* 'discard' rates: in effect bending to the rules of ecological entropy and linking this into bottom-up empowerment.[18]

> It is an ecological 'disadvantage' that New World populations are so highly urbanized (75 to 85 per cent) and are thus a fixed gross consumer of resources, and gross discharger of pollutants.

Issues of misunderstanding about responsibilities in relation to the *exploitation of resources* and the *discard of wastes* impact seriously as local matters. As already shown, the exploitation and discard activity arises because most individuals put personal gain before public interest, because most communities put local advantage before national interest, and because most nations put their sovereign rights before the global interest – *unless* checked and balanced by higher authority.

The global problem has been elegantly expressed by Herman Daly (1993) as one in which:

> The principal monetized 'internal burden' for the poorer 'southern' nations is the imbalance of within-nation income distribution, often with the top 10 per cent of income earners commanding up to two-thirds of the national wealth and income. The main monetized 'external burden' is the dominance of trade and prices by richer nations.

> The regenerative and assimilative capacities of the biosphere cannot support even the current levels of resource consumption, much less the manifold increase required to generalise the higher standards worldwide. In fact, free trade becomes a recipe for hastening the speed with which competition lowers standards for efficiency, distributive equity and ecological sustainability.

Economic growth, particularly under GATT, NAFTA, APEC, WTO and CER agreements, benefits some nations over the short term, but harbours the adverse potential to *environmentally* endanger, *economically* imperil, and *socially* disempower future individuals, communities and nations.

In terms of the Exploitation and Discard reasoning it is apparent that it is not realistically possible (in other words it is not readily within the capacity of any nation's collective and democratic conscience) to simply de-accelerate consumption and to reduce in this way the impact of finite resource extraction and the rates of pollution discard. This is from David Korten (1995: 98):

> Markets don't tell people with substantial incomes to consume no more than their rightful share of ecosystem resources. They don't tell retailers not to sell guns to children. They don't tell producers that their wastes must be recycled. They don't give priority in the allocation of scarce resources to the basic needs of those with little or no money before providing luxuries for those who have great wealth. Indeed in each instance, they generally do exactly the opposite.

What is called for in order to avert the previously detailed twin-tragedy and twin-dynamic syndromes is a socially acceptable alternative to the growth-on-growth mantra, represented here as *neo*modernism: a style of added-to modernity which both 'takes out of' and 'puts back into' the environment, the economy and the community. This environmentally neutral, socially improving paradigm, styled as conservation *with* development, is easy to comprehend even if, ecologically, it is challenging to effectively act out.

The core to a neomodern drive for sustainable conservation *with* development is widespread education and empowerment toward a steady state in which the consumer uptake of resources, and the discharge of waste outputs, are pulled into balance. There is a need to manage the resource production capacities, and the absorptive capabilities of the eco-environmental setting on an all-costs-considered basis. Current levels of low-density urban sprawl, and production-consumption-discard output, exceeds known utility supply capabilities and pollution-absorptive capacities, and accumulates as future economic environmental and social costs. It is this *un*sustainable style of modern resource exploitation, along with under-employment and pollution discard, which highlights the *neo*modernist challenge.

The settler-European populations of the larger towns and cities find it difficult to comprehend that it is they, the urban citizenry, who constitute the mass of consumers and the bulk of within-nation polluters. Additionally, there is a lack of understanding about the converse reality: that it is the surrounding countryside and the fresh water and saline water masses and the atmosphere, all acting as waste 'sinks', which receives everything the urban populations disown and discard as waste (consult Wackernagel and Rees 1996).

Global directives and state sovereignty are pitched one against the other. There are enormous practical difficulties to overcome in bringing nations under the umbrella of globally enforced legal instruments, particularly when more than half of them, comprising much of the recently independent Third World, are fiercely defensive of their hard-won sovereign rights.

A GOOD URBAN ENVIRONMENT IS A:
- nuisance-free environment
- healthful environment
- recreational opportunity environment
- housing opportunity environment
- health opportunity environment
- job opportunity environment
- school opportunity environment
- modern amenity environment.
- [Plus an all-accessible environment]

K.R. Cox, *Man Location and Behaviour*, 1972

The most significant confrontation is that of persuading, educating and regulating those who manufacture and discharge from urban places. The settlement populations have scant collective appreciation of food-producing chains, potable water supply ecosystems, waste disposal processes, fresh air replenishment exchange mechanisms, or any of the other dilution and absorption cycles which tie them to earth island in space. In short, it is important to push home to urban populations the message that if the biosphere sickens and becomes diseased, the conduit from nature to themselves will work its way through remorselessly as habitat denial, urban decay and social disorder. An ultimate irony in this regard is that nature as such has nothing akin to a 'soul' and does not, indeed cannot, in and of itself, 'care'. This dumps the responsibility for biospheric wellbeing firmly into the ambit of sustainability politics and development *with* conservancy practice.

Improvements in the take-up of the neomodern sustainability ideal are within the policy reach of OECD communities *provided* there is conviction on the part of the urban component in those societies to abide by the ecological rules and conform to the logic for upholding these values. If in its 'efficiency' urban society fashions a pea-soup atmosphere, a gormless suburb, or an industrial moonscape, so be it. In short, after human society reaps the harvest of its own landscape evisceration, destruction and poisoning, nature simply adjusts accordingly, degraded to be sure, and rolls on into a quality-reduced future.

For much of the richer nation OECD a worst-case scenario along the lines outlined need not be perpetrated. The Anglo settler societies have the resource capacity to retain a larger environmental conviviality (National Parks, Forest Reserves and the like) *and* a capacity for 'tipping the balance' ensuring that education for conservation is worked in with development, particularly for urban places.

Socio-Environmentalism: The New Reality

The day-to-day exigencies of the Commons Tragedy and Synergy Tragedy, and the Exploitation Dynamics and Discard Dynamics traversed earlier, fastens upon the four main resource categories (finite, renewable, heritage, free-flow); to which human communities are bound and by which they are nurtured. That resources set, implicated in development *with* conservation, is presented in box 3.2 as **Resources within ecosystems**.

European concerns in the eighteenth century related to continued survival for a global population of less than a billion people, which in lengthy hindsight shows how misinformed was the Malthusian perspective on resources, geographical space and technological potential. The specific projections made by Malthus in 1798 were from the data available to him about human numbers, and his understanding at that time of the remaining territories from which edible grains could be produced. His 'arithmatic' reasoning foretold the equivalent of a crossover when food production, which had previously kept ahead of population growth, would decline relative to population growth; assertions based on inadequate geographical facts, an inadequate insight into the future of agricultural science and ever-improving food storage science. But now, over two hundred years later, with the global population bound to grow beyond eight (maybe ten) billion, the scientific certainty is that there actually is no more geographical space, nor large and accessible oil and gas fossil energy sources, to exploit, although volumetric food production to feed that population is less problematic. Viewed from off-planet as it were, the challenge for twenty-first-century humankind is about a global course for survival. The macro-pattern role in this, for OECD nations, is to manage sustainable development, fair burden-sharing, North–South trade, and environmental conservation.

> Keynes, writing in 1933 (*Yale Review*, 1983: 758) on the social benefits of full employment, expressed the case for self-sufficiency in these words: 'let goods be homespun whenever it is reasonable and conveniently possible, and above all, let finance be primarily national. We do not wish, therefore, to be at the mercy of world forces.'

A Second Coming of the Malthusian apparition, this time altogether more scientific, was promoted in the 1960s and grew into a virtual 'limits to growth industry'. The seminal work was produced by a four-person Massachusetts Institute of Technology team led by Donella and Dennis Meadows. The early style of computer printouts, the large typeface and simple parables (for example, the lily plant exponential growth depiction) remain fresh and appealing. The Meadows text, *The Limits to Growth* (1972, followed by numerous reprints), was intended to be read in conjunction with other MIT works less charismatic yet also important, notably Jay Forrester's *World Dynamics* (1970). The

The Limits to Growth logo

provocative approach of the two Meadows and Forrester led to many counter-claims of 'doom watching' and 'Malthus with a Computer' vindicated, in the view of some, by the 'apparent' low-price fossil-fuel bonanza.[19] In 1992, Meadows and others in their *Beyond the Limits*, expressed the previous arguments again, notably as 'Overshoots' with all factors (consumer goods, services, food and *life expectancy*) in decline from about 2020.[20]

The main counter-thesis, Cole's *Critique of The Limits to Growth* (1973) was concerned to point out the 'tremendous potential of changing technology along with

Box 3.2 Resources within ecosystems

Conservation *with* development within a framework of generic sustainability acknowledges four categories of resource:

FINITE RESOURCES: those vital and non-replenishable resources of fixed quantity; primarily fossil fuels and some short-supply minerals. After stock depletion, and following entropic disorder (their disaggregation beyond recovery) that is it! At the point of individual consumption of finite resources the whole of humankind is about to enjoy the one and only opportunity it, collectively, will ever have to benefit from that item of resource.

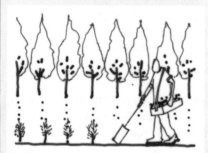

RENEWABLE RESOURCES are those retained primarily in the earth's outer 'onion-skin' the biosphere, comprising a global platform of soils, air, and water which, fired along by free-flow resources, maintains the planetary complex of flora and fauna. Maintained in good health, undegraded, unclogged and toxin free, they can be replenished and recycled (witness the success of indigenous peoples) millennium upon millennium.

HERITAGE RESOURCES fall into a 'not-to-be consumed' category under two subheadings. There is the 'natural heritage' comprised mainly within the remnant primordial landscape, coastal zones and water-covered areas, which are recognized as being of nature. The 'cultural heritage' comprises the artifacts and constructions put in place over time by human agency. To most communities heritage resources represent a spiritual underpinning for human existence.

FREE-FLOW RESOURCES comprise principally the continuing solar, wind, wave, magnetic and gravity forces: the solar input being the driving factor and energy feed-stock for photosynthesis and all life.

Box 3.2 *Continued*

Use of the expression 'ecosystem' in policy language is largely maladroit. In noting that 'balanced ecosystems' all exhibit characteristics of being 'alive' and 'reciprocating within themselves' and of being 'in harmony with other ecosystems' we observe merely that, for example, two river systems, one crystal clear, the other sluggish and eutrophied, are both functioning 'ecosystems' albeit of different quality. Nature does not 'care' about the diversity or otherwise of contrasting ecosystems, agricultural ecosystems, or urban ecosystems. The conclusion to which this reasoning is directed is that the word 'ecosystem' and the term 'landscape ecology' are frequently employed by policy makers in an anthropocentric manner. Leave ecosystems to ecoscience. Recall that in a world of accelerating entropy there can never be a globally normative end state, for we are bound never to attain a more optimal overall ecosystem to live in than the one we enjoy today! Environmental wellbeing is essentially a societal matter under human direction.

an accessory criticism relating to some of the data sets'. Cole et al. were partly correct on both counts, yet only for a period of time. Nuclear power, plant hybrids, the prospect of hydrogen-fuelled vehicles, and effective information transference all now exist, but with many more complications and costs attached than were foreseen in the decade of the two Meadows and their co-authors. Furthermore, the acceleration of lasting environmental degradation and climate change, both largely fringe considerations in the 1960s, are now back on the agenda as urgent and immediate twenty-first-century problems.

> Prevention is preferable to intervention. Better, always, constraint care and counselling at the top of the cliff than an ambulance service at the bottom.

From a post-World War II perspective it might possibly have been wonderful if the cheap high-tech presumptions had materialized. But the simple fact of the matter is that global population has increased exponentially at just that period in human history when fossil-fuel supply is approaching dramatic decline. This is illustrated in box 3.3 which offers a side-by-side depiction of **Global population and energy use** for the two centuries on which global society is now centred. Like Sahelian locusts and Scandinavian lemmings, the rush to produce a global population beyond the fuel resources and eventually the food capacity available, is a biological imperative seemingly bound to run its cata-

> Not only did population almost treble during the last century; the length of lives lived by wealthier peoples doubled over the same period of time; the main consequence being an exponential (twentyfold?) increase in the exploitation of 'finite' resources.

clysmic course. Yet, unlike locusts and lemmings, human communities actually *know* what is happening! Furthermore, nations of the Anglo New World kind still have the potential to live comfortably within their *renewable* resource context, and with a lower level of *finite* resource uptake, all the while 'exploiting' the *free-flow* resources.

The Meadows team's combination of hard science (country-by-country projections of over-population and over-consumption), and high morality (akin to the Malthusian predictions for 'global atrophy and societal decay'), had a good press but received an apathetic political reception. Their work also generated counter-enthusiasms from other people of science who were predicating the wonders of nuclear power 'too cheap to to be bothered to meter'; agricultural hybrids and genetically modified foods 'producing a bountiful bread basket for

Box 3.3   Global population and energy use

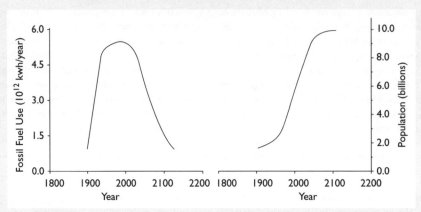

During the nineteenth century the increase in population numbers and the scale of fossil-fuel uptake were not in observable global conflict. Selecting AD 1900 as an assumed last year of *insignificant* competition between population numbers and fossil-fuel extraction, the graphs show that from 1900 onward, increases in the rate of fossil-fuel uptake outstrip the rate of population growth. The fossil-fuel-to-population crossover sometime after 2000 is a function of the global population still increasing while fossil-fuel extraction starts to dwindle.

In terms of this construct the high-volume oil-consuming nations will confront absolute fossil-fuel shortages early on in the twenty-first century, and oil resource scarcity will be a fact of global life by 2050.

The construct suggests also that the rate of fossil-fuel supply at AD 2100 (the end of the 'fossil-fuel age') will be about what it was only 200 years earlier in 1900 (at the beginning of that age). Furthermore, by 2100 both the fossil-fuel supply rate and the rate of population growth will have levelled off. But by then, according to this prog-

nosis, several times the AD 1900 population will be obliged to get by with only the 1900 level of continuing fossil-fuel supply.[a]

References: Meadows and others in *Beyond the Limits*, 1992; I. G. Simmons, *The Ecology of Natural Resources*, first published 1984. J. S. Steinhart and others *Pathway to Energy Efficiency*, 1987. Also from Brian Fleary, *Decline of the Age of Oil* (1998) 'Oil production in the major producing regions of the world is reaching its peak and beginning a decline . . . The former Soviet Union's production peaked in 1989 and has suffered rapid decline since. The remainder of the producing regions outside the Arabian Gulf are expected to peak by the year 2005. The Arabian Gulf region, with two-thirds of world oil reserves, is likely to peak last, in about 2020.'

[a] It is probable that hydrogen-powered vehicles of carbon fibre construction will be in mass production by 2025.

all'; and huge advances in medical science which would both 'constrain population size and prolong human life'. The reasoning, in short, was that resourceful humankind – as was usually, but not always the case previously – would find a technological 'fix'. The hopeful expectation from this counter-quarter was for a discovery or synergism which would extend the era of carboniferous capitalism beyond the period of concern for those now living, the mistake being that all this was done without taking into account that the numbers now living are not only of unprecedented magnitude but enjoy much longer lives as consumers, and that the rate of consumer uptake of fossil fuels is beyond previous historical levels.[21]

Resource depletion is a matter governments, in a global context, have been disinclined to heed. The push for *Agenda 21* (the 'Rio Declaration' summary given in the Appendix to chapter 5) is viewed as either 'helpful' or 'helpless' as suits the perception of the researcher; yet forceful, as a policy instrument, it is not. The pessimistic scenario has it that because essential life-support resources are either finite (as with fossil fuels) or largely irreplaceable (as with soils), the potential for a globally improved lifestyle, overall, is negative. The situation now is that the resource frontiers have either been reached or are well understood. Over the course of future time shortage-induced adjustments will arise, particularly in the overall consumption of fossil fuel. This, combined with the increasing presence of irreducible toxins in the biosphere, and a continuing reduction in biodiversity, erodes the overall quality of 'modern' human life.

Raymond Kopp (1992) explores the relationship between the use of finite ('inventory' to Kopp) resource uptake and renewable resource use, on the basis of these being partly private, quasi-public or pure-public in nature. 'Private goods (such as agricultural commodities) are exchanged in markets ... where one individual's enjoyment of them precludes all others' enjoyment. Quasi-public goods (such as water for irrigation) may or may not be traded in markets. Pure-public goods (such as aesthetic appeal) are not exchanged in [or protected by] markets.'

A global objective, were it practical to call into being a global resource policy, would involve the adoption of global controls, in effect regulating lifestyles in a way which coped with the regressive Entropy Laws, and applied the principles of sustainability. In reality most nations remain aloof on policy, and adrift with regulatory practice. With little more than glimmerings of pious hope for effective global enforcement, the actuality is that international councils have only coordinated *some* endangered species protection, and have been largely *un*successful with the control of toxins and harmful gas releases. Meyer (1993) makes the point that while 'the treaty text signed at the Earth Summit in Rio put out a legally binding commitment to strong and sustainable economic growth its commitment to the environment, a principal objective, outlined a weak non-binding option to limit CO_2 emissions to no more than 1990 levels'. He (Meyer) goes on to then establish not only a correlation between GDP, CO_2 and temperature rises, but also that *all three are increasing along with increasing world population growth*. In short, international protocols are proving impotent with regard to non-renewable fossil-fuel conservation, the limitation of Third World population growth, the control of pollution discharge, and the maintenance of bio-diversity: four significant counter-actions poleaxed by growth-and-discard practices. Even more sinister, the international agencies – global 'watchdogs' and 'whistle-blowers' – remain confused and ineffective in regard to controls over nuclear power generation, the dumping of nuclear wastes, and the disposal or containment of most toxins.

On a positive, selective, note: for some nations of the 'North' the record of attainment for environmentally progressive outcomes is partially better than the OECD average. This arises because some are *well placed* (for example Australasia's geographical isolation and low density of human population), or because they are *well poised* (an affordable North American environmental awareness). These placements and positionings enable these countries to pursue effective programmes to assist environmental conservation and hold to their current levels of human population.[22] This may be achieved: *first* through an elaboration of the largely social strictures which lie at the heart of concerns held by those now living, influencing the small-family option. *Second* through resource management, by simply doing much better in the pursuit of day-to-day policies for overall sustainable resource use.

The philosophy and science which characterized the first Malthusian round for the Limits to Growth prognosis, 200 years ago, is *now* an awesome technological assertion clearly at work upon the globe considered as an earthship. For a conjectural style of confirmation, look again at box 3.3 which hazards a conservative depiction of the twenty-first-century gap between remaining fossil-fuel energy stocks and a projection of population increase.

The political ecology of scale shifts

Scale shift is a local, regional, national, and global phenomenon. The national aspect of 'shift' is represented in figure 3.1 as **Scale and economy**. It took the efforts of the Club of Rome [1972] – recalibrating from Malthus to Meadows – to establish the obvious, that the planet itself, and the resources bound into it, were finite. The global scale shifts in the degradation of rural producer landscapes and growth in the size of urban consumer enclaves took place throughout the last century at a much faster rate, and on a relatively more dramatic scale, than in any previous century. And although it could be construed that putting together this listing relies on the use of shorthand expressions to dramatize a pre-indicated emphasis, it can also be held that it indicates clearly the scale of damage which 'pace and change' is dumping today onto states and communities, notably poor states and poor communities.

Small-scale past	Expansive scale present
'First-people' values	'Settler' values
For 'group' (community)	For 'self' (individual)
Rural dispersed	Urban concentrated
Stable population	Growing population
Labour intensive	Technology intensive
Pantheistic (with nature)	Theistic (above nature)
'Gift economy' past	'Gain economy' present
Self-sufficient production	Export-led trading
Every person productive	Massive unemployment
Discrete projects	Big enterprises
Community harmony	Individual profit
'Soft rustic' technologies	'Hard science' technologies
Agriculturally based	Industrially based
Production for satisfaction	Consumption for status

Figure 3.1   Scale and economy: characteristics of change

There is much analysis about *issues*; over-stocking, over-invest-ing, over-depending, over-producing, under-processing and under-employing, but there is little explication of much in the way of *remedies*. This has given rise to patronizing rhetoric along the lines that first some unpalatable 'medicine' will have to be taken in order for the environment to regain good health! Rela-tive to this simplification it is important to hold in view the general proposition that human optimism is always bound to eclipse here-and-now pessimism. It is helpful to be also aware of the prospects for continuous growth and profitability which can be obtained from the invention and profit-taking of environmen-tally benign technologies.[23]

The overall rate and scale of within-nation landscape change over the last one hundred years has been particularly awesome. The box 3.4 construct, **Soft pathways**, provides a representation of several technologies as 'soft' (benign? helpful? good?) and indi-cates others as 'hard' (mostly unhelpful! alien! bad!). In fact many a 'soft' technology has gone wrong (as with the introduction of alien weed plants and animal species to the New World); and sometimes a 'hard' technology is often helpful (as with the use of GPS technology).

In my circle a few people strive to live as 'sustainably' as practical. Gold and Webster (1990: 44) asserted that for the New Zealand case 'It is clear that the overwhelming majority (85 percent) are convinced of the urgent necessity for environmental protection.' Yet very few within this hefty proportion would be prepared, as a minimum, to junk their cars as a first serious move in the direction of 'sustainability'! Sustainability is an often misapplied and frequently misunderstood concept!

The prognosis given here and elaborated later involves, in large part, a slowing-down of finite (irreplaceable) resource consumption. What is called for is *a con-servative approach to the utilization of finite resources, the husbandry of renewable resources, a moderation of the rate of population added change; an endorsement of 'soft' production; and culturally linking the pursuit of an ecological balance with the environ-ment.* These strictures involve social deflections and social actions. They implicate agricultural production and an inventory basis of control for the utilization of finite resources, along with reduced reliance upon imported fossil fuels, fertiliz-ers and bulk foodstuffs. Also at particular urban issue are socially appropriate steady-state technological uptakes, energy-efficient building, and the retrofitting of sites and buildings for compact and energy-efficient (bio-harmonic) construc-tion and maintenance. Above all, toxins – those residues which degrade the ecology because nature cannot assimilate them – must not be produced at all *or* be tracked through to their neutralization.

An extension from the New-age pragmatics (box 1.2) is given in box 3.5, **Sus-tainable co-dependency**. This construct provides the rationale for incorporating sustainability into cyclical (seasonal) patterns. It also harbours concern for the wellbeing of people, and a reverence for historical precedent – all placed above short-term consumption and discard. Reinforcing the birth–life–death cycle, and traditional rural and urban values, is inherently worthy, as is the consolidation of a mainly natural growth of population. Co-dependency is a matter of putting power and decisions out to local levels of government (subsidiarity); to fostering less fiscal input from offshore borrowings, and advancing the utilization of within-nation renewable resources and finite resources. Co-dependency brings to closure

Box 3.4   Soft pathways

- *A scale pathway* which leads to technologies which bypass 'giantism' – thus avoiding 'thinking big' and offshore capitalization. Caveats swarm in, for of course not all 'big' projects are 'bad', nor is the participation of multinationals always harmful. This is where the utility of 'recipient' as well as 'donor' Cost Benefit Analysis, and Impact Abatement Assessment (chapter 4) are relevant and useful.

- *The pursuit of subsidiarity pathways* opts for local funding, local enskilling, local management, and local patents; *avoiding* external dependency, external profit-taking, external tax evasion, and the payment of external patent rights: and the external recruitment of personnel – although the immigrant inflow of outside expertise is often desirable and beneficial, most obviously so in the staffing of universities. Here also it is important to recognize and educate children as the role-modellers and stakeholders of the future, from which the current batch of adult decision-takers will in the course of time be duly retired.

- *Incremental pathway* applications engage technologies and skills which are a progression from proven techniques. An example is fish-farming born of family fishing experience; another is furniture-making as an outgrowth of sawmilling.

- *The selective use of high-tech pathways* which circumvent bottlenecks in contra-indication, on occasion, to the point above. Thus the controlled use of helicopter bulk transportation, waste management, toxin capture, and the engagement of other high-tech yet low-impact facilities can be of impressive utility. Every application for circumventing soft solutions should undergo Risk Impact Assessment.

- *Engagement of ecological pathways* which seek out benign technological applications (as with the use of a proven 'biological control' in agriculture) and the selection of options which avoid ecologically faulty technologies, especially those which leave behind synthetic residues and non-degradable toxins.

Box 3.4 *Continued*

- *Taking up conservative pathway* applications which favour the use of hydro-generated power, solar power and photosynthesized energy. The use of non-motor power along with the use of proven methods of low-sequestered inputs of energy in agriculture, horticulture and viticulture, as contributions to the reduction of greenhouse gas emissions.

- *Pursuing an equity pathway.* Seeking to avoid reversions to socially degrading drudgery (for example, hand tool agriculture), yet adopting work practices which engage local skills and traditional processes with an element of personal job choice.

- *Engagement of waste-avoidance pathways.* Viewing waste generation and abandonment as an abomination, and an admission of failure. Waste production to be regarded as an activity which harbours a potential for regains from waste minimization and waste recycling.

- *The pursuit of low-capitalization pathways* for plant installations with low start-up costs, minimal plant costs per workspace created, with low maintenance and operating costs, and above all achieve a high level of import substitution and inward investment.

- *Adoption of efficiency pathway procedures.* These engage technologies which improve, in terms of all the previous tenets, the efficiency and cleanliness of 'old' processes, particularly through the engagement of a new technology, import substitution, toxin control and rationalized cellular phone communication.

Box 3.5   Sustainable co-dependency

Among the environmentally knowledgeable, engagement of the generic expression 'sustainability' indicates the application of an attitude of 'balance' with regard to resource uptake and usage. But as was shown previously in box 3.2, *Resources within ecosystems*, the postures appropriate to the use of free-flow, renewable, finite and heritage resources are each different, being respectively to 'exploit', 'sustain', 'conserve' and to 'preserve'. Within this framework of usage, sustainability is seen to be a management tool for keeping the economy, not merely the ecology, healthy *and* above the margin of non-profitability or clean-up burden. What constitutes 'appropriate' sustainability can be explored further on two planes.

As *jargon*, 'sustainability' stands with the first and second development decade (1960s and 1970s) calls for 'modernization', 'excellence', 'integration' and 'comprehensiveness'. In line with the non-dictionary use of such expressions, 'sustainability' varies in meaning depending on the purpose or intent of the user! Thus a welfare beneficiary wants a 'sustainable' level of benefit; a consumer wants a 'sustainable' growth pattern; an environmentalist wishes to pass on the resource platform in a 'sustainable' condition. What they all do is promote the 'sustainability' of what it is they have an aspiration for, as with the ideals of 'comprehensiveness' and 'integration' in the past. Generic sustainability is probably impossible to achieve,

yet it can be held in view as a target or objective to strive toward, knowing it cannot be fully attained.

As *philosophy*, 'sustainability' is intended to reflect an epistemological realism, and here it runs into a conceptual wall: namely that it cannot reconcile the different pace of change between social and ecological processes. The era of fossil-fuel uptake enabled modern nations to skirt around that socio-ecological quandary; for pre-industrial age peoples 'social realism' co-related to 'ecological realities' and a human-environmental co-dependency was struck in a manner which was, for those times, 'sustainable'. But, fuelled by a hydrocarbon abundance which provided the surplus energy for twentieth-century consumerism, there has occurred a global cultural outgrowth (Westernism). The imbalance between a consumer-driven social system, and a carbon-regenerating ecological system, cannot be now closed by a superficial inclination toward 'sustainability', which does not, of course, deny sustainability as a worthy goal.

My predication is that a loosely applied usage of the term 'sustainability' will lead to the expression *either* eliding into misuse *or* to it becoming sidelined as jargon. The Anglo settler nations will hopefully evolve what might be indicated as *sustainable co-evolution*, a husbandry pattern for co-dependency, which strives to reconcile equitable socio-*economic* systems with harmonic socio-*ecological* systems.

---

the cynical claim of business and industry to 'trust us'; and engenders engagement of the wisdom to always ask enterprises to 'prove it'.

The co-dependency call is for diverse, fully costed, impact-assessed, socially analysed, locally sustainable projects. It also involves being wary of 'harder' technologies, particularly those producing discards which become embodied in the biosphere (non-degradable toxins and the time-bomb parts of discarded consumer durables).[24] Of course it also involves a factoring-in of conservation *with* development: safe and secure habitations, equitable economic growth patterns, natural population growth, environmental balance, and the reinforcement of what a district region or nation produces best. Local communities in the Anglo settler societies are democratically open and pluralist. They are blessed with an ever-continuing centrist potential to affirm themselves as co-evolving with nature on a co-dependency basis.

It is up to informed communities and their political leaders to stake a claim for conservancy *with* development, in effect heeding the lessons of history.[25] Never again to blunder on with lemming-like patterns of growth, consumption, environmental decay and entropic disorder.

Resource Guardianship: Principles into Practice

At every turn and during every hour of our lives each of us can identify personal gratifications deriving from an engagement of 'hard' technologies. These include ease of transportation (the owner-driven fossil-fuelled automobile), eating with convenience (prepackaged and ready-to-eat food from distant places), ablution comfort (potable water supply, and water-borne sewage disposal), trash discard (garbage collection and dumping), chemical weeding and pest eradication (herbicides and pesticides), home and workplace comfort (air conditioning and electric heating). Of course the list goes further than this selection.

In order to achieve sustainable urban outcomes the mainly *for myself* technologies for personal gratification must be aligned much more in the direction of de-mystified, functional and neomodern *for us* patterns. To do so need not raise the spectre of universal identity cards or whole populations pulling on hair shirts. The most favourable prospect is 'win-win' outcomes for all – *and* establishing and continuing that outcome with succeeding generations.

> 'There is an acute recognition within the environmental justice movement that the game is lost for the poor and marginalised as soon as any problem is cast in terms of the asymmetry of monetary change.'
> David Harvey, 1995
> 'The Environment of Justice'

The pursuit of actions beneficial to sustaining the natural resource estate, and for the wellbeing of the population at large, is open to adoption and pursuit by every individual and every community. It is already a motivating factor in the lives of many individuals and a few communities. Yet even the most ardent environmentalists never totally compromise their modernity by, for example, avoiding the use of petrol-powered automobiles or passing up jet vacations. The main difficulty is finding the means for getting from where matters stand, reduction of individual instances of energy profligacy and discard of toxins, to upholding fossil energy conservation and the use of benign biological control agents. A powerful accessory to the environmental justice movement, noted by David Harvey (1995) are those 'symbolic politics and powerful icons of pollution incidents. Toxins in someone's basement . . . (rather) than the diffuse clouds of ozone'. There is a difficulty of insubstantiality with ozone 'clouds' and multiple gas-guzzling automobiles, whereas with Harvey's 'basement toxins' there is a specific effect, obvious victims and a fairly obvious perpetrator.

The case for finite energy resource conservation is summarized in box 3.6 as **Kicking the energy-use habit**. The pattern under challenge is machine-driven and fossil-fuel sourced, which aggregates throughout the OECD as a profligacy. What is shown here are some pragmatic options for reducing energy consumption and achieving improved finite resource conservation. These options will turn into imperatives over time because, simply, the most easily installed hydro-kinetics, for example, have mostly been harnessed and the most easily won fossil fuels have already been tapped; and because each level of further exploration and exploitation reduces the ratio of recovered energy output relative to the energy sequestered into exploration, development and production. The imperative put here is to reduce the rate of fossil energy dependence, and eventually to reduce

Box 3.6   Kicking the energy-use habit

(Refer also to box 1.2 New Age Pragmatics)

The nub to progressively improved energy-use habits is a matter of downward adjustments to fossil-fuel uptake, coupled to an increased harvesting of free-flow energy resources. The 'energy-population' crossover difficulties shown up in box 3.3, *Global population and energy use*, highlights the fact that earth island is fast running out of yet-to-be-discovered oil and gas options. There is also an imperative rejoinder to any speculation that the likes of coal and shale might be used, for even were these reserves tapped, the further carbon dioxide and unscrubbed sulphur gas put into the atmosphere would vastly downgrade life for all, and literally drown human settlements in many low-lying estuarine areas and atoll locations, *and for this implacable reason is unacceptable*. From this premiss there arises an important trinity for action: fossil-fuel conservation, reductions in the rate of fossil-fuel use, and energy substitution from benign energy sources. Pursuit of this trinity would enhance, not impair, accustomed lifestyles, and do so by providing sufficient mobility with greater safety, and greater home and workplace comfort, enabling the money not spent on energy profligacy to be put into other aspects of lifestyle enhancement.

By what specific means?

- Through the importation and local construction of energy-efficient automobiles (improving further, as in the United Kingdom, upon the 1980s 30 mpg average car – already a vast improvement over the previous two decades – to a 45 mpg average car) *and* the phasing out of inefficient older vehicles.
  Coda: Improve the balance of trade, via reduced oil imports, at a stroke.
- By applying vastly increased petrol pump taxes (which would not so heavily hit fuel-efficient car owners) the increased revenue going toward other transportation schemes and pavement improvements.
  Coda: taxes as high as US$1.00 a litre are in place in car-loving Italy, $0.73 in Germany, and $0.67 in Britain. These induce car-using efficiencies, yet do not curtail lifestyle benefits from automobile utility.
- By legislating and enforcing the uptake of passive solar heat retention in buildings; installing high-rating building insulation, energy-smart glazing, solar water heating; also installing chip-controlled micro-climate management systems within larger buildings, heat-exchange pumps, variable speed electric motors, and halogen light bulbs among a host of energy-conserving soft-pathway technologies.
  Coda: about one-third of total electricity output in New World nations is consumed domestically, with about half that consumption for water heating, an obvious area of substitution and saving.
- By educating the energy-consuming public about the economic benefits and environmental gains which flow on from energy conservation policies.
  Coda: the UNESCO information sheet 'Connect' (produced separately in English, French, Spanish, Russian, Arabic, and Chinese) is one good example by which/world wide environmental educational publicity can be promoted.

Down which sectoral avenues?

From *urban lifestyle energy savings*, from *savings in primary production*, and from *savings within industry*.

- Because such a high proportion of the population within North America and Australasia is urban, the accumulation of urban lifestyle energy savings, when totalled, is impressive, particularly via the adoption of mixed-use zoning. Such savings are cumulatively significant: arising from the well-publicized litany of home insulation, solar hot water heating, car pooling, reduced out-of-home car trips, increased use of public transport, reduced water consumption, lowered product packaging and garbage output, and the installation of halogen lighting. Adjustments in these ways reduces fossil-fuel and hydro energy consumption at no loss to overall standards of living or human comfort, and largely awaits individual realization and personal action, coupled to official endorsement and inducement, which has not been forthcoming from energy suppliers.
- Energy saving in *primary production* (agriculture, fisheries, silviculture and forestry) involves the complexity of diverting away from fossil energy usage into a greater uptake and usage of free-flow energy sources. There are three policy possibilities: repressing the propensity to over-mechanize (the case against the likes of aerial fertilizer drops), to over-electrify (the case against mains-fed gadgetry), and to reduce

---

Box 3.6 *Continued*

chemical farming practices (cutting back on the use of herbicides, fungicides, pesticides), with a complexity arising from the fact that exchanging the trail bike for a horse, using sails for a fishing boat, and critical path adherence in exotic forestry, are not all that work-practical or cost-appealing. Nevertheless the ratio of fossil-fuel calories sequestered into the production of food calories and construction materials could be (say) halved (less use of tractors and trucks), *including* better storage and break-of-bulk patterning, *and including* a reduction in the mileage travelled for the notional standard food-on-the-lips-morsel (posited as 3,000 km on average): achieved by the adoption of a production-close-to-consumption policy. Improved management and a rationalization of machine-driven practices would produce both cost savings and energy savings for individual primary production units.

• It is with *manufacturing industry* that the proportionally most impressive and easily fashioned reductions in energy consumption, relative to output, can be obtained. There are programming tactics for cutting down on over-powering, over-lighting, and over-heating. To the credit of most larger enterprises they look to reduce these kinds of energy input, and to design a reduction of waste heat, frictional inefficiencies and waste outputs. Savings in industry also arise from two other seldom considered options: *First* the adoption of compacted production cycles (as with efficient operation of plants either 'full on' or 'full off') with production centred on spells of continuous operation; *Secondly* a reduction in the number of personal worker start-up days (three-day working week?) with longer hours per worker shift (12 hour aggregate shifts?). These arrangements generate worthwhile savings in industry, and they also harbour potential for both improved production and greater employee and employer satisfaction – but watch out for the twenty-first-century Luddites!

---

that dependency in absolute terms; ideally to *increase* per capita rates of employment and disposable income whilst *reducing* per capita levels of fossil energy consumption relative to each unit of productive output. By identifying the more profligate energy-using attitudes it becomes practical to target specific policy corrections along the lines presented in box 3.6, resulting in reduced levels of energy sequestration into projects, more benign technological applications in the home, the workplace and in transportation, and improved energy management within industry and on the farm; with, of course, a consequential slowdown in atmospheric degradation.

Attention now shifts to the means for putting these principles into practice.

Aside from the usually out-of-mind eventual and inevitable state of entropic disorder, reflection establishes that a unit of earth-bound fossil fuel can be used only once during the course of modern human history. This is so because there is, for practical purposes, one chance only to enjoy the finite quantity of energy stored up as fossil energy 'for us' by nature. In short, modern life cannot realistically be 'sustainable' in a contemporary, dominantly urban, way. Lifestyles can of course be modified to incorporate urban people within a *more sustainable continuum*, that which involves the attainment of a better balance between resource management, heritage conservation and communities of population. This implicates 'progressive change'.

Conservation *with* development is presented throughout these pages as the required *improving* vision, a multiple-belief *activity* instituting progressive change in the neomodern direction of a tolerable harmony. What has to be guarded against is the uneven application of resource-conservation and discard-reduction

At the crudest level of abstraction, a nation 'develops' if its gross national product per capita increases. Yet if a nation so develops, along the lines of New Zealand's one-off exploitation of native forest resources, Australia's one-off uptake of ground-water, Alaska's inflow of dollars to clean up oil spills, or the Philippines' acceptance of toxic industrialization, then the end result is inevitably a sorry mess, with an eventual reduction to the quality of life.

policies: to pursue an even application of sustainable urban planning. Within the wealthier nations these options remain still available: to develop and reduce consumption of 'finite' 'renewable' and 'heritage' resources, and increase the uptake of 'free-flow' resources progressively, as strategic choices. The following four paragraphs review these principles on a neomodern 'work-with and work-around' basis.

Conservative utilization of finite resources   (refer to box 3.2 previously in this chapter) requires that as irreplaceable fossil fuels and minerals are 'exploited', which is inevitably the case, this is carried out in a way which avoids balance-sheet demands to cut-and-run with the easily liquidated 10 or 20 per cent of such resources. For example: that mining operatives be constrained to glean their winnings patch by patch, abstracting these once-only resources as thoroughly as 80 per cent, all the while practising toxic waste containment and landscape restoration. The challenge to management is to set aside the 'that leaves little margin for profit' reasoning. Delay will lead to accusations that bureaucracy is impeding business; yet strategic 'delay' can be advocated for finite resource utilization on the basis that at some point of time in the future there will arise an optimal 'window of opportunity' and it is then, not imperatively now, that the winning of a non-renewable resource should proceed. It is simply no longer sensible (it never was) for nations to allow profligate finite resource abstraction, inefficient finite resource consumption, and widespread mineral waste by-

product abandonment. The utilization of finite resources, principally involving once-only access to fossil-fuel stocks and minerals (and for practical purposes, ancient indigenous forests), should be recognized as 'belonging to society', even though they frequently occur on or under freehold title. Communities must regulate access to these resources carefully and conservatively, and require them to be mined and used efficiently. Current procedures for winning the easily extracted portions thus impairing future access to the balance left in the ground, must be realigned toward efficiency in finite resource utilization, finite resource substitution, and a curtailment of rates of finite resource uptake.

Summary stricture: *manage and control the uptake of utilized-only-once finite, irreplaceable, earth-bound resources 'conservatively'.*

Sustainable engagement and use of renewable resources   (see box 3.2) is a matter of practising the life-holding stewardship of soil, water, air and indigenous flora and fauna. Refurbishment and renewal makes plain ordinary common sense *and* is sound longer-term business practice. Historically there has occurred a virtual 'mining' of agricultural soils, a heating, polluting and eutrophication of inland water bodies, and a degradation of renewable forest, fish, fowl and animal resources – under all manner of freehold, cognatic and state patterns of resource ownership. This adds argument to the case for imposing public controls over renewable resource-using actions. Movements in this direction by water catchment authorities, and by means of Landcare principles on freehold farms, are encouraging. Marketing the clean purity of diverse products from a toxin-free and genetically sound renewable resource base, managed without excessive applications of fertilizers herbicides fungicides and pesticides, is the 'clever' approach. Green marketing, admitting only to verified chemical interventions, adds to longer-term economic viability and environmental wellbeing. With renewable resources, particularly fresh water flows and soils, but also for indigenous flora and fauna, the societal ideal is to pass these on to future generations in a condition which will enable them, in turn, to maintain a level of productiveness or output equal to that enjoyed at present. The 'sustainable' contention in relation to renewable resources is that from any given point in time onward, the renewable soil, water and air

New Zealand (population close to 4m) claims the earth's fourth largest EEZ, and through a stuttering fish management quota scheme is set to increase the annual catch of most commercial species.

resources, along with indigenous flora and fauna, receive cyclic respect, are no further depleted or impaired, and are restored to ecological diversity and purity.

Summary stricture: *Coerce the restoration of degraded renewable resources; and guide the uptake from and replenishment of renewable resources 'sustainably' and 'indefinitely'.*

Preservation of cultural-heritage and natural-heritage resources in the neomodernist way (see again box 3.2 earlier in this chapter) gets to the heart and soul of human 'being'. Paradoxically, settler society administrations have previously done a good job at keeping up their birth-of-nation buildings, all the while flaying the natural forests and slaughtering the native fauna. Nowadays the situation is mostly reversed, with an often wilful destruction of the building heritage, yet a separate but considerable reverence for the remaining indigenous forest and avian life forms! The *neo*modern call is

Cultural heritage: former Post Office

for a preservation, for all future time, of the cultural *and* natural heritage, aligning and identifying with tourist pocketbooks, and the toxin-free demands of varietal lifestyles. The heritage resources policy set includes both a nurturing of the well-understood 'cultural heritage' along with a preservation of 'natural heritage' resources.

Natural heritage: wild coastline

Summary stricture: *revere, nurture and preserve cultural-heritage and natural-heritage resources with a respect for the historical past and a sense of the 'history' to come.*

Exploitation of free-flow resources (see box 3.2) embodies and engages the cleverly neomodern mode of progressive and allowable free-flow resource exploitation. Highly approved in this category are hydroelectrical generation, wind and tidal kinetic energy capture, photosynthetic food and energy productions, and the likes of passive and active solar energy capture (and natural heating and cooling systems) for buildings. Ingenuity may have to be constrained if it implicates denial of reasonable access to, or utility of, some other 'finite' 'renewable' and or 'heritage' resource, as for example with the likes of windmill 'farms' obtruding into the conservation estate, and the flooding which can result from the silting up of hydro lakes. But, on the whole, a loose rein 'exploitation' of largely benign free-flow resources has appeal, and great potential for human benefit. It is solely in relation to free-flow resources, provided from energy sources largely off-planet (the sun) and beyond human output control, that individuals and communities can be allowably profligate.

Californian wind farm

Summary stricture: *exploit, with neighbourly consideration, the uptake of free-flow resources.*

Communities tend to resist the idea of technological reversal and revisionism. With most new technologies 'going wrong' in one way or another, inspiration can be drawn from Kropotkin's nineteenth-century treatise (paraphrasing by Ward 1985) in which 'to get it right' Kropotkin made four points. *First* that:

> [P]roduction for a local market is a rational and desirable tendency. The *second* was that each region of the globe must feed itself, and that intensive farming could meet the basic needs of a country . . . The *third* was that dispersal of industry on a small scale and in combination with agriculture is also rational and desirable . . . and the *fourth* is that we need an education which combines manual and intellectual work.

By contrast to Kropotkin, the OECD categories of wealthier nation, expanding into the twenty-first-century, remain aligned to the notion of expressing farming efficiency in terms of high worker input-to-output ratios on an also high hectare-per-worker basis, *and* to allow the growth-on-growth model to enslave the consumer mind.

Much that was 'hard' and 'smart' with twentieth-century policies must eventually give way to 'soft' and 'clever' twenty-first-century practices. Yet, it is important that this should be achieved not by giving up on sophistication in favour of rusticity. A clever neomodern future retains the best of a traditional 'past' which is harmoniously organic and cyclic, and combines this with the best of the hi-tech 'present' in situations where this conjunction is economically feasible, socially appropriate, environmentally benign, and indefinitely sustainable.

The Soft Pathways Matrix

The pathways to a 'tolerable triple harmony' are as manifold and complex as is depicted in the vertical and horizontal array given as box 3.7 a **Matrix for conservation with development** – identified throughout this book as the **Matrix**.

It would deflect from my purpose were the main thread of the current within-nation and socio-environmental discourse to stray into the box 3.7 maze. The **Matrix** is there for the reader to scan and contemplate – according to the circumstance and situation being addressed. Attention to some key words and phrases within the ambit of sustainable co-dependency sets the context: 'quality', 'balance' and 'appropriateness' come to the fore.

Quality with respect to soft-path outcomes has been profiled previously. There can be fiscal savings, even gains, through the improved environmental *quality* which results from toxin-free and diverse production; an uplifting of the feel-good factor by celebrating the *quality* of a nation's natural heritage; and community pride can emanate from a flowering of the *quality* of human skills. There arises, of course, the correctional converse: avoidance of mediocre design and avoidance of shoddy projects which incur maintenance and which give rise to excessive operational and transaction costs. A quality-of-life pursuit within open democracies couples with the security of high levels of employment.

Balance targets the soft pathways pragmatically, threading in two components which incorporate some of the 'quality' reasoning, with a social leavening. In summary:

- *Balance factor one*: maintaining social wellbeing, along with material growth, within a context of work-routine security; positioning 'people place and community' alongside growth-for-profit.
- *Balance factor two*: maintaining resource and habitat equilibrium in line with the reasoning given earlier:

    Conservative uptake of once-in-history finite resources carefully and with respect for the future;

    Sustainably engage the use of renewable life-support resources, with consideration for the needs of generations yet to come;

    Preserve natural heritage and cultural heritage extrinsic resources as though for all future time;

    Exploit free-flow resources in a socially and environmentally acceptable way.

> 'If our species is to survive the predicaments we have created for ourselves, we must develop a capacity for whole-systems thought and action.'
>
> *When Corporations Rule the World*
> David C. Korten, 1995.

BOX 3.7 Matrix for conservation with development[a]

The POWERS section of the **Matrix** is on pp. 108–9.
The ACTIONS section of the **Matrix** is on pp. 110–11.

	NATIONAL[b] (For the nation)	REGIONAL[b] (Communities of Concern[d])
NEOMODERN POLITICAL PHILOSOPHY[f]	Pan-political guardianship Resource custody humbleness Equal liberty and general equity[j] Reduce external debt and dependency Maintain international parity Politics and policies of decentralization Impact defence: environmental, social, economic Independent and non-nuclear: reduce the military	Positioning: national, regional, local The regional spirit: a concomitant Attitude: progressive development Custodial regional politics Co-regional and within-nation dependency Husbandry in lieu of resource blowout Impact defence: the regional emphasis Attitude: multiplier development
SUSTAINABLE POLICY[g]	Biculturalism within multiculturalism Treat multinationals circumspectly Eschew indiscriminate growth maximizing Public ownership of common resources Promote energy-saving policies Advocate import substitution Promote societally useful policies Regard 'place' seriously Selective immigration and tariff policies	Reason regionally; act locally Regional: urban-rural symbiosis: a journey Seek to establish a dynamic harmony Dualistic: 'interventions' and 'controls' Recognition: no 'away' to throw waste 'to' Publicize energy-saving policies Impact-defence as regional policy Combat pollution and resource degradation State of the environment monitor-auditing Institute 'life cycle' analysis
NEOMODERN ECONOMICS[h]	Neomodernist: quality of life paramount Progressive employment and taxation policies Stop borrowing: reduce national debt Subsidiarity: self-service economic organization Inhibit unearned pathways to wealth Cut military expenditure drastically Within-nation ownership and profit taking Aged: GRI to be GNP and population indexed[k] Youth: priorities start with pre-schooling Fund environmental research	Promote 'basic' (export) development Integrate the regional economy Seek out regional self-sufficiencies Balance: ecological accounting Increase regional multiplier activity Low capital inputs per workplace Sustain within-region reinvestment Reject junk commerce[l] Conduct development multiplier research
SUSTAINABLE RESOURCE STEWARDSHIP[i]	Recognition: unemployment is mismanagement Shortened working week (longer working day) Integrity: political-bureaucratic-technocratic Resolve production and sales bottlenecks Quota management of common property resources Localize and privatize away from the centres Resource management and impact abatement Monitor environmental impacts and changes Nationally profitable may not be locally good	Development with nature: impact abatement Recognition: communities of concern overlap Promote bottom-up decision-making Enforce common property resource policies Resolve throughput bottlenecks Supply-side 'carrots' and demand-side 'sticks'[m] Establish development advice bureaux Labour-intensiveness avoiding drudgery Education: economics, ecology, development

P O W E R S[c]

BOX 3.7 *Continued*

LOCAL[b] (For the community)	HOUSEHOLD[b] (For Individuals[e])
Sustainable ideal is neomodern	Variety in all things: the spice to life
Community: the democratic core	Nature humanized yet revered
Regional-local-personal inter-dependency	Local dependency and cooperation
Stewardship: development with nature	Community betterment through social harmony
Think locally: foster community spirit and action	A 'postmodernist' household ethic
Community alliance toward sustainability	Husbandry: permaculture the ultimate
Purpose and design in development	Impact avoidance in the Conduct of life
Engage impact abatement assessment	Life as art: art in life
Sustainability in policy and practice	
Call the local political shots (subsidiarity)	Quality before quantity
Integrated collective trust	Honesty, affection, commitment
Strive for sustainability ideals	Cooperation with competition
People–place harmony	Foster community participation
Reciprocity: recognition of collective worth	Rely on proven experience
Attitude: everybody is useful	Waste minimization and energy saving
Policy: energy reduction practices	Self-servicing: minding, rosters, crime-watch
Policy: avoid waste generation	Pre-school benefit-link parenting
Treat waste accumulation as community failure	
Foster community independence	Work = income; income = dignity; work = dignity
Engage local know-how	Budget for self-reliance
Avoid drudgery: promote labour-intensiveness	Sustainability practice: an alleviation of ennui
Eschew self-serving professionalism	Integrate the informal economy
Police 'common property' regulations	Barter and exchange
Establish information skills exchange	Meet ecological debts
Enhancement through design excellence[n]	Skirt the money system – legally
Impact defence: locally applied and apparent	Small is best – usually
Environment–Economics–Equity–Efficiency–Education	Family-linked welfare support
Eco-manage: Economics ecology development	Development of person, place, self-reliance
Locally correct is usually nationally good	Self-sufficiency and household sustainability[o]
Balance: harmony; respect for tradition	Pre-schooling start: Self-reliance life skills
Take decisions locally: 'bottom up' (subsidiarity)	Eco-practice: care for the environment
Employ and purchase locally	'Bottom' place to start: pre-schooling, vegie patch
Low capital input for each workplace	Respect 'common property' policies
Recognize: quality of habitat reflects quality of life	Go for 'next step' technological innovations
Priority: early school provisioning excellence	Participate in community government
Foster a community-exchange economy	Beat consumer system: co-ops barter exchange[p]

Notes

[a] The Matrix suggests lines of approach vertically ('national', 'regional', 'local', and 'personal': and horizontally (engaging the available 'powers' and options for 'actions'): applied in the pragmatic pursuit of sustainable development practices.
[b] The nub to planned effectiveness of outcome across the nation-to-household spectrum arises, within Anglo New World nations, in two key within-nation contexts, regional and local.
[c] Worthy postmodern outcomes result from the use of powers coupled to follow-up actions, not as a consequence of the mere presence of statutes and regulations. The ethical theories and foundation principles identified with these powers and actions have been reviewed in ch. 1.
[d] Regions as 'communities of concern' can be both lesser and greater than 'administrative regions'. Thus there can be identified: catchment regions, climatic regions, metropolitan regions, urban regions, tourist regions, shopping regions, utilities service regions, social service regions, transportation regions and also the fortunate 'growth regions' and the less fortunate 'economically depressed regions'. See also ch. 4: Growth Pattern Management.
[e] Individuals as political and economic entities are the prime moving factor, 'presenting' as the major earning and spending (consumption and disposal) forces in society. Individuals are also the centre of proto-political power in society, and their role in resource management and in pursuit of sustainable development is very significant. The key influencing external input to individuals today is, of course, television advertising, which predicates the current style of conformity for management practices and development procedures.
[f] For a cross-reference connection refer to ch. 1: box 1.2: New-age pragmatics.
[g] See also box 3.5: Sustainable co-dependency earlier in this chapter.
[h] This expression is somewhat in line with Paul Elkins 'Conclusion' in *The Living Economy* (1986) thus national resource accounting and adjusted national product procedures; local revival of the local economy, local financing initiatives, promoting local public expenditure, and affordable basic incomes; health policy (but no mention of education!) and trade policy, all in the direction of self-reliance. Refer also to M. A. Lutz and K. Lux, *Humanistic Economics* (1988).
[i] Akin to the four resources (finite, renewable, heritage and freeflow) detailed in box 3.2: Resources within ecosystems (earlier in this chapter).

BOX 3.7 *Continued*

A C T I O N S	**RESOURCE UTILIZATION**[i]	Globalization of diversified niche excellence Accept 'limits to growth' as absolute Exploit 'free-flow' energy resources Conservation emphasis for 'finite' resources Sustenable emphasis for 'renewable' resources Preservation emphasis for 'heritage' resources Toxin production and use to be fully audited 'Polluter pays principle' an applied instrument Local growth population policy Resource self-sufficiency and self-reliance Hazards: defence force ever-ready	Development with nature: co-evolution Cleaner production: cleaner products Avoid ecologically faulty processes Exploitation of 'free-flow' resources Depletion planning for 'finite' resources Sustainable practices for 'renewable' resources Preservation practices for 'heritage' resources Levy pollution taxes and penalties neutrally Reuse; recover; recycle Tourism: approached regionally Establish an ever-ready hazards defence
	ENERGY USE and TRANSPORT[q]	Simplicity; Economy; Reliability Avoid 'giantism' and 'over-development' Mining: efficiency, plus restoration Progressively increase motor fuel taxes Depletion planning for fossil-fuels use Promote low-energy sequestration projects Energy-efficient automobile and highway policies Freight: truck, train and boat: localize Conservative commodity packaging	Appropriate technology a key factor[s] Low energy embodiments to agri-industry Photosynthesis, solar, hydro and wind systems Garbage sorting and recycling stations Waste-heat recovery bonuses Efficiency with fossil-fuel extraction Energy efficient building codes Reduce tonne-kilometres travelled Retain railway easements in public domain
	AGRICULTURE and INDUSTRY[q]	Simplicity; economy; sustainability Reinforce periphery–centre relationships Reinforce agri-industrial symbiosis Quality before quantity – profit from quality 'Think small' diversified processes and projects Decentralize agricultural processing Avoid ecologically faulty technologies 'Polluter pays principle' applies	Rural and urban: agriculture with industry 'Soft' and 'clean' technological applications Corporate Image: quality and excellence Polluter pays principle applied Sustainable diversified agriculture Food basket production close to settlements Trace toxins through to safe disposal Clean production: Residuals management
	URBAN and SUBURBAN[r]	Respect urban-rural inter-reliance Recognition: we mostly live in suburbia Promote urban self-reliance and containment Avert urban neurosis, alcoholism, crime, stress Retrofit suburbia and neighbourhoods Recognition: urban wastes go to open-area 'sinks'	Region: an urban-rural symbiosis Proximity: home-work-recreation Increase urban nodal densities: cluster Regard small towns as urban optima Revitalize mainstreet Refurbish suburbia: urban containment and focus Retrofit to light rail

BOX 3.7 *Continued*

Accept: everything connects to everything	Every action generates consequences
Respect for 'public' and 'private' domains	Exploit 'free-flow' resources (solar)
Exploitative use of 'free-flow' resources	Sustainable emphasis for 'renewable' resources
Conservative use of 'finite' resources	Conserve 'finite' resources
Sustainable use of 'renewable' resources	Preserve 'heritage' resources
Preservation of 'heritage' resources	Trauma-avoidance lifestyles
Consideration for community: the catchments	Retain, repair, recycle, re-use, retrofit
Enforce pollution taxes and penalties	Grow and make for personal use
Promote local hazards defence	Pursue impact defence: a local practice
Sustainability content to early schooling	Refurbish rather than replace

Proximity of home-work-recreation	Soft energy paths and energy savings[u]
Build to efficiency codes	Reuse and recycle affirmatively
Manufacture for long-term utility	Save on domestic energy consumption
Engage: solar, hydro, wind, photosynthesis	Reduce delivered energy supply
Waste: dispose as locally as possible	Natural heating/cooking/ventilation/lighting
Reuse and recycle	Reuse and maintain transportation stock
Practice low-energy project embodiment	Out of your car, on your bike, onto your feet
Practice waste heat recovery and utility	Dietary adjustment toward vegetarian balance
Promote minibus and light rail services	Car-pooling; minibusing; public transport

Rural 'feeds' urban: Rural 'receives' waste	Soft 'symbiotic' technological applications
Farmer-factory a co-function relationship	Interdependence within community
Reduce energy embodiment in all production	Labour-with-dignity practices
Design and build plant to last	Quality plus back-up: the secret to success
Extend the permaculture network[t]	Wholesome homespun output
Cradle-to-grave care for hazardous processes	Promote permaculture principles
Labour-intensiveness: yet drudgery avoidance	Accommodate benign 'outwork' practices
Pollution taxes and penalties enforced	'Peasants by Choice' reasoning

Recognition: urban is about community	Discover and 'work' the neighbourhood
Strive for 'focused' 'sociable' neighbourhoods	Design and build to last
Provide pedestrian and cycle accessibility	Use the home for benign out-work[v]
Reduce utility service run-lines	Use pedestrian and cycle accessways
Self-reliance: energy, water, waste disposal	Pursue on-site self-servicing
Urban silviculture: firewood and fruiting trees	Comfort goals before convenience goods
Urban horticulture: the edible townscape	Engage gift-giving support[w]
Avoid junk commerce and advertising	Foster the 'enjoyable' community

[i] Recognizably a 'Rawlsian' maxim; but this and other attributable precepts, hopefully adequately referenced in the main text, are not always acknowledged in this Matrix.

[k] The context for aligning gross retirement Income to the GNP and the changing population structure is examined in David Thomson's *Selfish Generations* (1991).

[l] 'Junk Commerce' for higher bands of taxation – a personal view – is commercial 'money-taking' activity without any tangible attempt to produce a corporeal product or community service. I would include 'cowboy companies', windfall profiteering from bonds and shares, consumer vanity advertising, gambling establishment profits.

[m] On a regional basis: encourage 'within region' supply-side activities, and discourage 'extra-regional' demand-side purchasing..

[n] A cross-reference to the 11-point listing in box 5.1 Urban social arrangement and style (ch. 5).

[o] Keyworded precepts to contemplate: 'include' reusing, repairing, recycling, conserving, organic: and 'to exclude ' toxins, synthetics, hard technologies, imports.

[p] The lawn needs cutting? The sustainably ever-worsening (but economically ever-increasing) options are (1) borrow a goat (2) the household kicks-in to mow it 'by hand' (3) a member of the household does the job with a motor mower, (4) a neighbour (who needs your complimentary skills) does the job on a skills-exchange basis, (5) a locally unemployed person is given cash to do the job on an 'illegal' basis within the 'black' economy, (6) a lawn-mowing contractor is called in.

[q] Derived from the principles expressed as the 'soft pathways' earlier this chapter

[r] Suburbs and other urban componentry are given attention in ch. 5. Urban Growth Management.

[s] 'Appropriateness' being a function of broadly 'social' criteria; specifically, as economically fair, environmentally harmonious and socially secure.

[t] An excellent text is Bill Mollison's attractive presentation (1988) *Permaculture: A Designers' Manual.*

[u] Consult the significant A. B. Lovins volume (first published 1977) *Soft Energy Paths.*

[v] The incorporation of 'outwork' into suburbia connotes the acceptance of compatible 'home-commerce' and 'light home industry' into the suburban scene; along with environment-friendly place-keeping.

[w] Important this for the low waged (an economic saving), and for the elderly (sociability). No day going by without some gifting/supporting activity: home-baked bread 'in', marmalade 'out' – fresh garden vegetables 'in', save a trip groceries brought 'in' – unstick a window, mind a pet, and so on.

This socially responsive listing for *balance* is of course more easy to set down on paper than it is to live up to because of the range of values involved, and the difficulty of establishing a clear understanding of what is meant by 'appropriateness'.

Appropriateness as a conservancy and developmental notion does not stand alone. Like 'sustainability', 'integration' and 'systems', *appropriateness* is an expression often used by conservancy and development specialists tautologically. However matters of *economic appropriateness, social appropriateness* and *environmental appropriateness* aggregate as a trinity of substance. What they turn on are actual methods of 'quality management' and 'balance management' including the pursuit of subsidiarity – that principle where 'higher' authority only processes those decisions which are beyond the decision capability and delivery capacity of a 'lower' agency.

Maintaining 'quality', 'balance' and 'appropriateness' requires more than attitude, calling for well-maintained levels of inward investment, all-costs accountability, and an all-parties style of evaluation and assessment, principally Cost-Benefit Analysis (CBA), and Risk Impact Assessment (RIA) – chapter 4.

For each of the procedures advanced there applies, separately, an auditing stricture, it being essential with all parties to any significant enterprise that their disparate actions are audited via an independent monitor. Risk Impact Assessments for donors and recipients must be carried out independently (albeit from the same data pool): the costs and benefits, for example, being each appraised and calculated from separate 'donor' and 'recipient' perspectives. And because these methods of accountability, evaluation and assessment are concerned to ascribe both real and shadow costs (and benefits) in monetary terms, the authorizing agencies must evaluate the 'economic', 'social' and 'environmental' impacts and risks. In this way impacts are assessed and risks evaluated not only by monetary criteria, but also in terms of socio-environmental factors, as a component part of socially responsible and environmentally appropriate decision-making.

In risk management there arises a political conundrum out of the difficulty that traditional parties, from both the left and the right, have with alignment to the positive success of environmental reforms, the attainment of success, not only for the environment, but also for the economy. In Easterbrook's colourful phrasing (1995) 'The *left* is afraid of the environmental good news because it undercuts (their) stylish pessimism; the *right* is afraid of the good news because it shows [them] that government regulations might occasionally amount to something other than wickedness incarnate [and be 'good' and societally useful]'. The professional-operational crux to all this is to shift the environmental focus from political categorization, doom-watching, hand-wringing and despair to a rolling celebration of 'win-win outcomes' called into being by communities of concern through their own actions and of their own volition, whatever their political stripe.

Getting the pattern of uptake and usage for the previous listing of 'finite', 'renewable', 'heritage' and 'free-flow' resources into socially appropriate balance is a complicated enough matter on its own account. Of greater complexity is 'where and how' in the multi-stage life cycle (of say, a toxic chemical product) is it best to focus controls and interventions? This is explained by MaCauley and Palmer (1992) as recognizing that:

> [P]otential for risks to health and the environment may occur at many stages in the [toxic product] life cycle – at the mine mouth [on the farm?] or during production of the feed stock, during production of intermediate products . . . during use by industry or households, and upon disposal. Thus regular intervention to safeguard against risk may be necessary at more than one stage of a [product's] life cycle and may have to take different forms.

Broadly expressed, the preferred approach comes down to the use of substitute benign products in place of those which are toxic; the engagement of recycling strategies such as deposit-refund schemes; *then* Command and Control regulations which target intervention and impose penalties for at-risk usage or the dumping of a product or a resource. This topic is addressed more fully in the Risk Assesment section of chapter 4.

Responsible neomodern sustainable decision-making comes down to approvals being given, and controls being engaged, for applying socially acceptable resource management use and discard practices. These practices also exhibit 'impact balance' and 'environmental quality' in line with the soft pathways reasoning depicted earlier in box 3.4.

The soft pathways listing could have gone further, although there is also the box 3.7 sustainability **Matrix** to tap into. Alongside principles of the diverse kinds shown there, real life comes down to practical realities, including survival for the very poor, and taking the cheapest option by the not so wealthy. As surely as past attitudes have been conditioned by political motivations, plunder practices and freedom-of-use laws, nations of the North American-Australasian kind will be obliged over the medium term, or forced eventually, to fall in with watered-down 'soft' pathways. Fortunate indeed are those wealthier nations for whom 'soft' pathways remain an option. Their situation contrasts markedly with the Third World survivalist circumstance where the imperative, for most people, is personal and family survival through the rest of a mostly joyless lifetime.[26] Not for them the option of resource conservancy although, unselfconsciously, they live lifestyles which are more sustainable than those pursued by people in the wealthy nations.[27]

The Kyoto Convention, ratified in 2002, was not signed by the United States, where it was viewed by George Bush Jr. as potentially damaging to the short-term economy, despite clear and irrefutable evidence from the US Academy of Sciences that global warming, with the US arraigned as the prime culprit, was the major contributor to climatic change.

The wealthy settler societies have the capacity (if not yet the will) to command levels of fossil-fuel resource use which can underscore a cyclical and thus sustainable, ever-continuing, pattern of conservation *with* development. To this end they will need, over the first two decades of the twenty-first century, to secure the particular advantages offered by their low-density populations and discrete geographical positionings, and to fall in with social policies and *neo*modernist strictures of the kind first introduced in chapter 1 as new-age pragmatics, culminating in the soft pathways and **Matrix** arrays given in this chapter.

As the population and energy construct given earlier as Global population and energy use (box 3.3) showed, the time ahead over the first third of the twenty-first century involves adjustments – environmentally, socially, fiscally – put in place by political pragmatists who comprehend the seriousness of the sustainability imperative. It will be necessary for soft pathways to be taken, *and* for a democratic mandate to be profiled and harnessed to the job of shifting closer and closer to living 'less off' finite resource reserves; and living 'more from' free-flow resources, and obtaining 'more out of' renewable resources. In short: there is, truly, no free lunch and there is no quick fix. Mortal planners cannot play God: and, more to the point, no President can become King Canute; for with global warming the tide will indeed rise higher and the ranch will either turn to desert or be deluged. Staying on target for that triple harmony – growth, community, environment – requires changes in policy understanding and political sensitivity. Mostly this comes down to common sense, responding to nature's wake-up calls, and taking socially appropriate actions down socially appropriate paths.

The New Culture: Balanced Harmony

At base the 'conservative use of *finite* resources', the 'sustenable use of *renewable* resources', the 'preservation of *heritage* resources', and the 'socially appropriate exploitation of *free-flow* resources' all comes down to political and public motivation in the direction of a paradigm for sustainable co-evolution. This, in summary, is an operational matter of conservation *with* development. The approach outlined in this chapter is essentially *neo*modern because it is about achieving a more tolerable harmony, calling for changes in the direction of being ecologically clever. It accepts, as a moderating imperative, the necessity of being and acting in a style which is sustainable in spirit. It is also about a future which engages 'softer' production, consumption and recycling practices as a matter of political policy. This sustainable and pragmatic style clearly sets out to render day-by-day living more beneficial for everybody, giving rise to cyclically reinforcing community outcomes. It positions communities where they can bind into a steady state culture where all individuals 'enjoy their environmental habitat while also obtaining nourishment from it'.[28] In other words, enabling communities to secure a sustainably conserved and developed habitat which does not exclude any other individual's rights of access to an enjoyable way of living.

Taking the longer view, this is not merely a matter of contemplation, an either-or-if option. The closed-off global ecological system, and the simple laws of entropic disorder, establishes an imperative, which further predicates a 'what to do' question. Moving right to the brink of inevitability for the hapless – those not yet born or the unempowered – seems crudely 'unintelligent' for a consciously generational species. Nature, in and of itself, has no mechanism, except the dilution of pollution and the entropy of resources, for adjusting to the hedonism of communities which maintain a consume now and discard forever folly.

The ten 'soft pathways' outlined in box 3.4 along with the guideline concepts listed in the **Matrix** establish sustainable economic parameters, sustainable ecological thresholds, and some sustainable social criteria. Can these avert the spread of the worst aspects of entropic disorder in a closed-off global system, an extension which produces the less desirable aspects of Californi-anization and Japanization? Avoidance can be achieved by cleaving to enlightened attitudes of national, regional and community self-interest. This involves the application of both regulatory (stick) and incentive (carrot) instruments for enforcing and coercing sustainability. A worst-case scenario can be avoided through a living education system which infuses a steady-state co-dependency (box 3.5). Success in all this, in the phrasing of John Friedmann (1987: 302) involves fashioning linkages:

> One aspect of Californianization is a decay of the traditional family household, with more single-person households being formed than any other category. One aspect of Japanization is the pressure population puts on space, which leads to an engagement of surrogates for sound, vision, smell and taste reality.

1 *functionally* between place of residence and place of work, and from work-place to work-place;
2 *horizontally* from community to community, and from region to region; and
3 *vertically* from community to region, region to nation, and from nation to groups of nations.

And from these fashionings, search out the ecological (conservancy) specifics, and the growth (development) opportunities identified within the **Matrix** and the 'soft pathway' constructs.

The reasoning set out in this chapter has been expressed from a within-nation perspective. The important national dynamic is to work *against* the Easter Island Syndrome, on which there is more commentary in chapter 6, pulling into focus the big issue problems which affect us all. Four prophetic writings shine out.

First is Herman Daly and John Cobb's *For the Common Good* (1989); second, is David Korten's *When Corporations Rule the World* (1995). These are both 'blooded within the system' (IMF, World Bank, Asian Development Bank) publications by practitioners who express some of their former agency's more enlightened policy standpoints, along with their own understanding of the need for wider reforms. Of the two, Korten's polemic cuts to the challenge with greater immediacy. From a partial selection within his passage on 'Doing the Possible' Korten polemic a clear case for the 'banning of arms sales', a 'tax on advertising to finance consumer education', 'international antitrust agreements', 'taxes on resource extraction and international capital movements'. Yet

> Herman Daly and John B. Cobb, *For The Common Good*, 1989. D. C. Korten, *When Corporations Rule the World*, 1995. John Ralston Saul, *The Unconscious Civilisation*, 1997; and also *On Equilibrium*, 2002. Paul Hawken, with A. and H. Lovins, *Natural Capitalism*, 1999.

this is not all, for in another passage entitled 'Agenda For Change', he spells out the fiscal 'regulatory', 'buyout', 'payout' and 'preferential treatment adjustments' needed. Withal Korten is pro-business and pro-market 'favour[ing] local over global businesses and markets ... provid[ing] employment to local people, pay[ing] local taxes to maintain local infrastructure and social services'. Prescient guidance also emanates from the third author, John Ralston Saul, who extols the importance to us all of participatory government, namely that 'The power we refuse ourselves goes somewhere else [and that] . . . If the citizenry agree to exclude themselves from any given area, they are automatically excluding the possibility that in that domain the public good could have any role to play.' It is also Saul's assertion that transaction costs – which includes the costs of criminal activities, crime prevention, and welfare support – is a 'superstructure now far too heavy for the producing sub-structure'. His call is to rail against corporatism and rally for participatory democracy. Finally in this quartet is the work on *Natural Capitalism* by Hawken, Lovin and Lovin (1999) which sets out the policy parameters for energy, food and fibre, mineral, water resource, mobility, construction, waste management and other aspects of sustainable production, consumption and discard.

> Between 1960 and 1990 I had opportunities to work with 'natural economy' communities in Sahelian Africa, Melanesia, Afghanistan at peace, and the upper Amazon and Rio Negro. These were opportunities to observe customary kinship clusters, with admiration for the adherence of my hosts to their environment as the guiding vector in their lives – not on a consciously sustainable basis, but simply as the way of life.

Daly and Cobb, Korten, Saul, and the Hawken, Lovins and Lovins writings arch over my **Matrix**. Savour the connection between their maxims and my assertions for conservancy *with* development.

Is pragmatic *neo*modernity as set down in these pages all that new? Logically considered, I think not, for there exists the precedent of a once better-balanced lifestyle in the Old World, and wondrous living examples of human harmony with nature in a few remaining parts of the low-economy Third World. These are available as working models, showing a previous way and current principle. A more sustainable future within the OECD generally – and the Anglo settler societies specifically – pleads for political and professional horizons to be widened; for the kind of service to communities which commits to providing householder variety and security, positioning every individual to feel certain and assured that their progeny can be socially secure within the habitat they will in turn duly inherit.

4

Growth Pattern Management

The focus with this chapter is larger than local, addressing development problems and growth potentials in a cross-jurisdictional context. It bridges between sustainability ideals and the irrepressible desire for consumer growth, fashioning a synergy between economic activity, ecological conservation, and social wellbeing. It is set out in two sections.

Information Needs and **Conservation with Development Basics** are examined in the first half of the chapter. The latter half addresses **Macro Practice Patterns**: Ownerships Interests and Rights, Urban-Rural Patterning, Coastal Zone Management, Agriculture and Forestry, Tourism Policy and Practice, Unemployment Alleviation, and Waste Management.

Growth pattern management and planning is approached in this chapter mostly as a multiplier process, combining conservancy *with* development. What is remarkable is that in the absence of much in the style of 'regional' growth pattern management in settler societies, particularly the United States read as a whole, there has been so much progressive gain. There are three contextual points to consider:

'Regional planning is different from other varieties of planning in that it is seldom related directly to the exercise of governmental authority, but revolves around the persuasion of many independent groups to act together [within cross-jurisdictional coalitions] to pursue the attainment of regional objectives.'

Frank So, 1986.

- *First* and particularly in relation to the transpacific New World, the landed platform on which development took place was acquired initially by the immigrant settlers at little or no cost: there was literally no initial raw land capital outlay of consequence.
- *Second*: in the bygone days of frontier expansion and resource stripping in the Anglo New World, impressive community and family wealth was made from mining, logging and fishing, and first-flush pastoralism; the one-off 'vent for surplus' model.
- *Third*: respect and historical recognition has to be accorded the pragmatic achievements of day-to-day local government in the settler nations.

After World War II until the 1980s local and regional government agencies were mostly left alone by central administrations to pursue incremental and correctional policies on their own account and in terms of their perceived interests. Up

Bruce Katz: 'The
fundamental premise of
regionalism is that places
have relationships and
connections to other
places that should not
be ignored.' Yet also to
be considered is 'If
regionalism is . . . [such]
a compelling idea and an
inescapable reality why
[has] the United States
almost no examples of
regional or metropolitan
governments?'
                    *Reflections on
                    Regionalism*, 2000.

Regional planning in the
United States received
early impetus from
Lewis Mumford and
Clarence Stein's
founding of the RPAA
(Regional Planning
Association of America)
which largely came
under the thrall of
urbanism. Peter
Calthorpe and William
Fulton's recent (2001)
publication of *The
Regional City*
reinvigorates the US
regional enquiry.
New Zealand and
Canada evolved
provincial regional
planning, with marked
success in Canada:
Gerald Hodge and Ira
Robinson (2001),
*Planning Canadian
Regions*.

until that time it was unlikely for these 'regional' communities of concern to obtain impetus for innovative growth from central government: the central bureaucrats were distant interventionists not always interested in being perceived as all-seeing and all-caring. But this created a frustration from the local grassroots in that there is little that local government unaided could do to initiate greater-than-local development or conservation, especially so when local tax revenues were low and borrowings high, and when plugging problems as they occur in poorer communities can be a full-time job.

Following an emergent pattern of mixed success with growth management practice (*circa* early 1980s) in a few of the United States, other state provincial and federal governments have sought to revitalize their city-centred growth management policies. This chapter identifies this macro-development activity as 'growth pattern management'; the regional component within the 'national-regional-local-household' **Matrix** outlined in the previous chapter. Within that construct the emphasis overall was on the attainment of a 'fair balance' which included economic gains, social betterment and environmental health, *predicated in this chapter on the premiss that if regions are to have conservancy success this must be mounted on a platform of well-balanced economic growth.*[1]

To the extent that growth is valid – and it is, provided within-nation and within-community harmonies and dynamics are maintained – then it is at the regional level of middle organization, where officials and developers are in touch both ways nationally and locally, that growth multiplier mechanisms can be effective, pushed along by that initiator and motivator 'community interest'.

Greater than local, rural-with-urban policy-making and plan formulation are positioned to seize and act upon conservation and development initiatives which cannot be delivered by central or state-level government, and which are beyond the capabilities of local government, most notably in poorly resourced situations. Regional agencies pursue material and social gains (jobs, community projects, and utilities servicing) along with maintenance of the wider multiplier benefits which go with the conservation of resources and the management of development. In short: worthy conservancy outcomes need the cash oxygen which economic growth provides.[2]

Policy markers

This chapter, generally considered, is about beneficially proactive sustainable development *with* conservation for non-metropolitan regions. It mostly addresses 'regional multiplier policy'. This is bounded by relevant 'multiplier' principles.

In the delineating context of these principles it is useful for developers and conservationists to have an understanding of the **Socio-ecological economics** reasoning given in box 4.1; and for these principles to find expression in operational mission statements, state-owned enterprise management plans, and the annual plans of larger corporations. Here, also, are eight policy markers.

1 Maintain a working relationship between territorial resource utilization and the conservation with development purpose.
2 Accept and promote an interpenetration of the production and welfare sectors and a variety of overlapping communities of concern.
3 Integrate and promote networks: the transportation channels and communication linkages.
4 Seek cross-jurisdictional solutions for cross-jurisdictional problems.
5 Reason periphery-to-centre for non-metropolitan regions; lending a rural and resource focus to development and conservation operations.
6 Work in accordance with the clustering concept which achieves production economies from the sharing of infrastructure and services in cognate sectors.
7 Attempt output and growth for a region's prime enterprise sectors at a rate that exceeds the national average; balancing between resource supply, processing positions and markets.
8 Consistent with the previous seven markers, pursue competitive reductions in regional price charges for goods and services as efficiencies cut-in: and be aware that whereas within-region communities often cooperate, regions mostly compete against each other.

In summary: what is recommended is that a growth pattern social contract is engaged which recognizes that all development and conservation efforts are inter-connected, holding to the principle that management methods, accountability attitudes, performance measures, profit-sharing and careers are bound up with sustainable planning practice.

It is salutary to consider how seldom the eight 'markers' or anything like the box 4.1 format are incorporated into growth pattern policy. Regional institutions are dominantly 'correctional' and 'regulatory' in character. The emphasis remains mainly with protectionist (liability avoiding) formalisms. There is not so much a case to be made against protection and procedural instruments, more a case for the embodiment of balanced conservation *with*

Regional is applied mostly to defined units of administration, for which regional development planning practice is of *strategic* importance. *Regions* in terms of practice, include distribution regions, supply regions, functional regions, tourism regions, activity regions, and of course administrative regions, all of which can stand alone and/or overlap.

Because regions are markedly varied, the focus within this chapter is 'growth pattern management' as a lead-in to Urban Growth Management in chapter 5.

Regions in a generic sense can be contemplated as *communities of concern* about which there are four significant characteristics of note: first, these 'communities of concern' can, and do, overlap; *second*, what happens toward the outer edge is usually relatively less important; *third*, administrative delineations tend to prevail; *fourth*, non-metropolitan regions are best contemplated periphery-to-centre.

'Acceptability across the spectrum of interests is the key characteristic of successful growth management policies.'
    Barry Cullingworth,
    Planning in the USA, 1997

Box 4.1   Socio-ecological economics

For indicative purposes relative to the sustainability ideal the overall 'socio-ecological-economic' effects of change in the dynamics of an enterprise or project can be indicated as an alternative to reward-for-failure styles of management. For clarity and simplicity these are presented as four factors for overall Production Gain [PG] namely the accumulated sum [Σ] of: Economy Equity Environment and Efficiency.[a]

Consider the problem of maintaining consistency with the socio-economic-environmental benefit and loss outcomes for a public supply (e.g. electricity utility) by identifying termly (usually annual) rewards and penalties connected to the output of overall Productive Gain. This could be categorized, positively-negatively, for the previously identified: Economy Equity Environment sectors, and in terms of Efficiency.

The rewards to management for 'getting it right' and penalties for 'getting it wrong' hinge upon an interplay.

- The concept of an *Economy* reward-or-penalty around which the level of fiscal profit 'this year' would be assessed relative to the past. By increasing gross income – in all probability the current reward scenario – management would continue to lose or gain bonus points in the time-honoured manner.
- An *Equity* factor would reward continuity-of-supply and evenness-of-price. Every supply hitch and price hike would incur a penalty, inducing constancy toward end-users.
- An *Environmental* penalty factor would be factored in for punishing irregular and/or low levels of delivery,

and for creating adverse socio-environmental situations – sheeted home to the assembly, delivery and retail sectors.
- An *Efficiency* bonus would accrue from improving consumer savings, achieving end-user economies, and for increasing worker output.

These four bonus/penalty entities would 'accumulate' in a mathematical sense – incorporating 'subtractive' penalties for 'getting some of it wrong', along with 'bonus' rewards for 'getting the rest of it right'. In this way, regardless of freak weather patterns, natural calamities and market vagaries, the all-up Production Gain can be expressed by a simple formula:

$$\sum PG = \text{Economy}(f_1 + f_2...), \quad \text{Equity}(f_{12} + f_{13}...),$$
$$\text{Environment}(f_{24} + f_{25}...), \quad \text{Efficiency}(f_{36} + f_{37}...)$$

Complex generation-delivery-retail-consumer-discard systems warrant a reward and penalty auditing arrangement – with the devil in the detail. This cannot be solely industry-regulated, indicating the need for an independent regulatory authority.

[a] Two other 'E' components which could be factored-in are 'engineering' (design), and sequestered 'energy'. For further reading: consult Edwards-Jones and Hussain, *Ecological Economics*, 2000.

Refer also to Kicking the energy habit [box 3.6], Risk Impact Assessment [box 4.5], and Soft pathways [box 3.4].

---

development policy formulations and plan preparations in macro growth pattern contexts. The complication is not always one of 'will' – the intention to establish growth pattern performance and to innovate to that end can usually be identified – the universal difficulty is one of establishing an understanding of and a locking onto multiplier processes which achieve conservation with development in a concomitant way. Attention now moves, with only a smattering of formulae, to an elaboration and expression of these principles.

Multiplier Principles

The objective for growth management in non-metropolitan regions is the attainment of improved regional and hence national wellbeing via the planned pursuit of *multiplier* positive-sum benefits. With the multiplier-within-sustainability

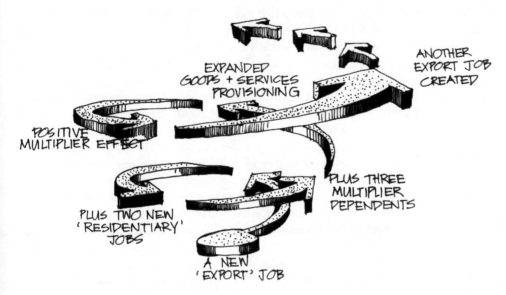

Figure 4.1 Multiplier spiral for development.

notion locked into regional administrations, their populations stand to be beneficially enriched, socially secure, and environmentally protected.

A failing with orthodox growth pattern endeavours is an assumption about economic growth based on extra-regional happenings which are beyond intra-regional influence. At worse this becomes planning by spin-off belief (hunch) where the imagery of a transport 'circulation system' (very little transport in fact 'circulates'), the opportunities for the appointment of an executive officer to operate like a 'captain of industry' (such executives have few opportunities to operate in such a manner), leaves regions pretty much unchanged and unimproved. An additional shortcoming relates to enforcement, which can be identified as a major complication for growth pattern management because, for most rural-urban contexts, and metropolitan tracts, the mandatory power to lock policy onto delivery is either weak or non-existent.

Symbolic imagery (for example sporting achievements) are often employed as a regional metaphor, with macro pattern ambitions depicted cartoon style. Pre-selected 'solutions' without an understanding of the necessary 'planning progression' (figures 2.5 and 2.6 in chapter 2) or an appreciation of the **Multiplier spiral for development** (figure 4.1) are inclined to put those implicated under the delusion of growth perpetually denied. The symbols of failure (goals underachieved, targets unmet, predictions unfulfilled) can leave a region marking time; and such failures, particularly for already poor regions, are bound to undercut confidence and morale and knock on to influence future endeavours adversely. Little wonder that the efforts of regional agencies, because they have so often striven to achieve hunches as though this expediency might result in attainable outcomes, have been unsuccessful.

In a *deterministic* context the outcomes sought are for improved levels of employment, higher levels of income-and-expenditure, more project start-ups, an ever-expanding and improving infrastructure, resource conservancy, heritage preservation and an increase in all manner of value-added flows in and out of a region. In more subtle *associationist* terms the emphasis is upon achieving a socio-economic-environmental triple harmony, calling into being operational procedures which display openness, political honesty, and produce a multiplicity of options.

Noteworthy to the reader interested in procedural theory is the fact that the figure 2.6 'planning' construct (chapter 2) is styled as a *progression*; whereas figure 4.1 is styled as a *spiral*. The two constructs infer an interface between 'planning' and 'development', although that is not the purpose of these distinctly different constructs.

The multiple spiral for development construct highlights the expansionist character of *basic* (export-model) and *residentiary* (consumer-model) economic growth theory. The *base export sector* comprises industries which earn income from 'outside' including those extra-regional tourism and business services where the receipts 'in' exceed the flow of import payments 'out'. The *residentiary sector* is supportive of the base export sector in that it provides services and collateral support for 'within region' expenditure and consumption. Both export base sector and residentiary sector spending is good for a region; yet it is 'base export production' and export-focused jobs which gear up the multiplier effect. This arises because the purchasing monies paid out for 'export' goods and services usually originate outside the region of supply. The economic base multiplier is the mechanism which makes a real difference through the generation of jobs which increase the economic base output overall, and through the addition of export units of product. In effect, when one export job knocks on to generate (say) two residentiary jobs (the economic base multiplier becomes 'two') and the total number of jobs created is three; and at say 4.25 family persons per breadwinner the aggregate number of spending dependents introduced into the regional economy is about 14 persons. The longer-term 'support' and 'induced' economic multiplier benefits of base export activities are of more permanent worth to a region than the initial or 'start-up' effects and returns.

Regional multiplier dynamics can be contemplated as a local engagement of Keynesian principles – to invest, create demand, and consume.

It is appealing to look at multiplier dynamics in terms of jobs. This, however, is seldom fully adequate because problems arise with fiscal accounting for trans-regional communities, and with the calibration of income from seasonal and part-time employment. Within-region value-added dollars are reliable indicators, with few data difficulties to overcome within already efficiently taxed administrations. A complication can occur in that although a 'basic export dollar' may be earned within a region, a proportion of that dollar will usually settle outside the region. Some federal tax policies applied to both 'basic' and 'residentiary' productions are ineffective when income flows out untaxed, failing the region where the earning was generated, although, to be sure, other pension and welfare dollars do flow into a region from outside. It can be seen that both the 'basic' export earning capacity and the 'residentiary' co-employment generated is beholden to 'rest of the world' open-economy trading policies.

Parallel to the 'base and residentiary' model is the categorization of the labour force two ways – there are the 'transformers' who produce the goods and services which society obtains utility from, and the 'transactors' who mediate and manage the producers of goods and services. The unemployed, the criminally engaged, general administrators, and data processors are also transactors; and as a rule of thumb, when transaction salary outlays relative to transformation salary outlays exceeds 1.0 (and also when the number of transaction workers exceeds the number of transformation workers) a sub-economy can be judged to be running inefficiently.

What supercharges the 'economic multiplier dynamic' is reinvestment and respending within a region. This of course relies on trading outcomes which produce profits. Such an outcome is facilitated by a frictionless, openly helpful administration which assists both 'basic' and 'residentiary' expansion, principally by going all out for the multiplier benefits of export job creation. Each growth pattern is unique and presents opportunities to expand 'basic exports' in ways that are specific to its community of concern, even if this is not always so good for the nation. Furthermore every region is a collection of overlapping sub-regions, a multiplicity of services, a host of manufactures, a mixture of government and statutory agencies. It is from the 'export base' – which includes tourism – that regional earning and spending growth dynamics arise, which is why the multiplier benefits of 'export base' employment is the harbinger of effective growth pattern management.

Problems arise when the 'export basis' involves 'finite' resources and a repatriation of profits arising from exploitations of the oil-minerals-gas kind; and even more visibly so with the exploitation of virtually 'non-renewable' living resources (such as indigenous forests and soils) for the short-term asset-stripping and employment opportunities provided. What has to be weighed up are gains over the short term from the extraction of 'resource capital' in the form of minerals, fossil fuels, and milled timber, against the longer-reach incremental gains from living off the 'resource interest' as, for instance, with tourism, selective indigenous forest logging, and production from fertile soils. This weighing-up defines a central principle of conservancy *with* development, living 'sustainably' from the natural 'resource interest'.

The call is for an 'associationist' approach which is mutually self-interested, particularly in relation to collaborative project formulation and design. The enrichment of life – the 'variety' objective – is of course more complex than problem-solving can address. It is bound up with the expansion of access to scenic resources and heritage sites, *and* the introduction of production opportunities, and the enhancement of social services. By these criteria, growth pattern development focuses on contributions to the material worth and variety of life, with 'enrichment of variety' involving a wide array of production and recreational options.

One 'associationist' procedure is to consider policy and design in a collegiate atmosphere on the understanding that the multiple generation of ideas from several people is more productive than an individual effort. Another approach is heuristic reasoning: the movement toward a solution by trial and error (trial and test) which in its ultimate sophistication morphs into the Delphi Technique whereby successive rounds of open discussion, followed by closed voting, moves thinking in a lineal way towards a supposedly optimal option. Gaming simulation, popular in planning education, is a further tool in the 'associationist' locker.

The centrepiece to 'economic multiplier' planning comes down, in practical effect, to 'employment multiplier' outcomes, emergent as the generation of gainful regional income relative to expenditure within a formal income–expenditure construct. Offset against the job losses resulting, for example, from replacing telephone operators with digitized exchanges, are the 'employment multiplier' benefits of employee-intensive activities, especially those achieved at modest rates of plant capitalization per job place created. The longer-term economic multiplier benefits – often of a residentiary kind – are frequently of greater overall worth to a region than the first-flush fiscal gains from once-off resource exploitation.

A problem with contemporary growth pattern management is adherence to the determinism linked into rationally comprehensive planning. Computer technology helps to store, retrieve, select, and compare factually accurate data, but can do little to help the regional growth pattern practitioner to think, reason, form wise judgements and consider wider alternatives. The 'enrichment of variety' approach implicates diverse production and welfare options, along with the enhancement of lifestyle variety, although it is often impractical to quantify. Either consciously or subconsciously, the regional multiplier specialist is ranging his or her mind over alternative options and considerations all the time, working within a conservation *with* development lattice.

In interim summary for this introduction to multiplier principles, growth pattern management can be reduced to a prime essential: promotion of socio-environmentally acceptable growth-based employment along the expansionist *export* lines depicted earlier in the multiplier spiral for development (figure 4.1). A growth pattern planning service, motivated by enlightened self-interest, can deliver 'positive' outcomes – the procedural steps depicted in the figure 2.6 planning sequence (chapter 2) and the figure 4.1 development spiral (this chapter). Moving on: the production of policy plans and projects at the regional level involves rather more, operationally, than is indicated with these two constructs.

Growth Pattern Information Needs

The previous section in this chapter profiled the 'development multiplier spiral' and revisited the 'planning progression', while the passage previous to that delineated the 'policy markers'. These reflect the *qualitative* characteristics of macro growth pattern (regional) planning. The practical part of that endeavour, regional development and conservancy, is *quantitative*.

At the heart of every project endeavour lies a quantification of data and a data analysis work unit, surely? In practical fact this is rare, most instances of non-metropolitan planning output being more like an intermediate level of government advisory service, and a fiscal conduit for central and local government contributions. The fiscal-administrative approach has of necessity, driven by inefficient resource exploitation, created an extractive approach to federal handouts in poor regions, an evasive approach to waste disposal in industrial regions, and an exploitative approach to resource consumption generally.

Growth pattern planning practice at the regional scale is seldom 'all of a piece'; indeed, there are several component parts to macro patterned development and conservancy. Always there exists a number of overlapping 'communities of concern within a region' all supporting the general case for an ever-continuing embellishment of raw data, an ever-refined calibration of the linkage analyses, and an ever-assertive use of rural-urban analyses. Macro-project 'big-hit think-big' projects are mostly *out*; policy prognoses for value-adding 'basic' multiplier processes are *in*; as is environmental conservation and social service provisioning. Consequent to the discreteness of the information clusters and the impermeability of much of the data, there arises a mix-and-share data need. This reflects the inter-penetrating interests of industrial and service establishments which contribute, with varying proportions of embodiment, to 'export' and 'residentiary' production, jobs and earnings.

> I worked with Victor Bartels on several southern Ghana regional plans – 1968 through to 1972 – within that nation's administrative boundaries. These, we found, were overlapped and interlaced with a complexity of river basins, the three-cities 'Golden Triangle', the savannah and rainforest zones, lowland and upland districts, a line-of-rail belt, the cocoa belt, the tsetse fly zone, and three ethnic tribal areas.

This inter-penetration is elaborated by way of a parable in the box 4.2 construct **'Export' and 'residentiary'**, predicated on the basis of an agriculturally styled notional region.[3] There can be no perfect net account, no truly economic or ecological balance, every discrete goal being an augmentation of growth for the subject region, preferably ahead of the national average growth rate as a target, and striving to achieve a competitive imbalance of trade in the subject region's favour. Fiscal growth is not the be-all and end-all of course, for to be 'sustainable' development projects have also to be environmentally balanced and socially uplifting. The important consideration is 'progressive improvement of the overall human condition', and the operational thrust is a mixture of emphases upon material growth retention, habitat equilibrium and social wellbeing.

The most significant information-processing components for macro patterned development planning and conservancy practice include: *data assembly and raw data analysis, linkage and pattern analyses, and rural-urban understanding.*

Data assembly and raw data analysis

Ever-improved raw pattern data and base pattern analyses can be identified as the operational core to getting quantitative programmes and projects up and running.

Raw data assembly compiles information as fixed data about 'stocks' (urban-and-rural, firms-and-farms and so on); and flow information about 'networks' (transportation, telecommunications, media and so on). In another format there is the appeal of the three-tier 'layer cake' developed by the McHarg consortium:

Box 4.2   Export and residentiary considerations relative to an agricultural region

Consider three familiar agricultural products, apples, potatoes and oranges – relative to a subject agricultural region, 'our' region of concern. Assume that the apples are highest grade and an excellent out-of-country export. The potatoes are categorized as high grade by other regions within the nation and from within our region. The oranges grown within our region are of poor quality and not acceptable in any other region.

Every 'apple dollar' earned from sales made beyond the nation is an 'export dollar' earned for the nation; and if it is reinvested in our region of concern it is a 'new dollar' from beyond, now embodied into the regional economy. This 'dollar' largely did not exist previously within our region. The stricture given out here is to maximize apple production for export on account of the value-added gain this brings both to the nation and our region of concern.

Every dollar's worth of potatoes sold on to consumers within the region takes a residentiary dollar out of one local individual's pocketbook and transfers it across to another individual's pocketbook. Even better for our region is the sale of as much of the potato crop to consumers in other regions within the national economy. Above all it is important to avoid importing from another region (or worse, from overseas), for both these actions result in a net-loss transfer payment out of the region.

The regional best-practice stricture is, sell as much local production as possible to the rest-of-nation market, withal making sure that local needs are met. Do not import from abroad. In the absence of a foreign export market for potatoes, view all the other within-nation regions as our offloader market, creating ex-regional income, pulled in across our regional boundary.

Every dollar paid out for imported oranges hurts our region and our nation. Our region's inferior oranges are locally available, and it is known that through plant selection, ripening in storage, and emphatic marketing that local consumers can be coerced into purchasing this product to the exclusion of imported product. This 'import substitution' is in opposition to the tenets of trade liberalization: so we have to 'dress up' orange production as a locally preferred product, when in reality it represents 'import displacement'.

Standing naked with a fine agricultural export product in the world market does not automatically catapult a region into prosperity. In order to prosper, the region described above should produce all the 'apples' it can for export; produce 'potatoes' for itself and the rest of the nation; and produce those low-grade oranges for within-region sale and purchase. In these terms our notional agri-region's horticultural sector will prosper.

Socio-cultural   ⎫   further and further
Biological   ⎬   elaborated and layered
Enviro-physical   ⎭   out into subcategories

This bio-regional approach, attributed originally to Patrick Geddes as the Valley Section, works well for physical analyses (the sieve technique for pragmatic problem-solving) but presents difficulties when the posited task is the development of potential.

The comprehensive approach, vindicated by exponential improvements in computer storage and retrieval, makes it appropriate to catalogue all manner of information of the kinds shown in box 4.3 **Pattern data: a dump listing**. It is important in relation to such a smorgasbord to caution against time-wasting and mechanical data assembly, particularly for project planning where the data needs are specific. In relation to generalized development and conservation it is necessary that data is held in an accessible retrieval system where it can be updated and cross-referenced, rather than being filed away as a paper record. In localities of previous data shortage the planning operative welcomes the elaboration of a data library containing all the information available, including 'weak' and

Box 4.3   Pattern data: a dump listing

Physical data: topography and climate

Drainage systems, ridge systems, slopes, coastal, wetlands: 'spot' features – outcrops, viewpoints, waterfalls: geology, geomorphology, minerals and soils: macro and micro climatic data: physical aberrations and anomalies. Climatic and seasonal weather information: flooding, cyclone, fire and earthquake periodicity.

Spatial data: ownerships, landscapes, land uses

Landownerships and other terrestrial 'interests'. Natural and reversion landscapes according to flora and fauna. Humanized rural landscapes; mining, quarrying and forestry; farming situations, types and sizes; rural access routes.

Urban landscapes according to extent, land-use placements, and locational arrangements.

Nodal data: rural and urban stocks

Open area components: Farms, mineral workings, quarries, dams, dumps, sawmills, processing plants and factories (by volume; stock units, tonnages, cubic measure).

Urban Components: urban rank and hierarchy; CBD componentry and services (by map and list); processing and industrial components (by output); suburban arrangements (by area, numbers, density).

Resource data: free flow, finite, renewable and heritage

Free Flow: the situation and extent of hydro, solar, wind and wave free-flow resources.

Finite (non-replenishable): estimated resources, previous extraction and current rates of extraction for fossil fuel and mineral resources (also long-lived tree species logged from natural forests).

Renewable: soils, flora and fauna condition, rates of erosion and depletion, rates of replenishment and resource sustention.

Heritage: preservation policies and success levels for the natural heritage (forests mountains and coastlines); and for the cultural heritage (sites and buildings).

Ecological data: urban and rural depredations

Urban: patterns of energy and water uptake, goods for processing, imports for consumption; urban waste disposal (sewage, stormwater, solids and atmospheric dispersal); waste disposal from manufacturing and processing plants.

Rural: patterns of herbicide and pesticide applications, nitrogenous and phosphate applications, animal manure toxifications; extent of liquid dumping and solid waste dumping from mining, sawmilling and other rural activities. Rates of ground and stream water abstraction.

Waste Absorption: take-up of urban and out-of-region waste (sewage, storm water, solid waste dumping, air pollution).

Network data: channels and communications

Channels: road, rail, waterway and airfield infrastructure; conduits (water, gas, storm water, sewerage), and by wire (electricity, telephone, cable TV); volumes and patterns of goods, energy, people and wastes moved in and out; journey to work and recreation patterns.

Communications: postal, telephone, email, FAX, cellular phone patterns; radio, TV, advertising, newspaper and community message flows; passenger transport routes and timetables; private vehicle social usage.

Linkage data: historical, economic and social interactions

Economic: exports–imports and value-added, production, product mix, pattern changes; capital-to-output ratios for firms, farms, production and processing plants; utility agencies; savings and investment patterns; credit and financing flows; income levels; plant valuations, commercial floor space charges, house prices and rentals; utilities installation unit costs; backward and forward production linkages. Economic links to other regions and the rest of the world.

Social: disposition of population 'urban' and 'rural' – also by age, income, wealth, cultural identity and gender; health, education attainment, work experience, skills

---

Box 4.3   *Continued*

acquisition; employment and jobless statistics; consumer preferences; population movements into, out of, and within a region; social and kinship services, and welfare facilities; recreational and vacationing patterns. Cultural connections to other regions and elsewhere.

Extrinsic data: government and institutions

Central government: interventions, controls and involvements. Procedures of Government Departments.

Statutory undertakers: roles, rules and activities. Services for health, electricity, water, gas, phone, flood control and emergency support.

Local government: obligations and ambitions. Status of the *ultra vires* and 'general competence' doctrines.

Information and Services: consumer bureau, police fire and ambulance facilities, sporting and recreational clubs, church and cultural organizations,

Accessory government service agencies: (e.g. Land Title Registry, charities, statutory commissions).

Commercial: Range and availability of goods and services.

The local-regional-central government connection. The roles of statutory undertakers and authorities. Local politics of decision-making and chains of command.

'suspect' data, knowing that the initial rough information can always be updated and improved.

There is an adage which holds that 'the worth of any planning prognosis is reflected in the quality of data available as the input for analysis and diagnosis'. But there is a corollary stricture about *relevant* accuracy, whereby the veracity of data is seldom accurately reflected in the eventual outcome. In other words, for the general conservancy or development situation, 100 per cent (even 90 per cent) data accuracy is *not* necessary. This is especially so in contexts where there are several unknowns, where fluctuations in the global and the national economies are likely, where the shifting sands of central government politics apply, and where there are uncertain population growth rates and population movements. Fully accurate sets of factual data are never parlayed into guaranteed or near certain outcomes.[4]

Additional to the usual flat depictions of pattern data, an inputs–outputs array can assemble and order economic information and thereby highlight the tactical significance of industry versus agriculture versus tourism within an overall matrix. While fresh initiatives will not be indicated from such static situational reviews, depictions from an input–output array can yield insights which benefit growth management policy through the identification of 'gaps': say, for example, no cement factory; or a service gap (a lack of a dentist or a weather forecaster?); a need for a locational improvement (fresh food grown closer to consumers?); or the facilitation of a latent industrial linkage (sawmilling and furniture factory sited in proximity to each other?).

For most non-metropolitan regions the activities which are profiled for input–output analysis are likely to include pastoral, horticultural, exotic forestry and fruit-growing activities; some resource extraction activities (indigenous and exotic timber exploitation, water abstraction, fishing, mining); some manufacturing and processing activities (food-processing, service and manufacturing industries); tourism and recreational activities; and several commercial and servicing enterprises (banks, insurance and brokerage agencies). Information about transactions are arranged around two sides of a square (or along the sides of a dog-leg) and are set out in a way which shows for the same material date, the sectors 'making' and the sectors 'receiving', illustrating, in effect, inter-sector connectivity.

The box 4.4 depiction of **input–output patterns** (p. 130) indicates the amount of 'input from' and 'output to' each different category of activity for a notional 'three-sector' agriculture–industry–tourism economy. Arrays of categories, and the iteration of costs leading from primary production through to household sales, can take time to produce, prove expensive to provide, and lead to a 'so what?' situation. Nevertheless a useful feature of an input–output patterning is that it identifies the proportion of a region's income accruing for each stage in the production of goods and services, up until the point of consumption. Such an array can suggest strategic opportunities for bringing an outside process into a region, and for expanding some forms of production. Little other use can be made of an input–output construct for tactical or predictive purposes; but it can be of indicative utility to conservancy practice when this is part of an income-producing tourism activity.

Linkage and pattern analyses

First, a truism: *each* of the six dimensions of any region – administrative, historical, spatial-topographical, temporal, economic, social – is linked to *all*. Relevance is the consideration here: thus from the box 4.3 pattern data listing, the linkage between 'geology' and, for example, 'residential floor space' may be nonsensical, whereas the linkage between 'residential floor space' and 'household energy uptake' is likely to be significant. Pattern analysis frequently commands enormous expenditures of time in the setting-up of information; the preparation of data-coupling comparisons of the 'geology–floorspace' type proving vapid. Yet, with the general availability of computer facilitation, why not store all the data possible (hence the completeness of box 4.3); and why not request the data library to present all manner of binary and multiple comparisons? Access to a host of questions and answers about data relationships can be assembled with computer assistance at fractional expenditure. Data comparisons should of course be always purposeful, policy-directed and plan-led.

James Corner views mapping in a way 'that both reveals and realises hidden potential . . . a productive and liberating instrument, a world enriching agent, especially in the design and planning arts.' James Corner, 'Agency of Mapping', 1999

In practice, regional planners have tended to list 'linkages' within physical data sets only. Thus the emphasis for Rondinelli and Ruddle (1978: headings only) was for:

Economic Linkages
Physical Linkages
Population Movement Linkages
Technological Linkages
Service Delivery Linkages
Political, Administrative and Organizational Linkages

Box 4.4   Input–output patterns

The table represents an agricultural region, with an urban-based agricultural service industry and a fast-growing tourism industry.

OUTPUTS ➤	Agriculture sector column I	Industrial sector column II	Tourism sector column III	Consumer sector column IV	Exports sector column V	
Agriculture level	200	1000	100	200	300	1,800 gross output
Industry level	300	100	150	50	300	900 gross output
Tourism level	50	100	150	50	350	700 gross output
Labour level	500	300	100	100		1,000

- The outputs from the *Agricultural 'level'* aggregate at 1,800 units of value: of which 200 units go back into agriculture itself (to plant nurseries, agricultural research etc.), 1,000 units go into the industrial sector (wool for making carpets, fruit for canning etc), 100 and 200 units are taken up, respectively, for local tourism and sustenance by within-region consumers, while 300 units of local produce is exported out of the region.
- The outputs from the *Industrial 'level'* aggregate as 900 units of value: going mostly to the agricultural sector (300 units for machinery maintenance, plant hire etc.), back into industry itself (100 units for buildings, plant maintenance and upgrading), to tourism infrastructure (150 units for providing accommodation and servicing facilities), direct to the consumer (50 units of locally consumed manufactures), and 300 units of niche machinery products for export.
- The outputs from the emergent *Tourism 'level'* of activity aggregates as a minor 700 units of value; with 50 units going to the agriculture sector (farm-visiting and rural home-staying), 50 units to industry and maintenance, 150 units to the provision of tourism facilities (infrastructure, buildings, training), 50 consumer units for purchases of local agriculture, and a very impressive 350 units (half the total) as 'export' earnings (money spent by out-of-region visitors on accommodation, transportation, fees and handicrafts).
- The *Labour 'level'* aggregates as 1,000 units of value; with 500 units going into the dominant on-the-land

agricultural sector, 300 units going into the agri-supporting industrial sector, 100 units to the emergent tourism sector (tourism services), and 100 units going into the consumer sector.

An important feature with this array is that exports from the historically 'dominant' agricultural level represents less than 19 per cent of gross output from that sector; whereas exports from the more 'clever' industrial level represents 33 per cent of the gross output from that sector (withal from only 10 per cent of the region's labour input); and that export earnings from the 'very clever' tourism level represents 50 per cent of the gross output from that sector, the most offensive blot on this success being the repatriation of some of the tourism earnings offshore.[a]

Assuming constant-scale characteristics for the model (adherence to 'linearity' and 'homogeneity') analysts can set out to ascribe outcomes which produce altered 'input' and 'output' figures: depicting beneficial outcomes from (say) reducing inputs at the agricultural level, and commensurately increasing inputs at the tourism level.

[a] 'Very clever' on two accounts: *first* because of the 'export' orientation of the tourism activity; *second* because of the modest level of capitalization per created workplace (contrasting with the higher level of capitalization involved with the creation of workplaces in agriculture and industry).

Such subsets have the potential to leave the planning practitioner operationally stalled. Of greater relevance, but still frustrating to development and conservancy, are Friedmann's (1966) exhortations for the detection of *intra*-regional linkages, mostly the identification of worthy outcomes for 'distressed' regions within an inter-connected 'core-frontier-distressed' regional set. While the dynamics of *extra*-regional and *within*-region data calls for analysis, it is easier to whistle up the general arguments than to perform the specified *analytical* tasks. In regional planning practice it was ever thus: the problem being to make the likes of ongoing seasonal flow data fit the rest of a calendar year, to render the vagaries of project invoicing amenable to the tax year, and to provide a depiction of all manner of employment and consumer data trends.

Extra-Regional Analysis of trading activity with the rest of the world is clearly focused on *between*-region linkages, the aim being to increase that outward trade by facilitating between-regional production and service activities. Conceptually, such an analysis attempts to render the whole of a 'region of concern' an a-spatial entity. A practical start can be made by setting up a tabulation of data which parallels the annual money worth of flows, both ways, across regional boundaries, supplemented by an assessment of equity and debt, and outflows and inflows of cash and cash-equivalents. This kind of data is generally available for a whole state or province. The quality of the information (gathered for taxation purposes and to serve industrial commercial and consumer groups) forms the basis of national assessments, and in these terms subset depictions are usually available.

The format devised is, of course, specific to each subject region. And provided consistent double-entry eliminating procedures are applied, and equal-valued 'profit' and 'loss' flows are cancelled, it is possible to establish a figure for gross capital production (exports less imports). This, when positive and increasing, is the harbinger of more projects and increased consumer spending.[5]

Within-Region Analysis of linkage and flow information highlights *potentials* for improvement, along with possibilities for *problem* correction. This is particularly the case for production activities where the flow of inputs into a plant, and the onward linkage from such a plant for product finishing, is essential pattern information. This is a 'production' emphasis. In terms of some 'welfare' facilities (regional hospitals for example), flow and linkage constructs have been in use for decades – operational experience which is often overlooked.

Questions to ask about the source and flow of inputs to an industrial production plant are: *first* in relation to raw materials of all kinds, their sources and suppliers, and the delivery costs; *second* to identify those raw materials imported to the region which could be made available locally (even at a cost premium); *third* to identify resources for which environmentally acceptable substitutes can be found where the preference for this is indicated. A major plant, for example, could take up hydro-generated electrical energy 'imported' from another region; or generate power from within-region sources (say, using 'brown coal'), then enter a 'mitigation of adverse effects' set of environmental and economic considerations to determine the net within-region costs and benefits.

Linkage studies set out specifically to assess the time taken, and the fiscal costs and time costs involved, at points (usually towns) for breaking down raw materials, storage for shipment, processing, waste disposal, storage again, onward shipment, and consumer marketing and trading. Fluctuations in consumer demand, raw materials availability, and labour periodicity can be identified.

Friction analysis sets out to identify the key factors inhibiting beneficial economic flows *and* to spotlight opportunities for facilitating greater beneficial interaction between regions. Bendavid-Val (1991: 62) establishes a basis for friction analysis by focusing upon a set of 'leading questions' organized under investigator headings – *what* are the regional exports? *what* are the intermediate imports? and *what* finished essential consumer goods have to be imported from without and are available within a region? A scientific analogy is illustrative for, as with physics, where the attraction of one mass to another varies in inverse proportion to the square of the distance between them, so too with friction analysis does the so-called 'friction factor' increase with the distances travelled and the volumes of exports and imports handled. For non-metropolitan regions it is practical to proceed directly to a study of commodity analysis, and an assessment of production and trading chains and the consumer spending patterns which indicate locational-preference patterns. The somewhat maligned inputs–outputs patterns array – offered previously as box 4.4 – has utility here.

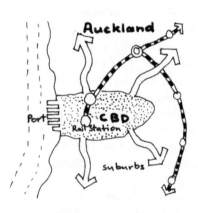

Finally there is the facility of 'Shift and Share Employment Analysis' to consider. The principle factor here being the regional share of employment in industry, agriculture, tourism and the service sectors (relative to the box 4.2 Export and residentiary construct) expressed as regional quotients.

These 'linkage and pattern' considerations search out ways to increase the employment absorptive capacity of a region, to improve the within-region supply of raw materials to all processes, and to facilitate all manner of resource, cash and commodity flows. Attention is now shifted to linkages viewed as part of the *within*-region (rural-with-urban) context.[6]

Rural-urban understandings

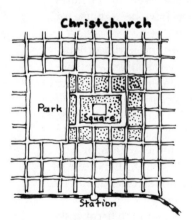

Port city and plains city

For rural-urban regions the historical emphasis has been centre-to-periphery for both orthodox 'port' and 'plains' cities. A converse suggestion in relation to the non-metropolitan contexts is to appraise such regions from periphery-to-centre: from the 'space-draining' productions of farming, forestry, mining, recreational and tourism, through to the 'space-organizing' activities conducted in the main centres and small towns.[7] In this way the normative central-place urban-hierarchy and size-and-rank analyses, although informative in a 'raw data' context, are viewed as questionable. One issue is to detect component shortfalls for either correction or substitution on an 'ought to be' basis, and to assess the componentry and trading potential on a 'new horizons' understanding. The overall objective is to enlarge upon economic strengths, enhance the quality of habitat, and attain improved overall social wellbeing.

Consider *service centre* studies. Normative topology assessments for attracting new businesses are obviously indicative and useful. The usual procedure is to look at the rank–size composition of businesses and services for the size of town under consideration, and then identify the gaps which ought to be filled. Such a scan makes comparative assessments relative to other settlements of similar function and size, and assessments of professional and commercial services, industry and agriculture support services, marketing services, transportation services, and welfare schooling and entertainment facilities.[8] For any given 'community of regional concern' this information can be entered onto a functional display (along the top) and a town sized display (down the side) *scalogram*. Smaller towns would, understandably, have fewer functions than a regional centre, with the scalogram highlighting anomalies, vacancies and situations of over-supply.

An elaboration of this form of array is often called for in the style of a *service centre services* analysis. This involves: *first*, assessment of the points of origin and termination of goods and services, including the volume-flows, transportation routes and communication-networks used; *second*, a determination of the fiscal accruals and community flows through each service centre; and, *third*, analysis of inhibiting frictions like comparative shortfalls in relation to like-sized centres, and the factors inhibiting transaction linkages and communication flows.

Turning to *access studies*, here appraisal involves 'gravity' considerations, accessibility being a function of settlement sizes and their distances apart. Of itself this information is of little more than situational utility. The 'basic' concern (as an *export* consideration) is the extent to which the distance-cost and time-cost of access inhibits rural-to-urban and urban-to-urban processing prior to regional export. In the local context, conducting surveys of users on typical occasions (usually weekdays) about the purchase of their goods and services (at the moment of departure from the source of service) makes it possible to 'pattern' the acquisition of those services and commodities, which enable analysts to form a view about consumer purchasing preferences and the extent to which access time and access cost are attracting and repelling factors within a region of concern. This is useful information for assessing the likely potential for extra trading activities, and provides vital information for enhancing within-region trading activities.

Growth Management Basics

Project propagation (generation)

The point and purpose of sustainable development and sustenable conservancy, and project initiation, is much more than change for its own sake. The point and purpose is a three-way improvement in the material wellbeing, the quality of the habitat, and the perceived sense of social security, with much of the emphasis on economic growth. It is possible that some kinds of project will lead to an overall decline in material wellbeing (for example the economically regressive features of some *un*employment, social investment and 'trading enterprise' schemes); and/or degradation of the habitat (for example, resource degradation or depletion); and, or also, social discord (for example, schemes that make presumptive decisions about who should be enskilled and who should not, and what they should be enskilled about).

One pragmatic emphasis for project generation is to extract positive support from government and local government sources. It is by means of promotional outreach and direct project propagation that growth needs are addressed, and direct actions and projects for growth are pursued and managed. This is a competitive, inwardly focused, within-region, process.

A question arises about the reasons for exploring the possibilities for development – and to a lesser extent conservancy – via project generation. Simply put, projects do not propagate themselves, nor are they necessarily positive. Generating a development and conservancy project inventory through the use of an 'ideas nudge list' is one way to start. This links on to suggest the utility of 'brainstorming' with all ideas received and considered openly in an atmosphere of mutual trust. The participants would include regional development and conservancy specialists, *and* educators, administrators, and executives in industry and commerce, involving a greater variety of specialists than the orthodox planner-economist-lawyer trio. Teamwork is clearly the combination-key to success, and the role of leadership is hugely significant within any team, described, at its most aggressive, as 'hard business networking'. Specialists are either directly engaged or consulted, and can include urbanists, statisticians and analysts, administrators, engineering architectural surveying and landscaping professionals, agronomists, pastoralists, silviculturists, hydrologists and other resource specialists, social workers and political analysts, education and health service advisers, geographer specialists, and civil-defence safety and security advisers. The difficult task for leaders of growth management teams is to keep focused on the 'multipliers' which will improve their region's *export* returns, while adding *residentiary* jobs to the production–consumption multiplier spiral (figure 4.1). The initial brainstorming search is for intervention opportunities, there being no established rubric; no concept is treated as absurd.

Economic development and resource conservancy agencies, and the project promotions they engage in, are a potent medium for political grandstanding. Nevertheless a political profile has to be identified as a component part of most economic development and resource conservancy projects. Indeed Levy's dictum (1990: Ch. 8) that 'selling is the single most important activity of most development (and conservationist) planners' suggests a reliance on political champions to identify with both economic development and resource conservancy case by case.

An operational dilemma which arises is how the planning practitioner engages and encourages political involvement. This comes into profile because most generative change, even in the private sector, needs political support to get going, which may be difficult to retract if the sooner-than-later indications are that a project should be abandoned. Shackling political support to a project at an initial stage, which later fails project evaluation, usually means a defeat for logic and reason when a fired-up political 'champion' is committed to holding fast to 'their' project. Much criticism is offered on the inanity of regional political input, but it has also to be taken into account that political representatives have not always been well served by their advisers. Of course technocrats declaim that politicians always 'go their own way' regardless of what they are advised. This quarter-truth serves to highlight an imperative, in the spirit of ethical integrity: namely, that the planning adviser must give a full range of advice to political mentors *and indicate and register their own technical preference*.

The regional planner-analyst who joins the political fray with his or her own personal assumptions 'predetermined' ends up in an ethical quagmire; whereas the regional analyst prepared to put up all the options and accept a setback when an indicated and recommended optimum is passed over, is always in the clear, ready to fight another cause on another day. Political involvement at the 'initial evaluation' stage is unavoidable: the planner's challenge being to provide politicians with sound advice.

Identifying economic development and resource conservancy project propagation as adviser-led and politics-driven is a useful operational starter. Indeed at the forefront of every regional agency there needs to be an effective political champion for every cause. This advocacy is best viewed as an adjunct to the regional interest, a driving part of the 'means' rather than a functional part of the 'outcome'. Another notion to scotch is that economic upsurge, in and of itself, is the main underlying reason for development, the *prime motive* being the generation of permanent 'jobs' – conversely understood as the alleviation of under-employment and unemployment. Holding out for job-creation consequential to growth, links with the observation that job seekers are frequently less than mobile, whereas many jobs are now highly mobile.

The emphases to flag are: *first*, that the lead focus to economic development and resource conservancy projects is the creation of new and additional employment opportunities; *second*, that a lower rate of capitalization per workplace has the potential to create more jobs – most perceptibly within conservancy, but also with the likes of tourism development. From this couplet there can be identified a tacit understanding that the bottom line determining factors are developer 'profit' and conservancy 'gain' generating more jobs, manifesting as a lowering rate of *un*employment.

Additional to low-capitalization job creation, satisfactory-to-the-community responses are required when the following four questions are put:

- Will the project be a net longer-haul contributor, or burden, to the national, local, and regional economies?
- Is there a valid expectation of social improvement to individual and community wellbeing, with betterment to the natural environment and the human habitat?[9]

- Is there potential for a useful synergy, or at least a complementarity, with other within-region activities?
- Can it be established that the project will *not* act to mutually deny any other gainful project?

New jobs and new projects (particularly export jobs and basic projects) are bound to have a number of economically beneficial, but also some socially adverse, impact.

Principal among the *beneficial* effects is an alignment of development and conservancy effort toward the marginalized, as with more work opportunities for women. Another job-related benefit may lie with the ironing-out of seasonal fluctuations. And beyond jobs, pure and simple, is the local benefit of increased property tax returns for municipal coffers. Indeed economic development in prosperous localities, already exhibiting low rates of unemployment, may be undertaken for this primary purpose alone. Another beneficial effect, and often the initial motivating factor, is the knock-on demand for more services, more residential property, and more consumption – all in addition to the creation of more jobs.

On the *adverse* downside, the listing is more disquieting than might at first be supposed. This could profile early as a squeeze on the local housing market, which proves tough on starter buyers, particularly local starter buyers. What also happens is that the inflow of incomers can adversely affect the proportion of local appointees to jobs, which, of itself, does not reflect the additional socially related costs of adjusting incomers into the local scene. There are also practical difficulties of cost recovery arising from the extension of utilities (water, power, waste disposal), and services (schools, clinics, public transport), to meet the expanding needs of incoming project participants. Additionally there are also the environmental degradation and resource depletion 'deferred clean-up costs' of many new production projects.

All the foregoing beneficial and adverse items need to be put into wide-horizon consideration, as factors for a recipient community to consider and accommodate. This process is addressed later as the Risk Impact Assessment problematic. Also, with new projects, it is necessary to assess and confront the competitive adverse effects of newcomer projects on already established commercial and industrial enterprises.

What, then, comprises the base set of operational guidelines for promoting growth?

- A first *normative set of* **Buttress Guidelines** centres around the notion of enriching existing processes, which includes enhancement of established activities, and the plugging of leaks within industry and business. This approach is examined first because an important lesson from experience is that it is much more likely that employment can be generated, that environmental values can be upheld, and a greater sense of social success can be created, through the expansion of enterprises already in place, rather than as a consequence of turn-key projects. An appropriate way to proceed is to seek out the processing and fiscal add-ons (value-added processing, along with an appraisal of tax incentives, local protections, inward investments) which are currently extra-regional, and attract them into a region's extant businesses.[10] The 'plugging leaks' angle also implies pulling processing and marketing activities back over a regional boundary as a form of import substitution. Adapting a phrasing attributed to the Rocky Mountains Institute, it is all a matter of avoiding the notion of 'your region being described as the bucket that

> A rule-of-thumb reckoning is that a workplace created in the tourism sector (for example) requires a capital outlay equivalent to 15 per cent of the capital outlay required to create a manufacturing sector job.

leaks'. Securing government contracts *within the region*, quashing pointless within-region rivalry, accepting value-adding challenges, providing locally available counter-attractions to extra-regional centres, and promoting within-region alternatives to 'out of the region vacationing' – these and other forms of 'buttressing' can be enhanced through enrichment, enhancement and efficiency actions.

- A second *progressive set of* **Betterment Guidelines** centres around the idea of investing and upgrading a region's infrastructure, image and services. In pragmatic terms this suggests improvements to road, rail and other transportation infrastructure, along with going to the next technical level with the postal, telephone, cellular phone, radio, television, newspaper and other communications channels. The 'frontier' style of region also benefits enormously from the provision of attractive if small shopping centres, the retention of postal, welfare, medical and governmental service agencies, the establishment of an enskilling and reskilling training centre, and the presence of some quality entertainment venues and eating-out establishments. Other possibilities, applied with varying degrees of success, include the provision of low-rent flatted factories, cost-reduced sites, utility hook-ups at reduced and preferential supply rates, and sites and services assistance, along with the more controversial possibility of start-up grants, tax-holidays and land tax rebates. No less pragmatic (and certainly less costly) is the facilitation of regional 'image' and 'ethos' through skilful conservation efforts, along with a preservation of the natural heritage and a profiling of the cultural heritage.

- A third *innovative set of* **Discovery Guidelines** sets out to attract new enterprises and external venture capital. A priority here is to work in parallel or on a joint-venture basis, to attract new business (including government-based enterprises) into a region, and also to expand private sector business. This is easiest to initiate at the level of niche tourism (the 'alternative' experience), difficult when attempting to attract specialist processing of within-region resources ('French' champagne produced from New World vineyards!), despairingly frustrating when the emphasis is on a major new enterprise expected to provide its own venture capital (such as a science park or a car assembly factory).

Within the three guidelines – Buttress, Betterment and Discovery – there is little point in exporting non-renewable resources or giving tax-breaks if there is only a modest internal rate of return and no eclipsing gain. This is especially the case when a project leaves an adverse legacy for the next generation to take on in the form of an environmental mess, or the kind of social upheaval which follows a completed hydro-dam construction or an abandoned mineral working.

The point of project generation, at the ideas stage, is the propagation of projects. At this level of endeavour there is probably more hunch than analysis, and more conjecture than science involved. Action follows, with the imputation at this stage of science logic taking over from human inspiration. In terms of that science logic, economic development projects and conservancy practice connects with the SWOT Progression (**S**trengths and **O**pportunities to seek out – **W**eaknesses and **T**hreats to adjust away from); *and* the 'Planning Sequence' (survey-analysis-prognosis-plan). Mistakes will be made and allowed for; but adherence to such 'progressions' and 'sequences' will reduce errors, and give rise to extra options. Community 'lessons from experience' should hold sway over 'formulaic presumptions' – particularly for smaller communities of concern.

Although there may be lashings of investment capital circling the globe looking for tax havens, investment holidays, low wage rates and relaxed labour laws, these are factors about the economic-climate over which development agencies cannot call the shots, any more than they can alter the weather pattern. In practical fact there are very few trustworthy footloose firms looking to make a start with a greenfield site in an unfamiliar region. This predicates caution. Agencies always flaunt any success they may have in attracting this or that big-name overseas company – but at what economic price, at what social cost, and in terms of what environmental reckoning? A factory will simply alight where land taxes, wage rates and union controls are favourable to them and the market they serve. A regional development or conservancy agency organizationally deludes itself if it believes, especially under GATT–WTO, that such firms will stay put when another, better to the firm, opportunity arises. Worse than the horror of such a firm not 'showing up' in the first place is the likelihood of their up-camp and departure once established at no notice, leaving in their wake social and economic discard and environmental hazards to clean up.

Of course when fiscal help comes from central or state government, then a subject region for whom this could be perceived as a windfall would be expected to take the helping hand – the only important operational criteria being avoidance of incentive packages which leave a residual legacy of social discord and environmental costs for the host community. To incoming investor enterprises, local incentive packages are actually a minor part of the overall deal. What is usually of much greater importance to them is practical help, such as cutting down on the lead time with 'permitting procedures', facilitating 'first people' protocols, introducing supply partners, opening market doors and providing procedural advice. A further point to note is that while overseas *marketing* is of 'basic' economic significance, attracting out-of-region or offshore *investment* often proves very daunting.

There is a need, even within small three-person planning agencies, for an openly accessed well updated data base. Such an information system should avoid over-embellishment and over-elaboration. On one plane there is the worth of being able to log into a pattern data library (box 4.3). More pragmatic is the creation of computer loaded spreadsheets keyed into prospective development sites, supplied from and tying back to all sectors. Levy (1990) puts much emphasis on the updating, new entry and editing of information, playing down the time-consuming and difficult-to-interpret graphics and fine-data tabulations, suggesting a 40-item maximum set of listings – but in most instances a lesser 20-item listing will prove adequate.

It behoves the would-be project-propagating agency to come to an understanding about the kind of economic development and resource conservancy projects local communities 'want' and 'need', and what planning information advises about the vindication of those 'wants' and those 'needs'. Is there a prevailing air of enlightened self-interest? Is there a 'co-active' spirit? Is there a 'reactive' willingness? Do sites exist or can they be produced? Is there a commitment to meet the demand for the utilities needs of new and expanding enterprises? Are the risk assessment and permitting processes facilitative? These are all important factors because in the GATT and WTO context it is the openly explicit and permissively helpful regional agency which is attractive to new business.

Levy also lends emphasis to what he depicts as the 'sales operations' and 'outreach activities' which both humanizes and politicizes the development process. It is his view that 'someone who is a great economist but a poor salesman is not likely to make a good (within-agency) economic developer' . . . (linking with a consequent observation that) 'the community is a product the development agency sells'. This is all part of a 'hard business networked' environment, to which spreadsheets, data libraries and procedural understandings are essential.

It is only possible to achieve success through the propagation of development projects if that operational procedure is bound into an effective agency. This aligns with the way outreach operators are induced to articulate value-adding channels for firms to expand or set up new branches, for bringing potential joint-venture partners together, for convincing a developer that sites will be found and utilities will be hooked up. The 'human face' of a development organization, a welcoming 'nothing is a problem' working culture, and its facilitation with language and protocol complexities, are the heart of successful agencies. Beware, in all this, of 'promising' what an agency may not be able to deliver, particularly with regard to sites that do not exist or cannot be produced quickly, cash grants which cannot be delivered, and utility hook-ups which are improbable. An ounce of person-to-person facilitation is worth a pound of paper projections, which returns to an acknowledgement of the significant accessory role of political figures, agency personnel, and public relations.

Risk assessment and risk management

Risk assessment and its corollary risk management are 'creatures of government' (Gilpin 1995) concerned to mediate the mainly adverse outcomes (externalities)

RISK ASSESSMENT
POSSIBILITIES
Cost Benefit Analysis
(CBA)
Environmental Impact
Assessment (EIA)
Social Impact
Appraisal (SIA)
Technological Impact
Assessment (TIA)
Strategic Risk
Assessment (SRA)
Total Economic
Evaluation (TEE)

of development and conservancy endeavours. These adverse outcomes can arise within one or a combination of three contexts: those affecting the project proponents, and/or the project recipients, and, or also, the project adjudicators. They can be understood as the 'costs' resulting from those project 'effects' which are not intended initially to be carried by a project's progenitor or a project's decision-granter (permitter). Risk assessment relates, historically, to the adverse outcomes associated with resource degradations and impairments to the environment, now extended to include trans-scientific determinations of economic risk and prognostications of social shortcomings. These risks arise from ethnic and equity imbalance, ecological damage, adverse economic outcomes, pollution hazards, and social impacts, reverse-imaging Elkington's 'triple bottom line' (1999).

The pragmatic bounds of risk assessment and risk management are both anthropocentric and ecocentric, *and* contingent upon ever-changing and emergent technology, *and now* delineated by the sustainability ideal, developer intent, and community ambition. A key generic consideration derives from the better-safe-than-sorry 'precautionary principle' which flags identification of potential harm and or also scientific uncertainty, and identifies the means to avoid that harm or uncertainty. In effect it is an application of the Pareto Rule: predicating that any project must ensure – by outcome or by means of compensation – that nobody is left worse off consequent to the project, at any foreseeable future time, and or also supposedly at any other place. In terms of risk management the application of this 'rule' requires that a project should only be approved if it is certain that the profit takers and the project adjudicators could if necessary compensate any socio-environmental loser or losers. Exporting a toxin waste manufacture, or situating a risk activity offshore – improving the health and reducing the risk 'at home' – violates the Pareto stricture.[11]

Because of these complexities the process of risk assessment is prone to be facile, a 'going through the motions' parody of fair procedural adjudication. There are always regulatory shortfalls (so far, but no further) and a tendency to grapple only with hard-facts physical outcomes – leaving the soft-facts social and aesthetic issues to be handled in some accommodating way. That matter of 'so far, but no further' suggests that a foreshortened horizon blinkers most risk-assessment procedures. This happens in ways which overlook the cumulative life-cycle consequences of project outcomes, particularly for those not yet born.

The risk assessment of fiscal benefits and disbenefits, environmental safeguards and enhancements, and social gains and losses, varies for the wider 'national' and the narrower 'local' and 'on-site' situations. In summary, risk assessment varies according to scale (national-regional-local-site) and according to participatory roles (provider–recipient–adjudicator). Concerning *proposals*, risk impact assessment will usually serve adequately to form a decision, or help decide on a preferable alternative. Relative to *procedures*, the 'precautionary principle' has utility. The introduction of DDT, CFCs, fluoridation and genetic modifications are instances where application of the precautionary principle – quarantine until a product or process is proved benign or acceptable – are justified. Yet there is a perverse 'risk' in that by fully observing the precautionary principle, innovation can be poleaxed.

Risk analysts and assessors must of course be wide-eyed and open-minded about 'which community of concern', and thus 'what constituency' they are evaluating and implementing for. Communities of concern vary as much as an individual, a landowner group, a for-profit agency, a river catchment population, a town and its hinterland, or a tourist attraction: all in addition to the formal local government and statutory delineations. Analysts and managers must be clear and frank about the tolerable thresholds of broadly acceptable social and environmental loss. This tolerance has to be balanced against the economic and social gains as viewed from the perspective of a project's progenitors (sometimes as donors) *and* the wider panoply of community recipients. A further complication is a tendency for risk and uncertainty assessment procedures to work tacitly to the assumption, before any decisions are made, that environmental degradation and pollution costs are *less* significant in poor neighbourhoods, poor regions and poor nations, a matter explored seriously for the US context by Robert Collin and Robin Morriss Collin in their 'Sustainability and Social Justice' (2001). An 'after the event' and an 'only if necessary' prolongation underscores evasiveness for at-risk situations in poor communities. It is clear that the tacitly decreed boundaries of 'tolerable risk' situates individuals differently to reject or accept what would be an 'unreasonable risk' situation. In short, unreasonable risk needs to be fixed for consistency by technical dicta, and not be allowed to stray into uncertainty or expediency.

The initial evaluation of risk needs to be conducted by an assessing authority in an all-accepting and defining-of-issues brainstorming style, intent on sifting 'project wheat' from 'project chaff' – hard facts from soft opinions. This *scoping* is in line with the predication that a preliminary review of the uncertainty involved leads to a more assured assessment of eventual and actual risk. From base information about a project, reflected against data received from the community of impact and concern, an assumption about probable effects can be formed: *first*, relative to the scale of the project plant and infrastructure and the utilities needed to service the proposal; and, *second*, relative to the short- and long-term acceptable and unwelcome effects. These are bottom line enquiries, applicable to any style of project. They are the kinds of initial evaluation of effects (adverse, acceptable, welcome) which would normally and rationally be 'scoped' in the first instance through an 'initial strategic risk evaluation'.

It is an indication of analytical poverty when an 'initial strategic risk evaluation' is not undertaken. An explanation for this can be that at the initial evaluation stage there are too many unknowns, uncertainties and externalities. Rather than come down clearly 'for' or 'against' a proposal, advisory personnel usually feel obliged to recommend that matters be put 'on hold'

The boundaries between NIMBY (Not In My Back Yard) positions according to economic standing, is of less significance than Not In Anybody's Back Yard community criteria.

while further enquires are made and more data obtained. Unfortunately this pro-crastination and uncertainty spurs the advocates for a proposal to take up posi-tions of conviction in favour of a project at the hunch stage – unconfused by too many facts!

A foundation reading is the Scott, MacArthur, Newbery treatise *Project Appraisal in Practice* (1976), which connected with an earlier OECD manual prepared by Little and Mirrless (*Industrial Project Analysis for Developing Countries*), 1968.

A next-level dilemma raises the spectre of an often phoney 'sci-entism' emanating from impact methodologies. Kelman's (1981) criticism, embracing cost-benefit analyses, establishes the main point of concern, that the 'conceptual framework is highly con-troversial in the discipline from which it arose – moral philoso-phy (and, to my way of thinking, economics!)'. The planning practitioner has a custodial responsibility to guard against giving pseudo-professional support for a procedure which aligns with questionable outcomes; like *more* pollution for the poor and inarticulate, and *less* pollution for the wealthy and well advised.

Expressed more forcibly, risk assessments are frequently biased, project defensive, and ethically questionable (refer also to the chapter 1, box 1.4: Ethical canon). A moral difficulty arises in project situations where an adviser *knows* intuitively in his or her own mind that the outcome of the burdens-to-benefits distribution pattern is adverse; for example, that a project owner's benefit will be outweighed by the longer-term community costs of clean-up and environmental restoration.[12]

A clear-to-proceed 'initial evaluation' leads to 'core analysis'. An important side consideration at this stage is the extent to which a project is 'export' or 'res-identiary' in character, because export projects (for example tourism in an ecologically fragile environment) may shift the level of risk tolerance from 'unac-ceptable' to 'tolerable' in the competitive context of trade and balance of pay-ments. This can be put into perspective depending on responses to questions of these kinds.

A What is the nature, form, function and purpose of the proposal? This calls into need all manner of information about capital and infrastructure, 'point source' and 'non-point source' pollution, physical resource demands, waste disposal arrangements, skilled and unskilled labour requirements, and a listing of preference-ranked options (for example: alternative sites, restoration plans, mitigation proposals).

B What are the potential outcomes from a preliminary impact assessment, some-times described as an Initial Evaluation? This assembles the likely adverse eco-nomic, social and environmental outcomes, together with preference-ranked indicators for handling adverse effects. There is no logic in pile-driving a core analysis which is counter-indicated by an unsupportive initial evaluation.

C Separate from, but accessory to core analysis, are project feasibility appraisals which look at technological feasibility (particularly for waste disposal, resource provisioning, and energy supply); skilled and non-skilled labour availability (engaging an employment assessment checklist); administrative co-support; public and political endorsement; and last but not least, long-term viability. A corollary involves getting an answer to the question 'Is there another, better, way or option?'

D Looking further out – possibly beyond – a project, there is a need for a data set which ensures that development agencies have information about likely adverse longer-term, intra-regional and national, and economic social political environmental outcomes.

A number of parallel formats can be identified in alignment to Strategic Risk Assessment core procedures – including Environmental Impact Assessment (EIA), Social Impact Appraisal (SIA), Technical Impact Assessment (TIA), and Impact Abatement Assessment (IAA). Aggregated, these combine as Total Economic Valuation (TEV). Some key questions for all manner of project proposals are:

- How are the risks apportioned?
- Are the risks at an acceptable scale?
- What are the objectors really saying?
- What are the longer-term 'legacy' effects?
- What are the project alternatives?
- Should a project be undertaken 'now', 'later' or 'not at all'?

From Otway and Fishbean, 1976. 'Risk research(s) . . . hidden agenda is the legitimacy of decision-making institutions and the equitable distribution of hazards and benefits.'

The construction given as box 4.5 sets out a skeletal format for the above, presented in the style of a **Risk Impact Assessment** (RIA) procedure. This includes notes relating to the 'Decision nodes' (in plain text) and the 'Processes' which take place between nodes (noted in italics). RIA sets out to facilitate, manage, and secure *development*, to serve *conservation*, and to support *growth* within a balanced combination of economic-social-environmental parameters and controls. An important accessory feature about the box 4.5 construct for an RIA is that it empowers both a 'call-in' of projects and a 'call-up' of input from local government, central government agencies, statutory undertakers (such as state-owned enterprises and research institutes) and other groups and individuals.

From this it is clear that additional to being 'environmental', risk assessment is concerned for social impact, which also implicates the economic gain-and-cost pattern. Keeping in mind a simple truism – that commercial development projects are beholden to shareholder profits – risk management practioners and adjudicators need to be diligent about adverse social injustice effects. The wrongdoer must clean up or pay – the 'polluter pays principle' – which may place some or all of the cost of environmental clean-up onto the consumer – doing so in accordance with the rationale that every citizen warrants equal protection from waste discard and environmental pollution.

In most instances the perspective of project generators should be counter-reflected by a mirror appraisal which reflects from and represents those being impacted upon. In essence, all parties to a project need, separately, to be aware of the risks and uncertainties and be equipped to respond to them in systematic, explicit, consistent and trustworthy ways which are co-reliant upon accurate data. This attendance upon an all-parties level of awareness about risks and uncertainties establishes, on the one hand, better-informed donors and recipients, while also imposing, on the other hand, *compliance requirements*. To the clearly up-front costs associated with the delivery of Risk Impact Assessment compliance, must

Box 4.5 Risk Impact Assessment (RIA): an agency perspective

◯ ADMINISTRATIVE NODES

[1] INITIAL EVALUATION
INVOLVES A PANEL APPRAISAL OF A
PROJECT: ARISING FROM GOVERNMENT,
WITHIN LOCAL GOVERNMENT; AND
WITH POSSIBLE PARTICIPATION BY
OTHER STATUTORY AUTHORITIES
AND NGOs.

[2] Facilitating.
Planner-friendly, user-relevant, helpful at identifying
interests and capable of encouraging projects and
proposals.

[3] CALL-IN OPTIONS
THE FACILITY AVAILABLE TO AN APPRAISAL
PANEL TO APPLY AN RIA TO ANY PROJECT.

[4] ACTIVATE PANEL
THE CORE PANEL WOULD COMPRISE
SPECIALIST ADVISERS AND CO-OPTED
EXTERNAL SPECIALISTS AS REQUIRED.

[5] Scoping.
Effective scoping involves an early identification of the
potentially intractable, the modifiable and the tractable
consequences arising from a project, as indicators for
base-line studies.

[6] BASELINE STUDY REQUIREMENTS
ECONOMIC SOCIAL AND
ENVIRONMENTAL IMPACT
INFORMATION WILL BE USUALLY
REQUIRED OF A PROJECT PROPOSER.

[7] Base-Line Study. Responding to base-line study
requirements is a project sponsor's responsibility.
Clearly inadequate, misleading, insufficiently scientific or
unconvincing base-line studies of little utility to the
panel, can be referred back for re-expression.

[8] RECEIPT OF BASE-LINE STUDIES

[9=] Public Notification and
Call for Responses

[9=] DISPERSE INFORMATION
OUT TO STATUTORY
UNDERTAKERS, NGOs AND
GOVERNMENT DEPARTMENTS

[11] Quantify Impacts and Compare Options.
The 'nub' of the procedure. Here the magnitude, extent
and time-scale of a proposal will be judged against
carrying capacities and likely outcomes. The positive
as well as negative considerations arise from
construction impacts, energy impacts, waste-disposal
impacts, economic impacts, socio-political impacts and
employment impacts. At this stage particular safeguards
against non-reversible and cumulative impact must
be detected for mitigation or prohibition.

[10] COLLECTION OF INITIAL RESPONSES

[12] COLLATION

[13] Write Working Documents.
Mitigating and monitoring measures are drawn up.
Prohibitions, design criteria, compatibility
requirements, minority safeguards, non-compliance
sanctions, insurance protocols, and disclaimers to
be prepared in clear legal language.

[14] RESOLUTION
ENTERING INTO DISPUTE
NEGOTIATION; PREFERABLY
MEDIATION RATHER THAN
ARBITRATION.

AGREEMENT ACCORD GOES BACK OUT
TO ALL RESPONDENTS; THEN TO LINE
AGENCIES FOR ADMINISTRATION.

be also added the *conformity costs*, those add-on costs of meeting the previously disregarded environmental and social provisions now considered to be part and parcel of socially acceptable sustainable development projects and conservation practice.

Considering that the broad aim of risk assessment is management of direct impacts and adverse effects for abatement, mitigation and possibly project denial, it necessarily involves the collation of a wide spectrum of economic, environmental and socio-political information. This subject is treated admirably in Neil Orloff's (1988) *Environmental Impact Process*, and is a matter continually under re-evaluation and up for re-expression at the Resources for the Future risk management centre (www.rff.org).

KINDS OF RISK
Insurance
Entrepreneurial
Construction
Technical
Environmental
Sociopolitical
Situation [Cultural-Racial]
Gender and Age
Actual and Perceived
Acceptable
Tolerable
Necessary

Breaking the Impasse,
Susskind and Cruikshank,
1987

The RIA process should be both purposeful and facilitative, with no dispiriting time lags. The assessment panel is expected, on the one hand, to be firm and consistent about the style and content of the base-line studies they require; yet on the other hand to be sponsor-friendly and generative in attitude. This matter of attitude is an important part of 'seed bed support', particularly in regard to being facilitative to project initiatives. Most Panels become stalled at Decision Node 12 'Collation' (the mitigating and monitoring measures), and Decision Node 14 'Resolution' (involving dispute negotiation and securing acceptable alternatives). Relative to the resolution-resolving process there is available the American-derived account by McCreary and Gamman (1990) 'Finding Solutions to Disputes'.[13] Impact abatement often comes down to 'who' can lay 'how much' abatement and enforcement on the line, which returns to the need to identify a regulated, in other words locked-on, set of socially acceptable policies for monitoring the progression, intervention, stop-notice engagement, mitigation enforcement and eventually the auditing and remedying of adverse outcomes. It is important to keep in mind that, locally ameliorative as Risk Impact Assessment procedures may claim to be, they are only a part of wider community impact, and are at best suspect, and at worst faulty, being, from my possibly cynical perspective, about 30 per cent sound science, 30 per cent economic speculation, and 40 per cent public relations hype!

Inducements, sweeteners, softeners, come-ons and bribes! Anything 'under the table' accepted by an official at any level of public service in a an open democracy, is criminal. All bribes are off. Yet 'understandings' are often entered into; and for operational personnel it is important to ensure that these are recorded and passed on for politicians to handle, advisedly.

A **Work and jobs checklist** of the kind cobbled together in figure 4.2 can also be usefully incorporated into the RIA process, for employment is the outcome most sought from growth patterning in both the realms of conservancy and development. Such an array can reliably inform impact abatement policy; yet very often such an exercise does little more than audit an investment recommendation for private enterprise investors. For Kelman (1981: see also Otway and

1   Number of new local jobs directly associated with operation of new project;
2   Number of new local jobs estimated to be created indirectly as a result of purchases connected with the operation of new project;
3   Number of new local jobs estimated to be induced by consumer purchases of the new employees: *less*
4   Number of local jobs estimated to be eliminated, directly and indirectly, by new project: (1 to 4 being the estimated number of full-time new jobs created)
5   Number of jobs estimated to be seasonal;
6   Number of jobs estimated to be temporary;
7   Jobs for which current unemployed are qualified;
8   Jobs for which displaced workers would be qualified;
9   Jobs filled by current local residents (rather than newcomers or commuters)

Figure 4.2   Work and jobs checklist

Fishbein, 1976) it is this ability to impute a dollar value for non-marketable commodities which lends tangible worth to benefit-cost assessment, for the recipients as well as the instigators of projects. Yet pattern analysts must discern, beyond the array of fiscal costs and benefits: 'what' the *community* gains and losses are in terms of basic-export or residentiary-service jobs and incomes; 'what' longer-term *social* complexities arise from the completion of, or a pulling away from, a project; and 'what' *resource* depletion and waste disposal burdens are to be left with future populations.

There is a gulf of difference between private enterprise accounting of a project's benefit–cost ratio (for the determination of investor benefits), and the community impact of these externalities and diseconomies which deny anything like all-round win-win improvements. Box 4.6 sets out the basis for a **Benefit-cost prognosis** as an extension to the previously depicted Risk Impact Assessment, and the box 4.4 depiction of input–output patterns. Most assessments of this kind skew away from balance; witness the early Scott, MacArthur, Newbury (1976) premiss, for Kenya, that 'The Green Revolution creates a real opportunity for cattle on feed grains to produce high value beef for export to sophisticated markets'. Such recommendations were loaded with unquestioned presumptions – the worthiness of fiscal gains from the 'mining' of Kenya's soils to produce high-value beef exports, the neglect of social consequences (for example land confiscation), environmental consequences (for example 'dust bowl' effects of tract farming), and economic consequences (*dis*economies for a tribally cultured society)! All of the foregoing underscores the need to have answers to wider socio-economic and socio-environmental considerations, wider, that is, than a project progenitor's profit-taking ambition. The assessment panel is expected, on the one hand, to be quite firm and consistent about the style and content of the base-line studies they require, yet on the other hand to be sponsor-friendly and generative in attitude. This matter of

Box 4.6   Benefit-cost prognosis

Benefit-cost prognosis is a pre-investment procedure. The main outcome criterion is usually that revenues exceed outlays – although, inevitably, there are external public effects (externalities) to incorporate into every assessment. Of course some benefits (and more usually some costs) arise well after a product has been manufactured or a service provided, and for these imputed values (shadow prices, usually costs) can be attributed.

Unlike an input–outputs array (box 4.4) which can be effective for a variety of sectors, and for a set period of previous time, benefit-costings relate usually to a specific project over the life of its output. This raises, for the public sector, the application of efficiency rules, most usually about the 'benefits' of shorter-term economic gain, and the 'costs' of longer-term social and environmental strain. It is a matter of overall importance to recognize that although pretty well every project imaginable has benefits to some, and losses to others, the societal need is for a project to exhibit an overall 'Pareto approved' optimality, with enforced transfers from the 'gainers' to the 'losers' if this is called for.

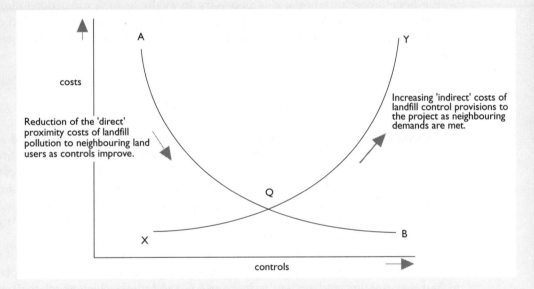

The construct offered here depicts the analytical basis of an economic assessment for a commercial landfill project. The perceived proximity costs to neighbouring land users diminish along the curve 'A to B' with every installation of controls. And the mitigation costs borne by the landfill operators increase along the curve 'X to Y' as each neighbourhood demand for more payouts and controls is met. The 'A to B' range of damage mitigation benefits are registered 'specifically' to affected neighbours: the 'X to Y' control expenses are recovered 'generally' from the community at large.

The construct implies that a balance would be struck at the crossover (Q), beyond which a left-to-right lessening occurs of the neighbouring land user benefits (the Q to B section of the A–B curve), and at which crossover point the rate of additional installation costs (the Q to Y section of the X–Y curve) start to increase prohibitively. There are two further features of note (1) that gross eventual benefits (greenfield factory site, housing tract, public open space), and gross eventual dis-benefits (property blight), be considered contextually over the longer term; and (2) that the shape of the curves is all important, *vide* a flattening, after Q, of the A–B curve, and a steepening of the X–Y curve: Q being the point beyond which neighbouring land-user complainants might reasonably be expected to ease off, and beyond which the landfill operator might start to consider relocation to an alternative site as a better option.

attitude is an important part of 'seed-bed support', particularly in regard to being facilitative to project initiatives.

At best benefit-cost assessments help project investors make sound, if greedy, investment decisions. At worst they fail adequately to inform a community about the protection of resources, about how to prevent adverse waste disposal, or about how to be more certain of future correctional costs (what will happen when there is a downturn in the longer-term economic situation?). Benefit-cost assessment provides cost and benefit information for investors, project donors and (sometimes) for project recipients; yet these assessments mostly fail to address the issue of 'regional yield' over the longer haul. They are usually predicated on only one value premiss, investor profitability, whereas a input–output array of the kind outlined earlier in box 4.4 makes an attempt to come to terms with wider economic and social outcomes. While it is possible to recognize many informational virtues with a benefit-cost prognosis, it is necessary to evaluate such indications more with the head than with the heart; keeping in view the question of which kind of benefits, and at what kinds of cost, and of course to whom such 'benefits and costs' accrue?

Project implementation

Development planning, and also conservancy practice, can be characterized as seeking answers to three basic questions: 'What do we have?', 'What do we want?' and 'What do we do to get it?' – this latter aspect being the nub of 'project implementation'. The three questions also identify with the more elaborate 11-step 'sequence' (figure 2.5 **Traditional planning sequence**) particularly the step 10 item – implementation – pursued in stages via the guidance provided by monitoring, evaluation and adjustment procedures.

Log Frame, from 'logical framework analysis' (not that it is at all analytical!) is a 1990s elaboration from the former MBO (management by objectives), PERT (programme evaluation and review techniques), GAM (goals achievement matrix), and CPA (critical path analysis) procedures. The LogFrame protocol can monitor and evaluate input to a wide range of project-donor schemes, particularly those involving the unilateral transfer from richer to poorer nations of fiscal and sectoral aid via specific projects. They also have a role to play in the monitoring of progress for conventional project enterprises, and joint-venture projects within commercial-industrial development projects and conservancy practice.

Project implementation centres on an 'If-Will' premiss: thus 'if' a project gets a go-ahead 'will' the project goals be sufficiently attained? LogFrame may contribute, via looping, to the 'planning sequence' (figure 2.5) but is largely confined to project monitoring during the operational life of an enterprise, and to project evaluation after the enterprise has reached its as-built stage. The box 4.7 construct **Log Frame project implementation** outlines the verification procedures involved. The procedure is applicable to any other sectoral or service activity (for example, education or health delivery) although in those cases care needs to be taken with the specification and monitoring of the throughput components.

Box 4.7 Log Frame project implementation

Structural arrangements	Verification procedures
TARGETS The 'problems' and the 'potentials' Solutions with minimum adverse effects. ↓	Potentials to be realized? Problems to be ameliorated? Externalities to cope with?

INPUT RESOURCES
Project designs, raw materials, skills, equipment,
   services, finance, public relations.
↓
	Quality, quantity and accountability
	   of inputs.

OUTPUT OUTCOMES Measurable benefits (profits/gains) and disbenefits (externalizations) consequent to the foregoing. ↓	How much throughput? At what cost and profit? On time? Adverse effects?
GOAL Terminal development outcome. Profits/Benefits.	Post-project evaluation (Utility to other projects).

Although project implementation is pursued in the direction Targets-to-Goal, it is first envisaged in the direction Goal-to-Targets. This can be elaborated in relation to a commercially operated landfill project, an extension of the study example selected to illustrate the Benefit-cost prognosis given as box 4.6 earlier in this chapter.

It can be assumed that the GOAL is on-site disposal (landfill, incineration, recycling) of urban refuse within agreed levels of environmental control, leading to the creation of a landscaped park, a housing tract, and eventually a sporting complex during the projects' terminal phase.

The OUTPUT elements include: (1) Park land, housing tract and sporting complex. (2) Safely landfilled refuse disposal. (3) Neutralized toxin disposal or containment. (4) Beneficial recycling. (5) Profitability with no comeback.

The INPUT resources include: (1) Good layout design and operational organization for the project, including access-to-site operating times and tolerances. (2) Plant provisioning and staffing. (3) Effective management and public relations. (4) Monitoring operations and profitability.

The TARGETS involve rubbish disposal within negotiated levels of impact tolerance, provision of a landscaped park, a housing tract and a sporting complex; along with profit-producing dividends.

Guiding the Log Frame project implementation procedure requires a stand-alone allocation of resources and personnel. It also requires empowerment of an agency with powers to apply intervention procedures including 'stop notices' *and* mediation. Above all else the Log Frame procedure will work only if the stated principles are adhered to, and are continuously improved upon, recalibrated, cross-checked and updated. If an outcome is found wanting, it will of course then be too late to do much about the matter. It is at the beginning of the Log Frame construct, with 'targets', that the eventual success or failure of a project, in terms of profits and protections, is cast and settled.

This passage – project propagation, risk assessment, project implementation – sets out some of the technical parameters which enable development and conservancy specialists to operate with integrity. Planning specialists seek progressive results, at the highest strategic level the enhancement of 'basic' export opportunities and 'multiplier' effects (money and jobs). This is a continuing theme with the pragmatic growth management practice passage which is to follow. The neomodern guiding context from *Agenda 21*, together with the sustainability prognosis, predicates that socially acceptable regional economic growth comes down, essentially, to the practice of conservation *with* development.

The second half of this chapter attends to development planning and conservancy practice in seven macro growth pattern contexts.[14]

Macro Practice Patterns

Of practical consideration for both development projects and conservancy practice are macro practice patterns relating to:

- 'Ownerships' and 'rights' (p. 151)
- Urban-rural growth patterning (p. 156)
- Coastal zone management (p. 163)
- Agriculture and forestry (p. 166)
- Tourism (sustainable tourism) (p. 169)
- Unemployment alleviation (p. 181)
- Waste disposal management (p. 183)
  (Urban Growth Management – chapter 5)

Holding to the ethical and sustainability ideals extolled in earlier chapters, while addressing the growth pattern management theme in this chapter, gives rise to conflicts between notions of development and conservancy, differing patterns of enthusiasm for regional growth and conservancy, different styles of transformer processing and transactor management, different forms of profit-and-benefit and loss-and-disbenefit, and different modes of procedure. Sustainable management is an ideal, impractical of full achievement in growth-on-growth and consumer-discard situations. Yet all of us can – some would have that as *must* – adjust our 'consume and discard' ways in the direction of styles of resource uptake which are more sustainable and more ethical in intent and execution. These attitudes can infuse conservancy practice and development projects in the style of re-education, retargeting and reclaiming, all served by flows of better information.

If behaving better as resource consumers and waste disposers is acknowledged as socially good, then this is best brought into the foreground than being obscured by a screen of deception about the potential of untapped resources and unproven technological fixes. There is another niggle: the reconciliation of sustainability ethics with growth, it being apparent in the real world that there is a large residual rump of opinion favouring continued growth-and-discard, come what may. Even though it is illogical, this hedonism exists as fact. Circumscriptions are set out in the seven listed policy sectors styled here as Growth Management Practice, their purpose being to signpost new directions for management in the style of sustainable planning practice, particularly sustainable 'urban growth management' practice (chapter 5). The signposts put up are large, clear and simple: each of the components in the listing deserving attention from the other writings noted in this review.

For the urban-living populations of the Anglo New World, but also for most of the OECD hegemony, coping with the 'ever-changing big picture' (box 3.1) comes down mainly to a matter of establishing a 'rural and urban' pattern of co-dependency along the lines indicated within the 'regional' column in the box 3.7 **Matrix** (chapter 3). In short, there is a need for federal-to-regional guidelines as well as regional-to-local guidance.

The seven paradigms reviewed in this passage exert inter-paradigmatic synergy one upon the other – reflecting a sustainable enlightenment.

'Ownerships' and 'rights' (introduced on page 16)

Historical shifts alter our perception of the 'ownership of resources' and 'rights of use' privileges relative to landscapes and waterscapes. These are significant and determining factors within growth pattern management. This comes home to an individual when a treasured open landscape in which they hold a community or personal 'interest', but not a property 'right', becomes cluttered with signage, hill-top shack constructions, exotic plantation forestry and abandoned consumer durables (particularly old motor vehicles), or gets plundered for its mineral or indigenous forest resources. These kinds of change come about because most open-area landscape activities in the New World are either un-regulated, or come under loose control, not only with regard to land usage but also with regard to the introduction of flora and fauna infestations and downstream-downwind pollution drift.

Underlying these open-area incursions is a division of the rural resource estate into its fee-simple freehold, conservancy commonhold, public land statehold and indigenous peoples (cognatic tenure) categories, which in turn become subject to interlevenings identifiable from the wider community – generally aesthetic, sometimes spiritual – 'ownerships', 'interests' and 'rights'. A case for growth pattern management policy and practice centres around the extent to which there is, or can be fashioned, a partial or controlling right to intervene in the management and enjoyment of those landscapes by the wider community, even though they are not of the public domain. As evidence, the widespread fudging of locked-on planning throughout the quasi-urban tracts beyond suburbia mocks most formal growth pattern management efforts.

Adjacent rural and urban locations are interdependent, yet each stands apart from the other functionally. This is clearly evident with post-World War II British planning which compartmentalized the urban and rural environments: indeed planning for urban areas, and non-planning the 'white' (on plan) rural areas.

Responsible open-area resource utilization is a matter of good land-use management pursued for a societal purpose. That purpose includes the primary production of food, water and fibre for the maintenance of human life. A secondary purpose includes the urban-recreational activities located in open area landscapes:

the urban playgrounds for golf, boating, horse riding, off-roading, walking, bird-watching, picnicking. The siting and appearance of rural purpose buildings, and control over adverse visual smell and noise effects, are controlled by regulatory mechanisms of the zoning and by-law kind – box 5.6, chapter 5. Within the urban-rural band the outcome is a mixed message – a person may believe they have left town, but in reality this is the beginning of an urban-rural landscape – a surrogate countryside. And if some of the often contrived 'rural' vistas over private land are attractive to the passer-by, then by all means look and enjoy, but do not touch, and do not feign hurt when the landowner decides to put up acres of glass housing, park some old cars, stable city folks' ponies, or allow trail biking on the weekend, or subdivide into broad-acre (lifestyle) homesites.

Some urban-focused people prefer to live in a quasi-rural way as urban-oriented non-farming residents. Their contention is that they have sufficient means and mobility to enjoy the secure and individualized 'rural' living ideal. A problem arises in that this 'ideal' can be at odds with national imperatives to ensure that good farmland is retained for food and fibre production and to meet the 'tourist gaze' (Urry 2002). The result: urban-rural houses get intermingled with a confusion of play spaces, dump grounds, glasshouses, training tracks, garden plant shops, commercial signage, and other footloose urban functions beached in the countryside. Within this quasi-urban belt some enlightened city administrations, and some city-state conjoint agencies have purchased tracts of rural landscape and waterscape as weekend playground space for city-dwellers and out-of-region visitors.[15]

Preserving Rural Character, Fred Heyer, 1990.

Beyond the peri-urban penumbra, in the full countryside, the dominant cropping is 'food and fibre' – or is it? Tourism receipts exceed 'food and fibre' income throughout rural swathes of the OECD. Here, and beyond, in the open area landscapes marginal to agriculture and silviculture, base ownership patterns begin to fade into other interests and rights. There arises a sense to the passer-by that this landscape partly, at least, 'belongs' to them. Sovereign or state land acquisition retains some marginal lands as public-owned national parks, forest reserves or wilderness spaces. But in these times of low intervention on the part of government (and state, provincial or regional) agencies, the worthy acquisitions have usually been already made, this being in its highest form the now publicly owned, yet in many ways artificially construed, National Park estates.[16]

A privately arranged conservation company (Marunui in Northland, NZ) in which my family has a shareholding and cabin (where much of this book was written) manages 2,000 acres of regenerating rainforest on land of no productive utility. The whole is covenanted to a 'conservation trust'. Throughout a 100-acre corner the 20 owners occupy carefully selected recreational cabin sites with vehicular access only. (See sketch in figure 4.4)

Ostensibly out of generosity, mostly on account of guilt, private landowners of sites of natural diversity and attraction, or owners of sites of first-settler or first-people historical significance, often bequest or covenant designated areas to the 'nation' a 'national' authority, or a local governing body. The cautious would warn those who bequest such a gift in one century to make legal provision to ensure that it cannot be sold on in the next! The proclaimed objective is for the private landowner to protect and conserve the natural heritage and cultural heritage landscapes for their own enjoyment *and* that of their progeny *and* the wider community *in perpetuity*. Hopefully, as is the situation with my own conservation group dynamics (see side bar). a treasured forest landscape can both be protected from clear felling, provide opportunities for recreational living, and contribute to overall environmental wellbeing 'indefinitely'.

A variation on the public-private open area landowning situation, in the direction of public rights and interests, arises within nature conservancy groups. These exist on a stand-alone basis in settler societies. Eve Endicott in *Land Conservation through Public and Private Partnerships* (1993) has editorially collated for the United States the public acquisition and private conservancy options, and detailed the legal, tax-saving, and partnership complexities.[17] The grandparent agency is the Nature Conservancy, which straddles all the United States and has a toe-hold in many other jurisdictions. In landownership contexts, these 'in cash' and 'in kind' benefactors are saving some of their corporeal landscapes, or salting away some of their ethereal wealth, for a land-trust cause. Nature Conservancy acquisitions and actions assuage 'settler guilt' about past enclosures, and their feel-good character can be uplifting to settler descendants, although to the likes of black Americans and indigenous first-nation peoples, they mostly engender indifference or annoyance. Indeed behold the Euro-wrath which descends upon indigenous peoples reaching for the settler's exploitation practices, doing as the settlers have done previously, namely cashing in the forest tracts and mineral potentials! And, of course, most nature reserves are beyond the means and access capability of a majority of the populations they have been set aside for. Nevertheless conservancy societies are a societally 'acceptable' way for the sensitive rich to contribute 'now' to the conservancy estate of the 'future' through the provision of greenways, bio-reserves and watershed protections.

> The Nature Conservancy website is www.tnc.org. Additional to the Nature Conservancy is the WCED (World Commission on Environment and Development); the UNEP (United Nations Environmental Programme); and the WWF (World Wildlife Fund).
>
> The Australian private enterprise company Earth Sanctuaries offers a negative investment opportunity to participate in land restoration. www.esl.com.au

Owners of landed property are conditioned by the fact (Denman 1962) that 'What a landowner has is not the land itself, but an amalgam of rights over the land'. The issue this exposes concerns the nature of what is usually characterized as the 'bundle' of ever-continuing interests which 'go with the land' supplemented by those shorter-term rights which 'go with the landowner'. There has arisen a slowly altering perception of community entitlement, in particular the public enjoyment of rural and wilderness landscapes. This is also the case with foreshore and riverine public land reservations where changes in attitude emerge: for example, moving away from free-for-all sand and gravel quarrying and refuse dumping, toward clean-up and conservation. The ownership of private user rights and public enjoyment interests are being continuously layered upon, and re-sectored throughout the rural-regional landscape. Such proprietorial changes emerge slowly.

Indigenous peoples – Maori in New Zealand, Aboriginal in Australia and native North Americans – have quite different resource-owning perceptions from the settler-incomers. The resources historically most compromised include the use and enjoyment of open-area land and waters by both settler and indigenous peoples for food-gathering and recreational purposes. To indigenous first-nation people looking out from the littoral, the ocean is perceived as a fish-food source; for the early settler-migrants looking in upon the same shore their emotions included delirious relief, now sanctified as hedonic sunning, swimming, lazing and fishing for pleasure. These perceptions are reconcilable, yet they will always be held separately.

Other public 'interest' issues include concern for a decline in general amenity values resulting from mechanized farming practices, low-grade rural-residential land settlement, exotic plantation forestry, and roadside commercialism with attendant chaotic signage. These are the negatively perceived 'add-ons' which must be linked to the also negatively perceived 'taken aways' in the form of the destruction reduction and desecration of indigenous flora and fauna. Ecologically flawed rural resource-use practices profile as clear-felled indigenous forests, over-stocked run holdings, soil and landscape erosion and strip mineral mining. These result in water quality impairment also associated with infusions of herbicides and pesticides, surface and ground-water abstractions, poisonings from mineral workings and fertilizer over-enrichments, and biological overloadings resulting from excess and uncontrolled animal waste disposal and run-off, sometimes interacting to produce a synergistic outcome worse than the sum of the polluting parts.

What follows are the available strictures which can be engaged to regulate or constrain land resource holders (cross-refer also to box 5.6: Planning in action):

Development levies, intended to benefit a community, are often unfair and frequently cause worthwhile proposals to go somewhere else.

Forward payments, demanded as a share of the cost of providing collector roads and trunk utilities, often profiles as an inflated demand; again a situation where the local governing body should take care to adhere specifically to planning principle.

1 Zonings for a district or a regional territory, often designated for purposes other than those preferred by a landowner, whether freeholder, community land-holder or an indigenous (cognatic) landowner.

2 Constraints upon the use of agri-chemicals; controls for detoxing and diluting the off-site discharge of animal wastes; regulation of water run-off and vegetation burn-off.

3 Land-use controls emanating from local government in the style of by-laws for proscribing the pattern of land uses which is to be practised; and in a format which protects against water-table, soil, aesthetic, noise and air pollution.

4 As-of-right easements for public utilities dug into land and passing over it, subject to due consultation and compensation for 'takings'.

5 Sub-leasing, licensing and letting agreements for the application of wider public controls.

6 The fixing of land prices and land rents – generally unworkable, and now usually unthinkable.

7 Expropriation of land; 'eminent domain' the 'taking' rights of the state for alienating land for functional public purposes.

8 Acquisition of land on the open market for public use and enjoyment.

9 Subjecting land to an official reallocation (remembrement) procedure, when holdings become minutely parcelled or held in multiple ownership – again generally unworkable, but a logical way to set serious 'wrongs' 'right'.
10 Protection Orders applied to the 'natural' heritage or the 'cultural heritage'.

Despite its length and complexity, the above list of essentially corporeal constraints over private property ownerships and resource uses does not include controls for protecting the ancestral interests and spiritual entitlements of indigenous peoples – or, indeed, the feral rights of indigenous flora and fauna.

Hofstee (1967) observed wisely if densely: 'that the rules a man [*sic*] has to obey, when he wants to establish continue or break a certain formal bond between himself and the land, without getting into conflict with his fellow men and the existing political powers, do not exist independently, but are related to society as a whole.' From this position he concluded: *First*, that the concept of private property is 'not the natural or self evident form of land ownership', challenging freehold land title systems which allow of 'ownership from the centre of the earth to the sky' as an ephemeral buyable-sellable-tradeable commodity. *Second*, he considered that 'private property in land as a system has already weakened' even though it is the cornerstone to all landowning democracies. *Third*, Hofstee concluded that in principle 'planning is considered as a legitimate action of the government, for which no compensation is due'. These three precepts collate as the basis of resource management – identifying and coding public interests and entitlements.

> Hofstee, a Hollander, alluded to the compromised degree of remnant land possession and enjoyment of so-styled Dutch 'landowners' and their 'landownership'.

Freeholder rights, so absolute in frontier times, can be codified and constrained by law, less effectively through covenants, by Landcare preference, and (relative to the all-important tourism industry) through an embellishment of community values and interests via conservation covenants. These latter involve the fashioning of voluntary agreements to protect natural landscapes against all future development *and* the enhancement and conservation of native flora and fauna in perpetuity.

The right to develop, exploit or conserve a landholding is regulated under planning and resource management statutes, conservancy laws, heritage statutes, mining and water-use controls, waste management strictures, and controls for downstream and downwind pollutions. Although of mainly theoretical interest it is helpful for practioners to contemplate the underlying systemic basis of planning control. What follows is a potted collation.

- Administrations in the poorer 'developing economies' do not have the benefit of much in the way of a system-basis to enforce development and conservancy rulings. Applying for approval to develop may arise as a formality, although obtaining an actual approval to proceed usually involves the engagement of agents and the payment of supplementary 'sweeteners' to third parties.[18]
- In 'command economies' the state owns all development rights. What the state decrees is absolute, which occasionally works well for the likes of macro-conservancy, but inevitably leads to on-site failures and shortfalls.

- In property-owning democracies of the Anglo settler society kind, 'landown-ership' is the cornerstone to land taxation, and land-use regulation through zoning.
- A sophisticated extension to the ownership basis for operational planning acknowledges the 'interests' which lie behind formal titles: these include indigenous peoples' residual rights and values, community aesthetic interests, airspace-above and below-ground ownerships, pleasure-using rights, and per-ceived feral rights – and there are surely others.[19]
- Another mode involves engagement of a 'control of effects' basis for the man-agement of planning operations via attachment to the land title registration and land tax systems.[20]

An undeniably beneficial and everlasting outcome of all planning is the conser-vation of open area humanized landscapes for aesthetic appreciation, food and fibre production, visitor enjoyment, and sustainable-as-possible urban residency.

Urban-rural growth patterning

(Refer also to the Urban Sprawl Control passage in chapter 5.)

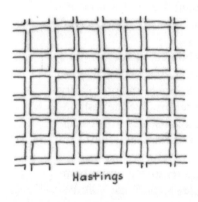

Hastings

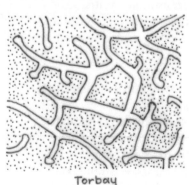

Torbay

Gridded and podded sprawl, NZ

Constraining urban sprawl is frequently addressed from the heart rather than the head, springing from the 'urban harbours evil' and 'rural is clean, green and good' sets of generalization.[21] An economic case for aes-thetic preservation, and against gridded and podded urban sprawl onto rural land can be made out. The eco-nomic-aesthetic concerns derive also from the simple fact that recreation and tourism activities throughout the rural landscapes of the Anglo New World are often as economically significant as agricultural production. There are three, often fiscally comparable, 'crops' to be harvested from the city fringe estate – food, water and fibre production dollars, tourism commodity dollars, and residential sprawl dollars.

The typical urban-into-rural crossover (also known as ex-urban, edge-city and peri-urban development) has taken place mostly by a succession of extensions to the urban growth boundary (UGB) on a 20-year look-ahead and leapfrog basis. The result: decreased densi-ties even for situations where the stated objective was density increase.[22] The physical outcome is illustrated as the urban-rural and rural-urban outliers in figure 4.3 **Periphery-to-centre city montage**. This depicts the befuddled territory which lies between the clearly 'inner suburban' and the clearly 'outer agricultural'

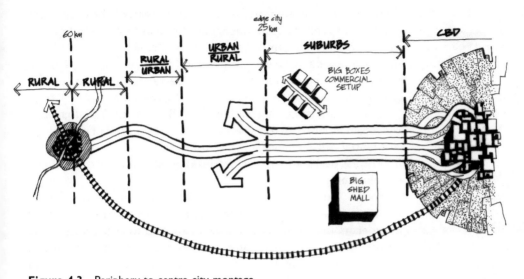

Figure 4.3 Periphery-to-centre city montage

land-use patterns, defining the location of the 'quasi-urban quasi-rural' problematic – the diseconomies and inconveniences of sprawl, the erosion of tourism attraction, resource degradations, and a loss of rural productiveness.

Dividing the urban-rural area into two parts, Bryant, Russwurm and McLellan (1992) define an 'inner fringe' which includes land of rural appearance which has been zoned in for eventual urban purposes, and against which arguments for the retention of rural character is futile, and an 'outer fringe' of rural land into which the infiltration of urban components is in competition with agricultural, recreational and tourism needs. In relation to both parts of the quasi-urban estate the initial infiltration includes hobby-farm, lifestyle (broad acre) and semi-self-sufficient occupation by urban-focused occupiers. Desires for privacy, the exercise of choice, extensive land proprietorship, easy access from blacktop roads, and the wish to be identified as residing in rural Arcadia, leads to the creation of urban-rural 'residential' environments. There are also the more legitimate yet awkward bulk acreage demands, at low-acreage cost, for animal kennelling, rubbish recycling, auto wrecking, garden sales, lumber sales, and horse-training.

Policies and plans for urban containment abound; yet quasi-urban extensions, driven by market demand against the trend of most planning recommendations, also abound. As a consequence most urban containment endeavours for both metropolitan and non-metropolitan cities are characterized by regulation entanglement and failure. Because of this, a clear 'rural-urban landmark' identity is underscored as the centrepiece to successful urban-rural pattern management.

An authoritative examination of the struggle to manage urban-rural patterning, together with a review of push-pull factors, and concluding with growth management practice options, is given by Tom Daniels *When City and Country Collide* (1999).

Here is Tom Daniels on sprawl into the urban fringe: 'Communities face a long run death-by-halves. The first twenty-year comprehensive plan envisions the development of only half of the [rural into urban] area, and the zoning ordinance then carries out that scenario. Twenty years later. . . .'

The spatially disaggregated support area required for a settler society city has been calculated, for Vancouver, as an 'ecological footprint' 180 times greater than the area that city occupies. Wackernagel and Rees, 1996.

Consult also the wider polemic advanced against urban sprawl in Eban Fodor's, *Better Not Bigger* (1999).

'The suburban developments of today and the shopping smarm that clutters up so much of the landscape in between them, arose from the idea . . . that neither the city nor the country was really a suitable place to live.'
The Geography of Nowhere, James Kunstler, 1993

The Queensland Regional Planning Advisory Group definition (1994) of 'growth *management*' posits growth management as seeking 'to redistribute growth and development in ways that minimise negative environmental or social impacts while achieving the maximum efficiency in the provision of services and infrastructure for the growing population'.

This is sought through containment, complemented by an urban corridor expansion component, accommodating the release of urban pressure in 'chunks' rather than in bands. This accommodation is essential (Weitz and Moore 1998) because 'UGBs are unlikely to keep development from leapfrogging when (urban-rural) boundaries are impermanent'. However, a problem with corridor expansion, highlighted by Barnett in *The Fractured Metropolis* (1995) is that it aids and abets 'a new kind of city, where residential subdivisions extend for miles and shopping malls and office parks are strung out in long corridors of commercial development'.

The UGB understanding and emphasis arose in Oregon (where urban-regional growth management has had marked success) as an economic-aesthetic imposition applied to either side of the urban fence. It is a residential growth management objective to nurture ever-sustainable food and fibre production from the rural landscape, coupled with an induction of improved livability within a more diversified and densified urban area. DeGrove's perspective (1984: 235) is that 'The process is a top-to-bottom and bottom-to-top effort which, in conceptual terms at least, is complete, rational, and comprehensive'. This has been further elaborated (DeGrove and Miness 1992) as a 'calculated effort by a local government, region or state to achieve a balance between natural systems – land air and water (conservancy) – and residential commercial and industrial development'. With regional growth management locked on, for reasons of 'economy sociability and livability', this calls into being arguments in favour of urban densification and diversification (infilling and layering).

Although the historical connections sourced for this text are mostly from within Australasia and North America, it is the outcomes of rural landscape management in the United Kingdom, including rural and urban separation and containment, which is of indicative value to the Anglo New World context.

With the exception of some outlier situations the contemporary level of regional consciousness in the British Isles is socially and geographically distinctive, boosted by a notable growth in regional identity following the EEC–EC generation of support policies for 'target' regions of need. The terra psyche of most British Isles populations reaches back to a separateness of function and identity between town and country, coupled to an effective locked-on anti-sprawl rural planning technique. Not to be overlooked is the long-term 'village' presence which provides British peri-urban areas with a protectionist lobby vector.

The British-European terra psyche derives from a rustic technological precedent which settled commons and pathways slowly from medieval field systems, abetted by an ancient (pre-orthoganal) landowning class system. Both the field system and the class system are imprinted upon the British (particularly the English) and much of the Western European landscape. A further point is that within Europe the rural landscape, although enclosed with many an injustice, was occupied in a manner which left remnant commons and public access ways, patterns which the contemporary population respects. No such social or historical legacy impeded the trowelling of suburban expansion over the peri-urban outliers to towns and cities in the New World. Hilltop and ridge top dominance (for the view), technicolour houses for the occupants to flaunt (for self-aggrandisement), and the treatment of soils and landed resources as playthings (for the kids), are the outcomes of a hedonistic and exuberantly unshackled mobility and wealth, pushed along by urban fears on the part of incomers, and windfall attractions for landowners. The landscapes of the New World involved the swift orthoganal 'enclosure' of aboriginal-peopled land from whom the settlers sought consciously to exclude the setting aside of common lands and pedestrian accessways. The dispossession of native ownership was sectioned off with such thoroughness that in most of North America and Australasia only 'badland' reservations were left in native people ownership, leaving some indigens landless in their own landscape.

It is a matter of operational interest for planners from the Anglo settler societies to understand more fully how communities of the Anglo culture-cousin kind maintain, in Britain, their urban *inclusionary* intensiveness alongside a rural *exclusionary* extensiveness. The European tradition for maintaining an urban-rural compartmentation is largely a consequence of having the 'correct' individual and community 'attitude', augmented by a procedural rigour. Yet within the British context it would be an error to assume that the battle for the countryside was a push-over. A conscious feature of modern libertarian Britain is that the custody of countryside values is *not* left to the vagaries of market forces. Central government interposes policy guidelines assertively into the planning system via Department of the Environment *Planning Practice Guidance* bulletins.[23] These recognize that the countryside is rich with historical and ecological associations as well as being of productive utility. There are guidelines to safeguard all manner of environmentally sensitive tracts: Areas of Outstanding Natural Beauty, Green Belts, Sites of Special Scientific Interest, Historical and Archaeological Sites, and the already extensively humanized National Parks. The bulletins set

Observing the Australasian scene: 'Balkan solutions produce Balkan outcomes of fragmented authority, rampant sectional interests and disregard of minority rights.'
    Phil Heywood, 'The Future Metropolis', 1994

Rural landowners in settler societies are loath to grant public access or designate public footpaths in the open landscape. A paradoxical consequence, observed by Elizabeth Aitken-Rose at Auckland University, is that comparing city with country, a much higher proportion of townscapes (up to 60 per cent) is available to citizens on a 'right to roam' basis than in the countryside.

An irony for the New Zealand context arose with the withdrawal of farm subsidies. This has led, over the last 25 years, to the abandonment of farming on low-return tracts. This in turn lent impetus to a peri-urban or quasi-rural crossover, *and ironically* gave rise to a massive regrowth of indigenous bush on the remaindered farmscapes. To a minor extent the unwarranted broadacre construction is offset by an also unexpected return of indigenous bush greenery.

The landscape imprint for the British Isles has been the beneficiary of massive and historically deep research culminating in the intricate *Studies of Field Systems in the British Isles*, edited by A. R. H. Baker and R. A. Butlin, 1973.

out to establish an agricultural rural emphasis. In relation to the control of building construction (Department of the Environment PPG 12: 1992) 'new house building and other new development in the open countryside, away from established settlements, should be strictly controlled. The fact that a single house on a particular site would be unobtrusive is not in itself a good argument; it could be repeated too often.' In contrast to an apparent narrow attention to the matter of housing PPG 12 establishes that 'Agriculture will remain the major user of land in the countryside, but a decreasing one' . . . (and that) . . . 'The guiding principle in the wider countryside is that development should benefit the rural economy and maintain or enhance the environment' – in a phrase that there is to be conservation with development.

The British system of development plans (comprising structure plans and local plans) is not overly prescriptive. They provide guidance, incentives and controls to an extent and in a way which ensures that developers cannot pursue or change the use of rural land for private reasons which are against wider public interests. The outcome imprinted so agreeably upon Britain's rural landscapes may not be procedurally adapted to the Anglo New World context, but the example is there, available as a cultural model to keep in view.

Sustainable farming, with an emphasis on food production for adjacent-city consumption is the catch-call emanating from the January 2002 United Kingdom *Commission on Farming*.

Robert Kaplan views the Northwestern United States growth management and urban conservation as a 'stagey perfection questionably difficult to transfer or replicate'.
An Empire Wilderness, 1998

With much of North America away from the western and eastern seaboards, and throughout Australasia, the quasi-urbanization of productive agricultural land is an incautious profligacy. The damage to the regional economy (transportation and utility provisioning costs), damage to the social community (atomized and isolated individuals distanced from community help), and damage to the environment (wrong land uses, free-enterprise soullessness and ugliness), all pile up as arguments against unrestrained quasi-urban development, and add to the case for sustainable regional growth pattern management. Yet figure 4.4, **Suburban-residential and rural-residential compared**, illustrates a perversity, the cost savings for a rural-residential arrangement relative to a suburban-residential provisioning.

Containment within agreed *urban growth boundaries*, and attention to the issues which are essentially urban (industry, utilities, housing, transportation, employment) is the nub to growth-managed urban-rural patterning. Of course recreation for the urban majority penetrates adjoining rural areas, and further complicates the case for an urban-rural distinction. Here Cullingworth (1997) notes that 'securing acceptability is difficult, enormously time-consuming, and fraught with political problems. . . . [yet] acceptability across the spectrum of interests is the key characteristic of successful growth management policies'.

In the Oregon context the set of 'attractive to business' policies is given expression in a total of nineteen goals, within which a set of five urban goals

During the 1990s I developed two residential sites: one an acre surveyed from a suburban title for city use, the other a residential site leased within a 1,400 acre rural conservation title for recreational use.

THE WEST AUCKLAND SUBURBAN-RESIDENTIAL ACRE

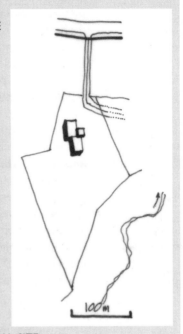

Rawland	20,000
Subdivision survey	3,500
Legal costs: titles, easements, liens	3,400
Geotechnic assessment	2,200
Engineer's plans: access and services	3,800
Clearing and earthworks	1,300
Access formation	10,700
Utllities: water, sewer, power, phone	5,100
Road frontage [proportion]	$20,000
All-up-cost: ready to build	$70,000

Annual 'provider' utility charges:

Water and sewerage set charges	600
Electricity and phone line charages	300
Local taxes [rates]	1,200
Annual ongoing costing	$2,100

THE NORTHLAND RURAL-CONSERVATION-RESIDENTIAL SITE

Rawland [1/14th proportion]	20,000
Formation of site access	5,500
Legal costs	500
Geotechnic assessment	400
Clearing and earthworks	600
Utilities connections	-nil-
All up costs: ready to build	$27,000

Annual site provider charges:
'Biocharmonic' house erected. No
public utility connections—

Local taxes [rates]	300
Access, fencing and maintenance fees	250
Annual ongoing costing	$550

Aside from aesthetic, best-use, and social reasoning arguments *against* rural-residential development, the perverse rural-residential living option is the cheaper alternative; withal being closer to the sustainable ideal than the suburban arrangement!

Figure 4.4 Suburban-residential and rural-residential compared

The USA and Canada contain about 45 metropolitan areas with populations in excess of one million. Soja (2000) lists the ten largest, each with a population exceeding three million, in ranked order:

New York
Los Angeles
Chicago
San Francisco-Oakland
Philadelphia
Detroit
Boston
Washington
Dallas-Fort Worth
Houston

Heywood (1994) shows that two-thirds of the population of Australia and New Zealand will be concentrated into only six polycentric cities:

Perth
Sydney
Brisbane
Adelaide
Auckland
Melbourne

The problems facing urban Australia are reviewed in *Australian Cities* edited by Patrick Troy, 1995.

'Regional planning has emerged time and again in Canada as the best perspective from which to to approach extra-municipal problems as well as sub-provincial and subnational dilemmas.'

Hodge and Robinson, *Planning Canadian Regions*, 2001

(*Urbanization*: the 'Key Goal', along with *Economy, Housing, Utilities*, and *Transportation*) range against the *Agricultural Goal* for which (De Grove 1984: 256) 'disallows the treatment of these lands as left-over areas available for (urban) development, and instead stresses their [for ever and ever] economic and social [aesthetic and recreational] value to the state'. The established Oregon experience 'mandate[s] that all urban areas designate urban growth boundaries (Goal 14) *and* exclusive farm use zoning (Goal 3) as soon as possible'.[24] Notable is the need for 'acceptability' – whole-government political commitment, whole-picture quality management, whole-region land-use designation, and an all-agencies-together funding; and the utility of PDR (Purchase of Development Rights), of TDR (Transfer of Development Rights), and SSZ (Sliding Scale Zoning) (box 5.6, chapter 5).

What is notable is that extensive sprawl leads to car dependence, social problems, and environmental impacts. Operational strictures have been assembled by John DeGrove and Deborah Miness in their *New Frontier for Land Policy* (1992: 161, reordered and summarized) which expresses six benchmark principles for Growth Management responsibilities, of which four are 'outcome-oriented'.

First, getting serious with the curtailment of urban sprawl through a mandatory application of rural subdivision standards – variable sizing as appropriate to the quality and extent of the rural resource – but seldom less than 20 acre (8 ha) subdivision blocks; the denial of urban sprawl to be concomitantly linked to compact urban development clusters at some discrete rural sites.

Second the inclusion of affordable housing as a major urban element thereby countervailing the rural shanty syndrome.

Third protecting the greatest of all assets, wholesome natural systems, by focusing on a conservation of wetlands, woodland, and viable farm and forestry holdings, along with urban containment within defined city limits and designated growth settlements.

Fourth promotion of overall win-win beneficial outcomes for both the urban and rural sectors as a broadly beneficial consequence of 'managing growth'.

The following two 'procedurally focused' principles are, arguably, the capstone arrangements for keying in the DeGrove–Miness strictures.

Fifth the 'concurrency' proposition wherein all the component parts of growth, particularly urban growth, are mandated 'all of a territorial piece': constituting an acknowledgement of the societal-economic-environmental necessity for a pre-planning pre-provisioning and pre-funding approach to urban growth management and rural retention throughout a whole regional territory.

Sixth is a 'consistency' requirement which, at a technical-legal level, underscores a mandatory necessity, conjoint state-regional-local participation in the foregoing policies and procedures.

Much mention is made of Oregon, particularly the 24 municipalities and the counties around Portland; particularly by a focus on an all-of-state application of the Growth Management strategy.

These six benchmark principles are dependent on some other significant inputs. The legal control factor derives from a mandated no-exceptions status. This recognition also calls into being an input of funding adequate for the job in hand and for a holding to that position within a future context of changing political orientation. One final ingredient, arising out of public sentiment and widespread education, is continuing political and public support and commitment, in a word 'acceptability' between all parties, but especially on the part of local government agencies.[25]

Other approaches, like the Queensland effort, are selective and partial. Another, much publicized, is the 'creative development' arrangement scoped by Yaro and Arendt for the Connecticut River Valley (1994) setting out to conserve existing woodlands, retain good quality land for agriculture, group any allowed housing into 'clusters', and prohibit building upon profiled ridgelines or close to roadlines.

Finally for this passage, and quoting again from DeGrove's seminal text (1984: 389): 'The days of fancy plans being developed every five or ten years, and then placed on the shelf, are giving away ... to plans that are linked both to state and regional policies, and the local implementation process.' The extent of resource degradation and amenity damage resulting as a consequence of the previous 20-year look-ahead pattern of ex-urban expansion, and recognition of the joylessness, dysfunction and diseconomy of much suburban and peri-urban life, focuses and underscores the emphasis within this passage on a *rural exclusionary* and an *urban inclusionary* basis to urban-rural patterning. These wake-up criteria are pursued *not* because land is in scarce supply, but because suburban sprawl and rural-urban sprawl is everlastingly costly, environmentally damaging and socially discordant.

The design issues associated with peri-urban growth management are addressed in the next chapter under 'Ex-urban Strategy'.

Coastal zone management

(Refer also to the Water's Edge Management passage in chapter 5.)

First a review of some positives. These arise within Anglo settler societies on account of the bi-cultural ('native' and 'settler' peoples) attachments to the foreshore landscapes and seascapes, and the established pattern of access and use, shown all-of-a-piece in figure 4.4 as the **Coastal marine zone**. Communities in all four Anglo settler society nations enjoy and flock to the water's margin.

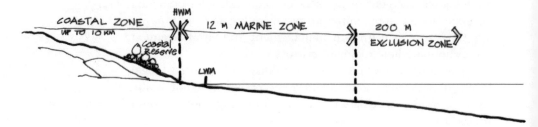

Figure 4.5   Coastal marine zone

A feature common to all coastal zones is their attraction for human habitation, which means competition for space on the landward side for buildings, recreation facilities, transportation and utilities structures, and waterside industries, and on the seaward side to fit in the ports and storage facilities associated with maritime harvesting, water-sport recreation and water-based transportation. The coastal strip to the landward side is the locus of maximum property investment and development intensity.[26]

The often quoted worst case sea-level rise is 0.88 m by 2100 – but half a metre is considered the more likely maximum.
International Panel on Sea Level Change, 2001

A foreshore should contain only the artifacts and structures that belong or need to be there. It is also the place where water-carried waste disposal is concentrated, where commercial fishing and fish farming terminates, and where water surface transportation and offshore oil and mineral exploitation is based. What further complicates matters is that the landward edge is suffused with cultural sentiment and attachment as well as being the preferred place of habitation. And a further complication for seaside margins is the phenomenon known as 'coastal squeeze', the inexorable sea-level rise, first recorded during the twentieth century and expected to accelerate over the twenty-first century.[27]

A primary issue is the indigenous first people's rights of use and access to the foreshore and the water beyond. This has brought about an emotionally charged complexity whenever indigenous first people and settler people are drawn together to consider coastal policy. Some settler stock people exhibit remorse over their forebears' acts of littoral theft, despoilation and commodification, not that the original indigenous populations were overly sensitive about resource depletion, for when fish stocks declined or seal populations dwindled they moved on or adapted to some other food source.

Individual freehold rights are expected, from the indigenous peoples perspective, to give way at the foreshore to common property 'interests' and indigenous 'rights'. Along the littoral, the historical privileges of indigenous first peoples are never fully extinguished, embodying spirituality and food-economy roles of historical significance. But along the intensely humanized sections of coastlines this recognition has been mostly subsumed: obviously so where reclamations have been made and port authorities have been empowered.[28] It is the suburbanized and rural-humanized sections of the littoral, where the shoreline has been less dramatically modified, that the traditional havens, food-gathering camps and landing places recalled by indigenous first peoples, remain remembered and recorded.

The development demands and conservancy issues inland from the high-water mark of the oceans and lakes are understood. It is when consideration is switched in the other direction, toward the inter-tidal zone, and beyond that to the 12-nautical-mile 'coastal marine area', that there arises human misunderstanding about aqua-diversity and rights of access to a supposed resource common. In place of the topsoil, bedrock and flora and fauna certainties of terrestrial management, there arise 'at sea' the much less well understood biological complexities of the marine environment. Here, over the last 200 years of farmland and urbanland creation in settler societies, the water-borne erosion of soils and clays, although clearly apparent on the landward side at the time of development, has disappeared from sight under the water's surface as a deathly silt cloak which lies on the seabed in a manner now well understood, yet not perceived at the time of deposit to be an interference to the marine ecology.

The waterland public resource estate is now guided by scientific indicators and the application of resource use procedures, and a better understanding of the way water movement patterns sometimes 'dump' and in other contexts 'move on' water-borne wastes and silt. It is a matter of relevance to coastal zone management, widely considered, to identify and plan for scientifically correct and culturally appropriate conservation with development, both inland and seaward.

There has been a century and more of bi-cultural complacency now going sour (over-fishing, foreshore rights abuse), and multicultural conflict (confused exploitation and conflicting enjoyment of the seaboard and marine resources). As a consequence the governments of settler-society nations of the transpacific kind are now attempting to impose an administrative authority to produce integrated coastal policies and plans – in the style of Coastal Zone Management Plans (CZMPs). These set out to achieve equilibrium between public and private rights over the 'subject to zoning' landward estate, and the 'subject to regulation' marine resources estate. In neither context do terrestrial local government authorities have an easy time of it. More particularly, the visual impact of buildings has been historically bereft of design direction and control; the subdivision of land up to the legal freehold edge has been largely unstoppable; and the exploitation of marine foodstocks and the out-of-sight-out-of-mind dumping of solid and water-borne wastes has gone on largely unchecked and unabated.

So, although coastal control intentions are mostly admirable, they arise from negative experiences and agency neglect. Unfortunately many of these adverse practices are difficult to take away from individual site users and harvesters of marine resources. Established ports policies, discharge practices, and fish-farming projects are also difficult 'resource common' attitudes to thwart, issues on which local and regional agencies seek 'big picture' guidance and bulletin style recommendations from central government for 'tipping the balance'.

One clear coastal zone management task is to improve the level of public understanding about the littoral bio-zone and the levels of public awareness about corporeal and customary property rights and responsibilities. This involves moving out of interventionist regulation toward integrated management: to achieve through proactive conservancy with development, and education, the outcomes and effects which are socially intended.[29] The entropic results of coastal wear-down calls for the regulation of adverse human effects, generating formal plans and guidelines and an interactive management process which is locked into a public coastal policy guided by scientific prognosis and an educational awareness programme. This must, as noted earlier, be followed up with an educational-informational policy package which improves usage patterns and provides design guidelines.

Agriculture and forestry

Pastoral, horticultural and silvicultural land use practice on separately parcelled freeholds is a feature of the humanized open-area landscapes of the New World. The enclosure of what is now humanized rural landscape was the consequence of a remarkably swift land capture, followed by an also rapid evisceration of indigenous forests, grasslands and their fauna. The early settler emphasis was on lumber (timber) needs with occasional shelter-belt and erosion-control tree planting relieving the landscape's bleakness as well as providing stock shelter. This pattern contrasts with the rural landscapes of Europe which benefited from slower rates of enclosure, slower exotic plant infestation, and slower technological invasion. Monocrop business agriculture in settler societies – agribusiness – is a style of food and fibre production bound to wither as soils decline in quality. When agribusiness fights against nature it will, eventually, atrophy; and as soils salinate or dry out and erode, or blow clear away, agribusiness simply loses out.

Agriculture and Forestry figures largely in Chapters 9, 10 and 11 in the Hawken, Lovins, Lovins book *Natural Capitalism*, 1999 viz.
- 'Nature's Filaments'
- 'Food for Life'
- 'Aqueous Solutions'

Enlightened New World farmers and agricultural officials seek to establish a better balance with nature, one approach being to retire rough, desiccated, infested, nitrogen-polluted, salinated and depleted patches of land and remnant wetlands into protected reserves.[30] Some farmers covenant remnant areas of indigenous forest and bush land to their local authorities or the state, seeking and obtaining some land tax relief as an accessory benefit. Another approach is to convert lands exhausted to the margin of agricultural productivity to plantation forestry or agro-forestry. Farm forestry is well suited to rain-sufficient regions, particularly the less intensively cropped, steeper graded and poor-soil farmscapes and the more remote sub-regions. This is a conservation approach to sustainable management of the overall rural estate, also, but separately driven by its tourism-commercial potential. The character and some aspects of the aesthetics of agro-forestry is the face of a New Agriculture, to fit alongside New Urbanism.

'Plantation timber production is regarded negatively by large consumers in response to pressure from environmental groups. This has given rise to an accreditation process for confirming the sustainable management of forest production.'
Forest Stewardship Council www.fscus.org

Agro-forestry is a triple-braided longer-term (25–35-year initially, thereafter ongoing) activity. The three braids are *profitability*, *sustainability* and *aesthetics*. In the mind of the agro-forester these braids are not necessarily linked. But for the wider community the three come together as benefits for the economy, conservation of the resource base, and as an enhancement of the overall regional environment.

Profitability. The historically narrow and always significant context of profitability comes down to the managed competency of agricultural, forestry or agro-forestry production from a combination of tree-cropping and pastoralism horticulture, *and* over the intermediate term, to the sequestration of carbon dioxide. Few cropping and pastoral activities are ecologically sustainable, simply because intensive agriculture is not part of nature. Beyond this obvious truth it can be deduced that the more economically successful a conventional profit-seeking farmer is, the more removed that farmer's position from sustainable rural land-use practice is likely to be!

This is the general situation, alleviated at the city fringe through commercial opportunities to engage in vegetable, fruit, nursery and greenhouse sales. The urban foodbasket emphasis is a notable feature of French sustainable food production policies, resulting in a knock-on reduction of foodstuff haulage and storage. The usual pattern in the edge city situation is conventional urban sprawl; a best outcome is rural retention of all the 'good' to 'excellent' soils for fresh-food supply to the adjoining city.

There are several obstacles to agriculture, obstacles co-associated with problems of commercial viability. Resistance to change on the farmer's part can be identified, which has to be balanced against the awkward position of agriculturalists and pastoralists as price-takers rather than price-makers, leaving them out-of-pocket in good and bad seasons alike. Truth underscores the adage 'that it is impossible for farmers to go-for-green if they are always in-the-red'. Consequently, out in the rural heartland, there resides a 'right to farm' ethos, interpreted by landowners as a freedom of unbridled choice to either farm or do anything else which occurs to them as a survival option. There are three worst-case practices: the nutritional wear-down and exhaustion of 'mined and dessicated' soils; the creation of tracts of salinated surface soil as a consequence of raised water (tube-well) irrigation; and the hyper-enrichment of waterways resulting from excess applications of nitrogen fertilizer up to the margin of farm profit.[31]

Pinus *radiata* in the New World context is a fast-growing, largely disease-free and genetically adapted and improved species which has the currently assessed potential to produce (NZ context) a $60,000 (2002 value) crop after 25 years for each hectare of managed plantation forestry. Agro-forestry (also known as farm-forestry) implicates conjoint farming and forestry practice on an inter-cropping basis.

In the general, extensive case, an unsustainable and un-aesthetic utilization of rural lands amounts to widespread non-point pollution. This line of reasoning has little meaning or impact for cash-strapped farmer-freeholders unless they either back an alternative tourism-type activity on their own account, or sell on their 'rights to develop' to a larger land consortium or a state or local government agency which is prepared to use the land less intensively. The point and purpose of such intervention is to maintain open-area land-use viability. The purchase of development rights (PDR) procedure is contentious – although the cycle from patterns of private misuse to public intervention is the reward of the patient and long lived.[32]

A return to the presumption that most cropping and pastoral activities are fundamentally unsustainable leads to a consideration of the policies of Landcare, a favoured Australasian institutional means for providing technical advice to the rural sector. In this way the cropping, pastoral, plantation forestry and agro-forestry combinations can be linked with erosion control and ground water retention while arresting weed infestation and combating fertility decline. Two complications are: *on the one hand* misguided official intervention and direction in agriculture through the application of subsidies, price-controls and tax breaks: *on the other hand* ineffective land-use planning and conservancy guidance. This is changing. What is now coming through is weed and pest control, riparian edge protection, catchment and groundwater management; and a conservation of the remnant indigenous forest heritage, regulatory controls and the uptake of best practice advice. The ultimate remedy for exhausted lands involves the buying-in of development rights, or the use of 'transferable development rights' for acquiring irrevocably decimated rural properties as part of the conservation estate.[33]

Maclaren (1993: 51) holds that 'The common belief that pines cause soil deterioration is not supported by soil scientists who have worked on the topic. There is, indeed, good evidence for the opposite effect.'

Sustainability.   Rain-watered agro-forestry can arrest the 'mining' of dessicated and infested rural lands, decrease the salinity of water tables, enhance soil productivity, and of course produce some timber.

Plantation forestry on former grasslands reduces the rate of water run-off and evens out flood flows, and is generally held to *not* adversely affect overall stream-water quality. Indeed agro-forestry and plantation forestry offers hope for continuing the productiveness of otherwise marginal rural landscapes while also contributing to the capture of carbon dioxide. The wider intent with pastoralism and agro-forestry is to avoid the overcropping of lands of declining worth and utility. This is an issue of national, regional and local importance over the longer haul, involving the fashioning, over time, of a balanced land-use regime. In these terms it is a clear planning option to conjoin conservation *with* development. There is, however, a complexity in that the lead time for agro-forestry exceeds the ever-foreshortening lead time set for attaining planning objectives.

Although a stand-alone rural hectare suffers a scale diseconomy, there are economies in favour of plantations only 10 ha in extent. In other words small-scale 5 to 25 hectare forestry plantation lots are a profit-taking option for medium as well as large-scale farmers, and in these terms they are realistically practical for hobby farmers. By 2050, clear-felled supplies from the world's remaining indigenous forests will either be exhausted or be subject to effective logging bans, *yet* the demand for wood-fibre will increase within those Asian growth economies with landscapes unsuited to, or unavailable for, forestry. The summary view of profitability, considered in the context of sustainability, is that allowing for a discounting of the cost of capital for plantation ventures, plantation forestry and agro-forestry involves modest initial outlays, low annual-once-over maintenance, and eventually impressive wood-fibre production *and* income yields associated with the capture of carbon dioxide produced as a result of fossil fuel consumption. The planning challenge, and a conservation with development planning complexity, is one of incorporating this significant export base activity into the within-region sequential spiral (figure 4.1).

Aesthetics. The aesthetic context, relative to the tourism enterprise, introduces considerations of profiteering and culture-impact, also examined next in a tourism passage. Aesthetic contradictions abound. One view is that tract forests, particularly *pinus radiata*, are dark and satanic, which needs to be set against the counter-argument for soil retention and profitable productiveness. There is a further aesthetic and soil erosion complication in that at harvest time agro-forests in the New World are usually clear-felled (clear-cut), the contra-indication being to execute pre-planned area-felling (patchcuts), an adoption of the screening practices followed routinely at timber harvest time in the United Kingdom and Scandinavia. Pockets of patchcut felling during summer, fall or winter, affecting up to half an area to be ultimately harvested, facilitates avian and small animal survival, sustains the local microclimate, and can reduce soil erosion *provided* operational procedures are in place to ensure that the patchcutting principle is not scaled up to masquerade as clear-cutting in practice.

Cultural and aesthetic concerns are valid, and the adverse impacts can be ameliorated in four procedural ways. *First*, by a patterning of the inter-cropped trees with pasture and horticulture for rotational tree harvesting, thereby softening and lessening the impact of commercial forestry. *Second*, accepting that mono-silviculture for adequately rain-fed temperate climates can be visually relieved, pines being supplemented with blackwoods, indigenous tree regeneration, and Corsican pine inter-plantings, along with some macrocarpa, willow, eucalyptus and Mexican cypress as is locally appropriate. *Third*, ensuring that plantations are fitted into the local geomorphological structure, with the engagement of landscape planning advice which softens hilltop profiles and merges or contrasts the pastoral-silvicultural interface. *Fourth*, ensuring that log-harvesting impacts are pre-considered, pre-planned and abated by adopting patchcut practices, and that harvesting is followed through with a 'clean-up green-up' regeneration and replanting programme. The overall objective is to maintain viable farm-sized agricultural units taxed at rural rates, rural-only zoned to ensure exclusive farming, and to inhibit non-farmbuilding activity on a non-variance basis.[34]

These observations on agricultural and forestry profile concerns about the longer-term absence of viability for mono-agriculture, and embody a pragmatic sustainable intent for 'agriculture with forestry' and various other mixed-farm combinations involving viticulture, horticulture and orcharding.

The dominant emphasis in this passage has been with the physical aspects of agriculture and forestry. Insights into the social needs of rural communities is provided by Jean Richardson, *Partnerships in Communities*, 2000.

Tourism

Tourism has an impact upon urban services, accommodation, and the built heritage as well as the open-area landscapes and waterscapes. It is a major economic

'TRAVEL AND
TOURISM. . . .
Is the World's largest
industry.
Employs 127 million
people. Accounts for 13
per cent of consumer
spending.' Will double
over the next decade.
         World Travel and
         Tourism Council.

'Artificialized
management has. . . .
paid dividends to one
citizen out of capital
stock belonging to all.'
     Aldo Leopold, *A Sand
     County Almanac*, 1949.

Tourism, by reason of
the inter-connectedness
of widely dispersed yet
co-related sites and
activities, can be usefully
reviewed in terms of the
practice procedures
detailed earlier in this
chapter: namely,
Multiplier Principles and
the passage on Risk
Assessment and Risk
Management.

Urry writes about the
infrangible, intrusive,
contrived, artificial,
unnecessary and trivial
character of tourism.
J. Urry, *The Tourist Gaze*,
2002.
See also *Flight to the Sun*.
Bray and Raitz, 2001

and selective land-use activity within all Anglo settler societies and most OECD nations. It has become an economic growth leviathan, which often neglects its conservancy origins. It is an activity prone to boosterism and 'boom and bust' vagaries. It is profusely written about. Tourism has emerged as the most diverse unruly and complex subnational planning policy process of all, because it implicates non-governmental organizations, local as well as central government, the private sector, those who own the tourism attractions and events, and of course the tourists themselves as consumers.

By broad definition (Mathieson and Wall 1982) tourism is 'the temporary movement of people (including business people) to destinations outside their normal places of work and residence, the activities undertaken during their stay in those destinations and the facilities created to cater to their needs'. The interdependence and interpenetration this gives rise to is introduced in a three-part dragram: figure 4.6, **Tourism industry: a construct** – depicting the structure of the tourism industry, demand and supply factors, and the effects of tourism.

Interdisciplinary professionalism and socio-cultural diversification is implicated and interwoven with tourism. The salient point to make, which has implications for all those who would plan for this industry, is that there is no single output; instead there is a variegated, ever-continuing provisioning and throughput. Clearly identified are the transportation, accommodation and victualling services; yet these do not comprise a 'tourism product'. The output product includes tourism attractions and events, imparted information, transportation accommodation and victualling; and the most important output of all, tourist satisfaction.

The *physical impacts* within settler societies can be identified directly from an abrasive clutch of motorized transportation modes: including, in addition to the usual cars, buses, trains, planes and ships, an array of helicopters, hydrofoils, jet boats, jet bikes, balloons, four-wheel-drive vehicles, trail bikes and motor skis. Noteworthy is their direct physical impact – as a conduit for the introduction of water-borne pests and diseases, destruction of flora and fauna, litter discards, sewage disposal, and vandalism. The *socio-cultural impacts* can be identified at destinations where visitor-visited contact occurs, particularly when indigenous first peoples are engaged commercially to provide entertainment in a context which commodifies and parodies their cultural heritage and debases the individuals involved. Tourist attendance at cultural celebrations and religious events, and their use of local recreational facilities (intensive as well as extensive) can degrade both the local people's facilities as well as the visitor's sense of welcome.

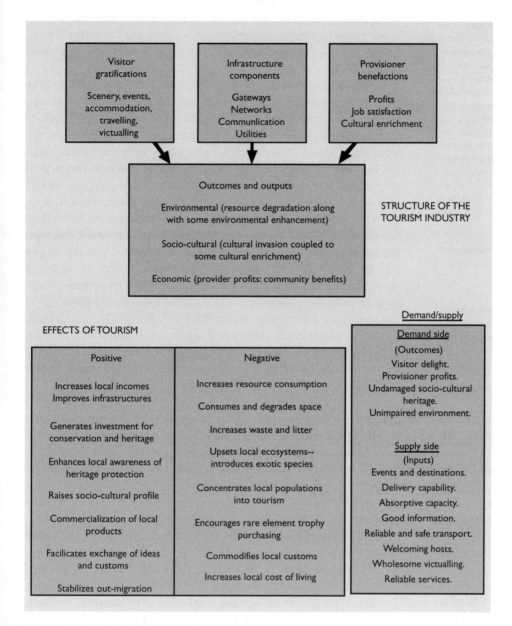

Figure 4.6 Tourism industry: a construct
Source: based on UNESCO *Environmental Education Dossier*, 15, 1994.

To these specific physical and socio-cultural interactions can be attached the wider all-public, all-services, all-infrastructural usage of utilities, enjoyment of the landscape, and input from several levels of government and business. There is a connection to the Hardin (1968) 'Tragedy of the Commons' maxim which predicates a wear-down of the very scenic and cultural ambience the tourists have come to join and enjoy. This wear-down of a landscape's enjoyability is usually

The overhead *gondola* has not been included in the listing of transport. With careful placement to ameliorate visual impact and meticulously controlled site construction, this conveyance mode has the potential to mass-transport sightseeing tourists through and in close proximity to a spectacular landscape with controlled impact.

Intensive: Playing fields, courts, public pools, public golf courses.

Extensive: parks, waterspaces, public woodlands, national parks, public reserves.

attributed to visitors; yet not to be overlooked are the likes of third-party commercial signage, put up in the countryside the tourist have paid to come and enjoy, by members of the host community!

In order to win-win with tourism one predication is that there must be everlasting growth-on-growth for the providers *and* continuing satisfaction-upon-satisfaction for the tourist participants. The implications are economically, socially and environmentally significant. On all three counts the impacts are intimidating, particularly for the most rapidly growing tourist-receiving regions of the world: South-Eastern Asia, the western US–Canada region, and Oceania–Australasia. Arrivals for this latter region have grown from 1 per cent of all international movements in 1960, to 3 per cent in 1970, 7 per cent in 1980 and 11 per cent by 1990, with the aggregate volume of this trend set to continue toward 15 per cent by 2010.[35] Two interconnected points to register are *first* that there is a marked degree of tourism market interpenetration into nations from their neighbours and, in the transpacific New World context, from other parts of the Pacific Rim; *second*, that growth in visitor numbers is dependent upon industrial and commercial prosperity at home (Japan, South Korea, Taiwan, China, Singapore relative to North America and Australasia) *and* continued visitor satisfaction.

Qualitative targets have a tendency to go awry within the tourism industry, markedly so when the number of annual visitors reaches or exceeds double that of the overall population size of the region being visited – with 'spot' attractions of the Niagara Falls kind excepted. Environmental impacts can be mitigated and diluted to some extent by a channelling and diversion of tourists towards new gateways and alternative destinations; but the onslaught of numbers eventually impacts adversely upon the destinations and events selected. The socio-cultural impact, unless carefully factored as an acceptable risk, is prone to introduce complications.

Visitor demand expectation is there to be met, not only through a planned supply-side provisioning of 'guidance transportation accommodation and victualling services' but also through the mitigation of adverse environmental impacts and the amelioration of sociocultural conflicts. Inbound (from offshore) tourist numbers per annum, when boosted to the equivalent size of the receiving state or provincial population, puts that region into a situation of tourism dependency, and induces a satiation which gives rise to socio-cultural conflict arising, particularly, on account of the intensive servicing demands of the industry. These overloads can also occur within free-access National Park and Reserves landscapes. These are some of the conflicts. In contrast, market force response mechanisms work well to meet transportation, accommodation and victualling demands.

Flagging the complications ahead for a growth-on-growth compounding increase in tourism indicates the need to backtrack into patterns and characteristics which can switch with little warning from a progressive to a regressive synergy. Although remarkable in its consistency of growth after 1965 the tourism industry, above all others, relies on economic growth offshore and tranquillity and security onshore – both sets of factor notoriously prone to change. On the *positive side* the basic multiplier benefits and knock-on increases in jobs are broadly beneficial and bring forward infrastructure and construction programmes of utility to the general population. On the *negative side* are significant fiscal leakages, such as taxes avoided through the use of pre-paid expenditure vouchers issued in the country of origin, degradation of the natural environment being visited, adverse socio-cultural impacts, and the inflationary effect of tourism on local residents.

1968 – Easter island. Soon after the completion of the international runway I visited this outpost of Eastern Polynesia with my family. Never before, or since so starkly have I personally realized and been able to foretell the awesome overwhelming impact of visitors upon hosts.

Expressed here as 'positive' and 'negative', a useful way to come to terms with the complexity of tourism enablement is to assess it with a parallel demand side and supply side analysis (figure 4.6). Of concern is the extent to which tourism growth expands in a largely unplanned, unstructured and uncoordinated way. Unbridled growth imposes itself upon regions with little understanding of the actual form and character of growth it would be actually desirable and acceptable to encourage. As examples: contrast package holidays which are short-stay and culturally compartmentalized, with backpacker-style visits which are individually organized, of longer duration and culturally well absorbed. Clearly much needs to be understood about demand side and supply side effects, and to determine via Risk Impact Assessment (box 4.5) the benefits and disbenefits to the providers and recipients.

The *demand side* to the tourism encounter is characterized by a two-part division. In one division there are within-nation sightseers, recreation seekers and visitors to friends and relatives; and in the other stranger-visitor sightseers and recreation seekers. These coexist as a mixture of pleasure-seeking, culture-relating, sun-seeking, photograph and video-recording, shopping, relationship-seeking, and nostalgia-reinforcing humanity. Many may achieve little more than a burnt skin, a depleted pocketbook and an upset stomach – along with some supposed enhancement of their home and workplace status. Yet their 'demand', however explicit or implicit, is that they experience cultural and also natural 'delights' which markedly contrast with those at home, and within a hoped-for context of conviviality, personal security, freedom of movement and ease of transportation. The initial challenge is to head off the bad experiences; but equally significant is the need to even out the peak-season and off-season demand side flows, and to achieve dispersal away from spot-specific attractions.

The *supply side* to the encounter centres, foremost, on the components of attraction; which at base comes down to natural phenomena, cultural events, pristine environments and the receptiveness of local communities. Attraction may take the form of an escape from northern or southern chills and picking up some sunshine while crashing out with relatives in southern or northern suburbia, which, although lacking in fiscal intensity, is bone fide tourism activity.

The challenge to tourism planning is to fit supply side provisioning and profit-taking to the demand side challenge; achieving customer satisfaction, and the avoidance of host community irritation, ensuring that the cultural environment is left unadulterated and the natural environment unimpaired. A wider objective is to implicate indirect beneficiaries (the general public) in an experience which is profitable to all. In the best outcome circumstance the customer obtains value for money and furnishes the provider with profits, while also enriching the cultural heritage both ways and improving levels of local access and visitor enjoyment.

Relative to high-volume mass-yield tourism, consult *Tourism: Principles, Practices, Philosophies*. Goeldner and Ritchie, 2002.

Enrichment of the cultural base for a receiving culture arises as a consequence of cross-cultural sharing and mixing – a both-ways shared exchange.[36] Conservation and enhancement of the natural resource base can arise from the installation of an improved infrastructure, landscape restoration, and the protection of flora and fauna.

SUBTLE MECHANICS
During the late 1960s–early 1970s the long-stay presence of cash-strapped, 'flower power' visitors to Nepal led the government to accept 'team' recommendations to hugely increase the cost of visitor visas, limit free movement to the Vale of Katmandu, and for government to own a large part of the hotel and the air transport services. The upshot for that decade: effective control of both tourist numbers, quality and profits.

Tourism encounters within the tourism-as-industry context are elective encounters. Tourism needs to be understood as a take-it-or-leave-it industry which can, and ought to be, subject to deft quota control by the owner-stakeholders. The extent to which the general population is predisposed or ill-disposed to accept and participate in the tourism encounter is a matter of contact concern to the visitor as consumer. The aspirations and attitudes of the 'hosts' can be manipulated, channelled, and factored in. The number of tourists (tourist-stay units) is the quantifiable element in the equation, giving rise to socio-cultural differences to reconcile and physical impacts to ameliorate. And it is because of these needs for amelioration and mitigation that attention needs to be focused upon absorptive criteria, the retention of intrinsic socio-cultural host worth, preservation of the cultural heritage, and conservation of the environment.

The 'absorptive' factor is significant in sparsely populated regions offering high levels of scenic attraction, where the amount of tax-bearing land is probably low. In this circumstance private-sector providers do well; but the infrastructure providers (local government and tourism agency) face funding difficulties. This leads inevitably to poor road maintenance, failed infrastructure, and serious mishaps. In this context tourism enablement has to be centrally assisted to avoid claims for damage against utility providers. At base the first need is for a sound estimation of demand, backed up with *either* a control on visitor numbers *or* the provision of amenities and utilities funding sufficient to keep ahead of that demand and meet the cost of mitigating visitor damage.

Calling into operation a 'dispersal' strategy creates little difficulty for the provision of accommodation for increased numbers of tourists, and, or also, for the management of increased tourism impacts. What is more challenging, and requires greater care and preparation, is the mitigation of strains on host conviviality, avoiding debasement of the host religious sporting and cultural ethos, ameliorating host denial of access to their own environmental hegemony, and a diplomatic handling of visitor offences whether these take the form of cultural, colonialist, unacceptable dress (undress!) behaviour, or what might be described as flashy fiscal ignorance and arrogance. The absorptive capacity of an overall physical landscape is enormous, whereas the absorptive capacity of any given spot attraction or community has discernible limitations.

An 'Index of Tourism Invitation' via Mathieson and Wall (1982 – connecting with Doxey's 'Irridex Model' 1975) categorizes four levels of social absorptive capacity, ranging from 'euphoria' through to 'apathy', 'irritation' and 'antagonism'. These conditions arise as a consequence of local community perceptions about social (cultural) and environmental loss and degradation. This potential for conflict can lead to a decline in tourist receipts, which lends emphasis to such matters as tourism number-balance, activity-harmony, and conservancy-development addressed within a quota framework.

Sustainable tourism specifics   A generic yet misleading label assigned to sustainable tourism activity is eco-tourism. This can be misleading because eco-tourism is seldom solely ecological, although it can approximate local sustainability. Sustainable tourism is a style of nature-based encounter which seeks to achieve host gain, some social enrichment both ways, and a conservation of the cultural and natural heritage. What sustainable tourism comes down to is environmental and cultural resource 'invasion' of an intensity which can be tolerated and managed without adverse effects. This must be organized in a manner which generates economic gain, yet impacts benignly upon the socio-cultural scene and the natural-heritage landscape.

> Urry (2002) identifies a 'shift from "old tourism" which involved packaging and standardisation, to "new tourism" which is segmented, flexible and customised.'
>
> See also *New Tourism* by Roger Bray and Vladimir Raitz, 2001.

A general connotation is that eco-tourism is environmentally friendly – sometimes indicated by it being styled as nature-based tourism – which it is certainly intended to be, although there are other dispersal, small-scale and pace-reducing factors which extend benefits from this style of tourism into the wider community and the general economy. The contrast between hard and soft tourism has been represented by Krippendorf (1982) along the lines re-expressed in figure 4.7 as **Hard tourism and soft tourism**.

There is also a need on the Demand Side for eco-tourism encounters of the sustainable kind to be small-scale, diversified, humanized, stimulating, physically challenging and above all within the absorptive capacity of the culture and environment being visited.[37] This is a topic aired in the Richard Voase text (1995) *Tourism: The Human Perspective*. The provider sets out to create nature-based attractions and culture-generated events which are experiential and enriching, even

Hard (enclave) tourism	Soft (benign) tourism
Aggressive (hard sell)	Cautious (soft sell)
Unchecked	Controlled
Overcomes environment	Fits into environment
About 'branding'	About 'ethos'
Large volumes	Small groups
Location-specific	Area-dispersed
International styling	Vernacular-styled
Corporate ownership	Local ownership
Menial local jobs	Skills-enhancing
Agency-driven	Community motivated
Sector-based	Entirety-predicated
Price-conscious	Value-conscious
Quantitative	Qualitative

Figure 4.7 Hard tourism and soft tourism

though this may be in a manner which proves physically uncomfortable and sometimes disquieting to visitors.

Where 'hard' formulaic tourism is often adversely synergistic, eco-tourism strives to be beneficially symbiotic. The challenge to tourism generally, and nature-based sustainable tourism directly, is a matter of responding to the following trinity (a summation by Voase 1995): '*First to recognise* that tourism benefits (to the tourists) are largely psychological – in the mind of the beholder: *Second* that the attractiveness of the tourism experience is determined by the culture and mores of the society which generates and provides it: *Third* that the competitive advantage in servicing the tourist consumer . . . will be gained by an instinctive passion for service.' Clearly 'tourism as place' (the earlier pattern of Old World holidaying) has evolved toward 'tourism as people', indeed as people-and-place, very much *with* local inhabitants *within their* living environment and on a sustainable-conservancy basis.

'Adverse' in the context, for example, of commercial formula Casino development which induces negative add-on recreational services (drug supply and prostitution) a pattern which then seeps into the host environment. 'Symbiotic' in the context, for example, of the limited-cost-small-return, yet widespread, homestay cultural vacationing.

The context of commercial formula 'hard' tourism (fixed itineraries, rapid transport, replicated accommodations) is exemplified by the 'packaged tour' experience. Tourism of this kind is bound to be often disappointing and unrewarding and to degrade the sites of concentration visited, eventually declining toward economic stagnation for the supply-side providers.

Nature-based tourists are prepared to put up with some hardship, even danger; also to pay more, and be basically victualled and considerably inconvenienced for that privilege!

Comparably, in the context of 'soft' eco-tourism, there is a green-politics preservation and a woolly-cardigan emphasis of the 'leave only footprints, take only photographs' kind, which needs to be understood in terms of customer and community satisfaction. Aldo Leopold (1949) evoked the following scenario: 'A piece of scenery snapped by a dozen tourism cameras daily is not physically impaired thereby . . . The camera industry (being) one of the few innocuous parameters on wild nature.' The main emphasis, and a reliable key-phrase for depicting contextually sound eco-tourism, is *authenticity of experience*. New frontier big-heartedness, spatial openness, open area access, first-peoples cultural traditions, these are all part of that authenticity which constitutes socially, environmentally and culturally acceptable (triple balanced) tourism. Whether it be styled with some inaccuracy as 'eco-tourism' or with some sense of Frontierism as 'adventure tourism' this nature-based experience can be identified as a preferred alternative to mass tourism. Most nations can contemplate a sorter-gate situation by which the tourism 'herd' can be channelled according to their sophistication and their wallets, upholding host concerns to reduce social and environmental impacts, with discerning sectors diverted to environmentally harmonious and socially low-impact, yet economically longer-term, eco-tourism options, notably a host choice put in place on a sustainable basis.

Above all else, as a broker would advise any risk punter, tourism is a fickle industry where speculators will suffer when the market falls and if there is a lack of diversification. It is also an industry where a 'getting it right as it grows' incremental expansion is important.

To the extent that there exists host-policy choice, there remains the situation, broached earlier, for consideration of absorptive limits relative to the amount of quantitative and qualitative impact that the receiving community is able to accept. The quantitative extent of these tourism encounters can be controlled, for the industry is indeed a both-ways elective. Cowgirl and cowboy operators, in solely for the profit can, in accordance with Hardin's resource commons dicta (1968) competitively wear down natural landscapes and debase cultural environments as though they were resource commons for competitive consumption. The profit motive predicates that benign hiking within the public conservation estate gives way to pony trekking, to trail biking and four-wheel drive excursions, and that activities such as river rafting along a nationally treasured waterway can be undone by jet boating. The point to keep in view is that the landscape and cultural contexts are of the public realm (especially so in National Parks, coastal fringes and scenic reserves, including their airspace) and should be subject to public policy rules, quota controls and regulation. The bottom line is that the community is the base-owner and potential regulator.

Aldo Leopold writing in *A Sand County Almanac* (1949) on 'symbols and tokens'.
'All these things rest upon the idea of *trophy* . . . a birds egg, a mess of trout, a basket of mushrooms, the photograph of a bear, the pressed specimen of a flower, or the note tucked into the cairn on a mountain peak is a *certificate*. It attests that its owner has been somewhere and done something.'

1960 Vivid memory. Climbed the then uncharted Mt Hopeless, at the northern end of the Southern Alps, my companion and I seeking a 'first' ascent. The summit, a large remaindered boulder, had a little cairn on top, under which was a tobacco tin containing a list of five names!

I was drawn into a tourism development *with* conservation operation first hand, during the course of a Dal Lakes (Kashmir) project, published as 'How To Justify Conservation in a Developing Country'. The adoption of eco-tourist principles provided an environmental foil against cultural asset-stripping and resource despoilation. The debasements and blights of 'hard' formula tourism were supplanted by a 'soft', yet also commercially viable eco-tourism, which included the sale of local handicrafts.

The Kashmir project generated two interesting disclosures. *First*, that the then (1985) sheer number of visitors to the Dal Lakes (0.3 million p.a.) wore down, fouled up and degraded the attraction. *Second*, that the economically significant foreign visitor component (40,000 persons) within the one-third million aggregate, were of 'basic' economic significance to both the tourism and the handicraft sectors.

Ecotourism Policy, Fennell and Dowling (eds), 2002.

Tourism is an industry where the prime attractions and some events are owned by the host nation, *not usually* by the commercial providers. The point here is that tourism, both quantitative and qualitative, is within public policy control. This gives rise, in regional conservation and development planning contexts, to a recognition that tourism encounters should *not* be left to the cannibalistic vagaries of the free market. We know the 'consumers are there', the imperative control factor being that the 'resource in question' is *owned* by the state, the region, and the community in combination as a limited supply asset. Obtaining growth and jobs from the tourism resource is centred on a finite resource. Tourism resource management, in line with other resource allocation quota can and should be planned and managed by the government, local authority, first peoples and NGO agencies as partners, and not directly led or initiated by tourism provisioners.

The general aim is management in a way which secures sustainable (return) tourism, sustainable (continuing) tourism, and socially sustainable (low host-impact with host-gain) tourism. Negotiating these visitor and host satisfactions is largely a matter of moderating unbridled narrow-sector 'growth' away from prime locations toward geographically dispersed regional alternatives, all of which is clever and neomodernist on account of its sustainable character and outcome.

Planning policies for the sustainable-in-spirit and authentic-in-experience tourism format leads to the identification of other planning objectives, which include:

- Legibility and 'sense of place' so that by means of information and signage tourists are always aware of where they are at; and
- Security of design at places and along routes which tourists use.
- Variety of options and a capability of these being connected to alternative tourism-as-discovery experiences.
- Permeability which enables tourists to disperse in search of variety knowing or feeling that they are secure wherever they are.

Unplanned and under-regulated tourism expansion, with little thought or heed for the wellbeing of the actual environment, the actual heritage, the actual communities being visited, or indeed the actual tourist's enjoyment, will wear down the very attractions on which the industry is predicated. The essentially physical and planable objectives are design components to lay over the delivery of an authentic experience (also consult David Weaver, *Ecotourism*, 2002). The collective considerations are depicted in box 4.8 as **Sustainable tourism policies**.

Box 4.8 Sustainable tourism policies

Government input: central, regional and local

The aim overall is to ensure that national regional and local tourism development agreements highlight sustainable tourism development policies and practices. Such an emphasis calls upon government agencies to select a societally appropriate balance between mass tourism and eco-tourism in accordance with the following principles.

1 Ensure that national and local tourism development agreements highlight a policy of sustainable tourism development, based on locality-specific as well as sector-specific assessments of the environmental and cultural tourism assets.
2 Ensure that all those involved in tourism at central regional and local levels of government are briefed on the concept of sustainability.
3 Ensure that aggregate tourist visitor days at destinations are well within absorptive capacities.
4 Establish educational-awareness programmes to connect people to sustainable tourism.
5 Support lower levels of government (subsidiarity) to develop their own sustainable tourism development strategies and conservation strategies and include tourism in the regional and local land-use planning process, *and* elaborate design and construction standards which will ensure that tourism development projects are safe and sympathetic in relation to local culture and the natural environment.
6 Enforce regulations to control illegal trade in historic objects and crafts; regulate against unofficial archaeological activities; prevent the erosion of aesthetic values and desecration of sacred sites; regulate and control tourism in environmentally and culturally sensitive localities.

And, where appropriate, also to:

7 Support the elaboration of economic models to define appropriate levels of economic activity for the natural and humanized areas visited by tourists.
8 Develop standards and regulations for environmental and also cultural impact avoidance, alleviation and mitigation.
9 Apply sectoral environmental-economic indicators and accounting systems for the tourism industry, including procedures for conducting the assessment monitoring and auditing of tourism projects.

10 Engage tourism advisory boards in public consultation in order to involve all stakeholders, including NGOs.
11 Develop tools and techniques to analyse the effects of tourism development projects on heritage sites and ancient monuments as an integral part of cultural and environmental impact assessment.
12 Ensure that tourism interests are represented at major caucus planning meetings that affect the society the environment and the economy.

NGO inputs

Non-government organizations (NGOs) represent and promote the interests of their community. They also have access to local information, expertise and labour.

1 NGOs are to be represented on tourism advisory boards at all practical levels of government and industry to provide input into tourism planning and development. This includes involvement in regional as well as site-specific development plans and the planning of appropriate land uses.
2 NGOs are to be engaged to seek local support for achieving socially appropriate tourism development as well as opposing inappropriate tourism development.
3 NGOs are to be encouraged to promote the use of local residents to assist in tourism research and data collection.
4 NGOs are to be involved in public education, highlighting the economic, social, and environmental significance of tourism development.
5 NGOs are to be encouraged to identify and communicate with regional and local agencies on issues related to tourism as well as providing an NGO viewpoint on solutions to problems.

Tourism industry inputs

The private sector is largely responsible for delivering products and services to the tourist as consumer. In this regard it is imperative that the industry 'players' support socio-environmental tourism development through the following actions:

1 Sustain the use of resources by ensuring a lasting openness of access to land, water, forests and the atmosphere.

BOX 4.8 *Continued*

2   Reduce and dispose of wastes by recycling, reusing, and reducing wherever possible and by having high standards for sewage treatment, waste collection and disposal.
3   Adopt energy-efficiency practices by maximizing the use of solar power, wind power and hydropower; and energy conservation.
4   Minimize environmental risks by minimizing environmental and health risks (e.g. avoiding hazardous locations, sensitive wildlife areas, unique features, fragile sites).
5   Undertake green marketing by promoting 'soft' tourism that minimizes adverse environmental and cultural impacts as well as informing tourists of the cultural impact of their presence.
6   Mititigate damage by replacing or restoring degraded environments and compensating for locally adverse effects – the 'polluter pays principle'.
7   Provide credible information to tourists by disclosing hazardous locations, and situations of potential cultural conflict.
8   Incorporate environmental values in management by ensuring environmental representation at the executive level in tourism provider-management groups.
9   Undertake and participate in an objective assessment of the social and economic effects and environmental change arising from tourism.

Tourist as end-user guidelines

As the ultimate user of the physical and cultural environment it is important that tourists be educated to undertake visitor activities in ways which support sustainable tourism. In this regard, their behaviour should be focused toward:

1   Choosing operators which have a reputation for being ethically sound and environmentally responsible.
2   Learning about – and being given information on – the human and natural heritage of the host communities, including the geography, history, customs and current local concerns.
3   Travelling in a culturally and environmentally sensitive manner, refraining from behaviours which negatively affect the host community or degrades the local natural environment. For example: carefully disposing of personal rubbish and wastes, conserving water and energy, consuming local food and drink, respecting local flora fauna and artifacts, purchasing locally made souvenirs; walking, canoeing and cycling.
4   Refraining from the purchase or use of those products, and means of transportation, which endanger the local ecology and culture, including the use of minimal-impact travel modes and adhering environmental regulations in natural areas and in culturally sensitive contexts.
5   Supporting official heritage conservation activities.

Based around the 'Globe 90' recommendations *Action Strategy for Sustainable Development*.

Additional reference source: *Dictionary of Travel Tourism and Hospitality*, S. Medlik, 2002.

SUSTAINABLE TOURISM
Local transportation
Locally produced food
Local 'home-stays'
Some participation
with
food and fibre
production.
Purchase of local
handicrafts
Photo-taking: footprint-
leaving

Sustainable tourism is about local people, local economics, local cultural and celebratory events, and the local environment. Indeed sustainable tourism is an enhancement to local wellbeing and local identity. The box 4.8 recommendations advocate a behind-the-scenes level of control at all levels of government; participatory input from NGOs; sustainable product and services inputs from the tourism industry itself; and a set of tourist-as-end-user responsibilities. The challenge is to trade away from volumetric 'spot tourism' in the direction of tourism which is based on an 'extensive' carrying capacity; working for scenic and event exposure which a host community can absorb *without* physical impairment of the attraction itself, and without adverse social degradation.

My cautionary end-piece 'rule of thumb' commentary is that annual offshore visitor numbers to a region of attraction should trigger defence strategies when the number of visitors considerably exceeds local population numbers, allowing that shorter or longer duration of stay, and visits to 'spot' attractions of the Niagara, Fiordland, Banff, Ayres Rock kind leads to management of visitor numbers well in excess of that figure. A supplementary concern can also be expressed when receipts from the tourism venture become more significant than the combined receipts from rest-of-region primary production. What can be described as dependency tourism is not able to provide economic coverage during inevitable periods of adverse trading health scares, climatic chaos, unruly conflict, terrorism or economic downturn. On the other hand, sustainable-in-spirit, socially acceptable, authentic-experience tourism has a degree of fiscal substantiality, induces social wellbeing, and enhances environmental conservation. This model, with its emphasis on expansion of the basic-export sector, is available over the longer-haul for multiplier employment and income generation.

Unemployment alleviation

Increasing the proportion of employed persons in a state, provincial or regional population is the major challenge to growth pattern management. It is achieved by 'somehow' increasing the proportion of the employable population engaged in gainful employment, which also includes those packaged into job experience schemes, and those engaged in marginally legal and maybe illegitimate projects. Claiming that unemployment is solely a national or a local matter does little to alleviate a problem which is of vital concern to urban-with-rural regions.

The eradication of unemployment is clearly not part of any realistic agenda, but project generation in line with the guidelines provided in the earlier Project Propagation passage (buttress, betterment, discovery) are available options, *along with* a consideration of adjustments to work durations and patterns. The direct job-generation prospects associated with low capital cost per job place for agricultural, forestry and tourism activities are other policy options. Reductions in the number of hours and days in the working week, also job-sharing and pragmatic job-generation, offers other prospects for enlarging upon employment options. Furthermore, mindful of the significance of basic-export multiplier benefits (figure 4.1: Multiple spiral for development) there arises a case for exercising export choice preferences for job promotion. This passage reviews the alleviation options which radiate out from those multiplier recommendations.

The most regionally significant yield of social wellbeing is that which arises from secure employment, not only as individual levels of disposable income, but also in terms of mana and self-respect. Subjectively, fuller employment is a major regional objec-

In the Northland region of New Zealand, where I live, cannibis-growing is often claimed to be the region's most economically significant product. There are advocates claiming much for the economic support and employment this provides to the otherwise jobless; on the other hand, there has been created in the eyes of other beholders, a substance-producing and guilt-ridden sub-culture.

tive, yet from the International Labour Office (Mayer) 'no regional development theory has been developed specifically with employment in mind'. Of course the social sciences supply a range of modelling instruments. But the ILO view is that 'employment specialists have in fact come up with very few analytical tools of their own'. The end result is levels of unemployment largely aligned with the job immobility of those on lower incomes and of lesser skill.

The corrections applied in OECD economies range from direct assistance for economically depressed regions, through to the introduction of welfare and social projects, right on down to almost nothing! The policy instruments put forward, often from an attitude of faith rather than conviction, stress the need for good forward and backward linkages, growth pole strategies, improvement of regional infrastructure, and employability-enskilling job-creation and starter-project schemes, all of which (excepting most growth pole strategies) cannot be gainsaid. Yet where are the 'real' jobs? Who might be the development or conservancy partners? What might be the development and conservancy alternatives? What are the potential regional cooperative venture initiatives?

Given that unemployment alleviation is the bottom line indicator of regional progress what, subject-specifically, are the top-down employment policies (additional to project generation) which are relevant and applicable? Bairoch (1988) invokes an implicit advantage in terms of the proportions employed in cities of the 300,000 to one million size-scale, although as a policy emphasis this constitutes little more than academic trivia for regional practitioners working in the service of already larger cities. More practically, regional administrators can work to strengthen forward and backward linkages, specifically between the rural periphery and the urban heartland, and from settlement to settlement, and for connecting development to conservancy projects.

There are some specific policies for priming and supporting enterprises which generate employment inducing linkages. Small-enterprise development and conservancy projects tie in with a 'mobilization' reasoning where for Maillat (1988) 'each job fulfils a function: it can provide stability, it can act as a springboard, or it can offer flexibility'. Co-related reasoning, connecting into enterprise mobility, invokes an emphasis on skill-portability rather than job-specific enskilling. Another ILO official, Lothar Richter, lays emphasis on the role of 'key informants' advising a 'recognition of the fact that there are many persons – business[people], farmers, officials, teachers in every country who, by virtue of their occupations, responsibilities and interests, possesses a wide knowledge of manpower and employment patterns and trends'.

At the softer informal scale the 'green economy' approach involves unemployed people exchanging goods and skills, possibly on a 'green exchange dollar' basis. More formally it involves official endorsement and some cash input to low-cost capitalization business start-ups.

Comment on employment alleviation needs to include the observation that within most OECD nations the traditional major sources of employment in primary production industries, like agriculture, have become streamlined and technologically refined – with considerable and permanent reductions in the numbers employed within those sectors. Of course growth in tourism, neo-technology service industries and agro-forestry will redress the imbalance to some extent – but a visibly long-term, permanently unemployed vector has become an established reality.

Conservative doctrines have often marginalized a proportion of the employable population to a near-permanent state of unrelieved despair. Libertarians would help a proportion of such chronically unemployed into a condition of self-determination through their individual exercise of enterprise and self-reliance. The importance, indeed the economic significance, of the green-economy initiatives (also known as the twin-economy approach) goes beyond the jobs which are created; it is a kind of inheritance which can induce commodity exchange, cash circulation, add economic value *and* boost human confidence.

The local-community, and household-individual, constructs given in the **Matrix** (box 3.7, previous chapter, along with the 'soft pathways' reasoning given in box 3.4) indicate some of the initiatives which can reduce household expenditure, produce household income, enhance individual satisfaction, and induce confidence and respect. Not, of course, that local employment initiatives compare with conventional job creation, or indeed does little more than dent the unemployed profile; yet these initiatives have a role in the context of the growth pattern problematic. In the absence of full formal employment, and in the context of continuing unemployment, any community-supported 'legal' job generation – whether in the formal sector or the informal sector – represents an economic good.

'Living Lightly' enthusiasts are mainly rural lifestylers who 'downshift' the conventional emphasis on employment; putting an 'upshift' emphasis on local exchange trading, co-housing and permaculture.
In regions of chronic unemployment this sectional concept has a clear function and a useful role.

Waste disposal management

A Maoist aphorism has it that the creation of waste – product residue for which no further use can be identified – reflects societal failure. Up until World War II ordinary settler society families did indeed practice frugality, handing down and extending the life usage of household items and clothing. But after World War II, consumer packaging and consumer durables got bound in with the business-smart practice of programmed obsolescence, which went on to became a significant part of modern economic 'success'. And as the ever-growing trash mountains and waterway waste loadings illustrate, Anglo settler society nations have not yet found a broadly effective way to 'recover, recycle and reuse' waste, let alone 'reduce' its production. The answer lies mainly in 're-education', and 'resistance' (desistance) to the generation of waste. Partly this can be achieved by giving some effect to the broadly acceptable tenets of 'green' policies. Consumers wish to be enlightened about packaging as a cost-burden and about waste excesses they can avoid, and want information about the purchase of consumer durables that will last and which can be home-serviced. Capitalism will not be threatened by more efficient waste disposal management practices; yet it can indeed be joined to the cause of waste reduction.

'Because economic consumption doesn't create or destroy matter but only changes its location form and value, the same tonnages that were mined from the ground as resources, treated, transported, made into goods, and distributed to customers are then hauled away again as waste or emitted as pollution.'
    Paul Hawken, Amory Lovins, Hunter Lovins, *Natural Capitalism*, 1999

Lean Thinking, James Womack and Daniel Jones, 1996

Waste disposal management is a conceptually simple yet challenging item within the overall regulative pattern. It is a matter not only of common sense and pragmatism, but also cleverness. The context is set by pollution and discard output, particularly for urban dwellers. In those terms pollution and discard are conscious and adjustable human actions. Control over these activities is also a co-component of growth management strategy for both urban and rural development with conservancy; especially so for rural areas and for water tracts in terms of impact, because these open spaces are the 'sink' for pretty well all urban waste. Urban sustainability, by even the most convoluted ascription, is an impossibility, yet it remains a legitimate ambition. Certainly urban-with-rural conservation *with* development is something to be striven for.

It is necessary to have a basic understanding of the distinction between the two main disposal–dispersal activities and the various levels of assumed responsibility for waste-handling activities. A 'point source' (end-of-pipe) waste discard activity amounts to a 'point blame' activity, which is discrete, identifiable and actionable. A pipe emerging from a factory, which discharges into a water table, is a 'point source' activity which can be cleaned up right there, so the emission generator can be prosecuted, licensed, ameliorated, taxed or prohibited as is appropriate to the circumstance.[38] Essentially this involves applying the polluter pays principle for establishing the polluter as also the owner of the problem: point-blame and point-clean-up at the point-source.

Recycler's World:
www.recycle.net

In the situation of 'non-point-source' pollution, consider the thousands of automobiles emitting exhaust gases as 'permitted releases' from a metropolitan automobile fleet, characterized by mobility multiplicity and intermittent discharge. The otherwise logical 'polluter pays principle' hovers ineffectually over these 'fugitive emissions' – examined earlier in a general way within the review of Consumer Dynamics and Discard Dynamics (chapter 3).

All of agriculture and all of industry aggregates as a non-point waste dispersal problematic. The issue in these wider contexts is not only that non-point sources are too numerous or cumbersome to itemize; it is also the difficulty of isolating different categories of polluter in correct proportion and administering the socially appropriate clean-up, taxing, alleviating and ameliorating, and prosecuting procedures. Because points of 'blame' cannot be readily isolated and dealt with, the punitive 'sticks' engaged to back up waste disposal management give way to inducements to good behaviour, the rewarding 'carrots'. People, the only conscious polluters in nature, must be 'potty trained', taught good manners, and enthused and educated to address waste disposal management in order to attain their due rewards of personal satisfaction and community approval.

Judith Petts (1994) provides a progression for planning waste disposal management: involving project definition, impact study, decision-making and implementation. Operating within this procedural construct, the main policy principles are paraphrased as follows:

- The *first* and societally most 'clever' principle of waste disposal management is the *avoidance of waste production* in and of itself, in accordance with the maxim that the most effective way to avert the sewage, garbage and gas emission onslaught is to not make so much of it. This resistance approach (precycling) can be induced (taxed against and rebated for) in manufacturing plants through the minimizing of both product and packaging, and by giving a 'societal seal of approval' to the manufacturing of recyclable and biodegradable products which use the 'cleanest available technology'.

- The *second* principle implicates manufacturers in producing consumer durables which are long-lasting, and energy efficient, to which there arises a concomitance: the attainment and endorsement of an energy-efficient and low-maintenance longer life-cycle for consumer durables.

- A *third* principle involves finding a way to *recover and reuse waste products*: thus paper discards may be reprocessed into the likes of egg-crates, and organic matter made into compost. It also involves the practice of 'waste forward exchange' involving the passing on (usually the on-sale) of waste from one source (baling station, industrial plant) as the input to another plant's product. Recovery and reuse also involves the engagement of 'takeback' policies and rules for the likes of containers, packaging, and outworn consumables, including the obvious reutilization of returnable bottles, reusable crates and packs, and burning combustible waste for the likes of district heating.

- A *fourth* principle involves the *capture of all hazardous and toxic waste for scientific neutralizing*, involving some possibilities for recycling, others for incineration and others for incarceration. The imperative in regard to hazardous and toxic wastes is to maintain a continuous 'audit' in recognition of the understanding that evidence of a lack of assimilability in nature calls for capture and diversion. The

Resist
Recover
Recycle
Reuse
Reduce
Re-educate
Rehabilitate

most important curtailment relates to radioactive wastes, toxic chemicals embodied in consumer durables, and certain fungicides, herbicides pesticides, and other other 'conveyor' products which are non-degradable (like CFCs) which disperse into, yet are not amenable to being recycled within, the landscapes waterways or the atmosphere.

- The *fifth* principle involves the practice of environmentally benign *safe disposal for solid, water-borne and gaseous terminal residues* and all other unusable trash.

This 'clever' approach – much dumping practice is not even 'smart', being in fact often 'dumb' – involves a mixture of desirable and imperative practices appropriate to modern hedonistic society. Better to promote a mixture of policies (reduction, reuse, recycle) on a rewarding 'incentive basis', and to enforce other policies for hazardous waste capture and recovery on a punitive 'disincentive' penalty basis. These approaches are the cornerstones to the five policy points which Bailey (1991) itemizes for the attainment of waste reduction and hazardous waste management: information, incentives, research and development, along with behaviour, correction, and controls. Important in every waste disposal management programme is the need to link waste management with a performance-auditing of fossil-fuel conservation and an overall fossil energy use curtailment, regulated by both policy and taxes

Procedures for endorsing environmentally friendly and environmentally preferable food fibre and durable goods production, attractively identified with a 'clean, green, caring' logo, are appealing and effective *provided* there is an official commitment to establish a publicly funded testing, registration and regulative service for monitoring such a process.

Finally, in addition to all the precepts of worthiness and goodness which underscore the waste disposal management theme, lies an emphatic case for 'enlightened self-interest'. This is that agricultural products, along with certain consumer durables produced from a 'clean, green and caring' environment, makes good business sense, especially for tourism within a generally over-populated and environmentally damaged global context.

Growth Pattern Policy Directions

It is open to any public authority or agency to:

- Commission studies and provide promotional information useful to developers, conservationists, statutory undertakers and utility and social service providers.
- Lay on education and training seminars and services for constituent local government agencies, utility and service providers, and for businesses.
- Provide a brokerage service to initiate development and/or conservation and provide linkage support for a community.
- Indicate local tax and levy ameliorations: provide relief, sites and services assistance, and funding promotions.
- Vertically integrate the strategic policy programmes of constituent local agencies.

Although largely promotional, these styles of agency reinforcement are able, even in the absence of 'powers of general competence', in other terms with subsidiarity powers, to graft and move for sustainable conservation *with* development. The question asked of central governments is, can they accept the premiss that their contribution is indeed about 'central' policy and assistance, *and* that it is their function to pass policy down to lower levels of regional and local government where the power gets ultimately delivered as action, and the responsibility stops? Only in those instances where central government accepts a subsidiarity positioning for local government can the empowerment of development planning and conservancy practice flourish.

One aim is to strengthen the output of central government guidelines and bulletins. Powerful metropolitan agencies can work these out for themselves, and address and fund their particular needs and circumstances. For smaller 'regional' agencies the objectivity and support of central government needs to be harnessed to the quest for guidance on growth patterning policies and practices. As examples, there can be useful practice notes for urban fringe growth management, for the management of tourism, conservation best practice, waste management, and for rural land-use practices – all contexts where outlier regional authorities stand to benefit from centrally provided regionally focused advice. By avoiding a legal prescription for such bulletins (which also ensures that they remain operationally innovative and challenging) they can be presented as best-practice indicators, serving regional, national and local sustainable intent backed up by the planning court system.

Well-staffed urban-rural agencies work on data, linkage and rural-urban analyses, and project generation and project evaluation as outlined earlier in this chapter. What is worrying is that the central governments of Anglo settler society nations still largely do not appreciate the potential of conservation *with* development. The modern-into-neomodern situation for a structural integration of central-local-regional administration, and the fashioning of sustainable urban planning needs to be better understood and practised.

What is at stake is improvement in the 'delivery' capabilities of political and planning agencies. The facts of the matter, simply put, are that:

- Rural-urban (regional) representatives are able to *integrate* a mix of actions with certainty of effect in those parts of a nation where central government is remote and misunderstood.
- Rural-urban (regional) agencies can *engage* development and conservancy stakeholders and go where central government cannot venture.
- Rural-urban (regional) organization is able to *control* from the middle out in development contexts where central government is obliged only to intervene from the top down.
- Rural-urban (regional) agencies *induce* the 'with a carrot approach' in contexts where central government can only indicate and berate.
- Rural-urban (regional) agencies *direct* using a 'with a stick approach' in both development and conservancy contexts, where central government can only be seen as a big-brother bully.

Macro pattern agencies – state, provincial, regional – appropriately empowered, can actually *attain* outcomes to which central government can only *aspire*, namely material progress, protection of the human living space and the natural habitat, and human security and wellbeing. Urban-rural administrations at a regional level of intermediacy are positioned to deliver nationally favoured outcomes and promote locally sustainable planning practices: those operations which achieve a triple harmony between patterned growth for the regional economy, a palpable sense of social wellbeing for the regional population, and the attainment 'indefinitely' of a healthy regional environment.

5

Urban Growth Management

The preceding chapters addressed big issues: the *Charter* laid out on a large 'canvas' in chapter 3, followed by an examination of *Growth Patterning* problems and potentials in chapter 4. Attention now turns to matters urban and suburban, concentrating on the home turf for Anglo settler societies. This is where most people live, and suburban dwellers are the people for whom planners mostly plan. Yet a caution: glance at the depiction of any land-use conflict in a community newspaper, or any development appeal ruling, and it will be clear that no single writing can supply specific direction to individual conflicts. This chapter explores the *Sustainable Urban Planning* pathway by attitude and ethical bearing, and through exemplars of practice.

'The suburb was instrumental in producing the architectural form of the bungalow, just as the bungalow was instrumental in producing the spatial form of the suburb. It was a process that, in the early 20th Century, was to be repeated in the suburbs of Anglophone colonial and most post-colonial countries worldwide: the United States, Canada, Australia, New Zealand.'
  Anthony King in *Visions of Suburbia* (edited by Roger Silverstone) 1988.

For other urban prognoses, together with other kinds of recommendation, refer to David Satterthwaite (1999).

Cities and large towns are growth assets: 'the engines of wealth-creation in modern societies'[1] and the 'building of houses constitutes the major architectural work of any civilisation'.[2] These urban places are resource-dependent upon the rest of the world, particularly their own hinterland, for their existence. A further consideration is that their outpourings of gaseous solid and liquid wastes are metabolized, dumped or diluted outside urban boundaries, in the open spaces beyond. Another organizational complexity is that within the urbanized settler societies of Australasia and North America planners have been positioned to do little and have got involved too late to improve urban efficiency, let alone induce self-sufficiency or enrich the liveability of cities and towns to any marked useful extent. Choosing a strategic way, and identifying a multiple-activity urbanism which is as sustainable as possible, is the challenge this chapter addresses, mainly from the perspective of where most settler society people live – suburbia.

Neomodern urban goals are relatively easy to explicate, to acknowledge as policy enactments of government, and to accept as *Agenda 21* protocols; but they are notoriously difficult for planners to lock onto as urban reforms. The 'sustainable urban paradigm' urges a response, a deflection from much of what has gone before, and seeks to attain a balanced relationship for society within nature. This largely becomes a matter of choosing a strategic way between urban achievements which have previously been considered 'smart', and the neomodernist delivery of that which is actually 'clever' – in a word, balanced. The chapter starts with an exploration of the urban multiple-belief ethos and the urban-humanized ecosystem, offering a critique and an urban sense of place, variety, community and uniqueness.

Yesterday's Solutions, Today's Problems

The periphery-to-centre city montage (previous chapter, figure 4.3) depicted the phenomenon of 'podded' and 'chunked' 20-year look-ahead developer-led urban expansion. This represents the modern – of the twentieth century – rural into sub-urban circumstance beyond which the Edge City and ex-urbanization phenome-non has become an extension.[3]

Suburban podding into tracts, ironically depicted as something they seldom are – neighbourhoods – was aided between the two World Wars by the mass pro-duction of automobiles and a reducing set of vehicle operating cost. From Peter Rowe (1991) there is the observation that:

> In 1925 the average automobile travelled some 23 miles per service dollar, sharply increasing to 112 miles by 1945 ... [and] ... vehicle operating costs plum-meted from between 10 to 18 cents per mile during the first decade of this century to slightly over 4 cents per mile during the 1930s ... [and] ... tyre performance increased threefold.

Consequent to these operating and servic-ing cost reductions, along with the bur-geoning pattern of post-World War I single-family household formations, there occurred (by the 1920s in North America, later in Australasia) a demographic crossover, after which the population of Anglo settler nations became forever more predominately urban than rural, and more middle-incomed than poor. Early suburbia represented freedom and became 'utopia' for these first-time incomers, a flight from rural drudgery and mid-city congestion.

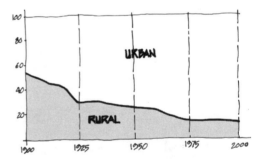

This pattern of suburbanization was initiated before World War I by tram and train rolling-stock transporta-tion, a phenomenon based on affordability of a car for each adult, succeeding the between-the-wars situation of one automobile for each household. At first the pat-terning became podded out, *not* in accordance with an 'onion skinned banding'. Suburbanization grew out of a nuclear-family urban settlement option and prefer-ence, and was 'chunked' into being as leapfrog zonings.

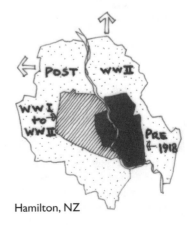

Hamilton, NZ

A pattern of self-organization for expanding New World cities goes some way to clarifying the inexplicable – the emergence of Los Angeles and Phoenix, as examples, beyond the bounds of climate geography and resources. Local government is never in full control of the situation or 'calling the shots' as thematically established in William Fulton's *Reluctant Metropolis* (1997). Researchers into city growth, at a loss for an explanation as to 'why?' can look to the self-organization swarm phenomenon ascribed evenly to human-peopled cities and to termite-populated anthills in Steven Johnson's *Emergence: The Connected Lives of Ants, Brains, Cities and Software*, 2001. Refer also to Mike Davis, *City of Quartz* (1990) and *Dead Cities* (2003).

But what started as shared enjoyment and conviviality in the era of public transport rolling stock, changed with an individualized discretionary use of the automobile into isolation, separation and anomie. After World War II this situation worsened as suburbs patterned into residential street layouts, often without sidewalks, but with road pavements wide enough for a garbage truck (Australasia), or a speeding fire appliance (North America). The houses in these suburbs were often contrived also to ensure that the in-front garage was positioned to avoid eye-contact between neighbours.

Up to the end of the nineteenth century 'the city' almost everywhere was compact, of high density, and comprised mixed uses. Urban life had been insanitary, but the technical solutions for trash disposal and sewer reticulation were well in hand by the beginning of the twentieth century. Then, at around the same time – the early 1900s – there occurred a surge in two mobility inventions of profound significance. One of these, the elevator, enabled the corporate fortresses and city-centre apartments to grow *up*; the other, the mass-produced automobile, enabled the residential fringe of these same cities to grow *out*. The major urban 'fractal' components (residential pods, schools, churches, civic realms, offices, shopping areas, open spaces, factories, hospitals) led the conditioned urban citizenry to behave in accordance with the dictates of a divide-and-control authority pattern. Later consequences of this authority were the large modern-era urban structures (malls, stadia, office towers) which have largely replaced the church and school as the social foci of communities.[4]

Tracked rolling stock and then the rubber-tyred automobile provided the mobility-mode for suburbanization. But that physical mobility fails to plumb the social motivation to give up on a compact Euro-urban tradition. One practical explanation was that suburban railways were available before sanitary sewers; another that for average soil types it was necessary to set free-standing houses on quarter-acre plots (approximately a tenth of a hectare) this being the area of land considered necessary to cope with a septic tank's through-flow.[5] A Fordist explanation would have it that the commodification of plots houses and automobiles was being simply customized and 'jobbed' as packaged entities, exemplified by the post-World War II Levitt housing projects in the United States, built rapidly with no architectural overview.

Although Levitt houses may not have been individually designed, the pattern was thoughtfully engineered, for by 1950, according to Avi Friedman (*Planning the New Suburbia* 2002: 30): 'traffic engineering studies revealed that the accident rate was substantially higher for grid-pattern subdivisions than for limited access [collector roaded] subdivisions . . . evidenced in the switch from grid to hierarchical road networks for reasons of safety.'

In all of this it is important, regardless of the quality of outcome, to be mindful of an 'idealistic' factor; that a clear majority of the immigrants to the New World were attracted by 'possessive individualism' and wanted never again to be obliged to integrate their domestic lives with others on a shared plot, in a shared building, and on shared transportation. What bliss to possess a freehold plot, a free-standing house, and for each adult to have discretionary use of a free-to-go-anywhere automobile, although James Kunstler (1993: 173) notes a downside in that the ever-questing 'obsession with mobility, the urge to move on every few years stands at odds with the wish to endure in a beloved place'.

The appealing image of suburban freedom has had to give way, in the round, to a sobering conclusion – that just as environment influences consciousness (Peter Jackson's *Maps of Meaning*, 1989) an atomized and socially sterile suburban 'bedroom' environment induces a flawed social consciousness and an urban stasis. Such after-their-prime suburbs are now redeemable only through revival – a process of nucleation (rescaling) and land-use mixture (variety) in association with the applications, where fitting, of Transport Oriented Developments (TODs), Mixed Use Developments (MUDs), and the likes of Co-housing – examined and explored later in this chapter.

A listing of presumed virtues for suburban housing prior to World War II would include: affordable, safe and secure, independent, comfortable and convenient, interesting, novel and lively, distinctive, individual and personalized.

The highest residential ambition for suburban living can be ascribed to the social and design concepts consolidated around the turn of the twentieth century by Ebenezer Howard and Raymond Unwin as the 'Garden City' ideal, along with Clarence Stein's identification (1929) of the 'neighbourhood unit'. Unwin's planning-out-of-architecture designs included a middle-class division of home access between the 'visitor' frontal façade and the 'trade person' rear access shown in figure 5.1 as **Radburn and Radburn rationalized**.[6] Howard and Unwin, both working in England, suggest British input to the take-up of the 'bungalow' (the North American ranch-style house), with Clarence Stein's 'Radburn' principles (New Jersey: and at Sunnyside, Long Island) ascribed to American origins.[7]

The earlier inference of poorly delivered 'blob' planning has its origin in either or both the 'non-planning' circumstance, or the 'formulaic planning' situation of yesteryear, inducing replicated gridded and podded patterns. Indeed most of today's inherited suburban development was out of date at inception, often sited in flood-prone or unstable locations, also costly to live in and service, resistant to adaptation, and largely beyond redemptive redesign. Regardless of planning legislation, planning personnel, zoning intent, shape of the landscape, or the inherited agricultural soils, the dominant influences at the time of rural-urban crossover were the already established landowner boundaries, entrenched developer preferences, and a local political orthodoxy where, 'at the developing edge the traditional model of zoning faltered badly' (Porter, Phillips and Lassar 1991: 6). Planning, as zoning, has not often played an initiating role, and has seldom harnessed the owner-contractor-councillor troika to good effect. These failings have been authoritatively listed by Charles Haar and Jerold Kayden in their *Zoning and*

Figure 5.1 Radburn: and Radburn Rationalized.
The left-side depiction of Radburn Place, New Jersey shows how the division of home access between the 'visitor' frontal façade and the 'trade person' rear access proved costly to implement. Yet when rationalized to a quarter acre (1,000 m²) Australasian situation (the right-side depiction) it can be seen that the area of a site required for rear lane access can be *less* than the area of site required for direct off-street access. This rationality is even more pertinent at higher densities.

the American Dream (1989) paraphrased here as 'failing to deliver high-quality urban environments', 'excluding low-income and minority families', 'engendering corruption', 'not dealing adequately with regional problems'.[8] To this listing can be added the findings of a Porter–Phillips–Lassar study on behalf of the Urban Land Institute (1991) establishing three main 'Arguments Against Traditional Zoning': that it is 'static', that it 'serves parochial interests', and that it 'cannot ensure high quality development'.

Assembly-line processing by local government functionaries, approving the conversion of raw rural land into suburbia, defies community reason. When the banality of pop-up suburban tracts are critically commented upon, local government functionaries blame 'the system'. They declaim that they follow orders from higher authority, without bothering to initiate changes in what they deliver and dump into people's lives.

Filling in edge city space piecemeal with low-density suburbia of the formulaic kind has proved less than satisfactory, both as a habitat for incoming multiple-belief residents, and by taking productive rural land out of food and fibre production *forever*. Of course much rural land is *not* usefully productive, and on those landscapes the case *against* tidily sporadic residential settlement falters, there being nothing wrong, within an open democracy, about opting for an ex-urban broad-acre lifestyle *provided* it does not impose any unfair community burdens on the neighbouring city or induce environmental offence.[9]

The New World suburban phenomenon can be contemplated from two other perspectives: *first*, in terms of it being a settlement innovation taken up for that particular small grouping of the global population which comprises these particular settler societies; *second*, in terms of it being inherently a product of the twentieth century, in other words a relatively new, clean-cut, quick-fix option and solution. The suburban style of road building, plot provisioning, and separated-use zonings associated with higher levels of car ownership and expanding rates of car usage arose, according to Hawken, Lovins and Lovins (1999) because 'Current zoning typically mandates land use patterns that maximise distance and dispersion, forbid proximity and density, segregate uses and income levels, and require universal car traffic'. Kenneth Jackson's *Crabgrass Frontier* (1985) identifies four 'distinguishing characteristics' of the settler society suburban experience:

- A strong penchant for home ownership.
- A widening disparity between residents of central cities . . . and those of their surrounding suburbs.
- The (considerable) length of the average journey-to-work, whether measured in miles or in minutes (and)
- The absence of sharp divisions between town and country.

Along the coded-in shopping strips *en route* to suburbia and ex-urbia lies commercial space, the 'big box' stores and cinema multiplexes and car saleyards surrounded by copious parking, which, at prime locations, has morphed into malls which now offer shopping as family entertainment. These compete against traditional urban centre trade and commerce by providing what downtown used to offer, out where the spending populations now live. What is forsaken is city centre liveliness, particularly for the first generation of malls because virtually nobody lives there. What malls do offer is tough competition to the crime-threatening and often dingy-dirty-scary traditional downtown city centre. Coming to the newer of these malls are clean service industries, office complexes and some residential accommodation.

Ex-urbanization now spreads well beyond the suburban fringe, extending as a quasi-urban penumbra to the further limits of whatever is regarded as the commuting range. Indeed ex-urbanization now represents the fastest-growing territorial change to North American and Australasian landscapes. Enthusiasm for ex-urbanization is identifiable as a wistful prolongation of the Arcadian ideal and an opportunity, for some, to remove themselves from urban crime, congestion, racial tension and pollution. The broad-acre (lifestyle) preference can be readily identified as also arising from affluence (unrestrained use of the automobile), good blacktop roading and lower vehicle operating costs (efficient vehicles and modest petrol tax) and for two diverse socio-economic groupings. The *first* includes those wealthy and informed persons setting out to live a technologically buttressed lifestyle of mock rusticity on some broad acres, with all mod cons close to hand. The *second* set includes

Joel Garreau, *Edge City*, 1992: The maximum desirable commute is expressed as forty-five minutes – notably not as a maximum distance or a limiting cost!

In the early 1990s the Auckland University Planning School invited some overseas candidates for academic interview. One of these was a woman raised and trained in Russia, but by then resident in the United States. A settling-in programme had enabled her to visit several non-metropolitan middle-American cities. Flying in to each airport she pointed a video camera out the window and simply recorded the quasi-urban scene that came into view. This video was part of her presentation. The hum of the engines and a frank commentary perfectly underscored the videoed confusion and chaos. For city after city we were shown a Dante's Inferno of scattered housing, quasi-rural living, industrial farming, recreation patches, scrap yards, commercial strips and an occasional horse standing forlorn.

lower-income ex-urban dwellers, people living a low-cost rustic existence beyond vigilant bureaucratic censure. For both sets of ex-urbanite dweller there is an avoidance of the costs of providing conventional urban utilities (roads sealed, garbage collected, water supplied), and or also for social support services (district nurse, welfare visitors, postal deliveries, policing). Many people become dispirited, some demented, by the isolation of the ex-urban broad-acre lifestyle, and householders soon tire of roof-water supply, septic-tank clean-outs, and dry garbage disposal, the concluding and frequent outcome being relocation back to the urban fold. The well-incomed category can organize all their social needs privately, but within the poor category the welfare requirements eventually become a cost-burden to the adjoining city.

This calls into question the economic disharmony and social undesirability of ex-urbanization and low density suburbanization. Thereby rests the case *for* Growth Pattern Management (chapter 4); and the Urban Retrofit Clustering strategy attended to later in this chapter.

Urban 'conformity patterns' and 'consumption cultures' are now offered and reviewed.

Urban conformity patterns seemingly furnish more space (bigger houses, larger sites), more mobility (privately owned cars), different houses (predominantly three-bedroomed), as though this is variety, when in fact all that is available is replication. Formulaic planning and building codes have delivered subdivision adjoining subdivision, from which there emerges what Australians describe as 'rat-run' urban sprawl. Malvina Reynolds (1963) cuts to the quick of the matter with the often quoted, very Californian, ballad *Little Boxes*:

Little boxes on the hillside
Little boxes made of ticky-tacky
Little boxes, little boxes
Little boxes all the same.

There's a green one and a pink one
And a blue one and a yellow one
And they're all made out of ticky-tacky
And they all look just the same

Reflect again upon the fact that over 80 per cent of settler society populations are urban living, and that in North America more than half that population is staked out on highly inter-visible noise-sharing plots at a low overall density, averaging – net of plots and half the adjoining street – ten to twelve (Australian) and six to ten (western USA) detached dwellings per hectare.[10] These low densities make public transport untenable, and, ironically, fail to meet either the *privacy* or *accessibility* ideals. These can be portrayed as the attainment of privacy and insulation against 'sounds sightings and smells' yet within neighbourhoods of sufficient density to support a viable public transport service which fits in with daily journey-to-work, shopping, schooling, entertainment, community watch, and recreational needs.

Change occurred for suburbs over the latter half of the twentieth century: throughout Australasia average plots halved in area, yet the houses built on them doubled in size, and the level of ownership and the usage of cars increased enormously. The suburban 'grey zone' (Belmont 2002) became the delivered and received pattern, with no consideration of any variety or alternative to the free-standing house laid out with a front lawn and back garden on a freehold title, the automobile transporting your body, and advertising transporting your mind. And were *you* in business to provide plots, houses, automobiles or appliances then, according to this prognosis, you would indeed be content as a supplier, for the resource supply has been captured and the market engineered. In short the formula suburb is a commercially corralled pushover, and urban dwellers in settler societies mostly find themselves believing that their trussed-up conformity is good fortune; that is until they visit a worthy alternative! The average suburbanite may prefer to not admit that they have been staked out in accordance with this pattern of urban conformity, but this is pretty much how it is in terms of the market-directed pattern on offer.

Urban consumption culture shoots home the conformity point. Given a plot-house-car lifestyle structure as dominant, plot-holding, home-owning, appliance-operating and car-running concerns take over suburban lives, pattern their consumption, and condition their thinking. The living-consuming-thinking pattern which has evolved is defined by child needs (pap food), child pleasures (low-gratification television), and child consumerism (plaything cars and dinky houses). The concur-rent 'freedom' to take your mind anywhere (multi-choice television channels and access to the World Wide Web), and the availability of an automobile to transport your person to all places as potential destinations, defines the supposed liberality of the suburban condition. In fact suburban residents are mostly contained within an 'automobile culture', 'bungalow culture', 'mall culture', 'television culture'.

In all of this television can be regarded as an essentially passive experience – although it is of course much more. On this matter John Friedmann (1987: 351) crackles with indignation and awe:

Day in, day out, individually or as a group, household members sit huddled in front of the screen that glows in the semi-darkness, gazing at the commercial entertainment, the news, and the sport along with millions of other spectators equally mesmerised, not talking with one another except for laconic exchanges during the numerous commercial breaks, each person silently absorbed into the images dancing on (their) retina.

For an interesting insight into the decline of social engagement and interpersonal connections largely as a consequence of electronic home entertainment, consult Robert Putnam's *Bowling Alone*, 2000

We now realize that television viewing is even less a shared encounter, being more a solo experience with 'laconic exchanges' taking place between the viewer and the TV set. Although slightly humorous in connotation, this situation also touches bathos, the point being that the 'programming collective' behind the screen is capturing the mass mores and influencing the mass preferences of viewers electronically, dispassionately, and at fractional cost, with low-brow televised soaps interspersed with excellently scripted commercials for products which induce dietitians and sociologists to cringe! The cartel of companies selling properties, automobiles, gasoline, and consumer durables are all reaching captive audience consumers. With media-directed consumerism and mail-shot advertising, the retail industry is able to boost shortfalls in the flow of profits and manipulate consumer spending responses, all neatly separated out, zoned into, and defined by car-plot-house conformity.

'Are we, I wondered, increasingly a nation of overworked, lonely people? . . . fleeing disorderly and tense home lives for the "reliable orderliness" of work (for) in the 1980s and 1990s the American worker's work year increased by a month.'
    Robert Kaplan, 1998

'Maintaining a fleet of cars to navigate among the housing tracts, commercial strips and office complexes of the American landscape now takes eighteen percent of the average family budget' [and all the while] 'California's population increased forty percent [during the period 1970–1990] and the total vehicle miles doubled.'
    'Paved Paradise', *Newsweek*, 15 May 1995.

In pre-automobile times family needs had to be met locally, mostly from within the household and the local community. Hence home entertainment, kitchen gardens, soap- and sauce-making and all the other trappings of family nostalgia. Now the postal service, courier van and household automobile enables suburban dwellers to obtain their goods effortlessly. Producers have used advertising to narrow the band of 'desirable' options and make consumer selection 'easier'. In this way manufacturers and suppliers arrange the mass production of a range of ostensibly different, yet essentially similar, consumer lines. These goods are always conveniently to hand in well-placed outlets, open seven days a week. And as the advertising volume can be turned up on command, the overall result is the conformity pattern and consumption culture outlined previously. All this, for an automobile-dependent, television-fixated, population – within which, an ultimate irony, settler societies put pride of emphasis on individuality and inventiveness.[11]

A characteristic of all that is conventionally suburban is conformity. Indeed monotony toned up as conformity is structurally laced and patterned into 'grey' suburbs displaying a repetitive permutation of streets, houses, berms, yards and lawns – all different, yet in reality very much the same. Always the questions asked are site differentials – 'what size of plot?', 'what width of street?', 'what yard dimensions?', 'what floor area?', 'what price?' Seldom asked are the questions 'why urban living in the plot-house-car replica pattern?' Why each house different (notably in Australia and New Zealand), yet all three-bedroomed stereotypes? Why curvilinear illegibility imposed upon gentle landscapes? Why so spaced apart yet lacking in privacy? Why so costly to maintain? Why no allowance for diverse accommodations and cultural beliefs? Why so little varietal mix of households by size, ethnicity and income?

It has also to be asked: is the received situation really all that bad, or all that wrong? Some American and Australian writing (Donaldson 1969; Stretton 1989; Bamford 1992; Garreau 1992) applaud aspects of the suburban lifestyle lampooned previously, and claim traditional-urban suburbs of the settler society kind to be the envy of people throughout the rest of the world. British writing (Gwilliam et al. 1999) extols 'the suburbs as vital components of the urban mix in economic, social, political and environmental terms' but of course British suburbs have been in place for a much longer period of time and are of intrinsically higher average density than those of the transpacific new world. French philosopher and sociological commentator Jean Baudrillard (*Amérique*, 1994) discerns, from a Euro-American per-

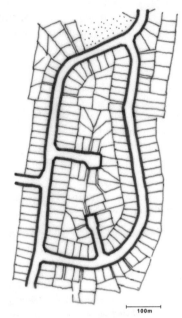

Large houses, small plots. West Auckland.

spective, the vast North American urban and suburban experience as an unpretentious cultural freedom – which of course it once was, being now morphed into low-rent 'grey zone' market-rate housing areas riddled with boredom, petty crime and family violence.

Strong pro-suburb reasoning is expressed in Greg Bamford's 'Density, Equity and the Green Suburb' (1992) a conference paper which argued that the case made against extensive urban sprawl is 'deceptively value laden'.[12] The case *for* standard suburbia he makes out hinges very much on the benefits deriving from property maintenance and gardening. Bamford also has a rosy view of the active recreational potential of low-density suburbia, and waxes lyrically on the value to children which low densities harbour for 'redressing some of the disadvantages of class'.[13] Wider claims for the virtue of the house-plot-car arrangement is that for other reasons – mall shopping as entertainment, tooling around in the family car as recreation, security – suburbs are the housing preference to which bread-winning adults in settler societies aspire. A two-car garage, an outdoor barbecue area, maybe a pool, access to a non-threatening mall – especially so in a sunbelt setting – defines an alluring settler society suburban 'reality and dream' combination.

All credit to Bamford (1992) for this shaft of prescience; the need to avoid consolidation outcomes which 'look as though someone put the plans for a conventional suburb in the photocopier and pressed the 20 percent reduction button'!

Settler society nation suburbs are profligate of energy resources on account of the car-based organization of life within low-density layouts. There is also the high unit service cost for piped-in and wired-along supply utilities, the high disposal costs associated with getting rid of the water-borne and dry-garbage wastes, and the community costs and social damage. To appreciate these shortcomings, as a

Refer also to Peter
Wolf's *Hot Towns* (1999)
not necessarily equable,
as in sunbelt, so much as
'places distinguished by
fine climate, awesome
physical beauty, abundant
recreation opportunities,
pristine air, pure drinking
water, relatively few
social problems, and low
crime'.
An alternative take on
urban desirability is given
in Richard Florida's *Rise
of the Creative Class*
(2002) for cities which
profile 'a creative people
index'.

'(C)ommand over money,
command over space,
and command over time
form independent but
interlocking sources of
social power.'
                David Harvey, 1985.

In contrasting perversion
to the long-term 'high
costs' of suburban living
it was the short-term
'low capitalization cost'
of suburban home
provisioning which led to
its proliferation in Anglo
settler societies. What
follows is a précis of
Kenneth Jackson's seven-
point 'cheapness'
summation (*Crabgrass
Frontier*, 1985).
• High per-capita
  wealth.
• The low cost of money.
• Low raw land costs.
• Low fuel costs.
• Inexpensive wooden
  frame construction.
• Deductible tax
  allowances (US mainly).
• Enterprise incentives to
  developers.

prelude to reviewing urban reform options later on, suburbs are now assessed via a social and environmental, as well as an economic 'cost' review.

Suburbia and Ex-urbia Costed

Most North Americans and Australasians live in suburbs; they will, most of them, die in suburbs; and the next generation will also mostly live and die in suburbs, although beyond that there cannot be certainty as oil shortages bite, new technologies evolve and populations possibly decrease. Cities are lived in and are of course livable, the oxymoron 'livable cities movement' being something of an admission of guilt about the monsters created, ostensibly for an exuberant and energetic family life – in reality security fortresses inducing much unfairness and isolation. The density component alone was specifically isolated in a Real Estate Research Corporation study (United States 1974) as 'costly' in energy, land resource and fiscal terms. Yet while it is a national and personal *economic* loss as well as an extravagance to bind into the suburban lifestyle, there are also significant *social* costs involved.

This situation will be taken to prognosis later. For now, mindful of the pattern of urban mistakes already reviewed, the cost reasoning is represented as a categorization of the adverse causal relationships which spring from the suburban way of life, and an understanding is sought as to how 'grey zone' suburbs learn, why some improve into 'green zone' suburbs with age, and why others decline and decay.

• Consider first the *fiscal-costs* into which the plot-house-car lifestyle shepherds suburban families and individuals. First comes plot provisioning, plus the costs of home construction, then the purchase costs of vehicles. The picture starts to clarify. This trap, which it proves to be in fact, is difficult to avoid. Yet on the fringe of the larger towns and cities, cross-commuting suburbia is still being put in place on rural lands lost to food and fibre production forever!

• Consider the *time-costs*, again particularly for the larger towns and cities, where some 80 per cent of the Anglo settler society urban populations live. Obviously the breadwinner's hour or so in the car each day is a waste of personal time. To this must be added the time-cost of child and other non-driver chauffeuring, shopping-trip time, and recreational-trip time. We all have an understanding of the time lost in getting to and from work; but this is only an individual component part of the personal time spent on the ten or more car trips generated out of the standard suburban household each day.

In the middle range $60,000 for a plot; $140,000 for a family home; $20,000 for a family car.

- Now consider the *stress-costs* arising from the way the preceding fiscal-costs and time-costs work. To live well in standard single-purpose suburbs, every driving-age person requires the use of an automobile; but when a second or third car cannot be afforded, or when a person is part of that one-third of society which is 'too young', 'too poor', 'too elderly', or 'too handicapped' to drive, then suburban life becomes suburban detention. Worse, an inability to budget for mothers to have discretionary use of a car induces a suburban neurosis that is the bane of family practitioners. Quite obviously, that inability to be in a position to drive away from the palpable boredom of the suburban home restricts social contacts and reduces social horizons to the solace of the television square as a surrogate for interpersonal socialization.

- Consider *institutional costs* in addition to the previously noted stress-costs, those expenses which come through as social care, involving the treatment of alcohol and drug abuse and the institutionalizing of those psychologically unable to get by in suburbia. Here too must be considered the costs of hospitalizing and rehabilitating the families of those who suffer or die from car accidents, particularly those accidents which result from otherwise avoidable car usage. There are also the policing and custodial costs connected with crime.

For the United Kingdom (1970s): more than 80 per cent of seven and eight-year-olds got to school without adult supervision.
By the 1990s: less than 10 per cent of seven and eight-year-olds travelled to school without adult supervision.

- Consider also the *separation-of-function costs* induced by a division of land users into specified-purpose cells (housing, commerce, industry, schooling); and the 'costs' which result from herding the lowest incomed and some racially distinctive groups of people into other specifically underclass ghettos.

- Consider *energy-costs* in terms of the profligate use of fuel sources, particularly non-renewable oil and gas reserves which nature allows human society access to once only during the course of recorded human history. Certainly these energy resources are there to be utilized by humankind; but apart from the pointlessness of wasteful use, their headlong uptake prejudices both future mobility and creates unsustainable places of residence for future generations. Simply expressed: lower urban densities generate proportionally higher levels of energy consumption. The most chilling prospect for cross-town commuting suburbanites is no automobile gas at the pumps, and to a lesser extent gasoline costing more than (say) five dollars a litre.[14]

Ironically *Neighbours*, a television parody of Australian cul-de-sac sociability, and the latter 'suburban' productions of *I Love Lucy* in the United States, portray low-density suburbs as socially exciting in a manner which grips its also suburban watchers during the window of time they might be socializing themselves, as in the programmes!

- Consider the habitat or *environmental costs*; the loss of indigenous floral cover and the urban transformation of usable agricultural land – productive assets forever lost whenever the urban commodification of farming land takes place. Then there is the extravagance of wastefully large (under-utilized) residential sections; the extravagance of one- and two-person households in three- and four-bedroom housing; and the high cost of long-run utilities and water-borne sewerage and storm water disposal services.

- Consider finally the *physiological costs* arising in low-density areas from the effects of toxins used in construction (such as formaldehyde and polyurethane), in housework (cleaning and pesticide chemicals), and in the garden (insecticides herbicides and fungicides). To these must be added the repair costs related to automobile usage – noise pollution, fume pollution, and other environmental impacts.

Aucklander's (*circa* 1.1 m pop.) often point out to visitors, with confused pride, that the territorial extent of their city is much the same as urban London, neglecting to note that it replicates the lost in space low gross density of Los Angeles.

The greatest failings are the separation of urban functions (including multiple housing zones), lack of attention to basic community needs, failure to green-link and community-focus neighbourhoods, *and* the action of contractors to minimize their contributions to the public realm. This is a situation which most commentators observe as regressive in terms of community populations and the built form delivered to them. It is easy to blame these unbalanced outcomes on the subdivider-developer, when from their perspective they pick up land titles as would any other buy-and-sell speculator, with a view to adding value and maximizing their return at the quickest fiscal velocity possible. If the outcomes are unfocused, car-dominated, lacking in green accessways and community facilities, they would argue that the 'blame' ought to be placed with local administrations first, and maybe planning incompetence second.

The genesis of suburban conformity and social problems can be sheeted home to the providers, those landowner, home-developer and local government personnel and politicians who, along with the vehicle manufacturing industry, and the beverage food and durable gadget industries, engineer and telecast it this way. Can we alter this conformity and the problematic list of 'costs' it generates? Not easily: although it is practical to 'work through' an improved pattern of variety and choice for greenfield suburbanization, and 'work around' the retrofitting of extant suburbia to attain a compaction which is well designed, carefully constructed and sociable. This cost-consciousness is identified, increasingly, with comments from the social welfare and security services, the medical and welfare emergency services, and the police, fire and ambulance agencies: those whose job it is to pick up the pieces and to console and band-aid the broken lives and attend to community disorder in suburbia.

'Place-making based on exclusion, sameness or nostalgia is socially poisonous and psychologically useless: a (person) weighted with insufficiencies cannot lift that burden by a retreat into fantasy.'
   Richard Sennett, 1995.

Throughout antipodean cities and larger towns there exists a home-builder handy-person commercial chain, supplying to the community as place-makers. From their mega stores women and men receive advice and take home materials for paving their patios, building barbecues, and for painting, planting, trimming, treating and generally adding lustre to their dream houses, yards and gardens. What has taken place in settler society cities and towns, following a nineteenth-century urban concentration, is a twentieth-century de-concentration, now tracking back again to a twenty-first century reconcentration. This physical emphasis on concentration (compaction) is one result of the lack of satisfaction with city suburbanization, where all those 'costs' reviewed earlier hit the pocketbooks of the 'placemakers', make inroads upon their relationships and marriages, and destabilize their personal perceptions of worth and achievement. It is problematic enough that modern atomistic living induces all manner of individual disbenefits and dissatisfactions; what is additionally apparent is that low-density suburban 'place-making' seldom induces *Gemeinschaft* – community exchange and interaction. The prognosis is a negative double whammy: *that* in addition to the marginal social utility of the fixed-option (plot-house-car) suburban lifestyle there exists career uncertainty; *and that* the suburban neighbourhood does not provide solace or support to individuals and families caught up in the tragedy of unemployment.

> 'The dream house is a uniquely American (also very Australasian) form because for the first time in history, a civilization has created a utopian ideal based on the house rather than the city.'
> Ralph Waldo Emerson quoted in Kenneth Jackson's *Crabgrass Frontier*, 1985

Within the living memory of most middle-income and mid-life adults their job satisfaction has been the handmaiden to job certainty. Careers, once 'for keeps' are now a feature of the past: and, ironically, just as people are living longer lives they have to make do with longer hours on the job (if they have one) *and* a shorter career path! Indignity is heaped upon indignity for those at the intersection of community indifference and job denial. Those worst affected are left, mostly in suburbia, with failed marriages, job redundancies, and the isolation of longevity. Of course suburbs and suburbia cannot be blamed wholly for all this, an underlying influence being the economic and employment sea-change. Service tasks, manufacturing skills and management operations are now transferable, transportable and transmigratory. A high proportion of the workforce is 'on contract' and 'on bonuses' for productivity. The workplace, now dislocated from the homeplace, has lost its central meaning. In a phrasing from Richard Sennett (1995) 'the market(place) does not nurture the dignity of the worker' nor, in corollary, does the suburban home place provide much support for the jobless person.

> *The Corrosion of Character: The Personal Consequences of Work in the New Capitalism*. Richard Sennett, 1998.

What is seldom realized by those who have grown up with generally dysfunctional tract housing is that there are better ways to arrange residential living, the alternatives available from the European, Asian, and African prototypes sketched out in figure 5.2 as **Urban morphologies**.

Dysfunctional North American and Australasian suburbs are evident. The sales hype suggests usually the contrary, that all is well. At issue is a large bundle of socio-economic habitat questions. In terms of Urban Growth Management a major challenge is the seeking-out of different and better ways for constituting residential living in a manner which facilitates exchange and interaction, reducing the amount of travel in order to get to work and school, and for enjoying the natural environment. Additionally challenging is the retrofitting reinvention and re-expression of established suburbia. To engender – not of course for itself, but for

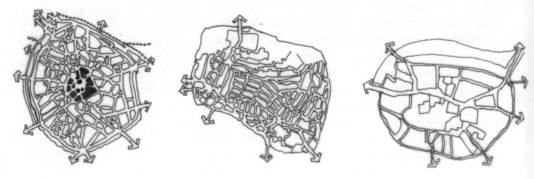

Figure 5.2 Urban morphologies.
European, Asian, African: different scales, perfect community creations contravening the planning
laws of Anglo setter societies?

its inhabitants – focus, legibility, personality, security and sense of place as an
alternative to single-use residential patterns.

Two interventions in the formulaic process which make up what is now the
suburban inheritance – neither of which I endorse – are the exclusionary 'walled
and gated' suburban enclave, and the imported 'mock historical' styles of tract,
although the latter, often styled as 'theming', does no social harm. Both are admissions of inadequacy arising out of new money and insecurity, explored in Phillip
Langdon's *Better Place to Live* (1995). A trading on fear emanates from gated
suburbs, a notably North American phenomenon now common in Australia, and
a phoney elegance wafts from revisited urban traditionalism. An evenly reasoned
yet emphatic opinion from Peter Rowe on the matter of walled and gated enclaves
(1991) puts the view that:

> LOCAL OBJECTIVES
> Neighbourhood pride.
> School and workplace
> satisfaction.
> Community identity.
> Flora and wildlife
> restoration.
> Compatibly mixed
> activities.

they should be of concern. On the face of it there is nothing wrong
with similar people congregating together in a spirit of goodwill
and common interest; in large part it is what neighbourhoods
seem to be about. There is, however, a problem when they band
together at the punitive exclusion of others. Less obviously,
perhaps, there is the further question as to whether it is actually
in the best interest of like minded citizens themselves to choose
to reside together at the exclusion of other members of society.

On occasion both these abominations (exclusionary-gated and
mock-traditional) are put together as a combination – mock-traditional behind
walls and gates. Maybe these arrangements, and the kinds of people who occupy
them, simply deserve each other.[15]

More functional and socially acceptable are the traditional 'neighbourhood'
themed, traffic-calmed, medium-density and usually entry-monumented new-
urbanist projects. Duany (in Krieger 1992; and in Duany, Plater-Zyberk, Speck,
Suburban Nation, 2000), Calthorpe (1995), Langdon (1995), Barnett (1995), Charles

Prince of Wales (1989), Krier (1979) are all
expressions of revisionist (traditional) styles:
narrow streets, often with rear lane garaging,
picket fences, meandering footpaths, tall
windows, front porches, tiny front yards,
tiled roofs, pastel-toned exteriors, and local
pocket-parks – that sort of mix. The layouts
are compact and well designed: not exclusionary, although there is an exclusiveness
based on price. They are an elegant riposte

Seaside, Florida. The best known of the new-
urbanism projects, used as the outside set for filming
The Truman Story.

to the failings of post-World War II suburbanism, and a pleasure to visit, providing networks of footpaths and narrow streets enticing car owners to park and
walk, and for many breadwinners to work from home.

There exists, in settler societies, a notion of the countryside as 'good, clean,
worthy' with the city as 'bad, dirty, corrupt'. This parody shakes down further to
the within-city belief of 'safety in the home' and 'danger on the streets', the actuality being all too often a cruel reverse – fear, claustrophobia and intimidation at
home, and freedom of expression and individualism out on the streets, albeit at
the right time![16] Security within an enduring sense of place is *all* in public domain
provisioning. Local neighbourhood pride, satisfaction about the home as an
adjunct to the school and workplace, sociability as a matter of community identity, retention and restoration of residual wildlife and flora, and compatible
mixtures of activities – these 'five worthies' are urban outcomes to seek out and
design. They cannot, and will not, just happen. Market forces, unfettered, will not
produce them. They have to be nurtured.[17]

Planners, developers, bureaucrats are the 'jobbers' with the organizational
ability and some of the design skills to fulfil this task – also ensuring that 'form,
focus, legibility, security, connectability, permeability, personality, security' and so
on are put in place along the lines detailed as Urban Social Design principles
in the upcoming box 5.1. Although these precepts, in and of themselves, cannot
produce urban functionality as an instant mix, they are the proven basic ingredients. It takes time, as much as or more than a lifetime, to achieve demographic
variety, a mixture of occupational and income classes, and racial heterogeneity for
middle Anglo settler society. This identifies the importance of fashioning worthy
places of residence, and aiding individuals and encouraging families grappling
with job insecurity and adverse personal misfortunes to build and maintain their
community scaffold.

Urban Reforms: Options and Actions

The eight sections which follow examine operational urban situations, the intention being to fashion recommendations for improving upon the general economic
substance, the social wellbeing and the urban environments which comprise community living places.

The recommendations start with a contextual scene-setting passage on overall urban social arrangement and style. They then track inward from the quasi-urban periphery to the centre, closing with shopping as entertainment.

Urban social arrangement and style (p. 204)
Ex-urban sprawl control (p. 211)
Small town conservation with development (p. 217)
Water's edge urbanization (p. 221)
Eco-village ideals (p. 223)
Raw land suburbanization (p. 227)
Urban retrofit compaction and clustering (p. 238)
Shopping as a leisure activity (p. 251)

Public housing policy and transportation provisioning, specialized accessory topics, do not form a significant part of these recommendations.[18]

Urban social arrangement and style

Recommendations which address the overall urban design problematic are collated in box 5.1 as **Urban social arrangement and style**, reasoning which owes much to Lynch's *Image of the City* (1960), the Bentley et al. (1985) *Responsive Environments*, and the US-based New Urbanism Congress (CNU) modelled on the European-initiated CIAM.

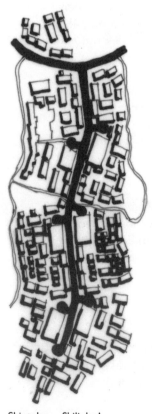

Incorporating design as a social dimension into urban layouts assumes that planners, engineers, surveyors, architects and to some extent landscapists are, or can be, trained and motivated to address and provide for urban social needs. In short, consciously to fashion a socio-physical platform for an urban lifestyle, avoiding patterned-in sterility and searching out designed-in sustainability.

A problem, even when urban designers and planners are motivated toward social goals, is that observational science has difficulty in identifying what neighbourhood morphology *actually is* in terms of 'appropriate' design – to distinguish in Kevin Lynch's terms (1960 and 1970) between 'practical automobile' city form and 'organic growth' urban form. Indeed, even when urban design (for a community, a subdivision, a housing cluster) 'appears' good, there is little understanding of why this is so, and why any such arrangement works. To Hjärne (1986: 206 Swedish context) it is not possible to demonstrate 'any simple or causal relations between physical environmental characteristics and the functioning of neighbourhoods' which, when considering Scandinavian enthusiasm for design, from freeways to furniture, is an indictment of

Skintebo – Skiljebo!

Box 5.1   Urban social arrangement and style

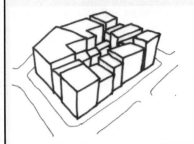

Form: the achievement of community scale and local identity (edges); and a wholesome building and massing identity for the urban landscape, with rectilineality a norm.

Focus: the attainment of a designed concept – inclining to some use of 'axiality' – for more densely fashioned urban places which enable the occupants to maintain a sense of 'where one is at' and what the district pattern is.

Safety and Sociability: the accommodation of a class, gender, family type, cultural, religious, by age and economic-class mix in secure urban communities.

Interconnectability: modal interchange and, of course accessibility; on foot, with cycles, by bus and train and, discretely, by motor vehicle.

Permeability: extending and identifying ways for people to gain access and move into and through the urban landscape, in their overall enjoyment and use of it.

Box 5.1 *Continued*

Ecological Harmony: good design, appropriate materials, wholesomely textured, sustainably landscaped, representing lasting worthiness and enhanced profitability.

Secureness: the conscious design of safe public areas and accessways, specifically for children, women, disabled persons, and the aged. Incorporating the privacy and personalization of home space.

Variety with Compatibility: providing for a wide range and choice of social and land-use activities and built-form options.

Legibility, Personalization and Robustness: establishing urban definition, richness and character; along with an exhibited sense of belonging; including occasional 'landmarking'.

Liveability and Seemliness: a sense of wholesomeness and tidiness (trash-cans off the street, no lifeless cars on the berm or in front yards, no dead fridges on verandas); in short good manners associated with local government support.

Component details for urban needs, urban users, and urban elements are depicted in David Sucher's *City Comforts* (1995). See also Lynch (1960) and Bentley et al. (1985).

designer intent in relation to worthy social outcome.[19] Withal it has to be understood that little can be done to impose 'good' design upon urban projects as a regulatory condition.

Many of those involved in urban design seem previously to have been military prison contractors, in line with this quote from the recent (2001) Australian Planning Institute's 50th Jubilee publication, that the Australian urban 'composition often forms one big rectangle – a town of rectangles. That was early town planning in Australia – planning undertaken by surveyors, often under the direction of soldiers.'[20] Of course all that is 'urban' has been 'designed' – even if with rulers, compasses and set squares, and the more inadequate the input to that design the more easily this can be detected.

> The best way to become appreciative of 'good' design is to visit acknowledged 'uplifting' urban places; and also to study model examples such as the 14 projects depicted in Steven Fader's *Density By Design*, 2000.

The 'ideal' suburban pattern, depicted in figure 5.3 as **Premier subdivision: Wellington 1960s**, begs many questions, one that is outstanding. This is, whether the people involved with producing these layouts at that time had any opinion about social goals of a community kind as they pulled this kind of physical arrangement into a curvilinear and podded outcome. One thing is certain, the planner-engineer-surveyor-architect-landscapist quintet implicated historically in outcomes of this kind were *not* trained to design for social effect,

Figure 5.3 Premier subdivision: Wellington 1960s.
The street toponomy (not shown) for this subdivision was based on exotic Caribbean republics, a choice marginally better than the selection of street names based on the now eviscerated flora and fauna! Automobiles in use to access all schooling, entertainment, shopping, repair and work functions.

On design, Alan Kreditor (1990: 160) observed that the staff of planning schools 'are valued on the basis of their research and publications' whereas the staff of architecture schools 'seem mostly valued for the buildings they have built' with the result that 'planners seem to have diminishing interest in design except for some broader environmental concerns; and architects remain dilettantes when it comes to serious urban analysis'.

A quietly voiced field trip comment: 'An hour out here on site is worth ten hours in lectures.'

People are known to be wary about densifying their way of life. In fact for the Anglo settler societies the post-World War II preference and provision has been the exact reverse, leading first to suburbia then ex-urban sprawl.

let alone meet the recreational needs of the 'baby strollers', the 'soccer mums' and 'frisbee dads'.

It is of course easy to decry replica suburban layouts after their replication! Those engaged in urban design should be able, when so trained, to discern the essence of good community outcome from physical layouts drawn on paper. We all have it within us to suggest and uphold 'key theme' excellence (the pursuit of neighbourliness, higher densities, urban design) believing or assuming that attention to these factors will 'magic into being' future improvements and higher on-sale property values. And we all, from time to time, harbour perceptions of designs which 'got it right' although we are less certain about the actual essence of that design correctness – be it street width, plot sizes, public space security, housing diversity, the landscaping, or a combination of these elements. And for well-styled neighbourhoods recognized as such, we are made aware of a connection between good design and social wellbeing without always understanding how this came about.

Additional to the box 5.1 principles it is important to ensure that urbanists exhibit 'good neighbourhood manners'. To that end a **Basic residential componentry** is presented as box 5.2. From a regional perspective the information given represents settlement detail: from an urban perspective these are core residential arrangements akin to the forethought of guilds in earlier centuries. The components given in box 5.2 all warrant elaboration in detail, although in the context of outcome, the key issues to highlight are sound policy and good design. There is also the matter of densification. The aim is for new suburbs to have more than 50 persons per hectare (more readily understood as 20 households per hectare – 8hh/ac – 'net' which *in*cludes adjoining access and *ex*cludes peripheral amenity spaces). This target density would generally be less, for practical reasons, in retrofitted suburbs; and preferably more for new development.

The box 5.2 litany implies cultural workability. In order specifically to identify the 'social' elements in urban residential design, it is helpful to centre in on the following four core design criteria.[21]

1   *That for each doubling of intended density there should be at least a fourfold increase to design input (or design care) – in other words a quadrupling of design effort for a doubling of density relative to a subject community, subject site complex, and indeed for the design of each subject building.* As a rule of thumb, practitioners are enjoined to 'design, design, design' higher-density projects in order to ensure that the living offered at those greater densities is indeed 'higher' living. This stricture is crude, but taken on board as social design effort it highlights the need for lavish inputs of time for handling the siting massing and materials

Box 5.2 Basic residential componentry

The following ten-point listing cannot bring about 'urban delight': but what follows are the key ingredients of good urban form, identifying both the policy parameters and the macro design principles appropriate to future urban communities, particularly at the time of rural-into-urban crossover.

1 Street patterns consciously, purposefully and logically focused, with some axiality, on a school-local shops-health clinic 'community' element; with public transport and put-down exchange points at each such focus (also encouraging reduced private car usage). Defining the identity, through walkability, of neighbourhoods.

2 Each residential urban community chunked into place (subject to topographical constraints) – with (for the raw land context) an outer farming 'broadacre' or amenity green belt, breaking down to a robust high-density residential 'band' around community clusters: the residential occupancy of suburban neighbourhoods being ideally at a density of around 70 persons per hectare – 28pp/acre – net (no less than 30 households per hectare – 12hh/acre net) with a view to creating sufficient opportunity for social contact, to induce an urban community lifestyle, and to attract the installation of a public transport service.

3 Planning and design to triumph over zoning. The objective is to establish a mechanism of 'landowner compacts' suited to a community purpose, leaving some land with native wildlife and flora or in agriculture, in exchange for a density increase or cash payback from some other part of a project. Allow 'double-designation' and 'deemed to comply' provisions, enabling well-designed proposals to exceed an 'as of right' zoned density.

4 Overcome discordance by setting out 'with the grain of the land' designs which heed what the landscape comprising each locality has to 'say', and 'listening' to the community into which it is to fit. Staggered gridding works well over flat-plane topography. Avoid the scraped-earth approach to subdivision, working with and deferring to land form.

5 Street patterns generally are best if interconnecting and formalized (straight and legible) rather than contrived on a curvilinear basis (unless this is dictated by topography). Also 'calmed' streets running in orthogonal sectors, generally of less than 15 metre (50 ft) overall width (down to 5 m (16 ft) for the carriageways.

6 Establish a walking and-or-also cycleway interconnectedness (particularly between culs-de-sac: conscious of topography and focused on transport pick-up points and the community core.

7 Adopt a precautionary approach to residential security. Design in a way which mollifies the criminogenic capacity of suburbs, mindful that 'permeability' can facilitate criminality, creating a challenge for defensible yet permeable design.

8 Accept chunkier smaller plots: 300 square metres (3,200 sq. ft), even 200 square metres (2,100 sq. ft) per plot for household clusterings which are well designed and accompanied by strata titling and other multi-level dwelling and ownership arrangements. Promote the living and aesthetic advantages of party-walling and building to boundary (zero lot-line construction) in designated instances; install common trenching for utilities, and make car garaging integral to the building frontage line, or to the rear.

9 Accept variably sized lots, mixed housing sizes and styles and compatibly mixed (adaptive) land uses: accommodating home-commerce, home-servicing, home-outwork and light home-fabrication.

10 Accept a mixture of houses and flats, comprising single to four-bedroom layouts, meeting all manner of household living preferences. Granny flats ('carriage houses' attached – and 60 square metres (650 sq. ft) maximum if detached) and loft conversions are acceptable. Housing to be organized in focused clusters as urban community artifacts which engender a sense of community.

Also consult App. 'A' (Traditional Neighbourhood Development) in Duany, Plater-Zyberk, Speck, *Suburban Nation*, 2000.

inputs at increased levels of density – and for resolving urban complications (through design) against noise-intrusiveness, unsafeness, and conflict.

2 *Involves consciously providing a community focus and having a sense of identity in mind; to include a mixture of compatible urban land-use types, and to allow residentially compatible functions to be incorporated into higher-density suburban layouts.* The objective is to work proactively to ensure in every situation that the noise, glare, smell and vibration effects of small homework businesses are mitigated. The most common among the totally unacceptable uses being the likes of backyard repair shops, fleet parking and gas stations. Design is engaged as the means for enabling residents within an urban neighbourhood to feel that they are also part of a community that is characterized by consonant vitality and variety. Such a community would comprise all manner of functional households and compatible work practices, along with an accommodation of a variety of places for cultural expression and interchange.

3 *Involves a harnessing of design consciousness to provide physical infrastructural easements and open space networks within communities in a way which facilitates 'permeability', 'connectability' and household 'defensibility'* (refer to box 5.1). Safety is also an issue here, the overall objective being to avoid the separation and atomizing of suburban people, and to provide them with access to a variety of workplace opportunities and services. In terms of 'detail' it is important to fashion and craft street pavements, street furniture and fittings, public art, plantings, heritage conservation, mixed land uses, signage, new buildings and traffic ordering in well-mannered and neighbourly ways (refer to David Sucher's *City Comforts*, 1995).

4 *To increase the overall density of greenery along with increases in density [!] and to resist any suggestion that this challenge is mutually excluding.* It is also an aim to protect existing shrub and tree planting, and to install additional street and public realm tree planting at every opportunity and in every available space. Beyond 30 households per hectare this challenge intensifies. One useful criterion is that the end result 'outcome' fulfils the pre-project landscaping parameters set for a project.

Physical design for pulling together a socially worthy urban outcome is a challenge for those managers, planners, engineers, landscapists and surveyors who would plan. The engagement of good design, along with an acceptable site-utility and land-use mix, induces the best that constitutes vibrant, wholesome and joyful urban living, accommodating work-at-home preferences, house-type mixtures and offering social choices. A difficulty with this emphasis on urban social design is that it works through as an aestheticism which is sought out, and in effect paid extra for, by those wealthy enough to afford it; but of course the need for good design is imperative for poor communities because it induces 'pride of place'.

Urban social arrangement and style leads to a consideration of the global edicts given out by *Agenda 21* (1992 United Nations Conference on Environment and Development: précis given in the Appendix to this Chapter) although this does not come to the universal aid of the urban cause because the urban design directives are not always clear, and the urban policy recommendations are far from specific. One reason for this is that *Agenda 21* is essentially a low-income nation 'agenda'; and in low income nations well over half the population is rural-living, leaving the lesser urban population to get by as best it can.[22] Thus rich and poor nations alike should not seek much in the way of direct urban social direction or actionable urban reform from *Agenda 21*.[23]

Ex-urban sprawl control

(Refer also to the Urban-Rural Patterning passage in chapter 4.)

Rural-residential settlement on land of marginal utility to farming is the only circumstance for accepting a discrete quasi-rural style of rural land occupation for city-focused dwellers desiring to live beyond the city fringe as an option of democratic choice in an open society.[24] Given the water-conserving, waste-management and solar energy collection technologies now available, it has become feasible for ex-urban lifestyler's to have no publicly provided and maintained services – aside from access to a legal road.

> Ex-urban: a band, ring or belt – but more usually corridors. The quasi-urban (also peri-urban) residential-rural living beyond the suburban edge of larger towns and cities, most notably within settler societies.

This means that whatever utilities householders connect to, they can be expected to make full payment for installation, including any requirement or preference for utility under-grounding. On-site services must of course be installed in accordance with local government conservation, building envelope, impact control rules, and residential-rural building codes. This constitutes the exceptional case for allowing discretely sited residential buildings in low-density forever, self-serviced, residential-rural broad-acre (lifestyle) zones, but again only for locations where the soils or topography are declared useless for agriculture.

'Scenic' Highway 16, NZ. A shifted on city house dumped on a hilltop.

Much housing already built in the ex-urban landscape is poorly sited, highly profiled, garishly decorated, awkward of access, neglectful of its landscape setting, and construed antagonistically in relation to any neighbours. Yet, in contrast, some residential-rural dwellings are placed as if by the hand of God: carefully profiled, sensitively clad and effectively landscaped into their setting. Additional to the physical considerations is a raft of socio-economic concerns, particularly for poorer

Again shifted on, but discreetly sited and landscaped.

families situated in remote quasi-urban locations where this is a lowest-cost option. The problem is that 'Out in two-acre (0.8 ha) zoning country old ideas of neighbourhood and neighbourliness are hard to sustain' (Barnett's *The Fractured*

Metropolis, 1995). Low-pension adults immobilized in retirement, and the denial of opportunities for children in younger families to socialize and enjoy outside play during the slush of winter, are also problems for poor families in ex-urbia.

Well-understood ex-urban policies can render it possible to achieve rural-residential conservation *with* development, involving no land taking, an aesthetically acceptable and environmentally benign outcome being the end result. Official controls are necessary simply because the operation of individual moral conscience is partial. There exists an exhibitionist-commodifier will on the part of a majority of ex-urban stakeholders to not conform, to profile their presence well beyond the title boundary, and also to take in what ambience they can enjoy 'free' from beyond those boundaries. Quasi-urban development on land not suitable for agriculture is acceptable and workable *provided* clear rules for siting, access, profile, appearance and landscaping – set out in figure 5.4 as **Ex-urban building performance guidelines** – are well understood, appreciated for what they are, and get enforced.

Care is necessary for this is the urban frontier, there are few watchdogs and no craft guilds at work here. Indeed Tom Daniels provides a five-page appendix to his *When City and Country Collide* (1999), entitled 'A Warning About Living in the Rural Urban Fringe', covering such matters as access and shared access, utility rights, ground water purity, noise (such as weekend go-karting), spray drift. And in a box he sets down a few notes on 'How to Tell if You Live in the Rural-Urban Fringe' (25-plus minutes' commute, on-site septic tanks, less than 500 people per square mile).

An advocacy for a 'rules' approach is contained in Randall Arendt's well-crafted *Rural by Design* (1994). His sliding-scale alters the rate of dwelling numbers

---

Much reference is given to Oregon in the rural-residential 'resistance' literature.

Also noteworthy, relative to the Connecticut River Valley, are the innovative 'work with the flow' guidelines put out by Yaro and Arendt (1994).

For *any* construction allowed under *either* a 'resistance' or a 'work with the flow' situation it is important, for the sake of local appreciation as well as the wider benefit to tourism, to conserve existing woodlands, retain arable and pasture land for agriculture, group any allowed housing into 'clusters' and to prohibit building on profiled ridges or close to roadlines.

Tracking down from these general design parameters: the attainment of rural building harmony predicates that attention be accorded the following on-site design and harmony factors for each individual siting situation:
- *Setting*: co-considerate discrete siting and clustering
- *Grouping*: buildings, garages, tanks, structures all-of-a-piece.
- *Positioning*: unobtrusive location, and heeling into the landscape
- *Profiling*: low-rise buildings, low-angle roofing; all below the skyline
- *Texturing*: surfaces low-sheen and non-reflective
- *Colouring*: use earth and woodland colorations on all buildings and structures
- *Parking*: out-of-sight, unobtrusive, screened
- *Utilities*: all within-site utilities under-grounded

Figure 5.4 Ex-urban building performance guidelines.

Tract (acres)	Dwellings permitted	Acres per dwelling
Up to 10	1	10 or less
10 to 21	2	5 to 10.5
21 but less than 35	3	7.0 plus
35 but less than 65	4	8.75 plus
65 but less than 105	5	13 plus
105 but less than 145	6	17.5 plus
145 but less than 185	7	20.7 plus
185 but less than 225	8	23.1
Thereafter an average of one dwelling per 50 acres of landholding		

Figure 5.5 Ex-urban density formula (patterned on Arendt 1994).
Applied in association with the performance guidelines given in figure 5.4.

within larger rural holdings – placing constraint on the division of large farms into minimum units by controlling the density of permitted dwellings. With this approach 'rural' plots less than ten acres (4 ha) in extent – the recommended minimum – are intended for sole single-household occupancy. Thereafter, through illustrations depicting 'Dwelling Yield and Acreage Protected', Arendt arrives at an array of the kind retabulated here as an **Ex-urban density formula** (figure 5.5) which could be elastically amended or compressed for sparsely wooded localities – my preference being that Arendt's 'acres' were applied as 'hectares'! This is not a quibble, for time and again in Barnett's 'two acre zoning country' the neighbours are in dispute about noxious, to them, land uses (intense chicken, goat, and pig penning), oversized buildings (feeding sheds, glasshouses), spray drift, and always noise. If you want peace and tranquillity, be advised to build in the middle of a large plot and take on some agri-silviculture, for, excepting well-wooded non-farm tracts, I would recommend the minimum desirable urban-rural retreat as 8 ha (20 acres) and advise that the figure 5.4 performance guidelines prevail as a minimum.

The figures 5.4 and 5.5 prescriptions work out acceptably for some landscapes, fail with others – notably coastal zones and sparsely wooded uplands – and are usually not sensitized to accommodate the vagaries of good-to-bad soil types, open-and-wooded treescapes, and flat-to-steep topography. It is always aesthetically desirable to cluster (group) the dwellings of adjoining titleholders together as much as possible, *and* to site all dwellings well back from public access roads, *and also* to closely regulate and monitor all manner of detail – massing, profile, colour, reflectivity, texture in accordance with the figures 5.4 and 5.5 criteria. The procedural basis for achieving a rural-in-character outcome involves adhering to a fixed exclusive rural zoning minimum – the economically viable farm size for operational and viable farming relative to a subject landscape. For large rural tract holders the only development option then comes down to assessing an estate break-up into minimum-sized economically viable farm units – thus far and no

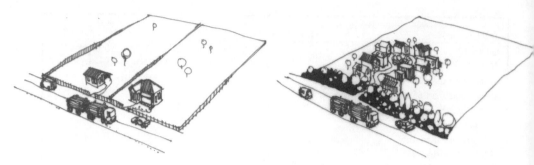

Figure 5.6 Rural road stripping and the cluster alternative.
Left: Scenic Highway 16 again. *Right:* not to be encouraged, but much better – a 20 per cent housing and 80 per cent rural ratio, retaining most of the land for agriculture, yet producing a bonus number of discretely sited, gravel-accessed plots for sale.

further – reinforced by binding all farm holders into a 'right to farm and nothing else' rural tax base.

At its most offending, ex-urban land commodification presents as 'ribbon development', an Australasian expression which transcribes expressively in North America as 'road stripping'. Figure 5.6, **Rural road stripping: the cluster alternative**, illustrates the recommended layout approach. Approval within such a compact involves acceptance of a deep frontyard set-back (50 metres minimum from the road boundary), designing multiple access and pan-handled rear siting, and achieving effective clustering, avoiding ridge-lines and hill-tops – and landscaped withal.

The most direct instrument to apply for averting the costs to a nation of taking elite soils out of food and textile production for ex-urban residential development, is simply to enforce an urban growth boundary decree, a rural tax-based growth prohibition against urban expansion onto land of either high productive character or high conservation value. The only ex-urban uses permitted beyond the urban growth boundary would involve pockets of agriculturally less productive soils of marginal agricultural utility. This approach accommodates the fact that those motivated toward an ex-urban lifestyle cannot be easily dissuaded from that choice, leaving this as a selective compromise option.[25]

The backgrounding to an extensive method of ex-urban sprawl control was examined in the 'Urban-rural patterning' section in chapter 4, signalling the ravages of sprawl and the benefits of growth management. *Turning growth management principles into growth management practice – in effect initiating extensive land-use planning – is one of the most exacting challenges of a planning kind confronting Anglo settler societies.* 'Exacting and demanding' because the emergence of growth management policy involves political partnerships, inter-governmental associations, technical competency, years of lead time, and the formulation of legal procedures of a magnitude unfamiliar to most local planning practitioners. The whole-of-territory imperative established in chapter 4 predicates that the growth management mandate exhibits a whole-state (whole province) attribute. In a text with the catchy title *Sprawl Busting* masking its serious polemic, 'mandate designer' Jerry Weitz (1999) reviews the learning paths and establishment successes acquired from beneficial growth management practice in the Pacific north-west and the Atlantic south-east of the United States. Newcomers to growth management practice have this precedent available, guidelining this multi-task, multi-year, multi-agency and geographically extensive procedure. The longer-term expectation is that growth management practice will evolve for all four Anglo settler society nations as a consequence of a maturity of outlook that time engenders.

Ex-urban siting criteria have been represented by Kendig et al. in *Performance Zoning* (1980) in a variety of 'exception designations' agricultural-district zoning, urban-rural district zoning, and conservation-district zoning, to be applied on a performance basis as is variously appropriate for rougher terrains and poorer soil localities.[26] These zonings accommodate some housing in peri-urban localities, with a spot-zone allowance for selected medium-density residential pockets on agriculturally insignificant soils, ensuring rural-only land usage for elite-soil landscapes.[27] This approach accommodates an inevitability, for some residential accommodation on non-productive open lands, conserving the best land for agriculture while also preserving the rural aesthetic comprising woodlands, meadows, plantations, orchards, ponds, streams, wetlands, outcrops and vistas. A format for breaking away from the 'by right' infilling of a rural landscape is depicted in figure 5.7 as **Trading rights for open space**: the aim being to allow only farm-buildings on farmland, in exchange for occasional, discrete, rural-residential pockets on land of less farming utility, with the balance acreage secured for farming or conservation.

In Randall Arendt's *Growing Greener* (1999, also his *Conservation Design for Subdivisions*, 1996) the slant is 'conservation subdivision', a four-step design

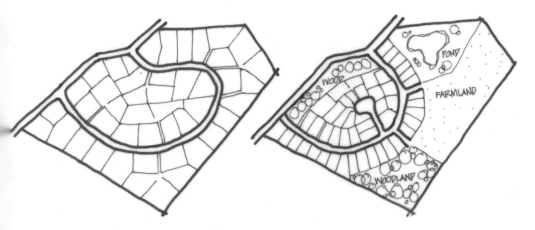

Figure 5.7 Trading rights for open space.
On the *left* small 'broad-acre' plots presenting as suburbia in the countryside. To the *right* a compromise; the same number of plots *and* some reserved woodland, *plus* the fertile area retained for agriculture.

approach – selecting areas for conservation and farming first, subdividing the remainder last – where much of the rural landscape is conserved or set aside for agriculture permanently. This approach does not involve any land taking. When and where professional initiative and political commitment is against growth management practice, a case-by-case pursuit of conservation subdivision is a useful alternative practice.[28] Arendt's advocacy involves trading in the broad-acre as-of-right zoning for compact clusterings, often for an increased number of dwellings, all sited within an appropriate sub-part of larger rural estates. These clusters might be locally of suburban density, yet usually *not* connected to water supply and sewage disposal utilities. These arrangements, like so much else that is well contrived, become exclusionary by price, a matter researched by Nancy and James Duncan ('Deep Suburban Irony', 1997) for Westchester County near New York.[29]

Planners in the Anglo settler societies have been stuck with precedent and constrained by utility providers *against* planning and implementing the likes of sustainable design and higher-density outcomes, sequested energy reductions, conjoint water supply and waste-water management and 'softer' materials installation. The challenge is for a conservator commitment, developer participation, and political will – backed by community awareness and endorsement of sustainability as a lifestyle exemplar.

Along with the negative economic effects of quasi-rural 'urbanism' upon agricultural production is an aesthetic despoiling of the countryside; the main lesson from experience being that rural-urban 'broad-acre' arrangements trend progressively toward higher-density quasi-urbanization on an 'as of right' presumption. Thus 20-acre (8 ha) blocks (which I am inclined to favour as sufficiently large to allay most agro-economic and aesthetic objections) get subdivided down to 10-acre (4 ha), then 5-acre (2 ha) and sometimes two-acre (0.8 ha) and one-acre (0.4 ha) blocks.[30] The consequence is that local government authorities are progressively cornered into permitting 'normal' residential infill, withal losing the opportunity to meet community space needs. The end result is sporadic urbanization, physically adrift from utilities and community services. Then, an ultimate irony, the hapless authorities who approved this pattern on a *laissez-faire* basis are asked to subsidize the installation of those utilities and provide social services and community facilities. In effect the territorial agencies end up paying much of the cost for installing the very suburban trappings the initiating lifestylers set out to be independent from!

Within the ex-urban band or corridors outside large towns and cities there are usually some small 'historic' settlements. The edge of such small towns are randomly configured because the shape of the towns are influenced more by the pattern of landownership than the defining topographical limits, water excepted. Ensuring that urban expansion at the fringe of small towns does not leapfrog beyond an Urban Reserve Area set by a growth boundary, is clearly sound policy, mainly to avoid the irrational extension of already capitalized utility services. It is important that urban expansion takes place as part of a defined and designated patterning, and that rural activities (along with appropriate recreational-rural activities) remain part of the rural scene. Small-town issues are addressed in the next passage.

A significant offshoot to ex-urban control policies involves recognition of the preference by indigenous first-settler peoples to settle down residentially upon cognatic owned peri-urban land for their own use on a community housing basis.[31] It is axiomatic that indigenous first-people settlements be required to meet the normal user costs of access and utilities provisioning, but with no application, in this context, of anything like a sprawl levy. The social issues involved are complex, but there is one certainty: that it is the right of indigenous first-nation peoples to exercise their preference, as an exceptional community value-set to reside within ex-urbia on a cognatic title if this is their inclination, or be provided with an acceptable exchange alternative.

A concluding emphatic point to make about ex-urban policy enforcement is that in order for it to really work it must be locked on comprehensively, as a complete package, throughout a whole territorial jurisdiction – the 'concurrency' and 'consistency' imperatives outlined in the previous chapter. Territorial plans which set out to enforce growth management must designate and specify separately for 'urban' and 'rural' land-use allocations throughout the whole territorial extent of a local-regional government jurisdiction. A consequence, following an effective lock-on of a rural-urban growth boundary, is that at the 'urban fence' the rural-side land values of the open-land areas only appreciate by some 10 to 15 per cent, which is much less than the valuation hike arising from the standard rural-into-urban expectation. Clarity of urban-rural distinction results in regional gains – reduced fossil energy consumption, better-quality local food availability, and constrains commodification of ex-urban landscapes against the state (provincial) and national interest.

In the greater metropolitan growth context it has to be accepted that accommodation of new households cannot be contained forever on an inward densification basis. It is an aspect of urban growth that cities be provided with some greenfield opportunities to 'let out the urban belt' in a planned and provisioned manner, and in pre-planned directions. This growth vector or corridor – for such it usually is – became a feature of the Doxiadis designs of the 1960s and 1970s of which I had personal experience at Tema (Ghana) and Islamabad (Pakistan), concluding that as automobile-friendly designs they exhibited some validity for communities of wealth, although they proved inconvenient for poorer people in those developing nation contexts.[32]

Small-town conservation with development

Small towns[33] have problems – sometimes remoteness, sometimes an abandoned mining logging or service-centre legacy, always economic insignificance and under-employment, often poverty. Yet they also exhibit several virtues, not least their compactness, accessibility, pedestrian scale, time-of-day friendliness, variety of building size and style, and mixed plot usage.[34] There are few production jobs,

The *Small Town Planning Handbook* (Daniels, Keller and Lapping 1995) offers a US-focused review of organizational and procedural issues, including a useful 'what can go wrong' checklist. The small-town scene is sensitively depicted in the evocative text by Kristina Ford, *Planning Small Town America*, 1990.

although many find ways to gain an income from working outside the tax-gathering system. In other words it is possible to be 'subsistence employed' in an often pleasant land-use environment which includes produce and exchange gardens, second-hand consumer-durable goods recycling, production from kitchens and sewing rooms, along with exchange skills and services of the 'piano lessons for child minding' variety. Social services are limited, yet even this drawback assists the formation of friendships and neighbourly support on a community-care basis, younger households keeping up a helping contact with the aged and isolated, and the aged supporting each other. Small towns harbour declining (increasingly aged) populations; yet these elderly are amazingly resourceful and capable.[35] There is no limelight, yet there usually exists healthy support for local football and basketball teams, an active and high level of participation in small-court sports and maybe golf, as well as good attendance at a variety of well-patronized historical and special interest clubs.[36]

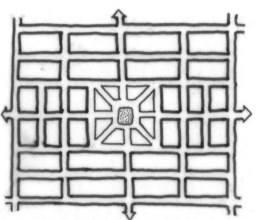

Martinborough, my family home town, a speculative nineteenth-century property venture by an Anglo-patriot. At a loss for a place name, Mr Martin chose Martinboro. At a loss for street names he picked world-famous locations. At a loss for a layout design, Mr Martin chose the British Flag! Martinborough is now a boutique wine-producing centre.

Small 'country' towns confront three main vectors for change, which challenge their viability and their future.[37]

- The least likely (ever-welcome when it is positive) change to the *viability of small towns* is that which arises from a gainful metamorphosis of the surrounding agriculture. Diversity within agriculture, ranging from intensive horticulture to extensive silviculture, has of course the potential to add value to the economic base of country service centres. On the distaff side there is also the global complexity of agricultural resizing to put into the equation; as has occurred throughout the 1970s and again as a consequence of GATT–WTO protocols during the 1990s and on into the twenty-first century. The denial of agricultural subsidies within agri-trading nations induces an upswing for only selective parts of the rural sector. More productively efficient agribusiness is likely to further centralize specialist agricultural services in provincial cities and larger rural towns, rather than in hamlets and small country towns, although in general the nearest small town is likely to remain as the schooling, watering-hole and small-goods purchasing focus for an adjoining rural community. In short, the economic prognosis for smaller country towns is: anticipate the rural economy to at best hold its own, but maybe to further decline, and do not rely on permanence from agribusiness.

- The most certain process of change for small towns is that which effects the *demographic trend* in the direction of school leaver out-migration and the in-migration of older-aged unemployed and retiring residents. The net result is an overall maturing of country town population structure, although the retired sector is a consumer force (and a skill resource) in its own right. Another low-income dependency group comprises solo-parenting and de-institutionalized persons. They are attracted to small towns because of low rents, the lower than large-town property prices, and low local property taxes. Future population size is difficult to predict for small towns because the fertile cohort is generally low.[38] Of course were a growth industry or a large service facility to alight, a younger job-chasing population would spring back into profile – but this possibility, as noted earlier, is unlikely. The overall population size of small towns well away from metropolitan centres will not change all that much, yet their age composition can be expected to vary as the out-migration of younger people puts reduced-value residential properties on the market, which may in turn be occupied by inward-bound low-income house-holders. Small towns can be characterized as physically unchanging places, prone to adverse variations of demographic composition; and it is their public service base, rather than their commercial component, which is most frequently in need of retention and refurbishment.
- Low levels of economic activity and an unfavourable prospect for natural population replacement underscores changes in public services. Settler society governments provide reduced public sector services in small towns, often cut back without consultation or anything like an open assessment of the likely impact. Rationalizations, as with the shrinking of rail networks, have poleaxed many centres, although the abrupt withdrawal of the likes of a postal agency can have equally devastating effects. Post offices and secondary schools come top of the retention list, followed by the need to retain citizen advisory services, banking outlets and medical clinics. These settlements offer a sense of community, a slower and well-ordered pace, certainty and security, and a clean environment – all desirable attributes beyond price. Small towns can survive economic-base changes, they can cope with demographic-base changes, but what shocks them to their foundations are draconian closures of public sector services.

Small towns are not economically significant, although they are usually socially viable on account of shared community knowledge, and to an impressive extent they can be self-sufficient in providing kitchen crops and property maintenance. This is not a case for denying them essential services (schools, clinics and the like) on the grounds of their low capacity; yet it has to be recognized that commercial and industrial regrowth for settlements beyond the magnetic pull of larger towns and cities is unlikely.

There is something else, a grass-roots capability, which implies for small towns a capacity to make something out of virtually nothing. This can also be likened to middle-out growth. There are vacant buildings and affordable services, and people with all manner of skills reside in these communities. The middle-out ideas, resources and energies are available as catalysts for local projects, most obviously in the style of craft outlets or museums, connecting with the Mainstreet concept reviewed later on in the 'Shopping as entertainment' passage. Small towns do *not* suffer a nation or a region with the excessive 'costs' of urbanization identified earlier in this chapter; indeed they are vibrantly self-sufficient and well poised to respond to any initiative which arises or opportunity which presents.

Maintaining the vitality of small country towns enjoins three notions which refute the usual concerns about population numbers and proportions, and commercial activities: namely small town 'attributes', 'activities' and 'attitudes'.

Attributes.   Country town futures are founded on in-place skills and within-community support systems. These, along with the attraction of a lower cost of living, proximate schooling, relative freedom from crime and an access to recreational facilities, add up to a neat, wholesome and mature urban package. To maintain these attributes small towns do *not* need to clutch at *any* kind of project, or be necklaced with amenity reducing quasi-urban smallholdings. At best they are 'in balance'; neither taking from, nor adding to.

Activities.   Small towns can 'own the idea' that their land-use approach is inclusionary, that compatible mixed land uses are acceptable and can be managed, and that tourism can be nurtured. There is always an edge-of-town potential for horse riding, golfing, and activities such as parachuting and gliding; and backshed light industry, retirement housing, bed-and-breakfasting can all be initiated provided there is a bottom-up tolerance.

Attitudes.   The country town capability of being able to fabricate and supply goods and services locally connotes the purpose-built context for following through on the vertical 'community' and 'household' columns outlined within the box 3.7 (chapter 3) **Matrix** for living a life which is sustainable in spirit. There is also the potential to profile the indigenous first people's history and the 'first settler' contributions to the changeover from a wilderness past to a small country town present.

Of interest to small towns is their tourism earnings potential, which can range from the attraction of an unhurried village setting, through to contrived features such as historical sites and museums, along with 'pay as you use them' recreation facilities. Two clear planning preferences associated with small-town tourism are, *first*, the separation-out of the bedlam elements (gas stations, fast food outlets) away from the core tourist attraction (museum, craft centre) and its support facilities; and, *second*, a bypass separation of through traffic from local and intentionally stopping visitor traffic.

Water's edge urbanization

(*Refer also to the Coastal Zone Pattern passage in chapter 4*)

Turn now the inquiring eye
To the sea's margin,
To the land's rough edge.

(Dennis Glover, *Enter Without Knocking*)

The conservancy and development issues which confront the ecologically fragile marine and lakeland shores – the marine, lake and river littoral – involves cultural heritage as well as the more tangible preservation of natural heritage and matters of biologically diversity. The chapter 4 (figure 4.5) depiction of the coastal marine zone illustrates the overall conservancy and development context of coastal regimes. The intrinsic worth of these environments includes sea food supply, visual and aesthetic appeal, transportation connections, recreational qualities, and historical associations, a fundamental *terra psyche* (box 1.2) for indigenous people, and a *landfall symbolism* to settlers. There is more at stake here than biological diversity, land protection, and silt and waste-water absorption. Water's edge management and the management of other extensive water-land uses are best mandated within a growth management (extensive land-use protection) context, as detailed in the previous chapter.

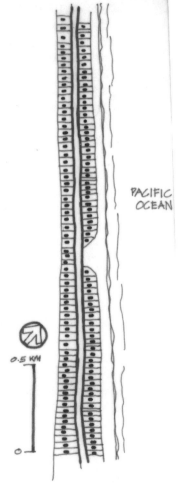

PACIFIC OCEAN

0.5 KM

Bay of Plenty!

Two questions: 'what is the coastal attraction?' and 'in what way is this an urban issue'. The 'attraction' is associated with the potential to gratify two base needs at the water's edge: to gain access to a place which offers the recreational cleanliness and sense of purification human beings associate with proximity to ocean and lake water; and to gain access to a food source of particular significance to indigenous first peoples. The 'in what way is this an urban issue?' is a function of landownership pressure up to the water's edge, and automobile mobility, combining to facilitate an extensive urbanization along the shoreline, even the remote shoreline.[39] Being close to the water is one compulsion, occupying and fencing the land as close to that edge as is legally allowable, is another.[40] These two factor-forces are embodied in the waterside holiday cottage, in the past absorbing all the waste materials, building-merchant 'special offer' leftovers and paints, and the limited spare time available from their second-mortgaged owners. In this context, Lucas (1970) recognized that:

> Sea coasts (and lakesides) are under pressure from people seeking to escape from an urban environment. The tragedy is that those who seek to escape, create another urban environment and all too often a substandard one. The result is that beautiful coastal areas are preempted for the benefit of a few . . . [and that] Key coastal areas should be retained for the use and enjoyment of the public, and typical examples of a country's shoreline should be preserved in as natural a state as possible.

What most inhibits conformity to the set-aside ideal is the pattern of freehold landownership, aided by a narrow 'painting by numbers' technique for the 'trend zoning' of land held in private freehold ownership along the littoral. A conservation vision (indeed a vision for preservation of the coastal heritage) is necessary because for all nations the coastal fringe is a national asset of fixed extent which, when obliterated from public use, becomes an asset forgone for public enjoyment, forever. In terms of this reasoning, public foreshore reservations – say 20 m minimum – need to be applied as the statutory norm along all of the coast, expanded upon by 'foreshore yard' provisions on designated private land where this is indicated. In 'soft and sensitive' residential-holiday localities a wider – 100 to 200 m – coastal reserve should be retained in public ownership. Another physical planning matter involves fixing a natural coastal hazard boundary limit in situations where the rising sea-level factor will lead to 'coastal squeeze'. In some situations this reality will eventually trigger 'managed retreat' (moving the building-line inland), 'adaptation' (raising building floor levels), or 'engineered protection' (seawall revetments and infill).

Although the coastal fringe ought to be recognized as part of the 'national heritage estate' along with National Parks and other kinds of forest and desert wilderness, it is mostly treated with less respect. Relative to the larger forest and wilderness heritage the water's edge is in fact both potentially more accessible, more fragile, and of fixed extent.

There needs to be an understanding and acceptance of variable controls relative to different foreshore situations. This can be incorporated into planning documents as a 'zone of vulnerability' established as a proscribed building limit (50 metres minimum, inland from the high-water mark) extending to 250 metres and more in visually, flood-prone and ecologically sensitive contexts. The performance guidelines noted in figure 5.4 are of crucial importance in CZM locations where building permission has been granted. In some jurisdictions (notably in Australia and New Zealand, in parts of Canada, but lamentably sparse in the United States) there are instances of mandatory public-owned littoral reserves over the band of land – often of legal road width – immediately inland from the high-water mark.[41]

The littoral has been subject to minimum at worst, mixed at best, official intervention in the past. Officialdom – a confused responsibility at the water's edge – has often turned a blind eye to amateur building construction, sometimes right into the foreshore reserve, and has failed to deter rapacious food-plunder practices both along the shore and offshore. What has to be taken on board is that water's edge development of all kinds is both a major attraction and big business. Developments here become urban centres in their own right. Smith (1992) picks up on this in his eight-stage documentation of the evolution of an unplanned water's edge settlement, from 'second home' strip development, through to the subsequent motels and hotels, to tourist domination, and urbanization, leading to environmental degradation.

Sustainable urban planning at the water's edge begs reversal of the unfettered commodification practices of the past – the neo-modern objective being to draw interested parties into benefiting from joint venture partnerships between landowners, developers, conservators and local authorities on an integrated win-win basis. Joint ventures are hard work, but the rewards include conservancy *with* development, improved public access, and an overall harmonization of the interface between land and water.

> A serious social failing is that the population of over-wintering water's edge holiday settlements can be as low as one-sixth of the summer holiday population. The low-density wintering population suffers from being identified as a remnant residual group with isolation and security fears along with winter weather desolation to contend with.

There are other dimensions to a water's edge urban strategy. These include such tangibles as the retention of coastal and lakeside biodiversity and richness; also the provision – sometimes compulsory acquisition – of public access, reinforcement of the waterline's legibility and personality, and above all an enhancement of the sociability of coastal and lakeland communities. Individualization of landholding needs to give way to legal certainty for public domains and public good. To elaborate on the joint venture suggestion made earlier, a key strategy involves cooperation between central and local government because this provides the springboard for government–developer partnerships which are otherwise notoriously difficult to initiate.

ECO-village ideals

Planning literature is larded through with concepts for new urban outcomes, some desirable, others highly speculative, few carried over to bricks and mortar.[42] There is *either* a lack of capability to set aside, out-purchase or override the profiteering orthodoxy of freehold landowners and the lineal certitude of local bureaucracies, *and, or also*, a lack of operational and political understanding, conviction and commitment to the negotiating deal-cutting and equity-adjustment potentials in joint actions and joint ventures.

In the essentially idealistic peri-urban category arises the eco-village, a new-urbanist concept often too difficult to achieve, yet too good to pass over. This new style of urbanism, known also as neotraditionalism, has been subjected to a lot of criticism, summarized by Larry Ford (2000) as a mode lacking in distinctiveness and authenticity, and exhibiting a marketing flirtation. The eco-village concept can transcend Ford's criticism, and is of course worthy, being *of* these technological times (proven-science, bioharmonic materials and techno-gadgetry) and *for* ecological balance and social harmony – albeit at a high unit cost. My preference lies with the neomodern prototypes invented from the present, rather than

NEW URBANISM
(A United States
selection of projects
which incline toward
the eco-village ideal)
Seaside FL
Kentlands MD
Laguna West CA
Windsor FL
Fairview OR
Southern Village NC
Northwest Landing
WA
Sunnyside OR
Celebration FL
Addison Circle TX
Belmont Forest VA

'The "new" in New
Urbanism . . . attempts to
apply the age old
principles of urbanism –
diversity, streetlife, human
scale – to the suburbs in
the 21st Century.'
Calthorpe and Fulton,
The Regional City
(2001: 279).

*Imported into urban
localities:* hydro-generated,
wind-powered, fossil and
nuclear energy; potable
water; fresh air; food and
fibres; consumer
'durables'.
*Exported from urban
localities:* waste heat,
waste toxins, waste
water, polluted air,
sewage, garbage.

conforming to a vision retrieved from the past. Yet all credit to the Duany, Plater-Zyberk, Speck revival of the Traditional Neighbourhood Development model, exemplified in the open-access settlement of Seaside, Florida (*Suburban Nation*, 2000).[43] Historically benchmarked, the eco-village ideal conforms also to the Geddesian ideal of a rapprochement between 'work place folk' for a countryside setting, described by Geddes in his prototype as 'the valley section'.

Eco-villages are predicated on the virtues of dependable and frequent public transportation, a within-settlement energy efficiency, pedestrian accessibility, waste reduction reuse and recycling, food and fresh water quality and semi-sufficiency, all laced through with greenways and backgrounded by a farming-woodland landscape. In this context the eco-village construct reaches back into history by replicating the decentralized, away from the city yet locally concentrated, global-wide rural village pattern. It also attaches to the neomodern principles of *Agenda 21* – taking care of the community and the habitat (Duerksen and others, *Habitat Protection Planning,* 1997).

Villages of the green-setting kind, peripheral to European cities and a few of the older cities of the New World, are locally dense habitations mostly established prior to the steam train, and certainly prior to the widespread use of automobiles. They are caricatured as being the distance apart, approximately, that a villager could return-traverse to market in the next town, on foot during one day. Their growth has been slowly incremental, often lineal. As they grew, they incorporated mixed uses (houses, small shops, light and service industry) and provided specialist services (of the blacksmith and bakery kind) which, previous to their consolidation as a village, may have been part of a farming hamlet. Those villages within an hour's drive of a large town or city have now become residential dormitories which offer aesthetically attractive, fairly private options for a mobile urban elite – at considerable social cost to the already established agriculture-serving population. In Britain various technical planning devices (the Green Belt, Rural White Land designations, Regional Growth Management practices; the delineation of Exception Areas, Areas Of Outstanding Natural Beauty and Sites of Special Scientific Interest) are used to limit the urban impact and prevent a suburbanization of the between-village space. One clear British objective is to retain good agricultural land, worked as living-producing household-farm entities. An accessory aesthetic objective is to leave these good-soil agricultural localities as agricultural and silvicultural tracts, avoiding the insensitive infilling of between-settlement landscapes.

What now mostly takes place throughout the quasi-urban freehold penumbra of settler society cities and larger towns is a patchy, individualized quasi-rural lifestyle, indiscriminately situated on agriculturally productive land. This squandering of a rural asset to satisfy an attachment to mock-ruralism has proceeded largely unchecked because there is no economic force (or Old World village protection lobby) to oppose a neither-town-nor-country commodification of the rural landscape. Effective 'growth management' of greenfield villages offers hope for a sustainably balanced alternative. This is optimal settlement living (approximating the European village model) in a New World greenfield setting, ideally as eco-villages – capturing the ambience and efficiency of sustainable town-with-country living.

What, then, characterizes an eco-village? First, they incorporate a mixture of the best design practices listed earlier and previously profiled in box 5.1 as Urban social arrangement and style. These design practices were further elaborated in box 5.2 as **Basic residential componentry**. For eco-villages a net density of 30-plus households per hectare is the ideal. Eco-villages also espouse a high degree of self-sufficiency of food production and water harvesting: are green canopied and pleasant to live in, are village sized, are largely self-reliant in the meeting of within-settlement food fibre and energy needs, and set out to recycle or reuse their waste. They are, for their inhabitants, safe, pleasant and interesting places in which to live – but they do not come cheap. In other words new urbanist settlements are not likely to provide any 'affordable housing' for low-income households, although moving in the direction of such a household balance is an objective.

Michelle Thompson-Fawcett (1996: 316) identified and collated, from several sources, the following set of recommendations relative to 'new-urbanism' principles. Rephrased, and recombined, these are as follows:

1 Personal vehicle mobility should not hold the status of a basic right.
2 Large houses on large lots is not an acceptable aspiration.
3 Diversity of residents in a community is enriching.
4 Lower land costs per unit can be achieved at relatively high densities while also ensuring an abundance of public spaces.
5 New urbanism's market is broader than is typical in conventional suburbia because of the diversity of accessible urban attractions.
6 Incorporation of a diversity of uses broadens the tax base for local authorities.
7 Higher-density development reduces set-up and maintenance costs of public infrastructure.
8 Neighbourhood shops do not require the extensive shared-cost furbishment which is common in malls.

From the UK Department of the Environment, *Regeneration Research Summary* (2000). Sustainable Community: Broad Themes:
1 Resource consumption should be minimised;
2 Local environmental capital should be protected;
3 Design quality should be high;
4 Residents should enjoy a high quality of life;
5 Equity and social inclusion should be increased;
6 Participation in governance should be broad;
7 The community should be commercially viable;
8 Integration of environmental and quality-of-life objectives.

Incorporation of these values and virtues into a sited-and-built greenfield village amounts, essentially, to using fewer *from without* resources and enjoying more *available within* potentials – achieving sociability along with improved sustainability. Thus less movement, less waste to dispose of, less utility dependency, and less heating and cooling of living spaces. Also *more* lifestyle variety, more community facilities, more social interaction, more environmental harmony, more toxin-free food and water, more human satisfaction from settling into local jobs.[44]

In a standard within-city suburban environment residents are disinclined to walk more than 300 metres to a local shop or community facility. Improve the ambient environment – safe and pleasant – and people will walk up to 400 metres to pick up a morning paper, visit the shops and access the local library.

In general terms 30 to 35 dwellings net per hectare (12 to 14 per acre *net* being the legal curtilage plot and half the area of the immediately adjoining access) has been recommended by Owens (1986) as an optimal density range when passive solar energy gain is an incorporated design objective. Rydin (1992) makes the point (connecting with Owens) that such settlement, at these sorts of density 'Offers the potential for greater energy efficiency. The actual outcomes depend[ing] heavily on households' and firms' resistance to distance [and that] where this resistance is low then such an urban pattern may encourage numerous inter cluster journeys and increase travel.' A benchmark feature for an eco-village in a greenfield setting is a minimum *net* residential density of 30 household units per hectare, which influences the siting massing and materials incorporated into buildings. This housing density is also dedicated to providing space for the incorporation of some compatible and benign mixed-use activities and home-working.

ECO-VILLAGE VITAL STATISTICS
50 hectares: 125 acres
Notionally: 800 m diameter (2,600 ft)
15 ha (30 per cent) allocated for community uses *(centre, collector roads, schools, pocket parks, utility needs, greenways)*
35 ha (70 per cent) used as residential *(home 'footprints', yards, half adjoining access street, residential parking)*
At 35 home units/ha: total 1,200 homes.
At 4.2 persons/home: 5,100 population.

Overall the eco-village size is a function of the walkable distance for an average pedestrian moving on foot or by cycle to and from the centre. This, in terms of the 'ideal' previously established, is no more than a maximum of six or seven minutes' purposeful walk, or about 400 metres (1,300 feet). As a circle-equivalent this works through as enclosing about 50 hectares (125 acres).[45] Deducting 15 hectares (30 per cent) for a community commercial-service centre, and for community pathways and collector vehicular routes, the area of the settled residential sector comes down to 35 hectares, and at an optimum 35 units per hectare net this calculates as more than 1,000 residential dwelling units in total.[46] Based on the standard family unit – the much-quoted 'woman and man plus 2.2 children' – as the start-up basis to an eco-village, the residential population would be around 5,000 people – sufficient to generate an employing base of critical mass, and to support a wide range of commercial and social services including pre-schools, one or two grade schools and a small high school.

With a 'footprint' for two-level housing at around 70 m² considerable curtilage space can be positioned adjacent to each home unit, leaving sufficient ground for recreational and kitchen garden usage (which, well designed, need only be 60 m²).

A minimum of 30 households per hectare, intensely designed, adhering to sustainable principles, passive solar energy retention, attention to bioharmonic building design and construction, some on-site food production, roughly summarizes the eco-village concept pragmatically. Eco-village sites would also capture and use natural rainfall as a source of water, and be served by a dedicated village sewage and nutrient recovery plant. In other environmental ways urban greenfield settlements would respect the natural heritage of their setting (flora, fauna, wetlands) during village construction, and at the landshaping, infill, construction and (particularly) at the residential occupancy stages.[47]

A sustainable-as-possible lifestyle can be incorporated into an eco-village when material inputs and outputs are brought into equilibrium – mainly by recycling, reusing, repairing and restoring. Such land settlement has been thought through in the Australasian context by Bill Mollison in his *Permaculture* (1988). Mollison's advocacy is for extra effort to be put into sewage digestion and bio-gas production, storm-water and greywater reutilization, and compost production along with other self-sufficiency and reduced movement and curtailed transportation practices. Given the obstacles strewn across the path of greenfield village projects, full-on eco-villages warrant respect and acclaim because their degree of sustainable attainment vaults beyond this book's advocacy for a tolerable harmony.[48]

Raw land suburbanization

This passage sets down guidelines additional to the basic residential componentry given already in box 5.2, the purpose now being to establish the ways and means to achieve legibility (communities instead of subdivision), cost savings, landscape enhancement and an improved sociability for the mainly suburban, rural-into-urban land transformation, emphatically argued against, but unstoppable!

A notable alteration in the progression of urban expansion over the last century was the ratcheting up of conventional subdivision standards, engaging regulations which were mostly a codification and accumulation of negatives, and a move away from 'deemed to comply' possibilities. For standard detached dwelling greenfield subdivisions the changes included refined provisions for larger houses on smaller plots with undergrounded utilities. In relation to house building, changes took the form of ever-increasing earthquake resilient, fire resistant, vermin-proof, thermal barrier, rot-proof, services-in/wastes-out, regulation.

Away from the inner suburbs through to conventional suburbia, there is the fringe, 'edge city', where the space opportunity provided by 20-year look-ahead zoning has been, historically, for maximum-sized urban lots. After 80 years of automobile use, suburbia acquired a fully vehicle-dominated mantle, often with the garage integral to the living rooms of the home in a manner designed to be a barrier to eye-contact with neighbours, further

'In 1949 a finished lot accounted for around 11 percent of total cost, increasing steadily to about 24 percent by 1982.'

Quoted by Peter Rowe, 1991.

From the United States (1996) *Congress for New Urbanism* 'Neighbourhoods should be diverse in use and population; communities should be designed for the pedestrian and transit (system) as well as the car; cities and towns should be shaped by physically defined and universally acceptable public spaces and community institutions; urban spaces should be framed by architecture and landscape design that celebrate local history, climate, ecology, and building practice.'

assisted by fitting remote-controlled garage doors! Despite local imperatives for growth containment (previously addressed) edge city in most metropolitan and large town situations is a spotty prolongation of quasi-suburbia set down in quasi-arcadia. In this manner edge-city green space was initially subdivided along rural-class roads into urban-rural plots. Typically these were the sites of large un-rural houses, the only plants and animals in view being for gratifications other than their eventual consumption as food or incorporation into textiles. Setting out to suburbanize in this incremental manner resulted in low densities for situations where it was hoped, at the outset, densities would increase.

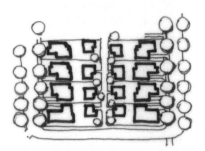

Aggie Village, Davis, California. Detail redrawn from Calthorpe and Fulton 2001, showing single-family houses with 'granny cottages' to the rear, which are linked to a pedestrian pathway.

The expansion of orthodox suburbia onto city-adjacent agricultural greenfields beckons as an opportunity in the eyes of landowners, urban developers and local government officials and politicians.[49] To them, historically, all freehold rural land, whether in active or passive rural use, and regardless of soil quality, was available for commodification and profit unless this was legally constrained. The question now raised is: what are the guidelines for ordained edge-of-city suburbanization, mindful of cost, conservancy factors and the achievement of social wellbeing for the future occupants?

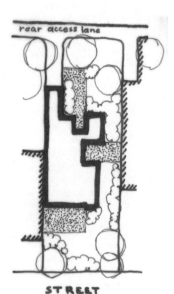

rear access lane

ST REET

Lot-line (built-to-boundary)

What is frequently sought is the doubling of previous standard suburban densities, by scaling down the average size of plots and the overall width of most kinds of residential street *and* through on-site design. Also included is the incorporation of some selective rear plot arrangements, the installation of user friendly greenway pedestrian access networks, a doubling-up of households (granny flats), and a scaling-up of housing vertically – part of a sustainable-in-spirit housing strategy.[50] Lot-line layouts on 350 m² lots (approx. 3,800 sq. ft) can provide all the benefits and space of fully detached single-family housing on larger 500 m² lots (approx 5,400 sq. ft); and on slightly smaller 300 m² lots (3,200 sq. ft) semi-detached housing can be sited to meet all conventional urban-living needs. Weak-link housing, compromising lined-up single and double-storeyed units in residential rows, need only occupy 250 m² plots (2,700 sq. ft); and town houses require no more than 200 m² (2,100 sq. ft), which includes the provision of integral garage space and a privacy yard. The illustration given as figure 5.8 **Density and design quadrupled** shows conventional

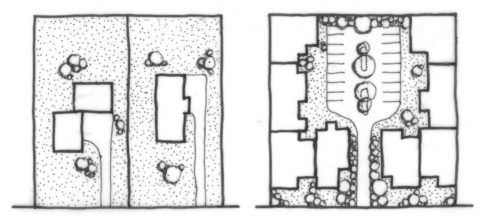

Figure 5.8 Density doubled and design quadrupled.

layouts, and potential layouts at a quadrupled density. This higher-density arrangement illustrates the improved safety, convenience, sociability and aesthetic appeal of cluster (pocket) layouts for raw land subdivisions giving enhanced street appeal.

Higher-density provisioning demands better and more design and landscaping effort. My rubric runs: 'the increase in design effort must be quadrupled as plot density doubles.' Or, more explicitly, a doubling of net density from (say) $600\,m^2$ (6,500 sq. ft) to $300\,m^2$ calls for a multiplied-by-four input of design at all levels, and also demands massively improved subdivision design, utilities design, landscaping, site layout and building design as well. The ideal *gross* density aimed for in the average 'raw land' context is in excess of 40 persons per hectare (16 persons per acre) which includes cycle–foot greenways and other community space provisioning. This works through in *net* terms, as 70 persons per hectare (28 persons per acre) where net includes plots plus half the adjoining access street. As it is not convenient to interpret the concept of persons per hectare or acre, this can be more readily understood as 30 households *net* per hectare (12 per acre) – a self-contained grandparent annex being also a 'household': again *net* (including abutting streets and pedestrian walkways, and *ex*cluding community land for arterial connections, public open space, playgrounds, schools and the like). Residential living of

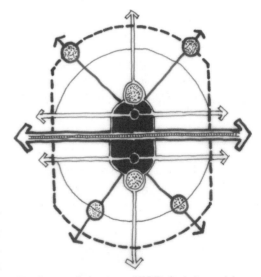

The frequently expressed TOD depiction originating with Peter Calthorpe.

these 'clustering' and 'pocketing' styles should be *less* than 400 m or 1,300 feet (six to eight minutes' walk time) away from pre-teen schooling, corner shopping, and a transit pick-up point.

The style of 'transport oriented development' (TODs) for a higher density walkable suburb (Calthorpe 1992 and 1993) exhibits internal logic, reducing overall energy uptake and automobile dependency, and increasing sociability, although in the often-replicated 'pedestrian pocket' depiction the outcomes can only be selectively nodal, leaving the lower-density between spaces stuck without much in the way of neighbourhoodness! The advocacy for existing urban nodes within extant suburbs is thus constrained in practice by the limited opportunities for selection and activation; for example, by the number of stations established along a railroad easement.

Accessory to TODs are MUDs (Mixed Use Developments) explored, for the United States context (1987 *Handbook*) by the Urban Land Institute, which was

Mixed Use Development.

followed (1991) by the Porter, Phillips, Lassar examination of *Flexible Zoning.* Mixed usage is a difficult concept to embrace for auto-fixated suburbanites willing to drive their cars at any time of their choosing to another zone to access their needs and wants. MUDs are in many ways tradition revisited, and the principles are sometimes incorporated into Traditional Neighbourhood Development projects.[51] The attraction of mixed use development is accessibility, without always involving a car, to a variety of shops and services – a huge advantage for that half of an average urban population which does not have personal discretionary use of an automobile. Mixed Use Development can allow the inclusion of a diversity of household types by income, composition, age cohort, and class; but also with a mixture of professional offices, artists studios, reception depots, entertainment and recreation places, motels and small hotels, churches and other community venues, pre-schools and schools, corner shops, and a

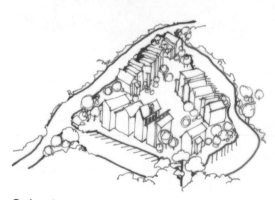

Co-housing.

wide variety of home-work establishments. Density and design are the keywords, and reduced business running costs the major incentive. Of course a 'free to locate anywhere' formula would be calamitous of outcome for residential districts, resulting in backyard (front yard!) auto-repairing, fleet vehicle parking, massage parlours, funeral parlours and small processing-plant operations. Carefully regulated and well-designed mixed use development is feasible and desirable, as indeed has been the previous situation, and ever will be, for the historical prototype, the European inner suburb.[52]

Co-housing, advocated by McCamant and Durrett (1994) in a book of that title, warrants co-consideration along with TODs and MUDs. Again this is a residential pocket arrangement for selected sites, which fulfils the needs of specific interests. Within those constraints it works well, achieving medium net density outcomes, maximizing at around 30 dwellings per hectare (12 per acre) for the site considered as a whole, the houses being a mixture of units with one, two, three and four bedrooms. Co-housing fits in some 'common' estate space – but *not* as public realm open space. Some of this common space is used for car parking at the edge-entrance to the site, with a larger proportion available for wider outdoor activities such as strolling, pooping the dog, improving golf swings, playing hide and seek and simply living a bit more of life outdoors. The pluses are, especially, the extra 'common' space and the added personal security, the big negative being exclusivity, for the extra space belongs to the group and is not of the public realm.

My colleague James Lunday's findings on sustainable urban design profiles the following as the suburban outcomes most sought by owner-occupiers: sociability, accessibility, healthiness, local identity ('legibility' to Lynch 1960), security, resilience (namely compact form and robustness), and a 'to hand' level of concentration reflected in accessibility and availability. Security is not about exclusion beyond the defensible home-space; it is more about occupation of the public realm and the presence of people in the 'third spaces' beyond home and work. To this listing I would add 'profitability' simply because for most suburban dwellers the home place is also a tradable, appreciating, capital commodity. Into the mix planners, bureaucrats and local politicians strive to achieve 'enjoyability' – an accessory to sociability – perhaps the least tangible, yet arguably the most significant ingredient.

What has to be acknowledged and lived with is that, as critical as one might be of suburbanization as a 'problem', it has been and largely remains for society at large the settlement growth 'solution'. This behoves planning operatives to do all that is within

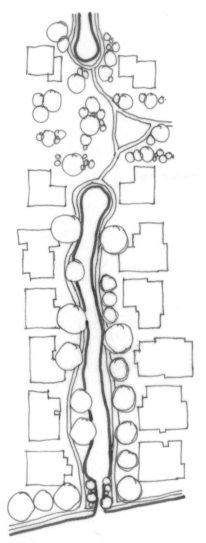

Cul-de-sac arrangements are preferred by many homeowners. A principle disadvantage is the way they concentrate onto collectors. But for many planners the neighbourhood-defining feature of collector roads supports the provision of a system of pedestrian-linked culs-de-sac and crescents. Vital to the induction of neighbourliness is the inclusion of pedestrian linkages. Layouts with all streets as through streets offer an unneighbourly way to even out a suburb's traffic load.

Box 5.3 Suburban design-detail code

(Refer also to box 5.2 Basic urban componentry)

1 Minimize residential vehicle access points entering onto traffic collector roads. Assign vehicle crossings to home access streets. Keep width of non-collector streets to a slow-down-traffic minimum – as little as 5 m (16 ft) with no parking, 6 m (20 ft) with one-sided parking.

2 Use chicanes, surface variety, raised and textured street patches, and kinked and constricted carriageway alignments to induce traffic calming for non-collector streets.

3 Design subdivisions with a range of lot sizes to accommodate a mix of house sizes; with provision for up to 20 per cent 'affordable' (starter) houses. Encourage the erection of live-alone annex constructions.

4 Use 'cluster designs' for urban focus and sociability. Aim to achieve small-town nodality for suburbs, avoiding monocultures. Position kitchen or living-room windows to maintain 'eyes on the street'.

5 Plant summer shade trees in the street berm. Use grass and shrubbed swales for storm-water control, and shallow ponds for storm-water retention and sediment settlement. Retain existing trees and other natural features, and create green swathes and pockets.

6 Accommodate building to the boundary (zero lot-line) positioning, common-wall provisioning, designate no-window and high-window walls and staggered site envelope designs as aids to the formation of some private outdoor living space within a plot curtilage. Avoid the useless front lawn: establish front-yards to a maximum 3 m (10 ft) to improve the rear-yard space (notably on the sunless side of streets).

7 Recess garages into one side, and aligned with the front façade, of each house. Best of all, provide rear-lane access to car parking, an attractive garaging option.

8 Design sites, considered one in relation to another, for and against sun, wind and noise penetration. Shape lots as often as possible in a manner which allows for an east–west axis to each house.

9 Provide chunky residential lots mindful of the preference for width (maximum 20 m–66 ft) rather than an emphasis on plot depth: but down to 10 m (33 ft) for smaller dwelling units, and as low as 6 m (20 ft) for some terraced housing.

10 Incorporate the use of occasional battle-axe rear plots but with a preferred maximum of four users sharing an accessway.

11 Adopt safe-at-night designs with entrapment-avoidance pathways and effective street lighting. Seek to attain 'permeability' with 'defensibility'.

12 Design 'landscaping to the curb' provisions; particularly for footpath-free streets. Curved footpaths flanking straight carriageways add character and accommodate parking inserts.

13 Provide for the common trenching of telephone, gas, water and electricity utilities; use flexible ducting. Handle storm water on a 'daylighting' basis and via permeable surfaces.

14 Conserve and incorporate the already existing landscape features, and flora, into the suburban scene. Maximize the planting of locally suitable trees and shrubs.

15 Harmonize design-materials-landscaping in either a regulatory code or guidelines.

16 Engage a variety of legally effective covenant restraint provisions: specifying building materials, external cladding texture and coloration, roofing materials and colour, window and door trim material and colour; and also design and profile parameters along with coverage, height, and siting and street set-back provisions, including a frontyard fencing prohibition, specification of the height and style of acceptable fencing; landscaping including mature tree preservation, large tree planting, native species emphasis and general landscaping guidelines.

17 Use cross leasing, strata tenure, lease holding and group titles (for community amenities) imaginatively: mindful of the social dangers of 'exclusionary' provisioning.

18 Allow designed-in home-work and home-office arrangements with separate front or side entrances. Accommodate the stand-alone 'granny flat' and the over-the-top 'carriage house' for elderly relatives or as rental or office-studio use.

their policy grasp and design power to improve suburban provisioning to the highest and best outcome, as well as rendering suburban housing economically affordable and ecologically fit. To that end the depiction given in box 5.3 as a **Suburban design-detail code** is a 'trigger list'.

At the highest level of new urban construction some localities can be given over to TODs, MUDs and Co-housing, and some others to the urban greenfield (eco-village) development ideal traversed earlier, although the main outcome will continue to be conventional street-frontaged housing 'densified modified and layered' and above all else 'flexibly zoned' and 'intensely designed'. These are some of the alternatives to orthodox raw land suburbanization. Also to be considered is the late Francis Tibbalds's (1992) statement on the 'Design and Evolution of Urban Design Codes' in which he advocated an 'inclusive collaborative approach'.[53]

Raw land subdivision economies.   Viewed objectively, there is no justification, in terms of sustainability principles, for urban expansion onto productive or potentially productive agricultural land, infilled urban housing being the preferred 'compaction and retrofit' option (reviewed in the next passage). A practical difficulty with the rural-urban crossover is that local government planning services have little power to effectively and consistently divert private property owners away from low-density suburbanization and greenfields expansion, or to influence and direct suburban expansion inwards toward the pursuit and attainment of densification. Given the inevitability of some suburbanization onto greenfield sites, it is pragmatic to outline the ways by which the best can be made of this contra-indicated process.

Developer-led raw land suburbanization can achieve some longer-term economies associated with sustainability goals, moving in the direction of utility economies, social service efficiencies and of course the attainment of everlasting environmental benefits. A prime focus, in terms of the sustainability ideal, is for land savings, essentially avoiding the uptake for suburbia of good agricultural land. In these terms, raw land urbanization should be confined to low-production land classes –

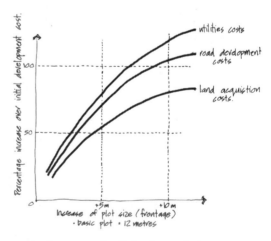

elite soils and most landscapes useful to agriculture and silviculture being declared off-limits, without waiver. Within-project land savings achieve further economies deriving from a reduction of the excess space allocated to plots, from a reduction of the length of utility runs, and savings from the reduced provision of road frontage and road width. Everlasting land savings are a move in the direction of the sustainable ideal and the intensification ideal combined – both being socially and politically sound outcomes. Most easily understood are cost savings. If the raw land cost of a 10-metre frontage is around half the raw land layout cost for a 20-metre frontage, then that saving is permanent and valuable simply because of the 'saved' land, the foreshortened run of utility lines, and the increased density of dwellings. Such a socially appropriate outcome has the added advantage of achieving ongoing occupancy and maintenance economies.

Energy savings, when projected through the lives of a succession of residential occupants, are also congruent with the 'sustainable in intent' ideal. Installations designed to maximize solar gain, warmth retention through insulation, less water consumption, harvested storm-water run-off, reduced sewage disposal volumes, and fewer shopping trips are all significant and continuing energy-cost reductions. Some occur at the construction stage, with really significant savings continuing throughout the ongoing occupation of residential buildings.

A sustainable-in-intent set of economies of the 'impact savings' kind are associated with raw land urbanization over four phases of sequestration:

1   From the time of raw land purchase up to the time when productive agriculture is abandoned;
2   When a raw land site becomes a road-and-utilities location;
3   When the site becomes a building and construction location; and finally
4   When it becomes a building construction site.

At all four phases there can be significant and everlasting softenings of impact. These may preserve some features of the cultural heritage (phases 1 and 2), conserve the flora and fauna natural heritage (phases 1, 2 and 3), restrain the run-off and end-disposal impacts of storm-water and waste disposal (phase 3), and also enhance the overall ambience (phase 4). However, as noted by Rydin (1992):

> There are two pressures working against successful implementation of [sustainable residential development] policies. *First* . . . the need to balance the claims of environmental policies against those for economic development and social equity . . . *Second* [that] the power of the planning system in controlling individual projects is essentially a responsive one.

There are other means by which local planners and administrators can influence the creation of better-balanced social and physical arrangements. Some of these are summarized and presented later in this chapter as instruments for planned change (box 5.6 Planning in action: the delivery of outcome).

The benefits of tree-foil.

Public open space provisioning. The greening of suburbia was the focus of my first paper, a 1960s article headed 'Open Space Requirements for Urban Areas'. It established criteria for urban open space provisioning under 'amenity' (aesthetic embellishment, and nature-wildlife retention), 'passive' (relaxing-recreational), and 'active' (participation-sport) criteria. In quantitative terms those recommendations enjoyed recognition, but in the context of quality (the positioning, design and utility of open spaces) the research was incomplete.

The contractor-provider preference, almost without exception, is to dump, gulch and creek marginal land into relatively useless and potentially unsafe 'reserves', although aesthetically these can often be quite pleasing, establishing a tall-tree foil and backdrop to the boiled lollies effect of suburban housing. But remnant plant habitats also become 'dump reserves'; local garbage tips, from which plant species threatening to the native flora and wildlife, proliferate. Worse, they may also become the haunt of the truant, the deviant, drug users and straying dogs, and are shunned as unsafe, unwholesome and generally undesirable. Children in most modern suburbs are enjoined to keep away from 'the reserve', to stay inside, to play in the backyard or, a parental irony, to play out on the street.

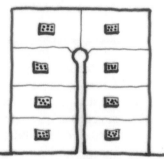

Ranch-style: Lots 75 per cent; road 25 per cent; open space nil.

Subdivision-of-land contractors have come to accept the allocation of 20 to 30 per cent of the most handsome parts of their raw landscape for streets, turning circles, car parks and utility easements; yet they have traditionally fought like ferrets against the lesser (around 10 per cent) statutory setting-aside of land – usually scrap land – for 'amenity' spaces (reserves in Australasia). The performance-based considerations were aired conceptually by Lane Kendig and others in *Performance Zoning* (1980).

- The detached ranch-style house has long been the preferred housing option for North Americans, and especially so in bungalow-style for Australasians. In a stylized depiction the space allocation on a notional acre (or half hectare) works through for eight houses as shown – with *no* accessible open space.

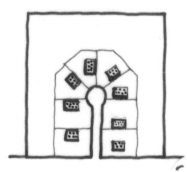

Lot-lined: Lots 50 per cent; road 20 per cent; open space 30 per cent.

- A built-to-boundary option (lot-lined in North America) puts all houses onto a boundary line, saving a side yard and maybe the front yard – allocating 30 per cent of the overall site as open space.
- The attached town-house (terraced) option, each dwelling provided with a small private walled-in outdoor living area, further reduces lot sizes and length of access road, leaving 58 per cent of the site as open space.
- The apartment option allows 75 per cent of the site to be allocated as open space. The last three of these options leads to a consideration of the use to which the left-over open space is put: the residential choice being for occupier usage, the community preference

Terraced: Lots 30 per cent; road 12 per cent; open space 58 per cent.

Apartments: Lot 17 per cent; road 8 per cent; open space 75 per cent.

being for public open space, and the developer preference being for an increased building allowance!

The traditional format compounds a serious failing with suburbia: a hollow semblance of green-city layout, but without open space provisions of worth and utility. This predilection for single-use zoning and low-density conformity stirred Jane Jacobs in her *Death and Life of Great American Cities* (1961: 15) to define standard suburban places as exhibiting 'a quality even meaner than outright ugliness or disorder . . . the dishonest mask of pretending order, achieved by ignoring or suppressing the real order that is struggling to be served'. The private home-ownership 'premier subdivision' shown previously (figure 5.3) is notably bereft of a community focus. The public-housing project shown in figure 5.9 **Olwyn Green** is an improvement, offering a well-designed layout with motor vehicles constrained (chicanes, speed bumps, road surface changes) enabling use of the street as a 'common living room' playspace.[54]

Conventional-density suburbs which maintain privacy spaces, utility spaces, and community spaces can be successfully designed and built, the key emphasis being the engagement of good multi-professional design skills.[55] Traditional subdivisions had the ingredients – private spaces and dwellings, utility spaces for vehicles and services, open spaces for recreation – but in the wrong juxtapostioning.

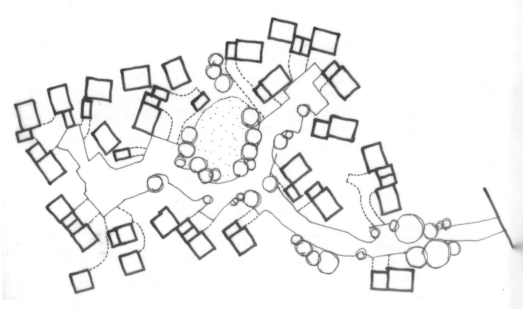

Figure 5.9   Olwyn Green: Hamilton, NZ.

The following three-part listing reviews the extent to which layout designers can be effective in providing focus and sociability through amenity open-space provisioning.

1 Turning to advantage the fact that contractors are obliged statutorily to sequest (with local authorities becoming the eventual community guardians) as much as 40 per cent of the raw land for access, utilities and reserves provisioning. Treat this as a composite handover where road takings are minimized, and community amenity space is enlarged and integrated. The ideal trade-off is *less* land consumed for access and utilities, and *better* land provided for actively used amenity spaces – thus with some overall reduction of the total extent of public land allocation and an overall increase in land residentially occupied. The issue here, as in much of suburban provisioning, is one of quality.
2 Give up on backland reserves (except for delineations along coastal, lake and larger river littorals and prominent ridge lines), concentrating on integral-to-the-community reserves as outlined in 'green street' recommendations, ideally with some floral and fruiting varieties.
3 Foster a leafy ambience, particularly by encouraging carefully positioned medium-to-large tree planting, along with the promotion (including some minor alleviation of land taxes as a community payback?) for private landowners who covenant the protection of tree species in backdrop-pockets. Trees and shrubs set within flexi-block layouts soften and subdue hard-edged suburban housing, and enhance property resale values.

Overall, in the particular context of amenity space provisioning, the most important open space design and social objective, is the location of actively used (soccer mum's and frisbee dad's) neighbourhood space, integral and connected to community schools, corner stores, local library and the like.

At the time of rural-to-urban crossover, the tensions between local governance and developer-providers linger on to haunt the communities served, unfortunately as irredeemable and everlasting mistakes. This beleaguering effect includes the provision of mindlessly curvilinear layouts superficially marketable at the time of sale, but exhibiting irrelevance as they mature. Part of the answer is purposefully orthogonal – not necessarily gridded – arrangements, providing a clear within-the-neighbourhood sense of structure and

Excellent indoor–outdoor New World detached dwelling living, in parts of nineteenth-century inner-city Sydney, Auckland and Melbourne, accommodates families with children, childless couples and retired people, with easy access to public transport, schools, medical centres, and local shops – on plots which average 150 m².

focus. Straightening out streets and orienting them in purposeful directions (toward schools, shops, workplaces) in association with green-way pedestrian and cycle links is important.

There is a need for more affordable (starter) housing and 'live alone' accommodation. The issues of 'what proportions?' and in 'which locations?' defy resolution with certainty. The political squint of left-leaning agencies sets out to achieve salt-and-pepper arrangements. With politically right-leaning agencies 'affordable' and 'live alone' housing will either be non-existent or will be sown like a self-conscious monocrop in redevelopment projects.

With urban transportation the choice of policy between cars or transit is hedged by two constraints. *First* is the received pattern of any given city. Those focused down to the water's edge, like most significant Anglo New World centres, constrain and concentrate their transportation problems into geographically limited corridors. And for any corridor where more than 20 per cent of the CBD-bound traffic is routed, there arise conditions for automobile gridlock 'problems' and an extremely costly transit 'solution'. The *second* complexity relates to the income class of the population within urban corridors. Where there is rail transit, for example, low-income populations generate low-usage rates and low returns on investment because poor people in the New World context own cars, and prefer the security automobiles offer rather than risk the violence of riding the trains. On the other hand 'white-collar' urban corridors harbour people who are prepared to use and pay for train-transit services, entrusting their automobiles to the transit station car park, and themselves and their school-bound children to the transit service.

When rural lands are converted into suburban landscapes, human intervention is of course dominant. Get the outcome wrong and it pretty well stays wrong. Inadequately contrived meso-density suburbs are difficult to undo, a mediocrity which gets enshrined for the rest of a residential locality's history – essentially the dumping of a wrongdoing from one decade into perpetuity. Finally, in addition to all that has been stated already, inherited suburbanization has been largely a product of the male imagination: the clear counter-predication is that the neomodern suburb for the future must embody feminist, elderly and child-scale desiderata.

Urban retrofit compaction and clustering

This passage heralds the most important, the least practised, and also the most woefully neglected urban growth management planning operation[56] – the retrofitting, upgrading, compaction and clustering of established suburbs. In his quirky and prescient *Edge City* the investigative journalist-author Joel Garreau (1992: 228) explains the transformation into neighbourhoods which takes place in the maturing of suburbs: 'Individual property owners continually upgrade their places. They look around at what other people are doing, decide what is good or bad, eliminate discordant elements, and bring their community closer to what is perceived to be the ideal.' What is heartening about property-owner participation and reurbanization over time is its connection to the ever-recurring family cycle – home place, workplace, school place, shopping place, and entertainment place – as the generator of urban habitat improvement. From that perspective suburbs contain both the modern problem – a lack of variety and focus – and harbour the neomodern solution – retrofit, compaction, clustering. An issue which then arises has been noted by Randall Arendt (1994: 229) as one in which: 'Once land is checker boarded into wall-to-wall house lots, it is nearly impossible to retrofit greenways, trails, parks and neighbourhood playing fields into the established pattern. The approved plot, for better or worse, is essentially chiselled in granite.' So, a caution: when suburban arrangements are in harmony – which is the situation with many between-the-wars (1918–1939) suburbs – leave well alone. Compaction is no panacea. Indeed the corollary to compaction, higher density, can exacerbate suburban crime and disorder. The greatest challenge is induction of neighbourhood clustering into the tracts of post-World War II 'zoned for housing only' suburbs. Rescrambling the urban housing omelette and reconstituting the urban transport mix are topics shot through with complexity and difficulty. Clustering at incipient neighbourhood centres is straightforward, leaving 'fuzzy' the bipolar situation which arises where neighbourhoods join and people are attracted either way to different centres.

Extant suburbs are places well-nigh impossible to undo and repackage. Planners may retrospectively rue inadequate provisioning at the historical rural-to-urban crossover stage; but the legacy now left for them to address is how to retrofit an often dysfunctional suburban inheritance. Hawken, Lovins and Lovins (1999) finger three urban crises: 'deterioration of the natural environment', 'dissolution into lawlessness despair and apathy' and a 'lack of public will to address suffering and welfare', which in its essentials mirrors Benton and Short's (1999) identification of three broad needs for the 'greening, detoxification and reforming' of the city. Combined, these six major urban challenges confront politicians, planners and local government administrators, particularly in relation to suburban retrofit.

Fortress enclaves are an execration, suburbs-within-suburbs shielding people and protecting property values behind walls, shunning the city beyond. Most planners with an ounce of social responsibility regard it as important, emphatically to resolve against closed-off, single-use, same socio-economic group, physically gated housing precincts. These exhibit as walled ghettos focused into private open space without two-way access to the public realm. Suburban layout should never be predicated on an exclusionary basis. This need for privacy and security has to be met firstly in the home, and if preferred, at high densities in condominia, and at lower densities in 'broad-acre' ex-urbia. Conventional separate plot layouts should legally and allowably accommodate culturally *mixed* households forms, for *mixed-income* households, and to include a *mixed* combination of home occupiers. Walled and gated suburbs are socially regressive:

Richard Rogers, Chair for the Urban Task Force in England set down (2000) these criteria for evaluating an Urban Regeneration Project:
- Does it combine live, work and leisure activities?
- Is it on recycled (urban) land?
- Is it socially mixed and inclusive?
- Is it served by a public transport system?
- Is it as compact as traditional villages?
- Is its construction and energy technology relevant to the housing problems of today?

'ghettos' because they accept racial division, ethnic exclusivity, pecking-order prissiness, and inculcate smugness.

Resisting exclusionary zoning as a part of density-increase reurbanization ushers in the reverse, a consideration of 'radical inclusionary development' styles which variegate, diversify and promote a differential character to suburbs, allowing a 'deemed to comply' accommodation of worthy alternatives to the orthodox. This proactive reasoning was first, to my knowledge, profiled in the 1961 writing of Jane Jacobs on the subject of urban diversity, her *Death and Life of Great American Cities*. In lieu of land uses compartmented into single-purpose 'everything according to code' zones, the need is for proximity predicated upon two main criteria – compatibility and neighbourliness. Those keywords embrace an operational conjoining – conservation with development *and* good design. This further indicates that inclusionary zoning is not some multi-purpose free-for-all of the commercial strip kind, where a jumble of land uses is allowed to pile up, obeying only utility and fire-safety regulations. Much more than this, 'inclusionary urban zoning' is set within a neighbourhood framework each containing a school and some pre-schools, benign work-at-home places, a clustering of local corner stores, places of worship, and other places for entertainment, cultural activities and leisure. The overall objective and predication is to:

- Achieve a medium to high density mix of house types and, by implication a mixture of households;
- To identify, endorse and build up neighbourhood 'centrings' – newsagents, corner shops, community buildings, pre-schools and a public transit pick-up point;
- To attain user-paying public transport servicing in line with density increases;
- To accommodate a mixture and variety of residentially compatible land uses;
- To move toward higher net density neighbourhood pockets, well served by user-paying public transport services; *and*
- To ensure that at least 10 per cent of the overall land area is acquired as amenity space in the public realm.

Density increase policies ('densification' and 'compaction' in North America, portrayed in Australasia as 'infilling') are the key to cutting back on a range of costs in post-World War II suburbs, characterized early on in that era by small houses (around $120\,m^2$ 'footprint') built on largish lots $600\,m^2$ plus. There can be savings with land provisioning costs, and utilities installation costs. This is not the sole intent, which is also to *improve* upon district nucleating, which engenders a sense of belonging, and reduces reliance on the use of individually owned automobiles to accomplish the daily living round. This is the economic and resourcing case *against* low-density suburban sprawl and the need, in response, for urban densification, community service clustering, traffic calming, landscape greening, and a transit-service. From Robert Cevero (1991: 127):

> The idea [being] that if the true social cost of building at low density were passed on to dwellers and developers, the market place itself would give rise to a built form

that respects the limits of natural environments and provides high levels of mobility. Indeed ... to remove some of the in-built subsidies that encourage [people] to live at low densities and drive their cars to all places at all times.

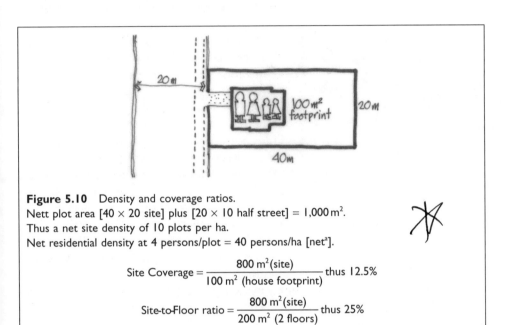

Figure 5.10 Density and coverage ratios.
Nett plot area [40 × 20 site] plus [20 × 10 half street] = 1,000 m².
Thus a net site density of 10 plots per ha.
Net residential density at 4 persons/plot = 40 persons/ha [net].

$$\text{Site Coverage} = \frac{800\ m^2\,(\text{site})}{100\ m^2\ (\text{house footprint})} \text{ thus } 12.5\%$$

$$\text{Site-to-Floor ratio} = \frac{800\ m^2\,(\text{site})}{200\ m^2\ (2\ \text{floors})} \text{ thus } 25\%$$

ᵃ Gross residential density embraces public open space, collector road space, community lots and local shops.

A technical problem with consolidation strategies is understanding some awkward notions, shown in figure 5.10, **Density and coverage ratios** as density (persons per acre or hectare: gross and net), plot coverage (the percentage of a site covered by buildings), and floor-to-area ratio (FAR – the amount of permitted floor space on a site expressed as a proportion of the total plot area). Suburban plot coverage below 'one-third' produces spaced-out arrangements which are culturally dysfunctional (characterized by householders frequently not knowing their neighbours); and such lower urban density lifestyles cannot support an economically viable public transport service. Although unable to identify the precise threshold of preferred intensity of land occupancy, my finding is that any net density below 35 persons per hectare (about 14 people per acre) lacks the population density to support public transport. From this premiss a further claim can be staked out, namely, that net densities of more than 60 persons per hectare (around 25 persons per acre) can and will positively generate neighbourly interaction, and provide the basis for a viable public transportation service pretty well regardless of the socio-economic group being served. Densities between 35 and 60 persons net per hectare (correlating roughly with 15 and 27 persons per acre) delimit a density trap – that band of densities where residents are denied privacy as well as the benefits of close-living urbanity. Unfortunately, it so happens that most established standard suburbs within settler societies fall within the category of being neither low enough in density to provide an Arcadian private ambience, nor high enough in density to benefit socially and economically from compact urbanity and public transport provisioning.

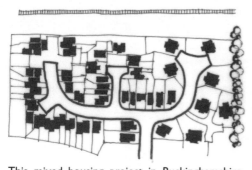

This mixed housing project in Buckinghamshire, England, comprises modest bed-sit and starter housing (terraced), through to four-bedroom double-garaged bungalows. Looks good, works well.

Because density of persons per hectare (or acre) is not readily understood, the reurbanization and densification goal is, as already noted, more usefully expressed as at least 30 households per hectare (12 hh/ac: 'net' of plots and the adjacent half of adjoining access roads). Consolidation also involves the acceptance of socially compatible land uses (mixture) and household variety (diversity), with the equivalent of 30 standard-family households per hectare (net as above) adhered to as the clearly understood minimum density. Proceeding toward a higher density can vary: from inducement (the carrot approach) where a local authority coerces landowners to design and work through and get special 'departure' approvals for higher-density and land-use mixes, to a penalty (stick) approach such as the application of arterial road tolls to pay for collector roads, and the application of higher land taxes for larger plots.

Mixed-housing policies, tied in with densification procedures and a 'working from home' acceptance, pull together the compaction and refurbishment case. Compatible mixed-use and 'working from home' practices are incorporated, not simply because this is a lively idea, but to provide a reason for a substantial proportion of the population *not* to have to use automobiles to get to work. If the dormitory and workplace parts of an urban framework are separately designated, people will cross-commute by private car, vindicating mixed land uses and mixed building-use design infusions. With a mixed-use pattern many car trips become unnecessary or get internalized (by pedestrian and cycle use). The main benefits from urban mixed-use higher-density development strategies within dominantly residential localities derive from enhanced lifestyle variety, improved opportunities for local

Helensville Montessori, located behind the family residence on a quarter suburban acre.

employment, and the housing of older couples, solo aged, and solo parented. Then there is the huge benefit from providing starter families with an actual start, and the practical advantages which accrue from a mixture of family types able to provide services to each other. Densification also achieves a more efficient use of the existing utility infrastructure, saves good-quality farmland from urban unproductiveness, and secures energy reductions. There is also the conservation benefit where densification leads to the reuse, rehabilitation and the conversion of derelict and under-used land which might otherwise decline into blight.

An interesting disclosure on this aesthetic matter comes from a Melbourne study (Swinburne Centre for Urban and Social Research 1990) which established that 'While there is no single answer to what makes medium density [housing only] development successful, landscaping around the individual units was the factor most mentioned . . . [and] from the resident's viewpoint, other factors in a successful development were a low level of noise and a layout which provided safety from traffic'. Thus against the all-Australian and general settler society preference for detached houses, the study concluded strongly (Swinburne 1990: chapter 8) in favour of medium-density housing which was well designed, mostly contiguous, well landscaped, and with some private yardspace for each residence.

A starting point for coming to terms with density-increase performance criteria involves the encouragement of urban government professionals to view their responsibility as one of promoting an efficient, enjoyable and rewarding compaction out of the received suburban inheritance. Local administrators and politicians should weigh up the prospects of increased revenues, as well as the lower unit servicing costs which higher-density urban infill generates.[57] Despite the complexity of the policy controls involved, the longer-term revenue prospects for local government are good; and when coupled to the avoidance of social damage and social gains the overall accumulation is impressive.

It clearly 'costs' greatly – environmentally, socially and in monetary terms – for the majority of settler society urban populations to live in low-density standard suburbs. It also vastly 'costs' nations in terms of land lost from agricultural production forever, as well as 'costing' heavily to patch up the lives broken through social dysfunction and isolation. The total excess works through as a national debit, which is something conceptually clear, although difficult to place a figure on with certainty. Yet it is possible to calculate the price of personal and family trauma resulting from each 'avoidable' automobile accident; the cost to victims of the larceny rampant in low density suburbs; and the total price of unemployability as a consequence of suburban isolation. In terms of household debit arising from low-density suburban life it is necessary to reckon in the price of *not* being able to organize work at home, *not* being able to get by on less than two cars per household, *not* being able to put down social roots, and on *not* being able to get into starter-housing. Box 5.4 detailed as **Compaction: an urban retrofit code** expresses the 'plussages' to seek out and apply.

Structuring the densification ideal comes down, strategically, to the identification and predetermination of potentials for extant suburbia, a realization and movement toward the installation of Co-housing, TODs and MUDs. The 'whole of suburbia' cannot be restructured, yet locations with 'nucleation' potential can

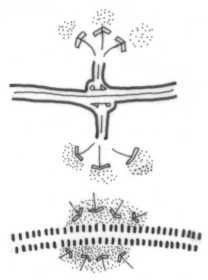

Above: 'dispersal' at an urban freeway turnout, which tips people onto streets. *Below*: 'nucleation' at a railway station, which tips people onto sidewalks.

always be identified and enhanced and the density for them can be increased, often by as much as 30 per cent without wholesale disruption. Out of this thinking has emerged the notion (somewhat fanciful because it fails fully to get around the overarching freehold-tenure fixity) which involves converting existing suburbs into suburban villages by reassembling them in better form. In the British context there was a compulsion to pursue a comprehensive approach consequent to World War II blitz damage. In settler societies, with no such compulsion, it is salutary to realize how unyielding suburbs can be. Daunting though the prospects for the creation of worthy neighbourhoods are, 'sustainable intent' and 'tolerable harmony' remain the driving-force factors for working the compaction and urban retrofit criteria (box 5.4) through one or a combination of Mixed Use Development, Co-housing, and Transport-Oriented Development schema.[58]

The urban retrofit and consolidation strategy, broadly considered, inclines toward overall sustainability, particularly when viewed in a regional context. It is important also to put into the equation the fact that within-urban ecosystems are, and ever will be, ecologically unbalanced in that they 'consume' inputs of raw materials, energy and food, and 'produce' gaseous discharges, putrescent liquids and generally useless solid wastes, incessantly. Sustainability is a desirable 'ideal' to be honed up, improved upon and striven for in differing neighbourhood contexts, and urban retrofit and consolidation contributes to that ideal through a promotion of resource conservation, community sociability and fiscal economy.

The retrofit progression moves from the inner city toward the brown-land band – then out to standard suburbia. It is in the inner-city enclaves where occupational, ethnic and religious diversity – and sexual diversity – is most apparent. In the 'brown-land' inner residential band (beyond the city core) 'diversity' is apparent to a lesser degree. Further out, in the standard 'grey zone' suburbs, families are moated away by their isolating yards 'front, back, side' – in badly ordered spaces which often prove unpleasing and seldom provide privacy.[59] Paradoxically the post-World War II plots in suburbia are often larger than what families want, yet too small to accommodate infilling. Working out from the inner city toward the edge, the Urban retrofit and compaction strategies are explored in three policy contexts: Inner-city rebuilding and retrofitting; retrofitting the inner 'brown-land' suburbs; retrofitting standard 'grey zone' suburbia.

Box 5.4   Compaction: an urban retrofit code

The recommendations offered in this box run with the set of Urban Social Arrangement and Style principles set out earlier in box 5.1; aligns with the design criteria set out in box 5.2 Basic residential componentry; and also connects with the Suburban design-detail provisioning components given in box 5.3.

1   A 'performance' approach

A deemed-to-comply 'performance-related' approach mollifies the inevitable injustices of 'prescriptive formulae' (for example density criteria, difficult to maintain); facilitating beneficial design innovations and on-site as well as beyond-site trade-offs including flexibility in site usage, enhanced off-street car parking, and higher-density site coverage.

2   Land-use mixture and clustering

It is important to avoid a housing monoculture; to accept a clustering of socially compatible mixed-site uses for professional practitioners, handicrafting, boutique food preparation, small hotels, and cultural, religious and entertainment venues with cooperatively shared parking provisions.

3   Walkability: pedestrians and cyclists: automobiles least considered

The top-down preference is to cater primarily for pedestrians, then cyclists, then motor vehicles. Public transportation is also a high priority. Provision for the private automobile is lesser ranked, and vehicle operators may suffer inconvenience.

4   Sociability

Conserving family privacy is easy to achieve at 70 persons (30 households) net per hectare, although it is necessary to provide increased design input in proportion to this density. Families living in proximity to other families fulfil lives of personal satisfaction, community utility, and personal economy, and generate sufficient customer-density to attract profit-making public transport provisioning.

5   Local workplace practices

Pretty well all local commercial enterprises, many local service industries, and a wide range of light manufacturing and outwork enterprises are, or can be, clean, quiet and compatible with residential life. The benefit is prox-imity of workplace to home place, and reducing the servicing and travelling costs associated with making an urban living.

6   Homestyle mixtures and household adaptations

Racially excluding and class-defined ghettos, whether in public housing or gated enclaves, are usually explained away and tacitly justified as economic segregation. Communities must, instead, encourage the accommodation of a mix of all kinds of residential household, including some 'starter' housing, extended family housing, and solo parent and other household types at various levels of affordability. As the needs of occupiers change consequential to the 'empty nesting', 'combo family', 'solo parenting', 'work from home' and 'boomerang granny' needs (*Planning the New Suburbia* Friedman et al., 2002) houses and households need to modify and adapt.

7   Reduced and constrained vehicle ownership and usage

Savings in household stress, and direct savings of time arise from getting by with only one car per household, along with the savings to society which arise from a use of public transport, and the further benefits which accrue from the provision of safe pedestrian and cycle ways. Traffic calming and urban greening are also practical contributions to the reduction of traffic stress.

8   Utilities management

Impressive savings in cash and kind can be attained by arranging the water supply and the sewage disposal systems conjointly: inducing savings in water resource uptake through a progressively increased and charged-price mechanism, which knocks on to induce savings in the reduced amounts of water-borne sewage put out for treatment.

9   Greening

Planting, particularly tree planting, softens the space between buildings, enhancing neighbourhood aesthetics, cooling out the habitat in the summer, increased community pride, and increased property values. Michael Hough (*City Form and Natural Process*, 1984) has observed that 'Two [forms of urban] landscape exist side by side in cities. The first is the nurtured 'pedigree' landscape of

Box 5.4 *Continued*

lawns, flowerbeds, trees, fountains and planned places everywhere that have traditionally been the focus of civic design. . . . The second is the fortuitous landscape of naturalised urban plants and flooded places left after rain, that may be found everywhere in the forgotten places.'

10 Design for densification

The disadvantages of higher-density living (noise, glare, overlooking, vibration) can be mitigated through improved layout design, site design, and unit design – provided this is also combined with the likes of traffic-calming and urban-greening.

. . . and, more generally

11 Remove obstacles

Review pricing for utilities connections to ensure the connector pays. Assist re-zoning to accommodate 'residential'. Assist recycling of warehouse, industrial and office buildings into residential use. Promote higher-density fringe residential projects. Remove penalty costs of non-conventional residential projects. Allow innovative reduction in standards (building-to-boundary and the like). Allow dual dwelling occupancy of larger lots.

12 Provide opportunities

Encourage residential construction within commercial and light industrial projects. Identify spot opportunities for higher-density residential projects. Provide higher rewards for affordable housing and higher-density residential projects. Reduce (or waiver) 'developer' fees to encourage selected initiatives for residential projects.

13 Assist the market

Undertake higher density demonstration projects. Promote public awareness programmes. Disseminate information on housing needs. Market residential innovations. Institute a public awareness programme which clarifies higher-density housing policy. Promote technical innovation and design diversity.

Inner-city rebuilding and retrofitting   is consonant with a city lifestyle preference, to live close by entertainment and information facilities and the commercial bustle and business hustle available in the city core 24 hours a day, seven days a week; and there is the convenience of being walkably adjacent to places of employment and entertainment. The inner city is a part of the urban scene where, in the phrasing of Joel Garreau (1992: 223), 'Development is very much a participatory sport'. It is a context where developers often say 'Forget zoning. There is no zoning, only deals.' Inner-city living is not so much 'planned' as 'negotiated'. It can include an accommodation of family life, although it is more usually attuned to the motivations of the upwardly mobile young professionals, and those involved with city-based entertainment and business. The clearest advantage accruing from inner-city living is that of being able to get on with whatever it is that is vocationally important without the hindrance of owning, registering, insuring, maintaining and garaging an automobile. While the sense of interrelational community is largely absent, there is a subtle sense of being part of a 'system' which provides surveillance for its co-inhabitants. The sustainability ideal is several removes from the conscience of inner-city lifestylers, yet the 'triple harmony' maxim is partly upheld because these individuals use less transportation energy per capita.[60] The European inner-city family lifestyle prototype is indicated for Britain by Baldock's (1994) 'hierarchy of residents needs: Accessible shopping and service facilities – Safety and security – Social, cultural, leisure and entertainment opportunities – Environmental quality and delight'. These criteria, with a raised profile for the environmental component, ring true for the inner-city parts of settler-society inner cities.

Infill on formerly built-on central city sites is one possibility. Also likely is the conversion of some floors in commercial office complexes into inner-city apartments.[61] Even more likely is that speculative office buildings for which office occupants cannot be found are converted to condominia and flats. Another popular variant involves the conversion of other non-residential buildings into loft apartments; for example warehouses of another age are overhauled and refurbished for inner-city living. Certainly a mixture of residential activities and land-use mixtures can exist alongside, and be layered into, the inner-city scene.

Early on in the residential retrofitting of inner-city localities there will arise shortfalls in the availability of corner shops, schools, clinics, and home supply stores, rectified gradually as the residential presence builds up. What cannot be easily established for the occupants of inner-city apartments is access to open space in the public realm. Nevertheless, in most settler-society cities, the civic parks provided in the nineteenth century are to hand, and usually there is access, or the potential to open up access to an urban water's edge.

Retrofitting brown-land inner suburbs arises for the localities which occur between the inner-city core and standard suburbia. Although mainly remnant first suburbs (sometimes villages) they are also infused with commercial and industrial activities. Atypical demographic forces are evident – fewer than average children per household, a large proportion of young professionals, many same-sex partnerings. There is also a recognition that the separate-uses concept which underpins single-purpose 'planned unit zoning' has given way to mixed land uses and population diversity. What often emerges is a multicultural household mix, along with a variety of household formations and intermingled commercial and light-service industrial land uses. The brown-land trending process frequently involves infill projects on land once used for a now-abandoned manufacturing or warehousing purpose. The urban design outcome for such solely residential projects is often exquisite. The results are profitable to the landowner and contractor, and meet a residential need. There are also new competitive land-use incursions: offices, light service industries and specialist commercial outlets. A high proportion of the residential inhabitants of brown lands are transitory, moving up-market, or renesting further out as children are born into their households.

> At their highest level of reordering, brown-land enclaves would have car-free zones, with peripherally sited carparking.

Brown lands offer culturally diverse and service-diverse regeneration (often disparaged as gentrified) opportunities within cities and larger towns.[62] Their positive virtues can be enhanced in ways which set out to retain most of the existing built structures and the local ambience. An objective is for through-traffic denial worked out on a precinct basis: pedestrians as the 'top priority', cyclists with public transport as the conjoint 'second priority', and service vehicles and private automobiles as a 'third priority'. A significant technical difficulty is that the pedestrianization of a former vehicular street is always of inconvenience to someone, and has the knock-on disadvantage of shunting more wheeled traffic onto the remaining thoroughfares. An advantage of traffic calming over full pedestrianization is that it allows vehicular penetration at a slower, quieter, safer and

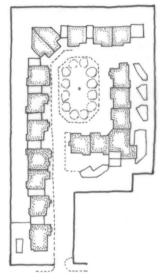

The 1853 Grace's Paddock allotment, Auckland, now the site of a townhouse cluster; probably the optimal replacement house-type in brown-land situations. The difficulty is that two hectare-plus chunks of usable land are needed for each cluster, and there are not all that many ex-breweries and former brickyards – or the like – being abandoned to provide space for cluster housing of this worthy kind.

Around 1970, following a reading of Jane Jacobs's *Death and Life of Great American Cities*, I visited the 'brownland' neighbourhoods of Boston's North End and Chicago's Back of the Yards.

more environmentally sensitive pace. Another objective is to enhance overall greenness both within the public realm and by means of 'corridor' and 'spot' planting on both public and private land, inducing a pedestrianization of the pace of life in brown lands.

The brown-land 'village' emphasis works best when established land-use intensities and transportation provisions come together at or around former villages, railway stations, abandoned electric tram stops, or surrounding a park or some other community facility. This can be pushed along by a local government administration in a number of ways (encouragement, advice, publicity) although the actual execution of regenerative change is mostly a function of returns to private developers and landowners of income relative to capital outlay. It is clear that hub-focused cluster projects, wholly desirable though they are, cannot infiltrate the whole of the inner suburbs; indeed the locating opportunities are limited.

Surviving urban 'villages' within the brown-land context usually exhibit outward signs of community and street life personality and a strong sense of place. This is particularly the situation with the generation of specific activities (places of worship and the like), and functions (shopping and transit exchange), and variety (mixed household types), and local jobbing (artisans and shopkeepers) when these are within easy walking distance of one another. These characteristics reinforce the sense of security, friendliness and calm, noted to be the hallmarks of 'urban village' living. At best brown-land neighbourhoods are interactive in ambience, legible in character, and highly permeable via interconnected and safe public realm spaces, also exhibiting an acceptance of mixed activities and mixed uses of genteel kinds (bakeries, realators (estate agents), small hotels, entertainment venues, handicraft centres).

Design excellence, in conjunction with the mixed-use and higher-density policies already reviewed, enable brown-land retrofits to avoid the fundamental layout mistakes which provide the context for street crime – 'opportunities', 'victims', 'offenders' (Zelinka and Brennan, *SafeScape*, 2001). In terms of physical design, the call is for the provision of well-lit public areas which ensure that there are no opportunities for entrapment, along with high visibility entrance–exit sight lines. These issues are important, but nowhere near as important as the need for root-cause social problem alleviation (most challenging, the eradication of drug dealing) centred on designing a sense of belonging, pleasure, liveliness and community. It is clear that were the cost of root-cause social correction compared to the cost of private surveillance provision, *and* the cost of contact-avoidance manoeuvres, *and* expenditures on institutionalizing, hospitalizing and counselling for both assailants and assaulted, *then* communities would get the mixed-use higher-density layouts and designs they deserve. This would also involve the activation of community-focused training and education, the incorporation of a safety audit (Zelinka and Brennan 2001: 174) and an increased and accepted obligation to keep an eye open for each other, as well as the promotion of a greater degree of civility in the public realm.

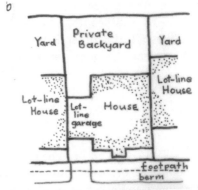

Design facilitating home security.

The inner suburbs are places where a mixture of household arrangements are positioned to support lifestyle objectives such as variety and conviviality, and which go some way to excluding the motor car and noxious land uses and socially unacceptable activities. Inner suburb villages improve on the unattainable urban sustainability ideal and are a major step in the direction of neighbourly urban form. Inner suburb villagization fulfils neomodern ideals, predicated on the lines of ancient guild-influenced inner-city living in the Old World.

Retrofitting, consolidating and revitalizing standard suburbia (Steve Belmont's 'Grey Zones', 2002) presents something of a curate's egg. Spatially considered, the partly-bad (usually post-World War II) patches which sprawl over most of lower-density suburbia, are adjacent or proximate to pockets of mostly-good urban living (usually built between the wars, 1919 to 1939). These standard suburbs can be partially remediated: rendered more affordable and economical, more safe and sociable, and more environmentally diverse and sustainable. Opportunities arise for 'citylets' through the design of within-city TOD and Co-housing projects. These work best when a public space or function lies at the heart of, or penetrates, such clusterings, although this is really only a worthy and purposeful outcome for select contexts. The 'bad news' is that the more recently built suburbs are inordinately transfixed, difficult to change physically, and do little to stir the political and administrative conscience or imagination.

With 'consolidation and densification' as a generally desirable objective, the straightforward housing infill approach runs head on into the also straightforward problem of utilities overload. Within low plot ratio layouts it is relatively easy to identify some backyard and frontyard infill building sites. Aside from issues of house-style compatibility (older bungalows juxtapositioned with new shift-ons?) a repetition of such infillings overload the pipe-and-wire supply services and the culvert-and-drain disposal services, and imposes increased residential street parking and traffic movement problems. Little wonder that local authorities which set off down the densification policy path for standard suburbs soon come to realize that there are wider aspects of neighbourhood resistance, ambience concerns, utilities upgrade, and transportation planning to consider. The cost of utilities refurbishment is inhibited by low investment returns on outlay over the short term, which of course deters investors.

One approach is simply to leave problem suburbia to stew in its original single-purpose layout, proposing little more for them than a landscape makeover. A cynical corollary is to beef up the marriage-counselling, gambling-counselling, vice-counselling, and drug-rehabilitation services, it being left to central government to provide the prisons, refuges and hospitals where the most irredeemably wrecked lives end up. The more positive longer-haul solution involves refurbishment in accordance with general rules (boxes 5.4, 5.1, and 5.2): to start with what is given and work toward a realistic, affordable and realizable neighbourhood recentralization and revitalization.

Infilling encounters three relatively intractable obstacles. *First* is the inertia of local residents and their local government agency overwhelmed by the tangle of the challenge.[63] *Second* is the tenural inertia whereby low-density freeholding induces an indifference toward community centring, it being reasoned that, as a consequence of the expanding use of the automobile, schooling, entertainment and employment can be accessed anywhere these happen to be located cross-city. *Third*, local government agencies avoid assuming a proactive indicative attitude, mostly preferring to adopt a 'you propose, we dispose' approach.

Garage and granny flat infill.

A rewarding collaborative outcome can be pursued on a joint-venture basis by neighbours activated by their local government council within a street block, combining their overgrown and disused rear yards into an amenity garden and playground shared space as shown in figure 5.11, **Creating an open space oasis**. In many respects, retrofitting and consolidating standard suburbia appears 'too difficult'. An alternative is for local authorities to operate on a joint-venture facilitative basis.[64] A supplementary approach for the attainment of prescriptive densification is land taxing calculated on a site-size basis whereby one household occupying a two-house site has to meet a two-house land tax bill thereby hurrying on infill. Greening the suburbs, planning plus planting, is a value-adding and ambience-refurbishment factor – and a can-do owner input option.

The sites of social services (play area, library, school, health centre, corner shop, church) are other nodal points available for the retrofitting and centring of suburbia through clustering and greening. These are the services which should have been planned in at the time of rural crossover – but they were not, are not, and probably never will be worked adequately into the standard suburb. This problem of community provisioning gives rise to a major challenge and question: how to

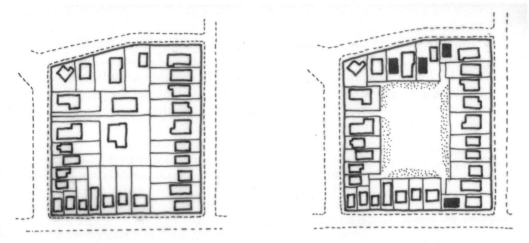

Figure 5.11 Creating an open space oasis
A conjectural depiction based on a starter effort by the Addigton Bush Society in Christchurch. Two houses removed. Four new houses inserted. Large, secure private open space created.

retrofit the social and utilities facilities *and* densify and partly repopulate in order to justify the investment called for. In all of this it is important to remember that the advent of an increased density demands a proportionally increased input of utility restructuring, public transport provisioning, and landscaping.

Urban density increase strategy, broadly contemplated, inclines toward urban sustainability, viewed from both a within-city and from a wider regional perspective. Urban ecosystems are, and ever will be, unbalanced in that they 'consume' inputs of raw energy, materials and food, and 'produce' waste gases, putrescent liquids, and generally useless solid garbage. Sustainability is a conservation *with* development ideal to be maximized, even though it may never be fully attained. The neighbourhood retrofit and consolidation process reviewed in this passage contributes additionally to revitalization through the pursuit of community sociability, amenity enhancement and compatible work-at-home arrangements.

Shopping as a leisure activity

Two countervailing forces, the protectionist urge to 'save' traditional central business districts and the profiteering urge to 'capture' middle- and lower-income consumers, are at work in the cities and larger towns of Australasia and North America. The United States and Canada have reinvigorated many small-city centres along the lines described evocatively by Franaviglia in *Main Street Revisited* (1996) and Suzanne Dane in *Mainstreet Success Stories* (1997). The main shopping opportunity for cities and large towns lies with 'big box' strips and within 'large shed' malls, usually at cheap and accessible locations in the suburbs or at the urban edge, every 'big box' and 'huge shed' provided with dedicated parking.

At a time before supermarkets and shopping malls, Plischke (1947) described the beginning of a central business district for a New Zealand mainstreet in his booklet *Design and Living*. The hastily developed gridiron settlement with its single-strip shopping centre was portrayed in a caricature of the informal expansion of antipodean town centres as they appeared to him:

Geoffrey Dutton (1964) provides this parallel Australian insight 'we've inherited the climate of Greece, the light of the Mediterranean, the colour of Italy and Spain, and we live in it with the fearful expectation of an audience gathered to hear Knox or Calvin thunder from the pulpit.'

A haphazard collection of all sorts of buildings and most of the styles of the last two thousand years strung along the road without regard to the size or character of the neighbouring buildings or the appearance of the street. The old hotel, a survivor of quieter and more settled times, is still there. The cinema is new . . . to glorify the product of a country thousands of miles away (the USA of course, and . . .) by far the most monumental building in the township is the bank. The end of the street leads up to a war memorial (World Wars I and II) and its formal gardens. On the whole, it is fair to say that this was a pretty true reflection of our civilisation.

With the passing of time most North American and Australasian small town centres have been rebuilt or retrofitted, with maybe the art deco cinemas given over to bingo or warehousing, and the classically façaded banks to a museum or craft centre. In the larger cities of wealth the demotion or replacement of these quasi-cultural icons is now substantially complete, it being an irony that the *more* prosperous the city the *less* effective the preservation of its heritage.

With the further passage of time, coupled to an enhanced nostalgia for the historical past, centres which have retained nineteenth-century and early twentieth-century building stock are undertaking heritage conservation, not only for the sake of the buildings, as much to hedge against competition from superstores. In out-of-the-way small towns blighted by above-average unemployment, derelict old buildings are converted into a modern building use – a former church or meeting chamber converted into a museum or used for storage.

Town centre 'heritage conservation' has now been packaged and marketed to appeal to commercial interests in the style of mainstreet improvement programmes, along the lines given in box 5.5 as **Mainstreet guidelines**. Small town business-centre retrofits of the kind detailed had their origins in the United States and Canada (National Trust Main Street Centre), initiated for Australasia by Anglin Associates mainstreet projects in the 1980s. Commercial boosterism – not really heritage conservation – is the principle motivation underscoring mainstreeting projects.[65]

The following rephrasing, from a UK Department of the Environment document *Involving Communities in Urban and Regional Regeneration* (1995) usefully supplements settler society experience with mainstreet projects:

1 Clarify community participation objectives.
2 Identify interests and interest groups.
3 Enlist community support.

Box 5.5 Mainstreet guidelines

Mainstreet improvements arise from both heritage pride and, particularly, commercial profit, bound together in one package. These strengths throw into relief two constraints. *Firstly* that the process has a limitation in favour of towns over cities because of their shared interests, knowledge and skills, and coherent community. Country towns and water's edge settlements are the kinds of place for which mainstreet guidelines are most effective. The *second* constraint is one of time; in effect an identification of the limitations of focused voluntary citizen input over one or two years. Of course good influences do last and linger; but it is important to recognize that most improvement is achieved over a short 'big push' phase, which eases into a 'rest on laurels' phase, with maybe a repeat resurgence at a later date.

Given the voluntary initiation of the mainstreet process, it behoves the initiators and motivators to start with a no-nonsense 'straight into prognosis' approach. How this is initiated and managed introduces complexity. The stimulus to activate mainstreeting could come from a local governing authority, a commercial syndicate, a heritage conservation group, chamber of commerce or indeed a combination of these.

The SWOT format (Strengths and Opportunities to 'enhance' on one side of the ledger; Weaknesses and Threats to 'correct' on the other) meets the operational situation admirably, but usually warrants some planner–designer–organizer input. The SWOT approach calls for 'savvy' as well as professionalism. The procedure builds upon the natural, cultural and historical heritage advantages as 'Strengths'; and an appraisal of where tourists and visitors are coming from and what they want to see and do, highlighted as 'Opportunities'. A 'miles off the beaten track' isolation will be a 'Weakness', as will the presence of unbridled larikinism work through as a 'Threat'. It is important to be candid about Weaknesses and Threats and the capacity to deal with them. With Strengths and Opportunities there are usually cultural-historical, natural-heritage and other interest groups willing to initiate action.

The next step involves moving from prognosis to planning. Participating citizen input is helpful, although business co-dependency is more significant and of longer-term utility. Participating businesses have organizational clout, so it is important to bind them into the process. They can be apathetic about outlay and involvement unless they are persuaded about the possibility that their project will become a fact and prove profitable. If a business community is reluctant to get involved with a mainstreet project then the all-consuming task of the initiating agency is to persuade it to come on board. Well-meaning citizens cannot achieve much mainstreeting good in isolation.

Following 'prognosis and planning' the next step activates the project as an enterprise. This involves direct work on such 'positives' as the cultural heritage, the natural heritage, the building heritage and landmark features: and direct work on such 'correctionals' as cleaning up on clutter, ugly signage, litter, building decay and unwholesomeness. At this delivery stage good design is not the whole answer, yet it is the catalyst for effective change. Neat and distinctive signage and information brochures are helpful, and a well-illustrated heritage trail is an attraction. Well-planted private gardens, careful repainting in 'heritage' colours, uncluttered frontyards and porches, and tidy berms and public places lend both local and visitor delight. Landmark trees, and street tree planting, add to ambiance. Local boat trips, aero club flights, visits to a period museum and, or also, the likes of a steam train ride are useful ancillary attractions. Pride and cleanliness along with a sense of making visitors feel welcome, and evident security, are also positive features. Litter bins are a pragmatic essential. Two cost-free ingredients hallmark an attractive and interesting small town: the calmness induced by canopy trees, and the friendliness of local people.

Assuming that there exists both the motivation and the capability to fit in with the above 'prognosis-promotion-project' format, there remains organization, management and funding. There is always a need for a marketing set-up, preferably working out of a mainstreet shop front, community hall, or an under-used landmark building. These organization and marketing units must, in support of their own credibility, monitor and appraise their achievements month by month, and 'one year compared with another' – proving current success and the benefits of soldiering on.

These are the headings for a 'four point approach' given in the US publication *MainStreet Success Stories* (Suzanne Dane 1997: 3–9): Organization, Promotion, Design, and Economic Restructuring. There are also 'eight guiding principles': Comprehensiveness, Incrementalism, Selfhelp, Partnerships, Assets, Quality, Attitudinal Change, Implementation.

4   Establish roles of the organizer.
5   Define levels of involvement.
6   Define the planner's role. ✓
7   Clarify the role of the community.
8   Identify techniques of involvement.
9   Document the strategy.
10 Establish a clear yet flexible time-frame.

The process of commercial district overhaul for larger service centres needs to be appreciated for what it is; a rearguard commercially motivated activity to reclaim middle-income customers now flocking to shopping malls and commercial strips in search of 'shopping convenience' and 'shopping security' in the case of malls for 'shopping as entertainment'. A significant attraction of strips and malls is that the household automobile can be safely parked adjacent to a shop or within or under a mall. These, being well lit and muzaked, exude secureness and cleanliness and replicate most of the shopping opportunities of 'mainstreet' under one roof.

The central feature of an effective mainstreet revitalization programme involves an accommodation of the motor car, coupled, perversely, with traffic calming and secure off-street parking. In what might be considered the most challenging shopping mainstreet circumstance, flanking a typical 30 to 40 metre wide commercial

Warkworth

easement, the former street space becomes a wide trench flanked by low-rise buildings. This becomes difficult to enliven and revitalize because it is aesthetically incoherent and lost in commercial space – offering counter inducements to go by car from 'big box' to 'big box' along a shopping strip, or to park and shop in the security of a mall. Pedestrianization of the typical mainstreet kind attains functional validity when the traffic lane is narrowed, the pavements widened, and street trees planted. Mainstreets are challenging to 'design' into life, especially so for those with a wider thoroughfare, although much can be achieved with the careful placement of kiosks, tree planting, bollard advertising and surface reconfiguration when this can be afforded. David Sucher's *City Comforts* (1995) illustrates the good manners and detailed components which induce a sense of belonging, security, peaceability, and orderliness in the shopping area context.

The main alternative to mainstreet treatment and central business district overhaul is the attraction of consumers to shopping malls and commercial strips. The socio-scientific context for both malls and strips, but particularly the latter, involves consideration of the shopping threshold range – the distance average travellers are prepared to travel to shop for high-order goods supplied at 'centres', with low-order goods supplied 'locally'. One way to cope with commercial strip problems of dispersal, chaos and traffic congestion is to accept the aggregation of these phenomena and to reassemble them along built-to-frontage arrangements with car parking to the side and rear – in effect converting them to something safer, more compact and more defined. These improvements include: placing parking to the rear and sides of the 'big boxes', landscaping, pedestrianizing and occasionally rebuilding up to the legal edge of the frontage road line; creating vehicle entry gaps every 60 metres or so; and varying the shop frontage setback line. Given that strip shopping is an established pattern of commercial life away from the central business district, then so long as automobile use in settler societies remains widespread and cheap, there is no likelihood that the commercial strip units flanking connector roads will fade into obscurity. Perversely there often arises a need to redeem 'ghost' malls and 'lacklustre' strips, stiffening their character, removing their worst dangers, and enhancing their level of convenience.

Strip commercial: nil-setback, rear parking. Improving street appearance and enabling shoppers to car-shuttle between stores without re-entering the collector road. See also the 'Ten Principles Pamphlet' in *Reinventing America's Suburban Strips*, Beyard and Pawlukiewicz 2001.

Shopping as entertainment has evolved as the principal family-focused outing from the suburban home (Bromley and Thomas 1994), the major attraction being to a shopping mall anchored by a major department store. Design manuals abound, for this is big business involving immense profits 'establishing shopping experiences and development profits – as the basis for a new way of life' (Crawford 1986).[66] Adhering to the principles outlined in box 5.1 as a set of urban social arrangements and style, attention is directed to the following critical characteristics:

- **Connectability**: between private car access and car parks, the bus stops, the taxi stands, and relative to the whole 'pedestrian' experience within the mall and along the strip.
- **Security:** convenience and safety for the parked car, the parked child, parked purchases, and for the pedestrian browser-shopper – all of which includes the avoidance of traps and danger corners, the provision of good lighting and clear signage;
- **Focus:** providing excitement and variety in a way which ties a mall into itself, but also reaches out and identifies with its urban setting; exhibiting and exploiting some form of 'landmark' along with a department store 'anchor'; rendering them appealing upon arrival for the shopping-as-leisure experience.
- **Visual Identity:** introducing an acceptable (usually fake) 'richness' along with a sense of (usually phoney) 'liveliness' and a presentation of (largely falsified) 'variety' to the mall user.

Additional to this 'theming' is the accessory attachment of entertainment (picture houses), and recreation facilities (fitness centres and bowling alleys) as integral mall components, leading, logically, to the incorporation of upper-level offices and professional agencies (doctor, dentist, optometrist) – in short all the retail, recreational and office components, and some residential accommodation, combined and integrated into the mall entity.

It would be a small-town 'real shops' conditioning in Britain and Australasia which inclines me to register some negativity in relation to the glitzy, themed, muzaked, air-conditioned and 'pocketbook oriented' environment of shopping malls. Nevertheless, it has to be acknowledged that the family car, consumerism, and the 'shopping as entertainment' syndrome do come together at landmarked malls. If this is to be 'romantically themed' on some simulation of an Arcadian or Old World surrogacy, orchestrated and paid for by entrepreneurs concerned with fiscal yield from high rents at considerable fiscal velocity, so be it. There are, of course, considerable shopper and security advantages to be noted in relation to strip and mall-shopping for a modern, mobile, urban-living consumer society. Indeed there can be some overall car usage reduction when malls are sited at or close to the 'centre of gravity' of urban populations. In existing larger towns and cities the shopping mall offers stiff competition to all but the most propitious local shopping centre and conventional central business district.

The mall is giving way, always the pattern with consumer capture, to large edge city epicentres providing mixed commerce, work, child care and entertainment – including within the most advanced prototypes, pre-schools, and higher educational institutions and some residential apartments. These mega-centres gain an increased sense of security in association with the increased density. At the edge of fast-growing metropolitan cities they are distinctive from ordinary malls in that they do have a life after dark, do provide conventional office jobs, and are within the commuter range of a mainly female workforce. To mall enthusiasts they are 'enjoyable' because they 'throb 24 hours a day: seven days a week' and because they are 'safe, secure and fun'. In effect they are places where retailers have figured out what people like and have set about giving it to them. As a consequence edge city mega malls offer formidable competition to metropolitan downtowns and small-town mainstreets. Some people will travel across town, even across a region, passing 'ghost malls and dead strips' to get to them.

Revitalizing and reclaiming the central business district in larger towns and cities is a multiplex planning-with-design matter which is well documented and prescribed for. Beyond the specifics given in the box 5.1 litany of urban social arrangement and style are some key heritage elements which warrant attention. These include the need to accord special protection to the places and precincts of historical significance (such as the nineteenth-century Victorian heritage in Australasia, and the 'Chinatowns' and other early settler heritage of western United States and Canada), to preserve the late nineteenth- and early twentieth-century narrow back-alley laneways, to protect significant vistas and landmark gateways and feature buildings, and to foster the revitalization of an inner-city residential lifestyle. Other aims include the need to park cars off-street and to plant trees on-street; to facilitate pedestrian movement and pedestrian activities in secure ways; and to enliven signage and frontages.

The greatest challenge of all for city centres is to reclaim them *from* the automobile and *for* the pedestrian. Transport Demand Management (TDM) programmes are quadri-polar: low-cost versus high-cost, and public-regulation versus private-control. Cycle park provisioning and car pooling are 'low-cost'; new expressways and subway systems are 'high-cost'. Law enforcement on parking violations and the spread of working hours are clearly matters of 'public regulation', while the induction of home-based outwork and the charging of parking fees by employers can be a matter of 'private control'. The dynamics of policy and practice within such a quadri-polar situation generates unexpected synergies like the Triple Convergence Syndrome (Downs 1973) where a new commuter route induces: (1) spatial convergence – diverting traffic from established routes to a new alternative; (2) time convergence – more drivers striving to commute during peak hours; and (3) modal convergence – taking people off public transport and into family cars.

Nowadays the historical centre of towns and cities is only occasionally claimed by 'the people' for victorious homecomings and protests. Mostly the 'mall' now prevails as the 'centre of community' functional space, flipping the traditional city-centre functions onto the newly built suburban shopping complexes. With the strengthening of urban identity through heritage conservation, plus the reintroduction of residential life to urban centres, city administrations hope that their commercial core will be reclaimed by the people as their 'polis' (or third place: 'third' that is, to home place and workplace). If the town centres are not reclaimed then John and Mary citizen will unconsciously stake out the shopping mall as 'their centre' – that *locus* where they are entertained, do their purchasing, and meet and encounter others in contexts where they feel safe and good and thoroughly up to date.

The Delivery of Outcome

The delivery of outcome is a techno-instrumental collation of the 'tools' needed to do the urban development with conservation 'job' for delivering 'results'. This is offered in box 5.6 as **Planning in action: the delivery of outcome**. This matter of 'delivery' involves the elaboration – in this context a summary listing – of the transactional instruments for planned urban change. Box 5.6 catalogues a selection of alternatives available for approaching the achievement and attainment of urban conservancy *with* development in sustainable style.

The local and regional planning official, previously hog-tied by administrative bureaucracy and politically unsupported, now connects with a better-informed public, is procedurally and technically better equipped, and is served by professional associations which have fashioned useful ethical guidelines. There remains

Box 5.6   Planning in action: the delivery of outcome

Planning for conservancy and development outcomes is an 'of the law' activity and a 'within the law' process. Much that is decreed within that activity process is not enforced because many planning instruments are enabling-permissive rather than mandatory. My predication is that, essential though the law may be for facilitating planning outcomes, the law, in and of itself, does not achieve good conservancy and development practice. This is a matter for the operatives involved to engage, manage, oversee and enforce, using the available instruments and processes.

Complexity and challenge arises from the reconciliation of two somewhat excluding verities. The *first* is for a light hand on the tiller, markets in free flow, trading deregulated, with only a few light and flexible controls. The *second* predicates, from scientific indicators, that consumerist and discard activities using biospheric resources should be subject to firm intervention and emphatic control. So, within settler societies there is this tussle between 'as of right' presumptions springing from such precepts as the sanctity of property-owner privileges and the likes of the US 'Second Amendment' as resource ownership and usage rights; and the 'highest and best use' interventions of good government in association with the use of enlightened subsidiarity.

The listing which follows is about matching up 'regulations' with 'regulating'. The big-stick options start with the powers of compulsory acquisition (eminent domain), progressing toward arrangements of the coercive kind, ending with some other less official ways to induce beneficial community outcomes.

EMINENT DOMAIN is the overriding 'sovereign' power held by a state to exercise its 'natural right' of property purchase: to take land (usually for compensation – hence 'compulsory purchase') for a worthy public use purpose as a 'taking'.

NEGOTIATED PURPOSE usually precedes and is usually preferred to compulsory purchase. In this way 'land' or the development-conservancy rights to a 'land use', are acquired by an arm of government which thereafter owns that use-right.

LAND BANKING is the exercise of governmental rights to acquire land in the marketplace for the purpose of protecting that land or securing its use in accordance with a pre-planned public purpose.

CENTRAL DIRECTIVE is the issuing of mandatory and enforceable change via statutorily authorized legal process. This takes the form of development and, or also, conservancy practice orders, rules, procedures and instrumental authority.

ZONING is a generic land-use planning tool for subduing land-use conflicts, grouping together complementary land uses, and for also excluding land or building usages designated non-conforming. Zoning sets down bulk and location rules, density parameters and building and land-use conditions. Although stylistically rigid, zoning practice can be varied and flexible.

- **Area-based Allocation Zoning** is usually engaged as a rural 'extensive' zoning tool for the broad-brush conservation of rural and natural heritage tracts, often allowing for some zoned-in residential units, usually clustered at designated locations.
- **Buffer Zoning** within urban areas divides benignly between conflicting land uses. Buffer zones for rural areas provide a green-belt expanse between settlements.
- **Rural Zoning** provides a rural-only barrier against urban-driven land uses, price rises and land taxes; allowing the division of land down to the minimum-sized economically viable farm unit, usually by decreeing the minimum economic agri-unit area of holding.
- **Spot Zoning** (in wider contexts PUDs – Planned Unit Development) denotes the selective and preferential designation of property for a chosen purpose. At worst spot zoning engenders 'do this for me' cronyism; at best it works effectively in a community's interest.
- **Cluster Zoning** also loosely fits the PUD (Planned Unit Development) concept, which accommodates the clumping together of a specified form of development (say residential) on one part of a site, reserving the balance for (say) open area enjoyment. Cluster zoning is often used to allow an above-average spot-density of built units along with a substantial area of adjoining open ground space.
- **Enterprise Zoning**: a non-specific administrative device for establishing the aptness of an otherwise aberrant proposal for a site.
- **Floating Zones** (also styled as Contract Zones) locks up land for a future designated purpose, subject to the terms of an agreement.

Box 5.6 *Continued*

- **Future Development Zones** (also styled as Contract Zones) lock up land for a future designated purpose, subject to the terms of an agreement.
- **Incentive Zones** allows contracting rights – usually in the form of increased floor space – in exchange for providing other, usually amenity, benefits (for example a creche in a city office block).
- **Up-zoning and Down-zoning** involves changes in the intensity of a zoning so as to increase or decrease the use of land, the site coverage and or also the bulk of allowable building on sites. Also known as Contract Zoning and as the exercise of Density Exchange Options.

GROWTH BOUNDARY is a legal 'fence' designated around an urban area within which the land uses are urban, and without which the land uses are rural. When applied strictly, land uses and land valuations (and taxes) switch from urban to rural at a growth boundary.

TRANSFERABLE DEVELOPMENT RIGHT (TDR) also styled as Tradable Development Right/Credit; a voluntary agreement brokered by a local government authority to facilitate the transfer of a right to develop (frequently airspace, but also the likes of coastal development rights transferred inland) from one site to another, sometimes kilometres away: hence a 'sending' site and a 'receiving' site. The 'transfer' can involve more, or less, development at the 'receiving' site than was traded in at the 'sending' site.

DEEMED TO COMPLY is a useful 'performance approach' which allows flexibility in the application of rules and standards; in effect 'deeming' a well-designed and generally beneficial proposal's approval by decreeing that it is adequately 'complying'.

WAIVERS (Dispensations and Variances) mostly indicate the foregoing of a local government rule to the specific benefit of, or to reduce the hardship for, a subject-site. Waivers are agreed to without prejudice or establishing precedence.

AS OF RIGHT involves two general 'freedoms': the 'right to develop' and the 'right to use', along with other specific categories of 'right' such as a 'right to farm'. Permitted Activities are a clearly understood form of prescribed 'right'.

PURCHASED DEVELOPMENT RIGHT (PDR) involves the forward selling (purchasing) of rights to urbanize, subdivide, harvest a forest, or mine for minerals (usually purchased from open area land holders).

CONTROL OF EFFECTS indirectly constrains land-use intensity, and site and building performance; and the intensity of allowable waste disposal and other 'effects' upon land and environment. The 'controls' are usually predicated on an 'activities' basis which allows a variety of overlapping and intermingling 'interests' in a property. These are regulated by means of 'effects criteria'.

BY-LAW an ordinance or code sanctioning what can or cannot be done. By-laws are mostly restrictive in intent. Although backed up with enforceable penalties they are frequently ineffectual. Many by-laws are observed in the breach, although others, such as building codes, are well observed.

EXCLUSIONARY COVENANTS are aimed at excluding a particular type of user (persons?) from living in or operating an activity in a specified area. It is usually couched in terms of minima: lot sizes, expenditure per unit, activity, density. 'Exclusionary' zoning – which is not usually designated explicitly as such – is also counter-reflected in the expression 'inclusionary' zoning. Walled and gated residential enclaves (including condominia) are the most usual form of exclusionary-inclusionary zoning.

USER LEVIES (also known as Impact Fees) are up-front charges or land set-asides, applied to a property developer (person or agency) to ensure that they meet the cost of infrastructure hook-up and provisioning. These levies are also applied to the recovery of up-grade costs associated with access roading and utilities provisioning.

DEVELOPMENT BONUSES (also Incentive Provisioning). Discretionary privileges (greater floor space, higher plot coverage) applied to specified sites for a specified reason and purpose. The provision of services and utilities to a project, by a local agency, as an inducement to develop, is a variant.

JOINT VENTURE PROCEDURES (also known as Integrated Ventures and Development Trusts) involve the pooling of expertise, money, property, by two or more people or agencies over a specified term, and with the

Box 5.6 *Continued*

clear intention that there will be a useful synergy. A public-private joint venture can deliver outcomes of benefit to the private sector developer (a useful 'buddy' relationship, generating certainty, priority treatment) and to the public sector (good outcome, effective control, environmental quality).

PRIVATE CONTROLS (also known as Covenants, Deed Restrictions, and sometimes as Private Zoning) are supplementations to the official regulation of development, particularly during a project's construction and consolidation phases. Private Controls delimit the land-use, landscaping, aesthetic and nuisance factors relating to the development and occupancy of a project. Covenants should run with the land title rather than a landowner.

JOINT OWNERSHIP is a style of co-ownership (as with co-housing trusts and in condominia) allowing for

individual ownership in association with a multiplex of other owners. Co-ownership arrangements usually define 'private' 'semi-public' and 'public' spaces. To be effective joint ownership projects and estates are controlled by an overarching managing unit.

References

D. Abbott, *Encyclopaedia of Real Estate Terms*, 1987.
Davidson and Dolnick, *Zoning Development and Planning Terms*, 1999.
J. W. Reilly, *The Language of Real Estate*, 1982.
J. S. Gross, *Webster's New World Real Estate Dictionary*, 1987.
For TDRs consult T. Daniels *When City and Country Collide*, 1999 (App. G).
For zoning options, see *Flexible Zoning*, Urban Land Institute, 1991 and M. Morris, *Incentive Zoning*, 2000.
On *The Takings Issue*, Meltz, Merriam, Frank (1999).

---

always the problem of how to get from 'here' (a patently unsustainable and socially ailing urbanity), to 'there' (prosperous socio-environmental urban harmony).

Scientific certainty is the anvil of generic sustainability on which the hammer-head of empowerment (knowledge power and outcomes – chapter 2) beats out policy guidelines and design actions. This is the essence of proactive sustainable urban planning and the future way ahead for local government.

Balanced Urban Living

There has been much conflicting community-level analysis of the urban condition. The information gap identified by Gerecke and Reid (1991) offers a view about those who would style themselves to be planners as 'Having no clearly defined goals, and still working very much with a discredited methodology . . . [further observing that they] are not handling the challenges of the city very well'. Certainly by most understandings of sustainability, cities and suburbs gaze across a gap of incredulity following decades of reactive local government administration.

Yet it is the city, more particularly the suburbs, that the standard settler society citizen is born into, lives within, and is usually cremated without. Suburbs are the focus and intent of majority life, and all is far from well in terms of their fiscal and energy drain, their social fragility, and for the suburbs themselves as physically organized places of habitation. There is also the peri-urban threat of forest fires in California and south-eastern Australia, earthquakes in central New Zealand and

California, flooding for major riverine settlements everywhere, hurricanes on the weather shores of the south-eastern United States, salination crises and fresh-water supply difficulties in urbanized areas bordering deserts, and an increasing likelihood of electricity blackouts, sewage surcharges, storm-water blowouts, traffic gridlocks and garbage mountains. Additional to the case for protecting potential victims from being burnt out, blown away, shaken down, is the counter-case for relieving the non-victim majority of the kinds of insurance payouts they expected never to have visited upon them. The above-listed failings lend a feral quality to much city, and particularly, suburban life. This suggests that the further perpetuation of city expansion on land patently unsuitable for urban development has to be slowed down, halted and reversed.

Existing suburbs are indeed cumbersome places, inordinately difficult to change. Yet communities cannot afford to continue with the social damage as well as the economic costs of their inefficiency. Indeed, because the benefits are greater, and the costs less, there is every incentive – not yet widely acknowledged – to make policy provisions and affect good design for *less* car dependence, *less* single-use zoning, *greater* housing choice, *higher* housing density, *increased* land-use variety, and *more* community participation – *and* a proactive use of the 'deemed to comply' principle for innovative and effective design alternatives. An irony is that those who live in settler societies know of, and have also often enjoyed, excellent urban experiences and stimulating urban living elsewhere, especially after visiting the European Old World. Despite this awareness, settler societies persisted in the twentieth century with a monot-onous and dysfunctional zoned-ahead pattern unsuited to the particular needs of singleton, solo-parented and one-car house-holds. It is a pattern predicated upon relative wealthiness, the 4.2 person housing norm, discretionary access to the automobile, and rural-into-urban land com-modification – the settler society 'received inheritance' and the Anglo New World 'urban tradition'. That inheritance and tradition now cries out for repackaging. The extant suburban and ex-urban style is dated and failing, exhibiting a need to be retrofitted, committing to urban development which is in good balance with nature, a social pleasure to live in, and economical to manage, albeit with some tidy and tucked away (self-served) ex-urban residential living on rural landscapes useless to agriculture.

> **CURIBATA**
>
> The Curibata experience in south-eastern Brazil has synthesized solutions to urban design, education, information, healing, safety and economy.
> An good explanation of these innovations is given in the popular Hawken, Lovins, Lovins text *Natural Capitalism*, 1999.

Governments should act custodially if the cost of the way in which people live is crime-burdened, drug-stalked, debilitating or debt-inducing, and do so for the national benefit as a whole. Individuals would make more commitment to com-munity affairs if there were alternatives to pawning their lives for a house and car with little else in the way of human investment and interest. How? Through avoidance of development onto known vulnerable sites – flood-prone, at fire risk, eathquake-prone. By increasing the density of grey-zone suburbia, then tempting people out of their cars, onto their bikes and on their feet. By providing user-funded public transport; by reducing waste and applying recycling policies. By capturing and using more solar energy in the home place, workplace and schools.

By production of food closer to the consumer. By reducing crime and poleaxing the drug trade. In summary, the need is to recognize and favour the longer haul, to go with the ecology, to trend toward a higher density and an urban harmony (refer also to the listing given in box 1.2, New-age pragmatics, chapter 1).

Furthermore, there is a community care factor to consider. Central and local government administrations regulate as necessary, and many would argue that they have little obligation to 'deliver', 'care' or 'intervene'. This distinction may lie at the heart of why there is, in settler societies, such a proliferation of culturally pitiable, uncaring, and dysfunctional households. Most city authorities have not previously been in a constitutional position to adopt a proactive policy or assume a subsidiarity preference. They have stuck – or been stuck – with traditional systems of statutory service provisioning and legally required quality constraint.

That urban situation is changing. Local government has been exhorted to adopt the *Agenda 21* desiderata (Appendix) although of itself that document does little more than show a way. Ultimately, what local administrators need is devolution of powers (subsidiarity) and the will and expertise to administer those powers.

The roll-over stage from 'open area terrestrial space' to 'urbanized place' is momentous in the history of a landscape's evolution. This is illustrated by our fascination with the late nineteenth-century urban-embryo photographs of the townscapes still inhabited today.

The greatest obstacle to change is the way that the corporate and private sectors in Anglo settler society administrations adhere and genuflect to exclusive landownership. This difficulty counter-informs the fact that when new urban land construction is being initiated on raw rural land the public imperative is to secure, ahead of that changeover and as a condition to approval, the appropriate heritage-conservation, public-access and public-space needs. The defining moment of change, the roll-over from an open-area rural space to urbanized occupation has, in the past, conformed to the principle (Parkinson paraphrased) whereby 'the most momentous decisions [about roll-over change] get taken with the least expenditure of time and effort'. The future imperative is that, precisely because these roll-over events are once-and-forever decisions of everlasting social and economic significance, they must be correctly detailed 'down' from a societally sensitive sustainable-as-possible policy toward an overall community 'best fit' practice. Urban administrations should exercise the interventionist powers detailed within the Place-making and urban reform reviews, and the 'boxes' and 'figures' of guidelines given earlier in this chapter. Anything less, and future generations will be forever short-changed.

There is no substantive way for the middle-serving building sector, left to its own devices, to meet housing clients, needs individually, to do by itself what ought to be directed through local government for communities of the future. The inhabitants of most of these suburbs will inherit a particular consumer-durable (their homes in their suburb) with a user span measured in lifetimes rather than decades. And although landowners and contractors may be aware of the contemporary solo-parenting and single-household patterns, they are not *of their own accord* about to provide houses which break away from three-bedroom designs, nor are they in step with the need to set about the provision of a joyful enriching and aesthetically refreshing urban lifestyle. To those landowners and developers who manufacture suburbia the business risks for innovation are inertial. Changes to the patterning and provisioning of middle suburbia, formerly matters of mere rote for local government administrators, call for social as well as physical design innovation on the part of technocrats, bureaucrats and politicians. These are the people positioned to ensure that the identified needs and wishes of future occupants are incorporated into future projects.

The point, the neomodern point, is that low-density wide-road subdivisions of once-rural land into plots, houses and mean-and-marginal public open spaces has run its relatively short and selective course in the transpacific (Anglo) New World. Past patterns of dreary suburbanization has given rise to a recognition that contractors and landowners and local government and central government (Federal and State) must be part of the urban reform options and flexible actions outlined in these pages. In broad effect: pre-design, pre-investment, and pre-development – thus 'pre-ensuring' for towns and cities of the future:

- That the focus and form (sense of place) components are agreed and set in place ahead of any necessary urban-fringe crossover from rural to urban settlement.
- That the mixture of up-coming generations in diverse households has housing choices and varietal land-use choices, at higher densities.
- That the supply of urban land be targeted *within* extant settlements much more than from the fixed and finite rural land resource. That an internal consolidation-diversification-makeover is the governing focus.
- That integrated public transport systems be justified and installed for higher-density tracts, and for the use of non-driver persons, against the day when profligate usage of private motor cars will become less practical as well as less affordable.
- That urban safety and security be addressed as a social need as well as a practical necessity.
- That green space 'public realm' components be pre-positioned to infiltrate suburbs and to achieve identity for urban neighbourhoods.
- That the level of local food and water provisioning and waste management, locally managed and conserved energy waste-reduction and recycling, and the panoply of sustainable-in-intent ideals, be ever improved upon and expanded.

Hope, incredible optimism, and the goodness of individuals, represents the ethos of settler society urban communities. Government, particularly better local government in all that is urban and suburban, is the instrument of managed intervention and strategic action. The challenge is to engage the minds of individuals to work out attractive proposals with communities, and then to adhere to the 'sustainability paradigm' for achieving balanced economic growth, social wellbeing and environmental husbandry. That trinity encapsulates this book's emphasis on balance and flexibility; the key phrase being *triple harmony*, the keyword being being *sustainability*.

APPENDIX

AGENDA 21
RIO DECLARATION ON ENVIRONMENT AND DEVELOPMENT

United Nations Conference on Environment and Development
The Rio Declaration, June 1992

Preamble

Principle 1   Human beings are at the centre of concerns for sustainable development. They are entitled to a healthy and productive life in harmony
with nature.

Principle 2   States have in accordance with the Charter of the United Nations
and the principles of international law, the sovereign right to exploit
resources pursuant to their own environmental and developmental
policies, and the responsibility to ensure that activities within their
jurisdiction or control do not cause damage to the environment of
other States or of areas beyond the limits of national jurisdiction.

Principle 3   The right to development must be fulfilled so as to equitably meet
developmental and environmental needs of present and future
generations.

Principle 4   In order to achieve sustainable development, environmental protection shall constitute an integral part of the developmental process
and cannot be considered in isolation from it.

Principle 5   All States and all people shall cooperate in the essential task of
eradicating poverty as an indispensable requirement for sustainable
development, in order to decrease the disparities in standards of
living and better meet the needs of the majority of the people of the
world.

Principle 6   The special situation and needs of developing countries, particularly
the least developed and those most environmentally vulnerable,
shall be given special priority. International actions in the field of
environment and development should also address the interests and
needs of all countries.

Principle 7   States shall cooperate in a spirit of global partnership to conserve,
protect and restore the health and integrity of the Earth's ecosystem.

In view of the different contributions to global environmental degradation, States have common but differentiated responsibilities. The developed countries acknowledge the responsibility that they bear in the international pursuit of sustainable development in view of the pressures their societies place on the global environment and of the technologies and financial resources they command.

Principle 8   To achieve sustainable development and a higher quality of life for all people, States should reduce and eliminate unsustainable patterns of production and consumption and promote appropriate demographic policies.

Principle 9   States should cooperate to strengthen endogenous capacity-building for sustainable development by improving scientific understanding through exchanges of scientific and technical knowledge, and by enhancing the development, adaptation, diffusion and transfer of technologies, including new and innovative technologies.

Principle 10   Environmental issues are best handled with the participation of all concerned citizens, at the relevant level. At the national level, each individual shall have appropriate access to information concerning the environment that is held by public authorities, including information on hazardous materials and activities in their communities, and the opportunity to participate in decision-making processes. States shall facilitate and encourage public awareness and participation by making information widely available. Effective access to judicial and administrative proceedings, including redress and remedy, shall be provided.

Principle 11   States shall enact effective environmental legislation. Environmental standards, management objectives and priorities should reflect the environmental and developmental context to which they apply. Standards applied by some countries may be inappropriate and of unwarranted economic and social cost to other countries, in particular developing countries.

Principle 12   States should cooperate to provide a supportive and open international economic system that would lead to economic growth and sustainable development in all countries, to better address the problems of environmental degradation. Trade policy measures for environmental purposes should not constitute a means of arbitrary or unjustifiable discrimination or a disguised restriction on international trade. Unilateral actions to deal with environmental challenges outside the jurisdiction of the importing country should be avoided. Environmental measures addressing transboundary or global environmental problems should, as far a possible, be based on an international consensus.

Principle 13   States shall develop national law regarding liability and compensation for the victims of pollution and other environmental damage. States shall also cooperate in an expeditious and more determined manner to develop further international law regarding liability and compensation for adverse effects of environmental damage caused by activities within their jurisdiction or control.

Principle 14   States should effectively cooperate to discourage or prevent the relocation and transfer to other States of any activities and substances that cause severe or irreversible damage, lack of full scientific certainty shall not be used as a reason for postponing cost-effective measures to prevent environmental degradation.

Principle 15   In order to protect the environment, the precautionary approach shall be widely applied by States according to their capabilities. Where there are threats of serious or irreversible damage, lack of full scientific certainty shall not be used as a reason for postponing cost-effective measures to prevent environmental degradation.

Principle 16   National authorities should endeavour to promote the internalisation of environmental costs and the use of economic instruments, taking into account the approach the polluter should, in principle, bear the cost of pollution, with due regard to the public interest and without distorting international trade and investment.

Principle 17   Environmental impact assessment, as a national instrument, shall be undertaken for proposed activities that are likely to have a significant adverse impact on the environment and are subject to a decision of a competent national authority.

Principle 18   States shall immediately notify other States of any natural disasters or other emergencies that are likely to produce sudden harmful effects on the environment of those States. Every effort shall be made by the international community to help States so afflicted.

Principle 19   States shall provide prior and timely notification and relevant information to potentially affected States on activities that may have a significant adverse transboundary environmental effect and shall consult with those States at an early stage and in good faith.

Principle 20   Women have a vital role in environmental management and development. Their full participation is therefore essential to achieve sustainable development.

Principle 21   The creativity, ideals and courage of the youth of the world should be mobilised to forge a global partnership in order to achieve sustainable development and ensure a better future for all.

Principle 22   Indigenous people and their communities, and other local communities, have a vital role in environmental management and development because of their knowledge and traditional practices. States should recognise and duly support their identity, culture and interests and enable their effective participation in the achievement of sustainable development.

Principle 23   The environment and natural resources of people under oppression, domination and occupation shall be protected.

Principle 24   Warfare is inherently destructive of sustainable development. States shall there respect international law providing protection for the environment in times of armed conflict and cooperate in its further development, as necessary.

Principle 25   Peace, development and environmental protection are interdependent and indivisible.

Principle 26   States shall resolve all their environmental disputes peacefully and by appropriate means in accordance with the Charter of the United Nations.

Principle 27   States and people shall cooperate in good faith and in a spirit of partnership in the fulfilment of the principles embodied in this Declaration and in the further development of international law in the field of sustainable development.

There are 40 chapters within *Agenda 21*: a United Nations agenda on environment and development for the twenty-first century. *Agenda 21* is a protocol – which ratifying nations could work within, although there is a leaning of emphasis in the direction of low-income nations. Behind *Agenda 21* lies the 1987 polemic from the World Commission on Environment and Development (The 'Brundtland' report) *Our Common Future*.

The Key Urban Principles from *Agenda* 21 (James Lunday of 'Common Ground')

Chapter 3 – Centres on the need for the poor to become more self-sufficient through community economic development, participation and access to learning.

Chapter 4 – Centres on the need to change patterns of consumption through encouraging environmentally sound use of new and renewable sources of energy, use of renewable natural resources and sustainable patterns of development.

Chapter 6 – Centres on social, economic and spiritual development and a healthy environment through clean water and non-toxic safe food, control of outdoor and indoor forms of pollution and safe disposal of solid wastes.

Chapter 7 – Is wholly devoted to creation of sustainable human settlements. Eight program areas are identified to guide cities along sustainable paths including affordable housing, resource inventories, citizen participation, integrated environmental infrastructure, sustainable energy and transport systems, sustainable land use planning and management and sustainable construction.

Chapter 9 – Centres on the protection of the atmosphere from greenhouse gases and from chemicals that reduce the ozone layer and other pollutants through new and renewable energy resources, efficient, cost effective, less polluting and safer rural and mass transport systems (transportation uses 30% of the world's commercial energy production and consumes 60% of the world's petroleum production), encourages forms of transportation that minimise emissions and harmful effects on the environment plan urban and regional settlements to reduce environmental Impacts of transport t)remote conservation of natural greenhouse gas sinks and reservoirs.

Chapter 11 – Centres on protection of forests through conservation, planting and greening of places where people live.

Chapter 14 – Centres on sustainable agriculture and rural development through increasing food production in a sustainable manner.

Chapter 15 – Centres on the conservation of biological diversity through encouraging traditional methods of agriculture, habitat protection, creation, restoration and rehabilitation.

Chapter 17 – Centres on the protection of marine resources through developing land use practices that reduce run-off of soils and wastes into rivers and seas.

Chapter 18 – Centres on the protection and management of fresh water supplies by recognising that rapid urbanisation is putting severe strain on water resources and environmental capabilities of cities, and by better management of water resources.

Chapter 21 – Centres an environmentally sound management of solid wastes through changing consumption patterns, promoting healthy, sustainable human settlements. user pays waste disposal, incentives for recycling and energy recovery.

Chapter 28 – Centres on the role of local authorities in making sustainable development happen through having consulted their citizens and by 1996 developing a Local Agenda 21 for the community.

Chapter 31 – Concerns the role of scientists and technologists in achieving environmental protection and human development. This group, including engineers, architects, industrial designers, urban planners and other professionals, should develop codes of practice and guidelines.

6

Tipping the Balance

Following on from the attention to detail in the previous three 'practice' chapters is this wide-horizon overview. Here a flag of conviction about 'tipping the balance' is nailed to the mast of social necessity, for fashioning a development process which is relatively far-seeing and sustainable – the paradigm shift. Not attempting 'everything' (a recognition that urban sustainability is somewhat of an oxymoron!) but 'something' balanced, reflecting in Conservation with Development the findings of science and the social realizations of these better-informed times.

This book has explored sustainable urban planning *principles* (the 'vertically partitioned' ethical, organizational, social, economic, political and environmentalist structures), following this with a review of *practice* (the 'horizontally arrayed' national-regional-local contexts). Politicians range to and fro across such 'horizontal' territories, and up and down the 'vertical' structures, rather as musicians practise scales and chords – each and both with little harmonious effect. The call put to new millennium politicians in the Anglo settler societies is to connect the stimulation and logic of the sustainability ethic with their ethos for political survival, providing a pathway which weaves them back to a basis of socio-political empowerment, with balanced growth the emphatic underlining. An objective is to position politicians to see and accept government as the handmaiden of pluralist democracy directed through the ballot box to achieve overall material well-being *and* social secureness within a stable habitat. It is important, for all manner of reasons grounded and proven in both socio-economic science and environmental science, to lay the institutional foundations for sustainable development *with* conservation, enabling communities within Anglo settler societies, specifically, to promenade the wealth of their technology, their tolerant consciousness, and sensitivity toward their habitat. This has been the through-line.

The Ends

Although global issues fall outside the framework adopted for this book, and my expertise, I engage the right of temerity to shoot home an overview and some concluding assertions.

'If current predictions of population growth prove accurate and patterns of human activity on the planet remain unchanged, science and technology may not be able to prevent either irreversible degradation of the environment or continued poverty.'
Joint Statement, *National Academy of Science* and *The Royal Society,* 27 February 1992

Issues of market failure are often expressed in environmental terms, but these are only the *symptoms* – environmental pollution, resource depletion – rather than the *causes*. These arise from the growth-on-growth mantra, now aided by fast and volatile stock option profiteering and a pernicious free-raider resource exploitation which rejects environmental constraint. Of all the species established on earth *Homo sapiens* is the most exploitative of its habitat, the most mindful of its destructiveness, yet the least effective at correcting its mistakes. And of course the human species is uncertain about the longer-term future for a global habitat punctured with ozone holes, melting ice caps, fresh water scarcity and the enduring retention and build-up of toxins. It is an irony that for wealthy and informed settler societies, and also for the stable and well-educated Old World enclaves, there is no problem of human over-population – which remains a Third World complexity – yet there is an acute awareness of dangers to the global habitat, most specifically as a consequence of toxin accumulations and nuclear stockpiles, along with global atmospheric warming.

The number of millionaires in the world grew, by the year 2001, to 7.1 million.
Cap Gemini, Ernst Young, Merrill Lynch.

As at 2002 the per capita global array of incomes for nation states, varies from a dollar-a-day on average as the lowest, to $112-dollars-a-day the highest.

- In terms of morality, people can be educated to live lightly on their home-scape.
- In terms of behaviour, individuals can be taught to correct unsociable actions.
- In terms of business, profits can be made from ecologically benign manufacturing processes.

Any modestly sized open economy in supposed fiscal control of its own destiny can find itself the subject of a stealthy buy-out raid or sell-out scam initiated by cash-loaded corporations and interlopers intent on asset-stripping and liquidation. Small nations and weaker states within large nations, striving to run open fiscal systems, induce an adverse knock-on effect, opening up their resource base to speculative exploitation. For all that the IMF and the WTO have willed fiscal openness and free trade, they never condoned its consequence, the predation to which turbo-capitalism has given birth – the skimming, trimming, gleaning, extractive raider processes visited upon the smaller, the weaker and the vulnerable.

One consequence is that a million or so multi-millionaires have emerged from cyberspace over the last two decades, in prosperous and poor nations alike. This is not just a 'that's how the cookie crumbled' scenario; it is more akin to the horror of giving a toddler matches in a fireworks factory. And when those quicksilver multi-millionaires and billionaires divert attention from the pursuit of gains, and direct their fiscal tsunami at real property, this happens in a way which hurts settler societies in their middle and poor sectors first and worst, with property inflation, resource depletions, consumer discards, socio-economic dysfunction, and habitat degradation, reversing the very determinants of balanced growth – property security, fiscal stability, contract validity.

So much for the global problematic, which can be largely laid at the door of the G7, IMF and WTO – whose almost impossible challenge, and one they have never

really warmed to, is control over unfair fiscal leveraging and arbitrage specula-
tions. In Korten's view (1995: 277) the choice for societies:

> Is a choice between organising for the human interest and arguing for the corporate
> interest. . . . [and] that *if* we focus on creating societies that enhance the quality of our
> living rather than the quantity of our consumption, we can move simultaneously
> toward sustainability and a better life for nearly everyone.

Most people would accept this reasoning unequivocally, and accord all power to
Korten's logic, although there remains embedded in his polemic the little itali-
cized word 'if', for nobody can envisage *when* the likes of the G7 – IMF – WTO
will tax inter-nation arbitrage and speculation – empowerments currently beyond
their delivery and enforcement capacity. Because we appreciate how much of a
struggle it has been to reduce the rate of environmental damage and to avoid some
singular kinds of environmental meltdown (for example, the prohibition of CFCs)
what chance is there for controlling fiscal outages and avoiding a fiscal meltdown?
Probably 'none' or 'little' which qualifies this urgency as an imperative for underscoring conservation *with* development as politically correct practice, *not* on an
all-or-nothing basis, but by tipping the balance toward a 'tolerable harmony' for
solid social reasons. The formula involves increasing returns by concomitantly
reducing the social risks: fashioning good design out of environmental dysfunction, and achieving wellbeing out of fiscal imbalance.

The overall urban and regional situation remains largely uncomprehended,
loosely coordinated and chaotically managed. It is all so incremental and
confusing – 'does it really matter?' Should the current generation simply get
by, and not be concerned that fresh water abstraction throughout semi-arid
Australia and western North America will eventually turn saline or dry out
the landscape? Does it matter that food production is becoming genetically
engineered?

The settler society environmental problematic profiles fertilizer-saturated soils,
the hybridization and genetic modification of flora and fauna, the mining of irreplaceable ground-water resources, the biospheric accumulation of irreducible
toxins; *and* the sprawl of low-density dysfunctional suburbia crisscrossed by
fossil-fuelled motor vehicles making often pointless journeys as a consequence of
workplaces, home places, school places and shopping places being situated within
separately zoned precincts. Furthermore much of horticulture, farming, fishing,
forestry and mining is practised unsustainably. Finally, unemployment increases,
trapping those lucky to have a job in a narcissistic '40-hour five days a week' work-
warp while the unemployed morph into the unemployable.

These are all recognizable flaws, and indeed they are frequently acknowledged:
yet nothing much changes. The significant point is that nations, within their sovereign boundaries and within their established systems, have 'ownership' of these
problems and are positioned to fashion within-nation solutions according to their
political persuasion. For this reason this concluding chapter seeks to profile the
'big picture' identifiers and motivation scenario for attaining the within-nation
sustainability paradigm set down in the earlier pages.

'Many disparate types of
theorists have analysed
the nature of democratic
government, but virtually
all are agreed on one
point: a true democracy
requires a small society.'
        Kirkpatrick Sale, 1998

The best head-start schooling possible, equitable employment with an emphasis on real-work jobs, environmentally balanced economic growth, participatory democracy, and guaranteed security in retirement are five cornerstones to a well-blended society. These cornerstones require governments to opt, on the one hand, to influence the 'transactors', and the 'transformers' in principled ways, by consulting and heeding those involved in local empowerment and multiplier processes. An accessory to all this is an imperative: to clarify areas of central and local responsibility, enabling government administrators to enhance their understanding of the role and strength of local government while also enlarging on cooperation and consultation between central and local government *and* the business community. The objective is to put regulations out to the places at which power is applied; to have less central government involvement; and to delegate subsidiary functions to local government – withal moving regulatory instruments away from formula controls to an 'each case judged on its merit' basis. This emphasis, which reaches back through this book to its opening pages, upholds human material needs in a growth context which is also socially responsible and environmentally sound – the outcome being an improved overall quality of living. To that end there has to be *less* emphasis on macro-corporatization, and *more* emphasis on the pursuit of small business seedbedding. These, then, are the essential attitudinal and motivational planes of neomodern social understanding: the discourse, policy pursuit and design which a triple harmony credo calls into being.

'A[ny] regime which
provides human beings
no deep reasons to care
about one another
cannot long preserve its
legitimacy.'
        Richard Sennett, 1998

'Liberal democracy
remains the only
coherent political
aspiration that spans
different regions and
cultures around the
globe.'
        Francis Fukuyuma,
        End Of History,1992

Why so? Well, simply put, open-ended consumerism which is good for an economy in itself is seldom universally good for all of society, because it puts harm in the path of future populations and is degrading for the environment on which we all depend. This is apparent and obvious. Ordinary people and politicians alike are not daft, although they have on occasion allowed themselves to be seduced by the presumption that government, *their* government, operates on a 'contestable' basis and that 'corporatization' will reduce both transaction and transformer costs and be of overall benefit. Of course there is already some success; but the deep-seated social problems of unemployment, underemployment and unemployability continue. Likewise, in being selective about environmental problems – saving an endangered species here, ignoring an endangered city there – governments degrade the wider setting in which their voters live. Yet 'why not' live for the enjoyment which economic growth can produce for consumers 'right now'? And 'why' address such issues as the vast number of computer-literate unemployable, unassimilable toxins, nuclear wastes, and degraded environments when these hard-basket issues can be simply dumped onto the next generation?

The answer to questions of these kind is bound up with a rhetorical conundrum. 'Why' produce children? And, having produced them, 'why' educate them? We, of course, produce offspring and educate them simply because we are mortal, and because we are biologically programmed to establish a successor generation. Children are in human terms *the* future, and in logic we would avoid polluting our contribution to that future by 'providing' or if necessary 'purchasing' for it and them, an economically stable, socially secure and environmentally healthy habitat. Our children will re-inherit, reside, recreate, reproduce and eventually return to this same space and place. What is good for the economy in accordance with sustainability precepts has to be tempered and fashioned to be also good for those children and the environment 'indefinitely'. And to the extent that the urban and regional planning service has a role in bringing about a triple-bottom-line advocacy, and to effect sustainability in a planned manner, it behoves local and regional planning organizations to define their operational role within the overall constellation of public policy providers. In short, planning operatives and conservancy agents act importantly for future policy in a political way which is large and meaningful to the communities they serve.

For a sense of hope from turncoats:
David Suzuki with Holly Dressel,
Good News for a Change, 2001.

For a 'no-worries' optimism:
Bjorn Lomborg,
A *Skeptical Environmentalist*, 2001.

For a pessimistic blast from the past:
Paul Ehrlich,
Population Bomb, 1968.

The Means

The attainment of generic sustainability has its social origins in a political and public motivation to undertake a style of resource banking for society.

The banking analogy is arresting, although there are key differences between the 'store of money' in fiscal banks, and the socio-environmental 'store of resources' in the environmental banking system. The fiscal growth process thrives in an open-ended non-planning and above all flexible context which moves quickly to downsize-upsize-restructure-relocate: in short to mop up gains, and take fiscal root wherever opportunity knocks. Fiscal stratagems and tactics are characteristically reliant on growth-on-growth with opportunism the key factor. Operationally, there is little enthusiasm for the niceties of socio-environmental values. Compatibility and reconciliation between the largely exploitative dynamics of fiscal growth and the sustainable dynamics of socio-environmental targeting is, in sporting parlance, 'a big ask'; yet such a balanced approach is the only logical way ahead.

Robert Heilbroner (1991) observes that some critics see 'Capitalism as one gigantic negative externality, in which the achievement of a high level of profitable growth is obtained only at the cost of an even higher, yet unnoted, level of public damage'.

From a historical perspective, people today can reflect on the injustices visited by their forebears upon indigenous peoples and the damage done to the landscapes of the New World. Modern societies have passed, and continue to pass, various points of no return, much as was the case for the isolated Easter Islanders before the visitations of Euro-explorers and colonizers. The call, in a phrase, is to 'indefinitely' pursue sustainability as an output; to fashion a capacity to empower and deliver plan-led conservation *with* development in a style which triple-balances growth community and environment. The Easter Island – earth

Indeed, such is the perverse perception of economic progress that the clean-up of humanly induced calamities – oil spills, for example – generates growth and gain, and is seen by some to be fiscally good for GNP.

Box 6.1   Easter Island – Earth Island

(Population late sixteenth century: 7,000. Population late nineteenth century: 110)

Easter Island has an area of 64 square miles. It is situated in the south-eastern Pacific Ocean, on the equatorial side of the Tropic of Capricorn, 1,400 miles from the next habitable landfall. Earth is 12,756 kilometres in diameter and moves on an orbit separated from other solar system planets, but they are of course *uninhabitable*.

In both instances, at either end of a normal human scale of comprehension, the incumbents – were (Easter Island), or are (Earth Island) – unable to leave their place of habitat. The outcome for Easter Island (despoilation, degradation, de-population, social disintegration, genocide) is a path the global system shows some inclination to replicate, wiping out forests and minerals, exploiting plants and animals to extinction.

On Easter Island the feller of the last tree knew it would lead ultimately to disaster for subsequent generations, but went ahead and swung the axe. This is what is so worrying. Humankind's covetousness is boundless. Selfishness appears to be genetically inborn. Selfishness has the allusion of leading to survival. The selfish gene wins. But in a limited ecosystem, selfishness leads to increasing population imbalance, population crash, and ultimately population extinction.

If the lesson of Easter Island's tragic mistake is not enough, it is difficult to ascertain what would constitute a wake-up call. It would seem nothing has been installed to alter earth's crash course with disaster. That is, until relatively recently, with the introduction of the sustainability concept.

Source: From Auckland University 'Planning School' student essays: Richard Turner, Craig Magee, Angela Davey. Source book: Clive Ponting, *A Green History of the World*, 1991.

---

island syndrome underscores the local-place need for socially responsible, environmentally compatible, and economically balanced conservancy *with* development.

Within the academy

Those who aspire to educate and communicate with those others who in turn aspire to bring about progressive change should know their existing development and conservancy legal framework, comprehend the sustainability ethic, appreciate the theory basis for planned change, and cleave to the ideal of vertical and horizontal integration. In short, humbly, yet with no false modesty, fall in with the philosophy and reasoning which involves 'tipping the balance' toward the conservation with development paradigm shift.

For the richer regions of the larger OECD nations and the smaller nations in that club, for most of the middle-order economies tied into global trading, and for the resource-rich regions among the poorer nations, 'growth' has always outvoted 'sustainability'; that is until either or jointly the economic and ecological bubbles burst. It is in the smaller intermediate economies, the poorer nations, and in the poorer regions of the wealthy nations, that the sustainability logic wells up in response to two forces. *First*, the 'force of argument' for clearly there is never going to be, for these transfixed contexts, a rapid growth quick-fix. *Second*, there is the 'force of disaster' arising out of grotesque economic, ecological, nuclear and ethical conflict.

A breakdown of the family unit and an individualization of the ballot are two causal explanations for the current levels of urban dysfunction, and an impediment to small open government. For a growing minority – the already convinced and converted – sustainable harmony is a welcome prospect. The problems of increasing human bad behaviour (crime and drugs), disease (Aids and cancer), poverty (unemployment and unemployability), points to the need for correction and change. The middle majority, particularly the comfortable middle-and-above income cohort within the wealthy nations, are the ranks from which emerge those who 'know' those who 'teach' and of course those seeking to 'learn'.

Design in its integrative and creative sense has been established as something planners and developers 'do and deliver'. Community design cannot be left with people without design-specific urban and landscaping skills. I agree with Carter (1993) who holds the view that 'The ability to manipulate [particularly in my view *design*] form and place should be the core definition of planning'. The practical reality is that teaching programmes weak or soft on design will produce chroniclers, administrators and transactors – rather than transformers – those who set for themselves the task of *delivering* a sustainable contribution to both conservation practice and development projects.

A teaching-place approach is needed which parallels the triple-balanced profile for 'sustainability' set down in these pages; to reposition planners, architects, engineers, landscapists and earth scientists – the 'design and delivery' agents – from being a 'modern part of the problem' to becoming a larger part of a 'sustainable solution'. This is necessary in order to tip the balance toward sustainable outcomes, particularly in regard to environmental and habitat issues, concerns and factors, yet also with a view to being in harmony with material growth and social wellbeing.

Environmental education and confidence-building for sustainable planning practice is crucial. The aim is to get young people, from pre-school through to the academy, *concerned* about social and environmental effects, and to engage their minds with improving possibilities. Blandishments, inducements and rewards, backed up by selective penalties, must be used in the manner of 'carrots and sticks', along with an ethical canon, to achieve a triple balance, and to deliver sustainable outcomes. In short, the call is for an educational approach which fosters an understanding of conservancy and developmental connectedness, an awareness of the cyclical socio-economic forces at work, and to inculcate competence for the delivery of a triple-balanced harmony.

Adverse environmental changes, for too long smoke-screened as value-neutral, are now profiled as value-burdening. Progressive top-down sustainable policy improvements are emerging, positively enhanced by some landowners and developers, yet still mostly observed in the breach by local and central government jurisdictions. Development practitioners and managers should not expect too much, too soon, in the way of results. There is

Big business has attempted a hijacking of the rhetoric of sustainable developers. Even Monsanto, the scourge of most environmentalists, has had a clumsy go at weaving sustainable language constructs into some position statements.

considerable hard graft and political contestability involved in latching onto the tenets of triple-balanced sustainability. Much can be done through the interdisciplinary enclaves and layers of the education system, working with pre-schools, through grade schools and colleges, right on to the graduate academy.

Trends and Changes: A Concluding Commentary

The 'dilemma of central-local relations' (Stewart 1981) is constantly being both added to and resolved. There is emerging evidence of less central government intervention, with local government more in control of its actions – sometimes perceived as an abrogation of central responsibility, but more thoughtfully endorsed as subsidiarity.

With improved and easier communication there is scope for greater consultation and cooperation between central and local levels of government, particularly in terms of sharing information and in shared work experience and personnel exchanges. As inter-government distinctions are clarified, public administration can move away from interventionist 'regulatory' controls toward a greater use of 'inducement' including deemed-to-comply procedures.

Misunderstanding between central government and local government professionals remains a complication for both conservancy and development. This derives usually from central officials viewing their role as an interventionist one, organizationally and in terms of the advice they give out. By contrast, local government officials are inclined to view themselves as geared to achieving transformational outcomes and 'getting things done'. Neither role is that clear cut. A case can be identified for pluralistic central-local working relationships which require that central government transactional and local government transformational efforts defer to a consideration of conservation *with* development. There is a need for policy to move in the direction of *neo*modernity – a matter of getting communities to work toward economic-social-environmental wellbeing. What is called for is a coordination of transactional policies and transformation practices: the overall objective being generalized improvement in lifestyle, particularly the improvement of urban lifestyle variety through the coordination of conservation *with* development

Viewed from a domestic perspective the households which comprise a locally governed community are 'paid back' through the non-profit services they 'invest' into. Year after year, this is the way local administrations operate. Unfortunately, performance for the whole of a community, involving a noble pursuit of the 'highest best use' principle for land, can be virtually unattainable within conventional local government practice. This calls for 'social profitability' to be factored in, so local government can register the success arising from a cleaving to those 'highest best use' principles.

There is certainly now a great deal more agency-to-agency as well as agency-to-public consultation than existed in the pre-Fax and email era, although much communication can be judged as lip-service consultation via sent, but unread, messages, with political leaders and public mentors 'looking through' and 'talking past' each other. Much of the talk about consultation, responsibility, linkages, sense of purpose, and sharing can fritter into shadow-boxing – metaphors hanging in the wind.

More than was ever the case in the past, there are niches of promise for conservation *with* development, horticulture *and* viticulture, forestry *with* pastoralism, owner-managed tourism, particularly ecotourism, and well-designed compact urban living in neighbourhoods.

There are also changes in the targeting of goods and services production, *and* with the transparency and contactedness of management procedures, in the exercise of unselfconscious green preferences, *and with* the indexing of welfare provisioning to longer cycles of understanding about gross domestic production. Adjudication as a result of economic-social-environmental risk assessment (not merely *appraisal*) is becoming increasingly mandatory, and the day of the development manager super-glued to market forces which replicate 'suburban' and 'sporting' stereotypes is on the wane. These are heartening indicators that management is now better positioned to 'close' on decisions of improved quality. Of course there remains a difficulty with follow-through services and back-up, and the maintenance of quota and quality controls, but the indicators are excellent and good outcomes are guaranteed.

Beyond the already identified difficulties of local-regional-central relations, it is possible to identify a range of not to be overlooked heavings within contemporary, predominantly urban, settler society communities.

- *Processing dynamics.* On account of greater mobility, and more effective communications, the second half of the twentieth century can be denoted the age of goods and data processing. The Saturday ballpark shuffle of the mid-century became the daily crush pattern for getting to work, going to school, doing the supermarketing, seeking entertainment, even holidaying. And it is in this 'processing' of people, goods and messages that new jobs arose, but only for those skilled to do them, while productive jobs (cash-in-hand 'real work' and 'real jobs' for less skilled workers) declined.
- *Employment dynamics.* Where, for most of the two-hundred years following Adam Smith's polemic, capital sought labour, capital now seeks technology and workers are disposable. The best of the capitalist heyday was characterized by worker satisfaction, product perfection and a sense of employer – employee linkage throughout a working life. This certainty has been removed by technological surrogates for labour, and with 'virtual realities' in non-participatory entertainment: machines doing the work and providing the leisure time distractions. The skill certainties and job securities of the mechanical-technological era are giving way to self-doubt. One consequence is that when a job comes up, proximity of work to home is not a consideration, further eroding the attachment of people to their settlement base.
- *Consumer dynamics.* While the level of per capita consumption increases, the landfills overflow, both outcomes being a manifestation of consumption in Anglo settler societies. Consumerism ensures that individuals and

profit-making groups maximize their resource-grab simply because, if they do not, a competitor will get in before them. And with the exploitation of resources there exists individual, corporate and in some cases a national compulsion to consume now, or lose out to a competitor. This regressive situation is exacerbated by the instinct of individuals, corporations, and nations, to dump their waste products and commodity discards into the atmosphere, the water bodies, somebody else's backyard, *anywhere* where the impacts of disposal are nil or negligible to the dumper.

- *Poverty dynamics.* It is an irony that as the consumption of material goods increases, so the proportion of the population trapped in unemployment, imprisonment, and social poverty also increases. The poverty issue has many facets. Prominent is the ageing of population, resulting in an ever-increasing proportion of those in retirement nibbling at a pension cake provided by an ever-dwindling proportion of taxed wage earners. This has the knock-on effect of ensuring an eventual backlash from an over-taxed and undersized workforce. More controversial is the emergence of an unskilled underclass merely living out their informal, sometimes illicit, but always desiccated, lifestyles. Pregnant teenagers do not get to that circumstance because their morals are lax; they are merely accessing a desperate support option when little else in the way of worth and identity is available to them. Other young people, particularly males, discover that they do not have the skills necessary for them to get a job. For them first, there is welfare support; then possibly crime or maybe the idleness of a retreat. All of this leads young adults to join a disaffected and largely disengaged underclass contained by extra enforcement and security personnel.

- *Property dynamics.* The poor and the rich will always be distinctively profiled within society; but when urban property holding, always selectively unequal, becomes more so, urban society as a whole slides into ghetto arrangements which compartmentalize and exacerbate the plight of the poor. Governments can bring into effect some changes – such as starter homes mixed in with conventional single-purpose housing projects – but powerful contra-forces deny major adjustments. Property proponents lobby for an unfettered pursuit of material aggregation and a regressive focus to taxation – and they largely succeed. In this way taxpayer preference largely influences outcomes in settler society nations. Wealth, connoting power, has come more and more to mean control; in short a property dollar vote has come to influence not only economic policy, but also social and environmental policy, far outweighing the influence of individual voters. Ethnic minorities are caught up in this circumstance, but so also in a general way are the under-educated, the unskilled, the aged, the children and the immobile.

- *Segregation dynamics.* The level of indigenous 'first-nation' consciousness, integral to North American and Australasian societies, is an ever-improving part of being, knowing and identifying with being North American or Antipodean. The indigenous first people's grievances and the inequities have left them disadvantaged and disempowered. Further apologies will have to be given and restitutions made.

• *Conservation dynamics*. Politics is slowly changing its political hue. The 'green' factors are associated with a small yet ever-increasing proportion of the generally better incomed who have the resources and mobility to access the likes of recycling stations in suburbia and national parks outside the city. The harrowing lessons of neglect and plunder from the past remain etched on the humanized landscapes. Only a few people, because the majority mostly live lives of insularity or impoverishment, are appreciative of nature or are in harmony with their environmental setting. Conservation dynamics 'shout' in a small voice, heard more frequently, but still with limited effect.

Balanced urban-with-rural Growth, Wellbeing and Habitat:

1 Support projects which require low investment per workplace created;
2 Network the local wealth of talent;
3 Support inward investment for farming, silviculture, viticulture, horticulture, construction, tourism and community care;
4 Moderate [watchdog] the electricity, telephone, water supply and waste disposal provisioners;
5 Enhance training programmes for providing and certifying core skills;
6 Protect rights: uphold political and property rights, safeguard libertarian values: *and as a result of all the above –*
7 Generate 'thousands' of additional, ordinary, real-work jobs: *thereby*
8 Reducing welfare dependents by the same number of 'thousands'.

The challenge now is one of putting a stop to being so settler society *smart*, and to learn how to be much more *clever*; sustainably and ethically through neomodern reasoning and enabling actions (property protections, low inflation, fair judiciary, scant corruption) expressed through open democratic government. The call is for jurisdictions to be fair, to pursue balanced growth, to design and provide security within society, to strive for capacity empowerment and capacity fulfilment, and to maintain a wholesome habitat. Most settler society governments know and heed all these strictures in the breach as a truism, yet most politicians genuflect still to big money and growth.

The changes which have taken place in the Anglo New World, particularly since the early nineteenth century, have been quick and remarkable. Some issues of conscience remain over illegal land appropriation of the first people's hegemony, and the reincarnation of their belief about who they are and what they stand for. There is no threat here, for the once frontier landscapes of settler societies are now largely a quilted patchwork of towns and farms, schools and factories, playing fields and parks, themselves quite stable. Land occupation, urban settlement and profitable productions – these are all well imprinted, flourishing and certain. Of course the future is never predictable; yet in pretty well every given situation, the settlement pattern is firmly established. Low overall population densities, resource richness, and geographical independence leave the Anglo settler nations well placed to 'tip the balance' for an ethically grounded triple-balanced harmony.

Producing out of, taking from, and putting organic waste back into the land-water-air resource base, and living lightly on the 'interest' available from the resource 'capital', is being approached more conscientiously and teleologically than before. Some parts of settler society communities are turning to the earth and the oceans after two centuries of exploitative resource quest, and many people previously aligned to a reactive style of governing are now being driven to realize (Saul 1997: 78) that 'the power we refuse ourselves goes somewhere else'. As a consequence reflective settler society jurisdictions are more conscientious about people and their communities after two or more centuries of reliance on the libertarian workings of a free market.

Wealthy people alight sporadically upon the rural and wilderness landscapes, but for the majority the urban pods proliferate. And in all of this planners mostly watch perplexed from the sidelines. The outcomes are messy, inexorable, interminable and often also excruciating, for while the dollars pile up for some, quality of life eludes many others. Understanding comes mainly from commentator-journalists – such as Joel Garreau and Robert Kaplan, and earlier on James Kunstler. They neither represent the female majority nor the pilloried minority. They have been sent out by their publishing houses to look, listen and report, advisedly. They serve up much despair, along with some hope, but provide no proven or lasting solution. But now the wealthier parts of the globe, through their democracies, have sufficient information from these authors and from scientific sources to wake up to the stark realities of water, soil, mineral and atmospheric loss and change – and adjust.

For some, mainly the flight-from-chaos people and the economically top-layered, life still seems materially good. For the poor, and socio-environmentalists, it is mostly perceived as unsustainable, characterized by low-grade ambience, low-variety urbanity, and low-intelligence transmissions through the ether. There is a *dis*harmony to challenge, and given the vast wealth of the Anglo New World the capacity is there to refashion, reconstitute and reconstruct that quest.

Tipping the balance involves devolution to smaller units and agencies of government (subsidiarity); clarification by governments of the wider powers and controls available to each unit of administration (general competence); and of course an adherence to due legal process (justice). The modern progression throughout the twentieth century, from smartness to becoming too damn smart – in essence behaving unsustainably – will give way to more 'clever' processes; implicating an ever-learning, ever-improving, ever-enabling and ever-empowering continuum. It is long term, a this-with-the-next generational matter. It engages trade-offs and compromises from economic growth in the direction of social fairness and environmental harmony, a paradigm shift for a balanced improvement to the overall quality of settler society living.

Bibliographical Retrospective

This retrospective highlights and celebrates the writings on development, conservancy and planning which underscore my experience.

North American writing is everywhere present. The socio-environmental luminaries include, in birth order: John James Audubon (1785–1851), George Perkins Marsh (1801–82), Ralph Waldo Emerson (1803–82), Henry David Thoreau (1817–62), John Muir (1838–1914), Gifford Pinchot (1865–1946), Aldo Leopold (1887–1948), Lewis Mumford (1895–1990), Ansel Adams (1902–84), Rachel Carson (1907–64), and Ian McHarg (1921–2001). And another collation, this time of, as far as I know, living American authorities on 'sustainability' 'urbanism' and 'planning', includes: Andres Duany, Barbara Ehrenreich, Paul Ehrlich, Francis Fukuyama, Joel Garreau, Garrett Hardin, Paul Hawken, Robert Heilbroner, Jane Jacobs, Robert Kaplan, David Korten, Amory Lovins, Kirkpatrick Sale, John Ralston Saul, Joni Seager, London-based Richard Sennett and Lawrence Susskind. In practical effect recognition of American sources goes wider, to the film directors, producers of sitcoms, and the newscasters and journalists whom, with varying degrees of humour, horror, sick humour and insight, depict and pillory the suburban scene.

Although far from literary masterpieces, the fresh and significant boundary markers from which this offering takes its contemporary cue are the *Rio Declaration* (usually depicted as *Agenda 21*, United Nations Conference on Environment and Development, 1992), which in turn took succour from the Bruntland Report, *Our Common Future* (World Commission on Environment and Development, 1987). Lesser known, but of structural importance to the post-modernist drift is Andrea Huysson's *After the Great Divide: Modernism, Mass Culture, Postmodernism* (1986), and David Harvey's *Condition of Postmodernity* (1989). These works possibly had part of their genesis in the likes of Fritjof Capra's 'The Turning Point' (1975) which was a stimulus for a host of writings on environment and development.

Overarching all on my account is Lewis Mumford's *Technics and Civilisation* (1934) first read during the 1950s in the Nelson College Scriptorium as a sixth former. My larger perspective also derives from Albert Waterston's *Development Planning* (1968), Clarence Glacken's *Traces on the Rhodian Shore* (1977), Eric Hobsbawm's *Age of Capital* (1975), Bernard Porter's *The Lion's Share* (1975). More specific and recent writings include Gertrude Himmelfarb's revelations of Victorian values, *Poverty and Compassion: The Moral Imagination of the Late Victorians* (1991), William Cronon's depiction of Chicago's expansion in *Nature's Metropolis* (1991) and David Harvey's paper 'The Environment of Justice' (1995). Books on the process of land enclosure in the New World include Howard's *Colonisation and Underdevelopment* (1978), William Lines's *Taming the Great South Land* (1991); and a useful trio of feminist perspectives and analyses, working back in time from Giselle Byrnes's 'No Holidays are Kept in the Bush' (1993, New Zealand), Kay Schaeffer's *Women and the Bush* (1988, Australia), and Annette Kolodny's *The Lay of the Land* (1975, United States).

The theory connections (chapters 1 and 2) were driven at base by Ralph Barton Perry's *Realms of Value* (1954). Broad, general and informative, are the likes of John Rawls's *Theory of Justice* (1971), Foucault's *The Order of Things* (1992); and a significant though unconnected (as far as I know) trio: Barbara Ehrenreich's *Fear of Falling* (1989), John Kenneth Galbraith's *Culture of Contentment* (1992), and Jane Jacobs's *Systems of Survival* (1992). As the notion of 'planners for responsibility' took shape, writings emerged which connected planning with ethics. These included Peter Marcuse's 'Professional Ethics and Beyond' (1976), Elizabeth Howe's 'Normative Ethics in Planning' (1990), Thomas and Healey's *Dilemmas of Planning Practice* (1991), Jerome Kaufman's 'Reflections' (1993), Harper and Stein's 'Centrality of Normative Ethical Theory' (1992), and Gerecke and Reid's 'Planning Power and Ethics' (1991). The normative attachments to lineal planning theory centre on John Friedmann's *Planning in the Public Domain* (1987), George Chadwick's *Systems View of Planning* (1971), and Le Breton and Henning's pragmatic *Planning Theory* (1961). The radical less-lineal attachments include Breheny and Hooper's *Rationality in Planning* (1985), Tett and Wolfe's 'Discourse Analysis' (1991), Hillier's 'To Boldly go where no planners have ever...' (1993), and Checkland's 'Soft Systems' output (1987 and thereafter).

The 'Charter' chapter 3 (with its Matrix) reflects personal empathy with the post-Stockholm output of: Eckholm (1976), Goldsmith (1992), Goudie (2000), Illich (1979), Lovins (1977), Meadows (1972), Odum (1976), O'Riordan (1976), Ponting (1991), Schumacher (1974), Simmons (1974) and Strahler (1973).

The growth pattern management (regional) passage (chapter 4) addresses an avalanche of writings, not all of them consistent one with another. Two significant 'commissioned' policy writings are: Frank So's *Practice of State and Regional Planning* (1986), and John DeGrove's *Land Growth and Politics* (1984). On the practice side there are two 'derived from official policy' pieces of note: Avron Bendavid-Val's *Regional and Local Economic Analysis for Practitioners* (1991), and John Levy's *Economic Development Programs for Cities, Counties and Towns* (1990). The 'delivery' section which address Regional Growth, Tourism Development, and Unemployment Alleviation (among other topics), draws on five notable writings: Jay Stein's *Growth Management* (1993); John Urry's *Tourist Gaze* (1990), Edward Inskeep's *Tourism Planning* (1990), the ILO compilation *Employment Promotion at Regional and Local Levels* (1988), and the 1999 edition of *Natural Capitalism* (Paul Hawkin with Amory and Hunter Lovins).

The lengthy urban chapter (5) addresses both the urban problematic and the practice of urban reform. The relevant literature is a deluge. The selected listings are portrayed on two fronts. First are identified those writings which best inform the urban condition. To start with are five sentinel texts in the order in which I encountered them: Lewis Mumford's *The City in History* (1961), Jane Jacobs's *Death and Life of Great American Cities* (1961) which led me to visit Chicago and Boston, Kevin Lynch's *Image of the City* (1960), and Spiro Kostof's *City Shaped* and *City Assembled* (1991 and 1992). Packed in around these sentinels are hundreds of urban New World writings from which a top-cut selection would include, in alphabetical order: Alexander and others, *A Pattern Language* (1977), Barnett's *The Fractured Metropolis* (1995), Boyer's *Dreaming the Rational City* (1983), Davis's *Quartz City* (1990), Etzioni's *Spirit of Community* (1993), Friedmann's 'The Right to the City' (1992), Garreau's *Edge City* (1992), Hall's *Great Planning Disasters* (1982), Jackson's *Crabgrass Frontier* (1985), Kunstler's *Geography of Nowhere* (1993), Leopold's *Sand County Almanack* (1949), Rep's *Making of Urban America* (1965), Sudjic's *100 Mile City* (1992), and Soja's *Postmetropolis* (2000).

Secondly, and to the point of practice, are writings about policy improvements and design changes for the urban condition. None has 'the answer' of course. The following, again in alphabetical order, are a stimulus to students of policy and design. There is the innovative Australian Government *AMCORD Urban* output (1992), Arendt's *Rural by Design* (1994), the Bentley and others' design-questing *Responsive Environments* (1985), Blower's *Limits of Power* (1980), Calthorpe's 'Pedestrian Pocket' (1992), Charles Prince of Wales's conservative-conservationist *Vision of Britain* (1989), Cullen's inspirational and ever-fresh *Concise Townscape* (1961), DeGrove's urgent *Balanced Growth* (1995), the British DOE's *Vital and Viable Town Centres* (1994), Engwicht's energetic *Towards an Eco-City* (1992), Fader's *Density by Design* (2000), Johnson's evocative and pragmatic *Green City* (1979), Kendig and other's realism-made-plain as *Performance Zoning* (1980), Krier's 'Tradition-Modernity-Modernism' (1987) together with his *Urban Space* (1979), Levy's pragmatic lucid *Economic Development Programs for Cities, Counties and Towns* (1990), Lynch's classic *Good City Form* (1981), McCamant and Durrett, *Co-housing* (1994), McHarg's durable *Design with Nature* (1971), Meier's stimulating *Ecological Planning and Design* (1993), Newman and Kenworthy's *Winning Back the Cities* (1992), Owen's analytical *Energy Planning and Urban Form* (1986), Rydin's 'Environmental Dimensions of Residential Development' (1992), Stretton's *Ideas for Australian Cities* (1973), Tibbalds *Making People-Friendly Towns* (1992), and Walter and others, *Sustainable Cities* (1992).

The novel as metaphor for New World utopia pervades. Joseph Conrad's (born 1857: New World) *Nostromo*; Samuel Butler's (1872: New Zealand) *Erehwon*; Robertson Davies's (born 1913: Canadian) *Cornish Trilogy*; Patrick White's (born 1912) Australian output; and from the United States John Steinbeck's *Grapes of Wrath* (1902–68), and Lewis Sinclaire's *Main Street* (1922).

Notes

Chapter 1   Sustainable and Ethical

1   See also Stern and Massengale's seminal study 'The Anglo-American Suburb' (1981).

2   Relative to 'certainties' 6 and 10 Megan Howell (School of Planning, Auckland University) observed direct to me (2002) that 'The fracturing of large states may not continue beyond the immediate future, particularly if globalization continues to erode the relevance of the state' and that 'Some [large] corporations are already more powerful than some [small] governments, and as global courts emerge corporations will find more space to exercise that power'.

3   Unfortunately an urban majority New World population could not, it would seem, *live* lightly and be also *governed* lightly!

4   Notably in suburbs where 40 per cent (US) to 70 per cent (NZ) of the population live in fully detached houses.

5   For even ardent 'greenies' jet about wantonly.

6   It being necessary with both definitions to go along with the North American way of understanding 'indefinitely'.

7   The market is of course an acknowledged mechanism of utility provided the democratic parameters within which it operates are clearly 'open'.

8   With reference to development law for any specified jurisdiction, the reader is advised to consult the national updating service (now usually on-line) for planning and local government management.

9   Also consult Krueckeberg's (1995) 'The Difficult Character of Property'.

10 Connections can be traced to John Stuart Mill, Jeremy Bentham and the early creators of the Model Industrial Town: Robert Owen, and Titus Salt (Britain), and Charles Fourier (France).

11 Used, I imagine, in support of the notion of 'general competence' for the likes of borrowing to finance land banking and similar initiatives.

12 This brought Friedmann (1987: 133) to observe that Lindblom presumes that 'legally constituted persons are expected to pursue their self-interest aggressively'. Friedmann's rather dismissive assertion (from p. 133 of *Planning in the Public Domain*) is that the claims for Lindblom's model embodies four major assumptions: (1) Society comprises 'legally constituted persons [who] are expected to pursue their self-interest aggressively'; (2) 'The policy context is always normal times'; (3) 'Access to power, including information, is evenly distributed'; (4) 'Society is not deeply divided over issues of class, ethnicity, or any other matter.'

13 The North American article referred to was 'The Ethics of Contemporary American Planners' prepared by Elizabeth Howe and Jeremy Kaufman (*APA Journal*, July 1979).

This data set was further elaborated by Howe and Kaufman as 'The *Values* of Contemporary American Planners' (emphasis added) in 1981.

14 Exemplified in the subtitle to Ann Forsyth's *Constructing Suburbs* (1999): namely, 'Competing Voices in a Debate Over Urban Growth'.

15 Charles Hoch examines (1988) the complex way in which North American planners are exposed to the risk of political conflict in their work, and addresses the need for more highly developed negotiating and organizing skills. His research, including some interesting case studies, is presented as 'Conflict at Large: A National Survey of Planners and Political Conflict', *Journal of Planning Education and Research*, 8(1), 1988.

16 The most apparent 'admissions bias' hinges around the assumption that 'straight' undergraduate planning courses produce operatives more/less useful than the product of hybrid courses offered to people with a cognate first degree. From my basis of experience there are operational presumptions in favour of both.

17 Martin Krieger (1988) reviews this problematic within a piece on 'Courage and Character in Planning' as 'depend[ing] on our commitments rather than on investment or materials; that failure and error are occasions for triumph rather than signs of exhaustion, and that devotion is more important than maximising. We also find that believing is more important than is skepticism, that power is authoritative rather than sovereign, and that we learn from poignant example rather than from abstract theory.'

Chapter 2   Knowledge Power Outcomes

1 Work on this book started during the antipodean summer of 1995–6. It emerged from papers on 'planning', 'conservation' and 'development' evolved at three universities (Newcastle-on-Tyne, Cambridge, Auckland) over three decades. This was teaching interlaced with practice and observation in the Anglo settler society and developing nation contexts, in both of which honourable planning intentions led frequently to disappointing outcomes! My contention was, and remains, that there is a bedrock need for every planning operator, despite the overwhelming demands of practice, to acquire a principled grounding in the theory of their craft, and for each individual practitioner to understand what they undertake public-policy intervention for. In short, to align with John Stuart Mill's dictum (1840) that 'sound theory is the only foundation for sound practice'.

Chapter 3   Charter for Conservation with Development

1 Over 30 years ago, in 1969, the references to 'development' in Albert Waterston's benchmark study *Development Planning* covered 21 pages.

2 The first edition of *The Wealth of Nations* by Adam Smith was printed in 1776. My own copy is a 1920 fifth reprint of a 1910 edition from which I gleaned this reference to The Invisible Hand: '[An entrepreneur] intends only his own gain, and he is in this led by an invisible hand to promote an end which was no part of his intention.' A contemporary selection by Kathryn Sutherland is available as *An Inquiry into the Nature and Causes of the Wealth of Nations*, 1998.

3 My preference is Bernard Porter's *The Lion's Share* (1996); and for an equivalent version written within the era of colonial expansion see Egerton's (1897) *Short History of British Colonial Policy*.

4 This path can be traced with profit from C. J. Glacken's *Traces on the Rhodian Shore*, 1977.

5 George Perkins Marsh was formally educated in the classics and Christian belief. The highlights of his career included election to the US Congress (1840) and ambassadorships to Turkey (1849) and Italy (1860). *Man and Nature* was published in 1864.

6 Ehrlich, Ehrlich and Holdren's *Ecoscience* (1970); Strahler and Strahler's *Environmental Geoscience* (1973); Odum's *Fundamentals of Ecology* (1959); Simmon's *Ecology of Natural Resources* (1974); Dasmann's *Environmental Conservation* (1972). More up to date is the work edited by Timothy O'Riordan (1995) *Environmental Science for Environmental Management*, and Andrew Goudie's *Human Impact on the Natural Environment* (5th edition 1999) with its accompanying *Human Impact Reader*.

7 Darwin was a significant influence, although of course Darwin's theory on evolution and what is described here as 'evolutionary', are quite different matters.

8 See Himmelfarb (1991), *Poverty and Compassion*, a magisterial reassessment of the supposed enlightenment of Victorian times; Himmelfarb's offering is a transatlantic interpretation of onward relevance to Australasia. Of direct historical connection, critically questioning nineteenth-century capitalist bourgeois culture, is Hobsbawm's (1975) *The Age of Capital 1848–1875*.

9 United Nations, *Human Development Report*, 1997.

10 In the opinion of Lang and Hines (1993) this predicates the need for the diametrical opposite of Free Trade: a 'new protectionism' for greater economic equity, for a healthy environment, for the sustainable use of replaceable resources, and for the careful use of non-replaceable resources.

11 If an individual's social experience has come from an upper income ghetto, that individual will be inclined to vote against social purpose funding; if another individual's business experience is predicated to profiteering they will be inclined to vote against resource conservation.

12 The 'county' in which I live (Rodney District) was judged 'dysfunctional' and disbanded in March 2000 by the Minister for Local Government, a quite rare ministerial intervention.

13 In global contexts this equates with the synergistic effect of CFCs on fixed quantity atmospheric gases within the ozone layer.

14 The connotation, thus far, implicates physical resource entropy. Interestingly, David Thomson's *Selfish Generations* (1991) offers a lucid assessment of future welfare provisioning. He engages the 'commons' hypothesis directly in a chapter 'The Problem of the Common' which parodies the pensioned aged as 'devouring its own young'; and by implication a synergistic hypothesis for the ability of welfare states to attempt the invention of an impossibility, perpetual care-and-support from womb to tomb.

15 'Global directives and 'state sovereignty' are pitched one against the other There are enormous practical difficulties to overcome in bringing all nations under the umbrella of a globally enforced instrument, particularly when more than half of them – comprising the recently independent Third World – are fiercely defensive of their sovereign rights.

16 Expressed in the past tense. Regional rules imposed for Rotorua since the mid-1990s have effectively addressed the Exploitation and Discard issues. One beneficial consequence, mid-2000, is that Pohutu Geyser in the Thermal Wonderland, occasionally active in the past, erupted daily throughout the first year of the new millennium.

17 The Wackernagel and Rees (1996) ecological footprinting demand was assessed for Vancouver City to be an area 180 times greater than the area of the city itself.

18 'Empowerment simply means awareness of self as a guide to action', a definition fur-
    nished by Kent Gerecke and Barton Reid (1991) in their 'Planning Power and Ethics'
    as coming out of the environmental, libertarian theology and feminist movements.
19 Critics of the oil shortage prediction mostly neglected to note that in terms of the
    known and proven oil reserves in the 1960s the Meadows prognosis was deserved.
    Much of that quantum of then known reserves has since been accessed.
20 The *Limits to Growth* scenario was less attentive to the effects of toxins, CFC disposal,
    carbon dioxide excesses, and now (2002) the vast Asian smog cloud.
21 Not to be forgotten were the vast landscape changes in the New World, the Levant
    and, in telling microcosm, on that most isolated Oceanic outpost Easter Island – refer
    to chapter 6.
22 A ten-point 'birth limitation' policy set, starting out with moral strictures approved in
    some parts of the Anglo settler society hegemony, then trending regressively, includes:
    (1) social approval of later marriages, (2) societal endorsement of singleness, (3) gender
    equality in the workplace, (4) societal condemnation of births outside marriage,
    (5) access to cheap and effective contraception, (6) access to free abortion services,
    (7) reduction of larger-family tax concessions, (8) increasing social service charges to
    larger families, (9) reduced housing provisioning for large families; (10) compulsory
    fertility control.
23 There is more than a righteous feel-good factor behind the involvement of oil compa-
    nies in solar gain and storage technology, and car manufacturers' development of
    hybrid and hydrogen powered vehicles. They are involved for the longer haul, when
    over the passage of time these will become the 'in' technologies, simply because they
    will become profit-making.
24 The bleeding of CFCs from old refrigerators in the OECD with historical success is
    now a serious issue to address on a potentially larger scale in the world's four most
    populous nations – China, India, Pakistan and Indonesia.
25 Expressed colloquially as: 'those who do not heed the lessons of history are condemned
    to repeat them!'
26 Of course, the 70 per cent of the global population which is of the Third World are not
    the gross per capital consumers of resources and discarders of waste. The future envi-
    ronmental prospects are relatively better over the longer haul for the Third World
    context than is the situation with the wealthy nations.
27 There will of course be an eventual US policy reversal or policy alignment to the
    Kyoto protocol; but by that date – 2005 for renegotiation, 2008 more likely if Bush Jr.
    serves two Presidential terms – the degree of climate change consequent to greenhouse
    effects will become a legacy of permanent damage beyond the influence of mere policy
    adjustment.
28 A parody on the old saw about 'having one's cake and also getting to eat it'.

Chapter 4   Growth Pattern Management

 1 These 'ecological-economic' components (see Robert Costanza's *Ecological Economics*
    1991; also Edwards-Jones et al. 2000) are identifiable within the 'regional' sector of the
    Matrix (ch. 3).
 2 'Regional income is determined by four types of spending–consumption spending,
    investment spending, government spending, [and input expenditure on] exports – that
    actually result in local income', which clearly includes informal sector gains (includ-

ing, for example the likes of cannabis cropping) provided the regionally earned profit
settles within the region. Quote is from Bendavid-Val (1991: 82).

3   Akin to the vast non-desert temperate regions of North America, New Zealand and
South Eastern Australia. 'Agricultural' in its broadest interpretation includes horticultural, pastoral, silvicultural, orcharding and viticultural activities.

4   Computer storage along with updating and retrieval systems, in an open and readily
accessible data library, is the heart and circulation system, and part of the muscula-
ture, of a growth management organization. These anatomical metaphors might be
extended: improvement to the overall regional 'body' involves close attention to the
'skeletal structure' (urban-rural resource base), the 'nervous' system (economic and
communication linkages)', and cerebellum (politics and administration).

5   Also useful is the preparation of Bendavid-Val's (1991) aggregate social accounts
devised to furnish technical advice on rudimentary linkages between an input–output
analysis 'set' and a conventional balance of payments 'account', thereby highlighting
beneficial adjustments and picking up on indicative trends.

6   See John Friedmann's (1966) recommendations for the linkage enhancement of 'frontier' and 'downward transition' regions (predicated on an extra-regional basis). For
New Zealand's best-known 'downward transition' region, the West Coast of the South
Island, during the period 1986–91 the population *decreased* 2.7 per cent; whereas for
the South Island as a whole the 1986–91 population *grew* by 1.3 per cent; and for this
reason the connection of the West Coast to the rest of the South Island was, in terms
of Friedmann's reasoning, of vital importance.

7   The 'space-draining' indication reasons that settlements can draw resources from the
countryside without reciprocally contributing to rural development.

8   Eric Pawson and Garry Scott illustrated the decline of public services in the context of
a dramatic West Coast (South Island, New Zealand) 'case study' ('Resisting Post Office
Closures' in Britton, Le Heron and Pawson (editors 1992) *Changing Places in New
Zealand*). Their data shows a decline from (1983) 45 outlets, to (1990) 14 outlets. Pawson
and Scott quote a newspaper reporting that 'most of the small communities found that
the post office is the only bank, and feel that reductions in services and closures will
herald the total decline of the communities as a viable proposition'.

9   The long-haul net deficit accounting process should always include post-operational
clean-up and landscaping.

10 An example is the internalization of part of an extra-regional indigenous forest log
export trade with diversion to within-region furniture crafting industries, maybe
avoiding a whole-log export tariff.

11 'Violates' leaves open the possibility that in some offshore situations the receiving
nation can be compensated adequately for the environmental risk and ambient degradation they allow.

12 Unless these are sheeted home to the project while it is ongoing.

13 See also the Fisher, Ury, Patton bargaining emphasis (1991) in their *Getting to Yes*; and
John Forester's 'Planning in the Face of Conflict' (1987).

14 An important component item not specifically itemized within the main text seven-
point listing is 'transportation' which is profiled in the Box 3.6 Matrix, fitting into the
regional growth management considerations which follow, receiving some further
appraisal in the next chapter, 'Urban Growth Management'.

15 During the 1970s the Auckland Regional Council acquired vast tracts – north, south,
east and west of the city – as Regional Parks. Although common practice elsewhere,
the geographical spread, and the huge acreage relative to the city population, was very
generous for its time.

16 On National Parks as a 'social creation' Benton and Short (1999) observe – in a manner which is relevant to all Anglo settler societies – that 'Each unit in the (national) park system is an expression of our political culture at a particular time in our history'.

17 There are over 1,000 private land protection organizations in the US.

18 Donor aid delivery is now often conditional on clean-dealing.

19 I enjoyed an association with my former colleague, Derek Hall, during the course of his doctoral work on the incorporation of an 'interests' basis to planning.

20 The 'regulation of effects' principle underpins the New Zealand 'planning' statute, the *Resource Management Act* (1991) which contrived, on its introduction, to avoid use of the words 'planning' and 'zoning'. What this massive statute (the Nation's largest) set out to do – avoid, remedy or mitigate adverse environmental effects – is ineffectual in many urban, all peri-urban, and most farmland contexts. Overall I rate the 'control of effects' generic underpinning as something of a 'legalistic rain dance' – much prolix and commotion failing to produce the intended outcome, avoidance of adverse environmental effects! A few of the detail workings are interesting (for example trapping silt run-off during subdivision and the control of industrial discharges), others are a sad joke (there has been no overall improvement in lowland water purity); and there has been an increase in the rate at which peri-urban landscapes are despoiled with haphazard subdivision and construction. Some pillory the Act, others fault the planning system, while some others have grown to appreciate it as a 'cash cow'. This earnest yet 'stagy' attempt at stewardship, here to stay on account of its pervasiveness, was and is too elaborate for the New Zealand context during a reformative land use policy period; and although devised by a left-centre government it snuffled the voice of the impoverished and marginalized; yet, perversely, has enabled those with fat pocket books mostly to get their way on legal appeal – albeit with complaints about costs and delays. My advice to outsiders contemplating the formulaic 'effects' medium as a basis to plan-making and development control? – some of the provisions are interesting, but be advised, don't go there!

21 For an indictment of sprawl in the United States consult *Suburban Nation* (2000) by Andres Duany, Elizabeth Plater-Zyberk and Jeff Speck.

22 Also, of course, the rural estate is the open area playground for a variety of low-density recreational pursuits: some benign (walking, cycling, horse-riding, golfing), others chaotic (dirt-tracking, small aircraft flying and parachuting).

23 For England (1992) PPG 12 *Development Plans and Regional Planning Guidance* and for Wales (1992) the PPG 7 *Countryside and the Rural Economy*.

24 Any impression that such an emphatic compliance policy would exclude the five, ten, and 20-acre quasi-urban 'broad-acre' lifestylers overlooks the fact that vast subdivisions of land have been previously approved and titled for this form of 'neither town nor country' sprawl.

25 For cogent reasons, not least 'self-interest', the regional growth management Commission in Oregon was held to its task by the '1,000 Friends Of Oregon' organization.

26 Described as the 'prelude to conflict' in Goldberg's *Coastal Zone Space* (1994).

27 Water temperature increases associated with global warming bulks up the global seawater volume. Accretions of meltwater from polar cap meltdown also adds slowly to the oceanic water volume. Both contribute to sea-level rise.

28 Early colonial governments, anxious to boost trade, granted wide powers of authority, mostly still extant, to port and railway enterprises, now of much reduced relevance to development.

29   The likes of the *New Zealand Coastal Policy Statement* and the Australian 'Coastal Zone Management' passage in the (1992) *National Strategy for Ecologically Sustainable Development.*

30   Guidelines for the Australian context have been fashioned within the 'Forest Resource Use' section of the 1992 *National Strategy for Ecologically Sustainable Development.*

31   In the distant past serious damage to the open landscape arose from the clearing of natural flora. In the more recent past damage arose from acid rain, sulphur dioxide in solution – now happily well on the way to mitigation in most OECD economies.

32   PDR (Purchasable Development Rights) can provide once only capital in the style of compensation for *either* not using a property for cropping or pastoralism of specified kinds *or* for managing a property in accordance with Landcare principles.

33   The purchase of development rights may be difficult to attain in situations where the rate of land loss to degradation (soil exhaustion, toxicity, salination) exceeds the rate of counter-preservation.

34   There will always be a case for the siting of urban-user recreational facilities, the most misfitting urban import to rural landscapes being quasi-rural residential construction.

35   *Courier* dossiers on 'Tourism': various dates.

36   Language, song and rhythm, food and drink, sports, religion, along with clothing and lifestyle traits.

37   ACE tourism combining Adventure with Cultural and Ecological experiences can, in its intense 'adventure' context (whale-watching, heliskiing) impact adversely on the enjoyment of the outdoors by others.

38   The corporate owners of a plant causing an emission are usually held responsible, although many a point-source corporate polluter will attempt to assign blame to an 'ignorant' worker or an 'errant' consumer.

Chapter 5   Urban Growth Management

1   From *The Richness of Cities: Urban Policy in a New Landscape* by Ken Worpole and Liz Greenhalgh, 1999. Also in my notes is this admirable phrasing '[Cities] are dazzling reflections of culture and in turn shape that culture, simultaneously evoking deep contempt and glowing admiration' which I have not, regretfully, been able to source.

2   Quoted from Lewis Mumford in Kenneth Jackson's *Crabgrass Frontier*, 1985.

3   Edge City has been investigated by Joel Garreau in a lively text *Edge City: Life on the New Frontier* 1992. For an earlier account of ex-urbanization see Arthur Nelson and Kenneth Dueken's 'The Ex-urbanisation of America' 1990.

4   Large indoor places and outdoor spaces policed by security people are now also under the surveillance of video cameras, the new form of controlling authority inducing a conformist behaviour pattern.

5   This explanation is probably an oversimplification, not least because efficient water-borne sewage disposal systems were being installed at a time when automobiles were still operating inefficiently.

6   What strikes the New World visitor to prototypical Letchworth (North of London) is that part of the town given over to a pre-World War I 'bungalow' competition, laid out on 'plots' which combine all the house-building variations of materials, layout, coloration and texture familiar to the urban populations of the Anglo-settler New World.

7 Not to be overlooked was a transfer of the bungalow to California from the place of origin for both the word itself and the design concept, namely the northern hill stations of India.

8 Along with a number of positives, particularly keeping incompatible uses separated.

9 Reasoning along these lines is included within the Regional Growth Management sub-passage in the previous chapter.

10 In Australia 'Over 77 percent of all homes are separate dwellings' (Anthony King in Silverstone 1997); and in New Zealand close to 80 per cent of all homes are single-storey detached bungalows.

11 Individuality and Inventiveness, my phrasing, is tongue-in-cheek mythology. The 1989 study of values (Gold and Webster 1990: xvii) summarizes thus: 'New Zealanders have a wait-and-see attitude to change and new ideas . . . most adopt an "it depends" attitude . . . [and there is only] moderate attraction to changes and the demands of fundamental reform.'

12 Within the same article Bamford denotes those who would promote urban consolidation as 'densifiers'!

13 It is also an irony that although to Bamford suburbs may have 'redressed some of the disadvantages of class' for incoming settlers, they present an almost impermeable barrier for Australia's indigenous first peoples.

14 At under a dollar per litre for gasoline it is possible to reason that the gasoline cost of automobile use is a relatively minor matter. At around $2 per litre car usage by, for instance, students would lessen, and at around $3 per litre serious car pooling would start to occur, and at around $5 per litre the suburbs would show marked signs of constrained mobility. Of course, with gasoline priced at that level there would be fewer jobs and a greater number of discontentedly unemployed – all grist to the mill for hydrogen-powered vehicle development.

15 Consult Blakely and Snyder, *Fortress America*, 1997. A gated neo-Georgian retirement home was chosen by former British PM, Margaret Thatcher. This led opposition MP Simon Hughes to define her choice as 'symbolic of the two nations constructed by [Margaret Thatcher's Conservatives]'.

16 'Buildings are where Americans spend about 90 percent of their time. They use . . . two-thirds of [US] energy.' Hawken, Lovins, Lovins, *Natural Capitalism*, 1999.

17 *Placemaking: The Art of Building Communities* (Schneekloth and Shibley 1995) is dedicated to the process of neighbourhood-building. In their Introduction they observe that 'the allocation of [placemaking] work [by architects, planners, builders, engineers and landscapists] is fundamentally disabling to others . . . which ultimately disempowers others'!

18 Consult *The Transportation Land-Use Connection* compiled by Terry Moore and Paul Thorsnes (1994).

19 The carefully designed Swedish (Gothenburg) layout for Skintebo is alliterated into *Skiljebo*, the home of divorce! Re-expressed from Bjorn Klarquist's 'The Neighbourhood Unit: A Social Mould?' (1991).

20 Australian Planning Institute, 2001. Bruce Wright, *Expectations of a Better World*.

21 Supplementary detail-design recommendations are listed in box 5.3, 'Suburban design-detail code'.

22 Thus even where useful recommendations for poorer nations might be anticipated (as with chapter 7 of *Agenda 21*, 'Promoting Sustainable Human Settlement Development') the central issue of 'land for housing' is not addressed at all.

23 The Appendix also contains James Lunday's listing of the Key Urban Principles emanating from *Agenda 21*.

24 A large proportion of the New World difficulties over suburbia, edge city, and ex-urbia arises from omnidirectional opportunities for peripheral expansion. However these open market choice situations are mandated *against* in a few situations, notably the north-west and the south-east United States: see the authoritative *New Frontier for Land Policy*, John DeGrove and Deborah Miness, 1992.

25 On the outskirts of Australian and Californian cities there are lengthy dirt tracks leading to residences lying within the heart of bushland, despite the known recurring danger and threat of brushfires.

26 Kendig et al. also even-handedly depict an 'estate-district zoning', a rural land commodification charter for enabling rural landowners to commodify their ownership into mansion-sized residential spreads, which I decided, selectively, to not make reference to in the main text!

27 In contexts where local government authorities acknowledge selectively specified ex-urban areas for future suburbia on some 20-year look ahead 'capacity need' basis, it is also possible for them to impose 'sprawl levies' as a user pays surcharge, which can be applied later to the purchase of amenity green spaces and the installation of utilities. Of course quasi-urban lifestylers under interim ex-urban zoning should be charged on a full service-cost basis for their low-density road installation and upkeep, and for contributions to the cost of water supply installation, long-run dry rubbish collection, and for low-density line-of-wire utility provisioning.

28 Writing from a country context, New Zealand, where neither 'growth management' or 'conservation subdivision' is much considered, might register my judgement presumptuous. Low densities and vast space offers some explanation for a tardiness of best-practice take-up in New Zealand, yet Australia and Canada have vastly more space – indeed the need for 'growth management' and-or 'conservation subdivision' is greater for New Zealand, considered as a smaller whole, than is the situation in the other three Anglo settler societies. My homespun explanation is that for New Zealand the lack of precedence for understanding is the consequence of a shorter settler history (exemplified by the still prominent conflict between indigenous and exotic flora and fauna) and this underscores a disregard for the damage being visited daily upon the humanized environment by the booster troika of 'landowners, developers and politicians'. Another 100 years may induce sensitivity; but, by then, will the humanized rural landscape be in a cherishable condition?

29 The Duncan and Duncan piece informatively contrasts wealthy Bedford Village with adjoining low-income Mount Kisco, noting that this zoning pattern 'effectively shifts the burden of providing housing for the County onto less affluent and politically less well-organised communities'.

30 The precedent was made legally respectable in the 1960s. Morton, Thom and Locker's *Seacoast in the Seventies* (1973) setting the scene for the 1980s and 1990s observes that: 'Once subdivision into ten acre lots has taken place it has been difficult for county councils to resist pressure to allow the land to be used for residential purposes and further subdivided lots can usually be shown to be uneconomic as farming units. This loop-hole has allowed land to be taken out of farming use prematurely, has contributed to the unnecessary high valuation of other coastal farmland and has prejudiced the success of local Council's attempts to plan their districts rationally.'

31 Within New Zealand there exists a papakainga group housing system for rural Maori comprising lower costing Euro-styled bungalow clusters; and in Australia the more 'rustic' yet socially more sensitive (sight-lined) ex-urban clusterings of Aboriginal ex-urban settlement. I harbour a sense of, but no direct knowledge of, this need in North American contexts. In the South African 'townships' and in the more populous low-

income nations the phenomenon is manifest in 'edge-city' shanties often physically desolate, yet invariably socially coherent.

32 The radiating-away designs for Tema Manhean, in Ghana and Islamabad in Pakistan have the disadvantage, which exacerbates over time, of increasing congestion at the tight, sharp centre of the urban arc – the main advantage being an exponentially increasing availability of land as the outer arc radiates further away from the centre.

33 In the United States 'small towns' are centres of up to 10,000 population, being settlements of lesser population (under 6,000) in the other Anglo settler nations.

34 One perception of the 'new urbanism' movement is that it is, at base, a harking back to the community ideals recalled from small-town living.

35 The small towns known to myself harbour all manner of practical horticultural, building, manufacturing, professional and commercial skills within the ranks of the 'retired' and the 'unemployed'.

36 Although small in terms of population numbers, the Kerikeri town and district (population *circa* 6,000) is hardly the archetype New Zealand 'small town'. Family sources have counted 'around 150' groupings of interest for land and water active and passive recreation, for indoor leisure and pastime pursuits, sporting clubs, and community interest groups replicating in terms of accessibility the social, cultural and sporting venues to be found in an average city.

37 The 'country' connotation excludes the special cases of mining, logging and hydro-construction towns built for utility, for which there is often no viable residual function to turn to in their afterlife.

38 Small towns, dormitory to larger towns and cities, buck the 'low fertility cohort' trend.

39 Whence 'leaving one suburban home, the holiday-maker went 100 miles to another at the beach'. Morton, Thom, Locker 1973.

40 Along the popular Californian Coast, for example, public ownership from the seaward side extends usually to the high-water limit, which is the general situation throughout mainland USA. In urban New Zealand, by contrast (with minor exceptions) a space 20 m inland from spring tide high-water mark is universally accessible to the public.

41 Referred to historically as the Queen's Chain – about 20 m, which is also the length of a traditional cricket pitch, reflecting British origins.

42 'Despite the buzz surrounding the concepts of ecovillages and eco-neighbourhoods surprisingly few are as yet being realised, and this reflects the inertia of public and private agencies.' Hugh Barton and others *Sustainable Communities* (2000: 84 quoted here) found a list of 55 examples, worldwide, of eco-neighbourhoods: many conjectural.

43 My first sighting of *Suburban Nation* was in mid-2002. Box 5.1 (Urban social arrangement and style) and box 5.2 (Basic residential componentry) are of a 'do this' character and remain unaltered; but the diligent reader is recommended to refer also to the Appendix 'A' checklist given in *Suburban Nation*.

44 Realistically allow for up to double the conventional capital outlay, incurred for each unit of accommodation provided in eco-village contexts.

45 The 'circle equivalent' is notional. The desired train-station or trunk road connection would usually be positioned tangential to the layout.

46 Implicated in this rough reasoning is some *ab initio* consideration as to whether there is to be enough three-bedroom family household units to support a primary school. This matter of the population needed to support a primary school was the basic issue determining population density and neighbourhood size in British New Towns, not, of course, that urban greenfield villages are anything like new towns in concept or size.

47   Yvonne Rydin's paper 'Environmental Dimensions of Residential Development and the Implications of Local Planning Practice' (1992) looks further into appropriate building materials, sequested energy, and avoidance of toxic materials. Refer also to Susan Owen's admirable *Energy Planning and Urban Form*, 1986.

48   The most likely future move in the direction of 'urban greenfields village' development will probably come from the private sector. The principle problem, unless the developer owns the whole of the surrounding greenfields estate, being one of keeping conventional suburbanization and edge-city broad-acre urbanization at bay.

49   With some local government administrations the GIS mapping of infill capacity (Land Capacity Analysis) is used to do the realtors' land supply job without attempting to address the determination and provisioning of site needs in anything like a socially focused way.

50   An effective provisioning for raw land subdivisions (also of considerable utility for infill situations) is the Victorian Code for Residential Development (VicCode 1992). See also *Residential Streets* by Walter Kulash (2001) for recent US contexts.

51   TNDs – see *Suburban Nation*, Duany, Plater-Zyberk, Speck 2000.

52   There can arise a down-side to work-at-home arrangements; sometimes missed supervisor feedback, certainly a lack of personal inter-reaction between workers. Often there are complaints about *courier* traffic, and of course the curse of malfunctioning technologies.

53   Tibbalds set down a design management listing which included the following items: consider places before buildings; learn from the past and respect your context; encourage the mixing of uses; design on a human scale; encourage freedom to walk about; cater for and consult with all sections of the community; build legible environments; build to last and adapt; avoid change on too great a scale; promote intricacy, joy and delight.

54   A visit to Olwyn Green was disappointing. The plots are well sited and the buildings craftily oriented; but there is an evident lack of upkeep-pride. This project was initiated as public housing.

55   An Australian publication of interest is the Victorian Ministry for Planning and Environment 1989, *Planning Guide for Urban Open Space*.

56   Excepting, to the way of thinking for many, ex-urban sprawl!

57   What they must avoid in the pursuit of compaction is policy simplicity of the formulaic kind once applied in my then home jurisdiction. There in the 1980s it was decreed that provided a 12 m × 12 m square could be fitted into any suburban backyard or front yard (and the total area of the new plot exceeded $250\,\text{m}^2$) there was an 'as of right' infill approval regardless of any aesthetic or good-neighbour consideration!

58   Recent study projects from Melbourne (Albert Park, East Malvern, Armadale) are indicative of the potential for Transport Oriented Development in the service of suburban densification. Commendable and worthy as the Transport Oriented Development ideal is relative to the nodal entities from which they radiate, they leave considerable expanses, particularly in the outer suburban reaches, unbenefited.

59   Privacy is entirely a matter of building and landscape design. In well-considered English suburbia the niche gardens and patios incorporated within $250\,\text{m}^2$ sized plots allow their occupants secluded sunbathing in the altogether, with a privacy impossible to achieve in New World frontyard-backyard-sideyard suburbs.

60   This supposition being blown away of course when inner-city lifestylers disappear to their remote weekender cottages, or power away from it all in cabin cruisers!

61 At its most intense and costly is a conversion of the nineteenth-century Exchange Building in lower Manhattan: net density 605 units per acre – a Costas Kondylis project depicted in Steven Fader's *Density by Design*, 2000.

62 This is one area (the other being the standard suburb) where according to the 1999 (UK) 'Rogers Report' 'over the next 25 years 60 percent of new buildings should be built on previously developed land'; which addresses the sociological threat of urban decline while factoring in sustainable ideals.

63 There are few opportunities for reinvestment which produce a payback. Between the wars suburbia was short-changed at inception (unusable backland reserves, low-grade utilities).

64 This is denied as an option when advisory initiatives are regarded as open to legal risk, implicating officials or their administration as a result of the modern complexity for withholding actual practical advice on how and what to do.

65 There is also the British tradition of town centre revitalization, summarized in the UK Department of the Environment 1994 report on PPG6 *Vital and Viable Town Centres.*

66 Available in soulless electronic form to the housebound and carless, and the rural poor, by the pernicious EHS (electronic home shopping) service.

References

Abbott, D. *Encyclopaedia of Real Estate Terms*, Gower Press, 1987.

Abernathy, V. *Population Politics*, Insight Books, 1993.

Abert, J. G. (ed.). *Resource Recovery Guide*, Reinhold, 1983.

Adams, W. M. *Green Development*, Routledge, 1992.

Adler, J. 'Bye-Bye Suburban Dream – 15 Ways to fix the Suburbs', *Newsweek*, 15 May 1995.

Aldus, A. *Urban Villages*, Urban Villages Group, London, 1992.

Alexander, C. *A New Theory of Urban Design*, Oxford University Press, 1987.

Alexander, C. with S. Ishikawa and M. Silverstein, *A Pattern Language: Town Buildings Construction*, Oxford University Press, 1977.

Alonso, W. 'Urban and Regional Imbalance in Economic Development', *Economic Development and Cultural Change*, 1969.

Altshuler, A. 'Review of the Costs of Urban Sprawl', *American Institute of Planners Journal*, 33 (2), 1977.

AMCORD (Australian Department of Health Housing and Community Services). *AMCORD Urban* (Part One 'Planning and Implementation': Part Two 'Draft Code': Part Three 'Support Material') 1992.

American Planning Association, Theme Edition. *Strategic Planning*. Contributions by Bryson and Einsweiler, Bryson and Roering, Kaufman and Jacobs, Wechler and Backoff, Nutt and Backoff. *APA Journal*, 53 (1), Winter 1981.

Ames, S. C. (ed.). *Guide to Community Visioning*, APA Planners Press, revised edition 2001.

Anglin Associates. *Main Street New South Wales* (Handbook), Department of Planning New South Wales, 1989.

Appleyard, D. with S Gerson and M. Lintell. *Liveable Streets*, University of California Press, 1981.

Arendt, R. *Rural by Design: Maintaining Small Town Character*, Planners Press USA, 1994.

Arendt, R. *Conservation Design for Subdivisions*, Island Press, 1996.

Arendt, R. 'Basing Cluster Techniques on Development Densities', *American Planning Association Journal*, Winter 1997.

Arendt, R. *Crossroads, Hamlet, Village, Town* APA Press, 1999.

Arendt, R. *Growing Greener: Putting Conservation into Local Plans*, Island Press, 1999.

Arnstein, S. R. 'A Ladder of Citizen Participation', *Journal of the American Institute of Planners*, July 1969.

Arrow, K. *Social Choice and Individual Values*, New York, Wiley, 1951.

Auckland Regional Council. *Regional Growth Forum – Toolbox of Techniques*, 1997.

Australian Government. *National Strategy for Ecologically Sustainable Development*, Australian Government Publishing Service, 1992.

Bacon, E. *Design of Cities*, Penguin, 1976.

Bailey, M. *Producing Less Waste*, Ministry for the Environment, Wellington, 1991.

Bairoch, P. 'Employment and Large Cities' published in *Bringing Jobs To People*, ILO Geneva, 1988.

Baker, A. R. H. and R. A. Butlin (eds). *Studies of Field Systems in the British Isles*, Cambridge University Press, 1973.

Baldock, J. 'Pecking Order Principles' (on Town Centre Management) *Planning Weekly*, Royal Town Planning Institute, 17 November 1994.

Bamford, G. 'Density, Equity and the Green Suburb', Conference Paper, Royal Australian Planning Institute Congress, Canberra, 1992.

Banfield, E. C. *Moral Basis of a Backward Society*, Free Press, 1958.

Baran, P. A. *The Political Economy of Growth*, London, Penguin, 1972.

Barbarasi, A.-L. *Linked: The New Science of Networks*, Perseus, 2002.

Barbier, E. B. with J. C. Burgess and C. Folke. *Paradise Lost?* Earthscan Publications, 1994.

Barnes, F. 'Me and my cars', *The New Republic*, 1 June 1992.

Barnett, J. *The Fractured Metropolis: Impropving the New City, Restoring the Old City, Reshapimg the Region*. Harper Collins, 1995.

Baross, P. *Action Planning*, Institute for Housing Studies (I.H.S. No. 2), Rotterdam, 1991.

Barrett, C. D. *Everyday Ethics for Practicing Planners*, AICP, 2002.

Barrett, S. and C. Fudge (eds). *Policy and Action*, Methuen, 1981.

Barton, H. with Geoff Davis and Richard Guise. *Sustainable Settlements: A Guide for Planners Designers and Developmers*, University of West of England, 1995.

Barton, H. (ed.). *Sustainable Communities: The Potential for Eco-Neighbourhoods*, Earthscan, 2000.

Baudrillard, J. *Amerique*, Grasset et Fasquelle, Paris, 1994.

Baudrillard, J. *Simulacra and Simulation*, University of Michigan Press, 1994.

Baum, H. S. 'Ethical Behavior is Extraordinary Behavior', *APA Journal*, Autumn, 1998.

Bauman, Z. *Postmodern Ethics*, Blackwell, 1993.

Beatley, T. 'Applying Moral Principles to Growth Management', *Journal of the American Planning Association*, 50, 1984.

Beatley, T. 'Environmental Ethics and Planning Theory', *Journal of Planning Literature* (USA), 4 (1), 1989.

Beatley, T. *Ethical Land Use: Principles of Policy and Planning*, John Hopkins University Press, 1994.

Beauregard, R. A. 'Between Modernity and Postmodernity: the Ambiguous Position of U.S. Planning', *Environment and Planning* D, 7, 1989.

Beder, S. 'Engineers Ethics and Etiquette', *New Scientist*, September 1993.

Behler, E. *Irony and the Discourse of Modernity*, University of Washington Press, 1990.

Belmont, S. *Cities in Full*, APA Planners Press, 2002.

Bendavid-Val, A. *Regional and Local Economic Analysis for Practitioners*, Praeger (4th edition), 1991.

Bentham, J. (original 1789) *An Introduction to the Principles of Morals and Legislation*, New York, Hafner Press, 1948.

Bentley, I. with A. Alcock, P. Murrain, S. McGlynn and G. Smith. *Responsive Environments: A Manual for Designers*, Architectural Press, 1985.

Benton, L. and J. R. Short. *Environmental Discourse*, Blackwell, 1999.

Berry, B. J. L. and A. Pred. *Central Place Studies: A Bibliography of Theory and Applications*, Regional Science Research Institute, Bibliographic Series No. 1, 1975.

Berry, W. 'Out of Your Car: Off Your Horse', *The Atlantic Monthly*, February 1991.

Beyard, M. D. and Michael Pawlukiewicz. *Reinventing America's Suburban Strips*, Urban Land Institute, 2001.

Binford, H. C. *The First Suburbs*, University of Chicago Press, 1985.

Blainey, G. *Triumphs of the Nomads: A History of Ancient Australia*, MacMillan Press, 1975.

Blakely, E. J. *Planning Local Economic Development: Theory and Practice*, Sage Publications, 1989.

Blakely, E. with M. G. Snyder. *Fortress America: Gated Communities in the US*, Brookings Institute Press, 1997.

Blaxter, K. *People, Food and Resources*, Cambridge University Press, 1989.

Bloom, A. D. *The Closing of the American Mind*, Simon and Schuster, 1987.

Bloomfield, P. *Edward Gibbon Wakefield, Builder of the British Commonwealth*, Longmans, 1961.

Blowers, A. *The Limits of Power: The Politics of Local Planning Policy*, Pergamon Press, 1980.

Bolan, R. S. 'The Structure of Ethical Choice in Planning Practice', *Journal of Planning Education and Research*, 3, 1983.

Bookchin, M. *Remaking Society*, Boston, South End Press, 1990.

Bosselman, K. *When Two Worlds Collide*, RSVP Press, Auckland, 1995.

Boudeville, J. R. *Problems of Regional Economic Planning*, Edinburgh University Press, 1966.

Bowie, I. J. S. 'Non-Metropolitan Regional Planning in N.S.W., Victoria and N.Z.', Charles Sturt University (mimeographed), 1990.

Boyer, M. C. *Dreaming the Rational City*, MIT Press, 1983.

Brammell, A. *The Fading of the Greens*, Yale University Press, 1994.

Bray, R. with Vladimir Raitz. *Flight to the Sun; The Story of the Holiday Revolution*, Continuum, 2001.

Breheny, M. *Sustainable Development and Urban Form*, Pion, 1992.

Breheny, M. and A. Hooper (eds). *Rationality in Planning: Critical Essays on the Role of Rationality in Urban and Regional Planning*, Pion, 1985.

Breheny, M. with I, Gent and D. Lock. *Alternative Development Patterns*, HMSO, 1993.

Brindle, R. 'Toronto: Paradigm Lost', *Australian Planner*, September 1992.

Brisbane City Council. *Urban Renewal Report*, 1991.

Britton, S. with Richard LeHeron and Eric Pawson (eds). *Changing Places in New Zealand*, New Zealand Geographical Society, 1992.

Bromley, R. D. F. and C. J. Thomas (eds). *Retail Change: Contemporary Issues*, 1994.

Brooks, M. P. *Planning Theory for Practitioners*, APA Planners Press, 2002.

Brown, A. J. with H. M. Sherrard. *Town and Country Planning*, Melbourne University Press, 1951.

Brown, L. R. with others. *The State of the World*, Norton, 1991.

Brundtland, H. *Our Common Future*, Oxford University Press for the World Commission on Environment and Development, 1987.

Bryant, C. with C. H. Russwurm and A. G. McLellan. *The City's Countryside: Land and its Management in the Rural-Urban Fringe*, Longman, 1982.

Bryfogle, R. C. and R. Krueger. *Urban Problems*, Holt Rinehart and Winston, Toronto, 1975.

Buckingham-Hatfield, S. and Bob Evans (eds). *Environmental Planning and Sustainability*, John Wiley, 1996.

Buder, S. *Visionaries and Planners*, Oxford University Press, 1990.

Burnley, I. and J. Forrest. *Living in Cities*, Allen and Unwin, Sydney, 1985.

Burrows, L. B. *Growth Management*, Centre for Urban Policy Research, New Brunswick, NJ, 1978.

Bushman, R. L. *The Refinement of America: Persons Houses Cities*, Knopf, 1992.

Byrnes, G. M. 'No Holidays are Kept in the Bush: Surveying in Taranaki and the Discourses of Colonisation', *Archifacts*, April 1993.

Calthorpe, P. 'The Pedestrian Pocket: New Strategies for Urban Growth', in *Sustainable Cities* (ed. Walter Arkin and Crenshaw) published Eco-Home Media, 1992.

Calthorpe, P. *The Next American Metropolis: Ecology Community and the American Dream*, Princeton Architectual Press, 1993.

Calthorp, P. with William Fulton. *The Regional City*, Island Press, 2001.

Campbell, A. with C. Keen, G. Norman and R. Oakshott. *Worker-Owners: The Mondragon Achievement*, Anglo-German Foundation, 1977.

Campbell, S. with Susan S. Fainstein (eds). *Readings in Planning Theory*, Blackwell, 1996.

Campoli, J. with Elizabeth Humstone and Alex MacLean. *Above and Beyond*, APA Planners Press USA, 2002.

Capra, F. 'The Turning Point', *Science, Society and the Rising Culture*, Berkeley, 1975.

Carlson, D. with Don Billen. *Transportation Corridor Management*, Institute for Public Policy and Management, 1996.

Carson, R. *Silent Spring*, Houghton Mifflin, 1962.

Carter, E. J. 'Toward a Body of Core Knowledge: A New Curriculum for City and Regional Planners', *Journal Of Planning Education and Research*, 12 (2), 1993.

Cartwright, T. 'Planning and Chaos Theory', *Journal of the American Planning Association*, 57 (1), 1991.

Catonese, A. J. *Planners and Local Politics: Impossible Dreams*, Beverley Hills, Sage Publications, 1974.

Cavanagh, J. and F. Clairmonte. *The Transnational Economy*, Institute for Policy Studies, Washington, 1982.

Cervero, R. 'Congestion Relief: The Land Use Alternative', *Journal of Planning Education and Research*, 10 (2), 1991.

Chadwick, G. F. *A Systems View of Planning*, London, Pergamon Press, 1971.

Chárles, Prince of Wales. *A Vision of Britain*, Doubleday, 1989.

Checkland, P. B. 'The Application of Systems Thinking in Real-World Problem Situations: The Emergence of Soft Systems Methodology', in *New Directions in Management Science* (ed. M. C. Jackson), Gower, 1987.

Chiras, D. D. *Lessons for Nature: Learning to Live Sustainably on the Earth*, Island Press, 1992.

Chisholm, M. *Regions in Recession and Resurgence*, Unwin Hyman, 1990.

Christaller, W. *Die Zentralen Orte in Sutteutschland*, Jena, 1933.

Cloke, P. and J. Little. *The Rural State? Limits to Planning in Rural Society*, Clarendon Press, Oxford, 1990.

Coates, G. J. (ed.). *Resettling America: Energy, Ecology and Community*, Brick House Publishing, Mass., 1981.

Cogan, E. *Successful Public Meetings*, APA Planners Press, 2000.

Cole, H. S. D. with P. Freeman, M. Jahoda and K. L. R. Parfitt. *Thinking About the Future: A Critique of the Limits to Growth*, London, Chatto and Windus, 1973.

Collin, R. W. and R. M. 'Equity as the Basis of Implementing Sustainability', *West Virginia Law Review*, 96 (4), 1994.

Collin, R. W. and R. M. 'Sustainability and Environmental Justice: Is the Future Clean and Black?', *The Environmental Law Reporter*, 31 (8), August 2001.

Connerly, C. E. with N. A. Muller. 'Evaluating Housing Elements in Growth Management Plans', in *Growth Management* (ed. J. M. Stein), Sage Publications, 1993.

Conzen, M. P. 'Morphology of 19th Century Cities', in R. P. Schaedel (et al. eds) *Urbanization in the Americas from its Beginnings to the Present*, The Hague, Mouton, 1980.

Corbett, M. N. *A Better Place to Live: New Designs for Tomorrow's Communities*, Rodale Press, Pennsylvania, 1981.

Corner, J. 'The Agency of Mapping: Speculation, Critique and Invention', in *Mappings* (ed. Denis Cosgrove) Reaktion Books, 1999.

Costanza, R. (ed.). *Ecological Economics: The Science and Management of Sustainability*, Columbia University Press, 1991.

Costanza, R. co-edited with B. G. Norton and B. D. Haskell. *Ecosystem Health*, Island Press, 1992.

Cowell, A. *The Tribe That Hides From Man*, Bodley Head, 1973.

Cox, K. R. *Man Location and Behavior*, Wiley, 1972.

Coyne, J. P. E. 'Resource analysis as an alternative basis for project evaluation', doctoral thesis (unpublished), University of Cambridge, 1981.

Craig-Smith, S. and C. French. *Learning to Live with Tourism*, Pitman, 1994.

Crawford, M. 'The Mall and the Strip: From Building Type to Urban Form', *Urbanistica*, November 1986.

Crane, R. 'Cars and Drivers in the New Suburbs', *Journal of the American Planning Association*, 62 (1), 1996.

Cronon, W. *Nature's Metropolis: Chicago and the Great West*, Norton, 1991.

Crosson, P. R. 'Sustainable Agriculture', *Resources for the Future*, 106, 1992.

Crosson, P. R. 'Is U.S. Agriculture Sustainable?', *Resources for the Future*, 117, 1994.

Cullen, G. *The Concise Townscape*, Architectural Press, 1961.

Cullingworth, B. *Planning in the USA: Policies Issues Processes*, Routledge, 1997.

Dalkey, H. C. *The Delphi Method: An Experimental Study of Group Opinion*, RAND Corp. 1969.

Daly, H. E. 'The Perils of Free Trade', in *Scientific American*, 1993.

Daly, H. E. with John B. Cobb. *For The Common Good: Redirecting the Economy Toward Community the Environment and a Sustainable Future*, Beacon, 1989.

Dalziel, R. 'Patterns of Settlement', in *New Zealand Atlas*, Government Printer, 1976.

Dane, S. G. *Main Street Success Stories*, National Trust for Historical Preservation (US), 1997.

Daniels, T. *When City and Country Collide*, Island Press, 1999.

Daniels, T. L. 'The Purchase of Development Rights – Preserving Agricultural Land and Open Space', *American Planning Association Journal*, Winter 1997.

Daniels, T. L. with J. W. Keller and M. B. Lapping. *Small Town Planning Handbook*, APA Planners Press, 1995.

Darwin, C. *Narrative of the Surveying Voyages of H.M.S. 'Adventure' and 'Beagle'*, London, 1839.

Darwin, C. *Origin of Species*, London, 1888.

Dasmann, R. F. *Environmental Conservation*, Wiley Press (3rd edition), 1972.

Davidoff, P. 'Advocacy and Pluralism in Planning', *Journal of the American Institute of Planning*, 31, 1965.

Davidson, M. *Glossary of Zoning Development and Planning Terms*, APA-PAS, 1999.

Davis, M. *City of Quartz*, University of California Press, 1990.

Davis, M. *Dead Cities*, New Press, 2003.

Dear, M. *The Postmodern Urban Condition*, Blackwell, 1999.

de Bono, E. *Parallel Thinking*, Viking Press, 1994.

Debord, G. 'The Society of the Spectacle' (1967) translated into English as *Comments on the Society of the Spectacle*, 1989.

DeGrove, J. M. *Land Growth and Politics*, Planners Press, USA, 1984.

DeGrove, J. M. *Balanced Growth: A Planning Guide for Local Government*, City Management Association, 1995.

DeGrove, J. M. with P. M. Metzger. 'Growth Management and the Integrated Roles of State, Regional and Local Governments', in *Growth Management* (ed. J. M. Stein), Sage Publications, 1993.

DeGrove, J. M. with D. A. Miness. *The New Frontier for Land Policy: Planning and Growth Management in the [United] States*, Lincoln Institute of Land Policy, 1992.

Deelstra, T. 'An Ecological Approach to Planning Cities', *Town and Country Planning*, April 1988.

Deelstra, T. *The Resourceful City: Management Approaches to Efficient Cities Fit to live In*, 'Proceedings of the Man in the Biosphere – 11 Workshop', Amsterdam, 1989.

Denman, D. R. 'A Classification of Universal Land Problems', in *Contemporary Problems of Land Ownership*, University of Cambridge, 1962.

Department of the Environment (UK). *Development Plans and Regional Planning Guidance*, Planning Practice Guidance 12, HMSO, 1992.

Department of the Environment (UK). *Vital and Viable Town Centres*, 1994.

Department of the Environment (UK). *Involving Communities in Urban and Rural Regeneration*, HMSO, 1995.

Department of the Environment (UK). *Regeneration Research Summary*, HMSO, 2000.

Department of the Environment (UK Welsh Office). *Countryside and the Rural Economy*, Planning Practice Guidance 7, HMSO, 1992.

Department of Health Housing and Community Services (Australia). *AMCORD Urban* (Part One 'Planning and Implementation'; Part Two 'Draft Code'; Part Three 'Support Material') 1992.

Department of Housing and Regional Development (Australia). *AMCORD 95: A National Resource Document for Residential Development*, Australian Government Publishing Service, 1995.

Department of Industry Technology and Commerce (Australian Government). *Australian Model Copde for Residential Development*, 1990.

Department of Planning [Sydney]. *Residential Development Controls* (Six Booklets) Crown Copyright Publishers, 1990–3.

Department of Planning and Housing (Victoria). *Victorian Code for Residential Development*, 1992.

Department of Planning and Housing (Victoria). *Melbourne Planning Scheme; Central City Planning and Design Guidelines*, 1991.

Dickman, S. *Tourism: An Introductory Text*, Edward Arnold, reprinted 1994.

Dike, R. *Architectural Common Sense: Sun, Site and Self*, Reinhold, 1983.

Dixon, J. M. *Urban Spaces*, Visual Reference Publications, 1999.

Dolnick, F. with M. Davidson. *Glossary of Zoning Development and Planning Terms*, 1999.

Donaldson, S. *The Suburban Myth*, Columbia University Press, 1969.

Downs, A. *Opening up the Suburbs: An Urban Strategy for America*, Yale University Press, 1973.

Dowson, E. and V. L. O. Sheppard. *Land Registration*, HMSO London, 1956.

Doxey, G. 'A Causation Theory of Visitor – Resident Irritants', *Proceedings of the Travel Research Association*, San Diego, 1975.

Dryzek, J. S. *Discursive Democracy*, Cambridge University Press, 1990.

Dryzek, J. S. with D. Schlosberg (eds). *Debating the Earth: The Environmental Politics Reader*, Oxford University Press, 1998.

Duany, A. *Towns and Town Making Principles* (ed. Alex Krieger), Rizzoli Press, New York, 1992.

Duany, A. with Elizabeth Plater-Zyberk. *Towns and Town Making Principles*, Rizzoli Press, 1992.

Duany, A. with Elizabeth Plater-Zyberk and Jeff Speck. *Suburban Nation: The Rise of Sprawl and the Decline of the American Dream*, North Point Press, 2000.

Duerksen, C. J. and others. *Habitat Protection Planning*, APA-PAS, 1997.

Duncan, N. G. and J. S. 'Deep Suburban Irony: The Perils of Democracy in Westchester County', in *Visions of Suburbia* (ed. Roger Siverstone), 1997.

Dunlop, B. 'Breaking the Code' (reviewing the work of Andreas Duany and Elizabeth Plater-Zyberk), *Architecture*, April 1990.

Dutton, G. *Russell Drysdale*, Thames and Hudson, 1964.

Easterbrook, G. 'Waste Energy', *The New Republic*, 18 March 1991.

Easterbrook, G. 'Here Comes the Sun', *The New Yorker*, 10 April 1995.

Eckholm, E. P. *Losing Ground: Environmental Stress and World Food Prospects*, Pergamon, 1976.

Ecotourism Society (eds P. F. J. Eagles, P. Nilsen, N. Kachi, and S. Buse). *Ecotourism: An Annotated Bibliography*, Ecotourism Society, Vermont, 1995.

Edwards-Jones, G. with S. Hussain and B. Davies, *Ecological Economics: An Introduction*, Blackwell Science, 2000.

Egerton, H. E. *Short History of British Colonial Policy*, Methuen, London, 1928 reprint (first edition 1897).

Ehrenreich, B. *Fear of Falling: The Inner Life of the Middle Classes*, Harper Perennial, 1989.

Ehrlich, P. *The Population Bomb*, Ballantine, 1968.

Ehrlich, P. with A. H. Ehrlich and J. P. Holdren, *Ecoscience: Population, Resources and Environment*, San Fransisco, Freeman (first published 1970), 1977.

Elgin, D. *Awakening Earth: Exploring the Evolution of Human Culture and Consciousness*, William Morrow, 1993.

Elkin, T. and D. McLaren with M. Hillman. *Reviving the City: Towards Sustainable Urban Development*, Friends of the Earth, London, 1991.

Elkington, J. *Cannibals with Forks: The Triple Bottom Line of 20th Century Business*, Capstone, 1999.

Ekins, P. (ed.) . *The Living Economy: A New Economics in the Making*, Routledge and Kegan Paul, 1986.

Elliot, J. A. *Introduction to Sustainable Development*, Routledge, 1994.

Endicott, E. (ed.). *Land Conservation Through Public/Private Partnerships*, Island Press, 1993.

Engwicht, D. *Towards An Eco-City: Calming the Traffic*, Envirobook Publications, Sydney, 1992.

Enzensburger, H. M. 'A Critique for Political Ecology', in *The Political Economy of Science*, H. Rose and S. Rose (eds), London, Macmillan, 1976.

Etzioni, A. 'Mixed Scanning: A Third Approach to Decision-Making', *Public Administration Review*, December 1967.

Etzioni, A. *The Active Society: A Theory of Societal and Political Progress*, New York, Free Press, 1968.

Etzioni, A. 'Toward a Theory of Societal Guidance', in *Societal Guidance: A New Approach to Social Problems*, (ed. Heidt and Etzione) New York, Cromwell Publishers, 1969. (Landcare Research Ltd).

Etzioni, A. *The Moral Dimension: Toward a New Economics*, Free Press, 1988.

Etzioni, A. *The Spirit of Community*, Gown Publishers, 1993.

Ewing, R. *Traffic Calming*, Institute of Transportation Engineers, 1999.

Eysenck, H. J. *The Psychology of Politics*, Routledge and Kegan Paul, 1968.

Fader, S. *Density by Design*, Urban Land Institute, 2000.

Fainstein, S. S. 'Planning in a Different Voice', in Campbell and Fainstein (eds). *Readings in Planning Theory*, Blackwell, 1996.

Faludi, A. (ed.). *A Reader in Planning Theory*, Oxford, Pergamon Press, 1973.

Faludi, A. 'The Return of Rationality', in *Rationality in Planning*, ed. M. Breheny and A. Hooper, Pion, 1985.

Featherstone, M. (ed.). *Nationalism, Globalization and Modernity*, Sage Publications, 1990.

Fennell, D. A. with R. K. Dowling (eds), *Ecotourism Policy*, CABI Publishing, 2002.

Ferguson, G. *Building the New Zealand Dream*, Dunmore Press, 1994.

Fernandez-Armesto, F. *Millennium*, Black Swan, 1997.

Fischel, W. A. *Economics of Zoning Laws: A Property Rights Approach*, John Hopkins Press, 1985.

Fischer, F. and J. Forester (eds). *Confronting Values in Policy Analysis*, Sage Publications, 1987.

Fisher, R. with W. Ury and B. Patton. *Getting To Yes: Negotiating Agreement Without Giving In*, Penguin Books, 1991.

Fishman, R. *Bourgeois Utopias: The Rise and Fall of Suburbia*, Basic Books, 1987.

Fleary, B. J. *Decline of the Age of Oil*, Pluto Press 1998.

Florida, R. L. *The Rise of the Creative Class*, Basic Books, 2002.

Fodor, E. *Better Not Bigger*, New Society Press, 1999.

Ford, K. with James Lopach and Dennis O'Donnell. *Planning Small Town America*, APA, 1990.

Ford, L. *The Spaces Between Buildings*, John Hopkins Press, 2000.

Forester, J. 'Critical Theory and Planning Practice', *American Planning Association Journal*, 46 (3), 1980.

Forester, J. 'Planning in the Face of Conflict: Negotiation and Mediation Strategies in Local Land Use Regulation', *American Planning Association Journal*, Summer 1987.

Forrester, J. W. *World Dynamics*, Wright-Allen Press, 1970.

Forsyth, A. *Constructing Suburbs: Competing Voices in a Debate Over Urban Growth*, Gordon and Breach, 1999.

Foucault, M. *The Will to Truth*, London, Tavistock, 1970.

Foucault, M. 'The Subject and Power', *Critical Inquiry*, 8, 1982.

Foucault, M. *The Archeology of Knowledge and the Discourse on Language*, Random House, 1992.

Foucault, M. *The Order of Things*, Random House, 1992.

Foyel, J. 'Planning in the Rural-Urban Fringe', *Australian Planner*, March 1992.

Franaviglia, R. V. *Main Street Revisited*, University of Iowa Press, 1996.

Fri, R. W. 'Sustainable Development: Principles into Practice', *Resources*, 102, 1991.

Friedman A. with D. Krawitz, M. Senbel, D. Raphael, J. E. Steffel, J. S. Frenchette and J. Watt. *Planning the New Suburbia*, UBC Press, 2002.

Friedmann, J. 'The Core Curriculum in Planning Revisited', *Journal of Planning Education and Research*, 15, 1966.

Friedmann, J. *Regional Development Policy: A Case Study of Venezuela*, Cambridge, Mass., MIT Press, 1966.

Friedmann, J. *Planning in the Public Domain: From Knowledge to Action*, Princeton University Press, 1987.

Freidmann, J. 'Discourse and Praxis', *Journal of Planning Education and Research*, 8 (2), 1989.

Friedmann, J. 'The Right to the City', *Society and Nature*, May–August 1992.

Friedmann, J. and W. Alonso (eds). *Regional Development and Planning: A Reader*, Cambridge, Mass., MIT Press, 1965.

Friedmann, J. and W. Hudson. 'Knowledge and Action: A Guide to Planning Theory', *American Institute of Planning Journal*, January 1974.

Friedmann, J. and C. Weaver. *Territory and Function: The Evolution of Regional Planning*, London, Edward Arnold, 1979.

Friend, J. K. and A. Hickling. *Planning Under Pressure: The Strategic Choice*, Pergamon Press, 1987.

Friend, J. K. and W. N. Jessop. *Local Government and Strategic Choice*, London, Tavistock, 1969 (second edition 1977).

Fukuyama, F. *The End of History and the Last Man*, Free Press, 1992.

Fulton, W. *The Reluctant Metropolis: The Politics of Urban Growth in Los Angeles*, Solano Press, 1997.

Furtado, C. *Development and Underdevelopment*, Berkley (in translation), 1964.

Gabor, D. with U. Colombo, A. King and R. Galli. *Beyond the Age of Waste*, Pergamon Press, 1978.

Galbraith, J. K. *Economic Development*, Harvard University Press, 1964.

Galbraith, J. K. *The Culture of Contentment*, Houghton Mifflin, 1992.

Garreau, J. *Edge City: Life on the New Frontier*, Anchor Press, 1992.

Geddes, P. *Cities in Evolution*, Williams and Norgate, London, 1915.

George, H. (1839–97). *Henry George's Progress and Poverty*, Published for the Henry George Foundation by Hogarth Press, 1953.

Georgescu-Roegen, N. *The Entropy Law and Economic Progress*, Harvard Univversity Press, 1971.

Gerecke, K. with Barton Reid. 'False Prophets', in *The Canadian City* [edited] Black Rose Press, Montreal, 1991.

Gerecke, K. with Barton Reid. 'Planning Power and Ethics', *Plan Canada* 31 (1), November 1991.

Giddens, A. *The Consequences of Modernity*, Polity Press Cambridge, 1990.

Gilbert, A. G. 'The Arguments for Very Large Cities Reconsidered', *Urban Studies*, 13, 1976.

Gilpin, A. *Environmental Impact Assessment: The Cutting Edge For The 21st Century*, Cambridge University Press, 1995.

Girling, C. L. and Kenneth Helphand. *Yard Street Park: The Design of Suburban Open Space*, Wiley, 1994.

Glacken, C. J. *Traces on the Rhodian Shore*, Los Angeles, University of California Press, 1977.

Gladwell, M. *The Tipping Point: How Little Things Can Make a Big Difference*, Little Brown, 2002.

Glasson, J. *An Introduction to Regional Planning*, London, UCL Press (6th Impression, 2nd edition) 1993. First published Hutchinson, 1975.

Glasson, J. 'The Fall and Rise of Regional Planning in the Economically Advanced Nations', *Urban Studies*, 29 (3 and 4), 1992.

Gleeson, B. and Nicholas Low. *Australian Urban Planning: New Challenges New Agendas*, Allen and Unwin, 2000.

Gleick, J. *Chaos-Making a New Science*, London, Sphere Books, 1990.

Globe 90. *Action Strategy for Sustainable Tourism Development*, Tourism Stream Action Strategy Committee, Vancouver, 1990.

Glover, D. 'Enter Without Knocking' (poem: 2nd edition) Pegasus Press, 1971.

Goeldner, C. R. and Brent Ritchie. *Tourism: Principles Practices Philosophies*, John Wiley Press, (9th edition) 2002.

Gold, H. and A. Webster. *Values Today: Report of the 1989 NZ Study of Values*, Alpha Publications, 1990.

Goldberg, E. D. *Coastal Zone Space: Prelude to Conflict?* Unesco Publications, 1994.

Goldsmith, E. *The Way: An Ecological World-View*, Rider, 1992.

Goldsmith, E. 'Ultimate Freedom', *Fourth World Review*, 92, 1998.

Goodman, R. *After The Planners*, Penguin, 1972.

Gore, Al. *Earth in the Balance: Forging a New Common Purpose*, London, Earthscan, 1992.

Gore, Al. *Earth in the Balance: Ecology and the Human Spirit*, Plume Press, 1994.

Gottdiener, M. *The Social Production of Urban Space*, University of Texas Press, 1985.

Gottdiener, M. with C. G. Pickvance, *Urban Life in Transition*, Sage, 1991.

Gottlieb, J. *Forcing the Spring: Transformation of the US Environmental Movement*, Island Press, 1993.

Goudie, A. *The Human Impact on the Natural Environment* (5th edition), Blackwell, 1999.

Greed, C. H. *Women and Planning: Creating Gendered Realities*, Routledge, 1994.

Greenbie, B. *Spaces: Dimensions of the Human Landscape*, Yale University Press, 1981.

Greentreet (Australia). *Australian Model Code for Residential Development*, 1992.

Greenpeace (Australia). *Ecologically Sustainable Development*, Greenpeace, 1992.

Green Street Joint Venture. *Attidudes to Housing in Australia*, 1991.

Gross, J. S. *Webster's New World Illustrated Encyclopaedic Dictionary of Real Estate*, Prentice Hall, 1987.

Grumbine, R. E. (ed.). *Environmental Policy and Biodiversity*, Island Press, 1994.

Guha, R. 'Thinkers: Lewis Mumford', *Journal of Socialist Ecology*, 2 (3), 1991.

Guha, R. 'Towards a Cross Cultural Environmental Ethic', *Alternatives*, 16 (3), 1990.

Gunn, C. A. *Tourism Planning: Basics Concepts Cases* (3rd edition), Taylor and Francis, 1994.

Gwilliam, M. 'Recognising Good Urban Design' in *Planning*, Issue 1315, 1999.

Haar, C. M. *The End of Innocence: A Suburban Reader*, Scott Foreman Company, Illinois, 1972.

Haar, C. M. with J. S. Kayden. *Zoning and the American Dream*, Planners Press, 1989.

Habermas, J. *Communication and the Evolution of Society*, Beacon Press, 1979.

Habermas, J. *The Theory of Communicative Action*, Beacon Press, 1984.

Habermas, J. in 'Life Forms, Morality and the Task of the Philosopher' [edited P. Dews], in *Habermas*, Verso Press, 1986.

Haeckel, E. H. *Natural History of Creation*, Jena, 1868.

Hall, P. *Great Planning Disasters*, University of California Press, 1982.

Hall, P. 'Planning for a Golden Age', *The Planner*, 75 (29), 1989.

Hansen, N. M. (ed.). *Human Settlement Systems*, Ballinger Press, 1978.

Hardin, G. 'The Tragedy of the Commons', *Science*, 162, 1968.

Hardin, G. *Living Within Limits*, Oxford University Press, 1993.

Harper, T. L and S. M. Stein. 'The Centrality of Normative Ethical Theory to Contemporary Planning Theory', *Journal of Planning Education and Research*, 11, 1992.

Harper, T. L. and S. M. Stein. 'Normative Ethical Theory', *Plan Canada*, September 1993.

Harris, R. *Unplanned Suburbs: Toronto's American Tragedy*, John Hopkins Press, 1996.

Harrison, A. *Economics of Land Use Planning*, Croom Helm, 1977.

Harrison, J. F. C. *Quest for the Moral World: Robert Owen and the Owenites*, New York, Charles Scribner, 1969.

Harvey, D. *Social Justice and the City*, Edward Arnold, 1973.

Harvey, D. *Consciousness and the Urban Experience*, Blackwell, 1985.

Harvey, D. *The Condition of Postmodernity*, Blackwell, 1989.

Harvey, D. 'The Environment of Justice', in Merrifield and Swyngedouw (eds), *The Urbanisation of Injustice*, Lawrence and Wishart, 1995.

Harvey, D. 'On Planning the Ideology of Planning', in Campbell and Fainstein (eds). *Readings in Planning Theory*, Blackwell, 1996 (Original 1985).

Haughton, G. *Sustainable Cities*, Jessica Kingsley, 1994.

Hawken, P. *The Ecology of Commerce*, Harper Business, 1993.

Hawken, P. with Amory Lovins and Hunter Lovins. *Natural Capitalism: The Next Industrial Revolution*, Earthscan, 1999.

Hayden, D. *The Power of Place: Urban Landscapes as Public History*, MIT Press, 1995.

Hayek, F. *The Road to Serfdom*, Routledge, 1962.

Hayward, R. and S. McGlynn (editors and co-authors). *Making Better Places*, Butterworth, 1993.

Hazeldine, T. 'The New Zealand Economic Revolution After Ten Years' Working Paper 161, Auckland Business School, 1996.

Healey, P. 'Change in the British Planning System', *Town Planning Review*, 60 (2), 1989.

Healey, P. [in Huw Thomas and Patsy Healey], *Dilemmas of Planning Practice: Ethics, Legitimacy and the Validation of Knowledge*, Gower, 1991.

Healey, P. 'Planning Through Debate: The Communicative Turn in Planning Theory' in Campbell and Fainstein (eds). *Readings in Planning Theory*, Blackwell, 1996.

Healey, P. *Collaborative Planning: Shaping Places in Fragmented Societies*, Macmillan, 1997.

Healey, P. with S. Cameron, S. Davoudi, S. Graham, and A. Madani-Pour (eds). *Managing Cities: The New Urban Context*, Wiley, 1995.

Healey, P. with Paul McNamara, Martin Elson and Andrew Doak. *Land Use Planninig and the Mediation of Urban Change*, Cambridge University Press, 1988.

Healy, T. 'Conservation and Management of Coastal Resources: The Earth Science Basis' published in A. G. Anderson (ed.) *The Land Our Future*, Longman Paul, 1980.

Heilbroner, R. *Business Civilization in Decline*, Norton, 1976.

Heilbroner, R. 'Reflections: Economic Predictions', *The New Yorker*, 8 July 1991.

Hendler, S. (ed.). *Planning Ethics: A Reader*, Centre for Urban Policy Research, 1995.

Heyer, F. *Preserving Rural character*, APA-PAS Planners Press, 1990.

Heywood, P. 'The Administration and Planning of the New World Metropolis', *Australian Planner*, 31 (4), 1994.

Heywood, P. 'The Future Metropolis: Planning for Metropolitan Growth Management in the New World' (typescript) Queensland University of Technology, 1994.

Hillier, J. 'To boldly go where no planners have ever . . .', in *Environment and Planning D: Society and Space*, Pion, 1993.

Himmelfarb, G. *Poverty and Compassion: The Moral Imagination of the Late Victorians*, Knopf, 1991.

Hirschman, A. O. 'A Generalised Linkage Approach to Development', from *Essays on Economic Development in honour of B. F. Hozelitz* (ed. Manning Nash), Chicago University Press, 1977.

Hjärne, L. 'Planning for Community in Swedish Housing', *Scandinavian Housing and Planning Research*, 3, 1986.

Hobbes, T. (first published 1651). *Leviathan*, Clarendon Press, 1909.

Hobsbawm, E. J. *The Age of Capital 1848–1875*, Weidenfeld and Nicholson, 1975.

Hoch, C. 'Conflict at Large: A National Survey of Planners and Political Conflict', *Journal of Planning Education and Research*, 8 (1), 1988.

Hoch, C. 'Commentary' *Journal of Planning Education and Research*, 12 (2), 1993.

Hoch, C. *What Planners Do*, APA Planners Press, 1994.

Hodge, G. with Ira Robinson. *Planning Canadian Regions*, UBC Press, 2001.

Hofstee, E. W. 'Land Ownership in Densely Populated and Industrialised Countries', in *Land and People*, Leonard Hill, 1967.

Hough, M. *City Form and Natural Process*, Croom Helm, 1984.

Howard, E. *Garden Cities of Tomorrow*, Faber and Faber, 1946; first published 1902.

Howard, R. *Colonisation and Underdevelopment in Ghana*, Croom Helm, 1978.

Howe, E. 'Role Choices of Urban Planners', *Journal of the American Planning Association*, 46, 1980.

Howe, E. 'Normative Ethics in Planning', *Journal of Planning Literature*, 5, 1990.

Howe, E. and J. Kaufman. 'The Ethics of Contemporary American Planners', in *Journal of the American Planning Association*, 45, 1979.

Howe, E. and J. Kaufman. 'The Values of Contemporary American Planners', *Journal of the American Planning Association*, 47, 1981.

Hudson, B. M. 'Comparison of Current Planning Theories', *American Planning Association Journal*, October 1979.

Huisingh, D. 'Cleaner Production', Course Outline for the Erasmus Studiecentrum voor Miliekunde, University of Rotterdam, 1992. In English.

Hunter, A. 'The Role of Liberal Political Culture in the Construction of Middle America', *University of Miami Law Review*, 42 (1), 1987.

Huyssen, A. *After the Great Divide: Modernism, Mass Culture, Postmodernism*, Indiana University Press, 1986.

Illich, I. *Tools for Conviviality*, Fontana-Collins, 1973.

Illich, I. *Energy and Equity*, Marion Boyers, 1979.

Illich, I. with I. Zola, J. McKnight, J. Caplan, and H. Shaiken. *Disabling Professions*, Marion Boyars, 1977.

Inskeep, E. *Tourism Planning: An Integrated and Sustainable Development Approach*, Reinhold, 1990.

International Labour Office. *Bringing Jobs To People: Employment Promotions at Regional and Local Levels* (ed. Jean Mayer), ILO Geneva, 1988.

IPCC. *Climate Change 2001: The Scientific Basis*, Intergovernmental Panel on Climate Change, 2001.

Isard, W. *Location and Space Economy: A General Theory Relating to Industrial Location, Market Areas, Land Use, Trade and Urban Structure*, Boston, The Technology Press of MIT and John Wiley and Sons, 1956.

IUCN/UNEP/WWF. *Caring for the Earth: A Strategy for Sustainable Living*. Gland, Switzerland, 1991.

Jackson, J. B. *The Necessity for Ruins*, University of Massachusetts Press, 1980.

Jackson, K. T. *Crabgrass Frontier: The Suburbanisation of the United States*, Oxford University Press, 1985.

Jackson, P. *Maps of Meaning*, Unwin-Hyman, 1989.

Jacobs, A. B. *Great Streets*, MIT Press, 1993.

Jacobs, J. *The Death and Life of Great American Cities*, Random House, 1961.

Jacobs, J. *Cities and the Wealth of Nations*, Viking Press, 1985.

Jacobs, J. *Systems of Survival*, Vintage Books, 1992.

Jantsch, F. *Technological Forecasting in Perspective*, OECD Paris, 1967.

Jarvis, F. D. *Site Planning and Community Design for Great Neighborhoods*, Home Builder Press, 1993.

Jenks, M. with E. Burton and K. Williams. *The Compact City: Sustainable Urban Form*, Spon, 1996.

Jensen, M. N. 'Ecology Moves Downtown', *Planning*, July 1999.

Jesson, B. *Behind the Mirror Glass: The Growth of Wealth and Power in New Zealand in the Eighties*, Penguin, 1987.

Jewkes, J. *Ordeal by Planning*, Macmillan, 1948.

Johnson, L. (ed.). *Suburban Dreaming: An Interdisciplinary Approach to Australian Cities*, Deakin University Press, 1995.

Johnson, P. and B. Thomas (eds). *Choice and Demand in Tourism*, Mansell Press, 1992.

Johnson, R. *The Green City*, Macmillan, Australia, 1979.

Johnson, S. *Emergence: The Connected Lives of Ants, Brains, Cities and Software*, Penguin, 2001.

Johnson, T. *Professions and Power*, Macmillan, 1972.

Jones, W. W. and Natalie Macris. *A Career Worth Planning*, APA Planners Press, 2000.

Jung, C. G. *Psychological Types*. Re-expression of *Psychologische Typen* undertaken by R. G. C. Hull, Princeton University Press, 1976.

Kaplan, R. D. *An Empire Wilderness*, Random House, 1998.

Katz, B. (ed.). *Reflections on Regionalism*, Brookings Institute Press, 2000.

Katz, P. *The New Urbanism*, McGraw-Hill, 1994.

Kaufman, J. 'Reflections on Teaching Three Versions of a Planning Ethics Course', *Journal of Planning Education and Research*, 12 (2), 1993.

Keeble, L. *Principles and Practice of Town and Country Planning*, The Estates Gazette 1969: first published 1952.

Keller, A. G. 'Introduction' to *The Challenge of Facts and Other Essays*, AMS Press, 1971.

Kelly, G. C. 'Landscape and Nature Conservation', in *Land Alone Endures* (compiled by L. F. Molley) DSIR, Wellington, 1980.

Kelly, K. *Out of Control: The Biology of New Machines, Social Systems and the Economic World*, Addison-Wesley, 1994.

Kelman, S. 'Cost-Benefit Analysis: An Ethical Critique', *Regulation*, the United States Journal on Government and Society, February 1981.

Kelsey, J. *Rolling Back The State: Privatisation of Power*, Bridget Williams Books, 1993.

Kemeny, J. *The Myth of Home Ownership: Private versus Public Choices in Housing Tenure*, Routledge and Kegan Paul, 1989.

Kendig, L. with S. Connor, C. Byrd and J. Heyman. *Performance Zoning*, American Planning Association, Planning Press, 1980.

Kennan, G. F. *Around the Cragged Hill: A Personal and Political Philosophy*, Norton, 1993.

Keyfitz, N. 'World Resources and the Middle Class', *Scientific American*, July 1976.

Keynes, J. M. 'Economic Possibilities for Our Grand children' written in 1930: presented in *The Collected Writings of J. M. Keynes*, Macmillan, 1971.

Keynes, J. M. 'National Self Sufficiency', *The Yale Review*, 1983.

Kilmartin, L. and D. C. Thorns. *Cities Unlimited*, Allen and Unwin, 1978.

King, A. D. *The Bungalow: Production of a Global Culture*, Routledge and Kegan Paul, 1984.

Klosterman, R. E. 'Arguments for and Against Planning', *Town Planning Review*, 56 (1), 1985.

Klarqvist, B. 'The Neighbourhood Unit: A Social Mould?' Department of Urban Design and Planning, Chalmers University, Sweden (mimeographed Occasional Paper), 1991.

Knaap, G. 'State Land Use Planning and Inclusionary Zoning', *Journal of Planning Education and Research*, 10 (1), 1990.

Knox, P. and J. Cullen. 'Planners as Urban Managers: An Exploration of the Attitudes and Self Image of Senior British Planners', *Environment and Planning A*, 13, Pion Press, 1981.

Kolodny, A. *The Lay of the Land: Metaphor as Experience and History in American Life and Letters*, Chapel Hill Press, 1975.

Kondracke, M. 'Neo-politics', *The New Republic*, November 1991.

Kopp, R. J. 'The Role of Natural Assets in Economic Development', *Resources for the Future*, 106, 1992.

Kornai, J. 'Appraisal of Project Appraisal', *Academic Press*, 1979.

Korten, D. C. *When Corporations Rule the World*, Earthscan, 1995.

Korten, D. C. *The Post-Corporate World*, Berrett-Koehler, 2000.

Kostof, S. *The City Shaped*, Thames and Hudson, 1991.

Kostof, S. *The City Assembled*, Thames and Hudson, 1992.

Kreditor, A. 'The Neglect of Urban Design in the American Academic Succession', *Journal of Planning Education and Reseaarch*, 9 (3), 1990.

Krieger, A. (ed.). 'Since [and Before] Seaside', in *Towns and Town Making Principles* (author Andreas Duany), Rizzoli Press, New York, 1992.

Krieger, M. H. 'Courage and Character in Planning', *Journal of Planning Education and Research*, 7 (3), Spring 1988.

Krier, L. 'Tradition-Modernity-Modernism: Some Necessary Explanations', *Architectural Design Profile*, London, 1987.

Krier, R. *Urban Space*, Academy Volts, 1979.

Krippendorf, F. 'Toward New Tourism Policies', *Tourism Management*, 3 (3), 1982.

Kropotkin, P. *Fields Factories and Workshops Tomorrow*, Freedom Press, 1985 (first published 1889).

Krueckeberg, D. A. 'The Difficult Character of Property: To Whom Do Things Belong', *American Planning Association Journal*, Summer, 1995.

Kuenstler, P. 'Local Employment Initiatives in Western Europe', in *Bringing Jobs to People*, ILO Geneva, 1988.

Kulash, W. M. *Residential Streets*, Urban Land Institute, 2001.

Kunstler, J. H. *The Geography of Nowhere: The Rise and Decline of America's Man-made Landscape*, Simon and Schuster, 1993.

Kuik, O. and H. Verbruggen. *In Search of Indicators of Sustainable Development*, Kluwer, 1992.

Landes, D. 'Rich Country, Poor Country', *The New Republic*, 20 November 1989.

Lang, T. and Colin Hines. *The New Protectionism: Protecting the Future Against Free Trade*, Earthscan Publications, 1993.

Langdon, P. *A Better Place to Live: Reshaping the American Suburb*, Harper, 1995.

Lash, H. *Planning in a Human Way*, Macmillan, 1976.

Le Breton, P. P. and D. A. Henning. *Planning Theory*, New Jersey, Prentice-Hall, 1961.

LeGates, R. T. and Frederic Stout. *The City Reader*, Routledge, 1996.

Lennard, S. and H. Lennard. *Livable Cities*, Gondolier Press, 1987.

Leong, K. C. 'Partnerships in Sustainable Development', Keynote Address on *Community Participation*, 15th EAROPH World Planning Congress, 1996.

Leontieff, W. W. *Input-Output Economics*, 1966.

Leopold, A. *A Sand County Almanac*, Oxford University Press, 1966 (New York, Ballantine Books, 1949).

Levy, J. M. *Economic Development Programs for Cities, Counties and Towns*, Praeger (2nd Edition) 1990.

Lewis, S. *Main Street*, 1920 (Dover 1999).

Lim, E. *The Economic Impact of Tourism in New Zealand*, New Zealand Tourism Department, 1991.

Lindblom, C. E. 'The Science of Muddling Through', *Public Administration Review*, 19 (2), 1959.

Lines, W. J. *Taming the Great South Land: A History of the Conquest of Nature in Australia*, Allen and Unwin, Sydney 1991.

Little, I. M. D. and J. A. Mirrlees. *Manual of Industrial Project Analysis for Developing Countries*, OECD Development Centre, Paris, 1968.

Locke, J. (first published 1690). *Two Treatises of Government* (ed. P. Laslett) Cambridge University Press, 1970.

Lomberg, B. *The Skeptical Environmentalist*, Cambridge University Press, 2001.

Lorenz, E. M. 'Climate Change as a Mathematical Problem', *Journal of Applied Meteorolgy*. Vol. 9, 1970.

Losch, A. *The Economics of Locations* (translation), New Haven, Yale University Press, 1954.

Lovins, B. *Soft Energy Paths*, Ballinger, NY, 1977.

Low, N. P. *Planning, Politics and the State: Political Foundations of Planning Thought*, Unwin Hyman, 1991.

Lucas, P. H. C. *Conserving New Zealand's Heritage*, Government Printer, 1970.

Lucy, W. 'APAs Ethical Principles Include Simplistic Planning Theories', *American Planning Association Journal*, Spring 1988.

Lutz, M. A. and K. Lux, *Humanistic Economics*, The Bootstrap Press, 1988.

Lynch, K. *The Image of the City*, Harvard University Press, 1960.

Lynch, K. *City Sense and City Design*, MIT Press, 1970.

Lynch, K. *Good City Form*, MIT Press, 1981.

Mabo (1992 legal judgement). *Mabo and Ors v State of Queensland*, 175 CLR1; 107 ALR1, 1992.

McAuslan, P. *The Ideologies of Planning Law*, Pergamon Press, 1980.

McCamant, K. and C. Durrett. *Co-housing: A Contemporary Approach to Housing Ourselves*, Habitat Press, 1994.

MaCauley, M. K. and Karen L. Palmer. 'Incentive-Based Approaches to Regulating Toxic Substances', *Resources for the Future*, 107, 1992.

McCreary, S. and J. Gamman. 'Finding Solutions to Disputes', *Planning Quarterly*, December 1990.

MacDonald, H. I. 'A Retrospective View from the Top', *Plan Canada* No 24 (3/4), December 1984.

McGill, D. *Ghost Towns in New Zealand*, Reed, 1980.

McHarg, I. L. *Design with Nature*, New York, Doubleday, 1971.

MacKinder, H. J. 'On the Scope and Methods of Geography', *Proceedings of the Royal Geographical Society*, London, March, 1887.

Maclaren, J. P. *Radiata Pine Growers' Manual*, New Zealand Forest Research Institute, 1993.

McLouglin, J. B. *Urban and Regional Planning: A Systems Approach*, London, Faber and Faber, 1969.

McLouglin, J. B. *Shaping Melbourne's Future*, Cambridge Press, 1992.

McLoughlin, J. B. and M. Huxley (eds). *Urban Planning in Australia*, Longman, Melbourne, 1986.

Maillat, D. 'Mobility Channels: An Instrument for Analysing and Regulating the Local Labour Market', in *Bringing Jobs To People*, ILO Geneva, 1988.

Malthus, T. R. (first published 1798, Johnson, London). *An Essay on the Principle of Population*, Everyman's Library, 1914.

Mannheim, K. *Ideology and Utopia*, New York, Harcourt-Brace, 1949 (originally 1929).

Mansson, T. *Ecocycles: The Basis of Sustainable Urban Development*, Environmental Advisory Council, Stockholm, 1992.

Mantell, M. A., with S. F. Harper and L. Propst. *Creating Successful Communities*, Island Press, 1990.

Marais, J. S. *The Colonisation of New Zealand*, London, Dawsons 1968. (First published 1927).

Marcus, C. C. *People Places: Design Guidelines for Urban Space*, Reinhold, 1990.

Marcuse, P. 'Professional Ethics and Beyond', *Journal of the American Institute of Planners*, 42 (3), 1976.

Markandya, A. with Julie Richardson (eds). *Environmental Economics*, Earthscan, 1992.

Marsden, K. 'Creating the Right Environment for Small Firms'. *Finance and Development*, 18 (4), 1981.

Marsh, J. L. (ed.) with J. D. Caputo and M. Westphal. *Modernity and its Discontents*, Fordham University Press, 1992.

Marsh, G. P. *Man and Nature*, 1864. Reprinted by Harvard University Press, 1965.

Martin, B. and S. Mason. 'The Future for Atractions', in *Tourism Management*, Butterworth-Heinemann, 1993.

Martin, J. E. *People Politics and Power Stations*, Bridget Williams Books, 1991.

Marx, K. (first published 1867). *Capital*, vol. I, Penguin, 1976.

Maslow, A. H. *Toward a Psychology of Being*, New York, Reinhold, 1968.

Masnick, G. and M. J. Bane. *The Nation's Families: 1960–1990*, MIT and Harvard Press, 1980.

Mathieson, A. and Geoffrey Wall. *Tourism: Economic Physical and Social Impacts*, Longman, 1982.

Mattera, P. *Off the Books: The Rise of the Underground Economy*, Pluto Press, 1985.

Mayall, W. H. *Principles in Design*, Van Nostrand Reinhold, 1979.

Mayer, J. 'Theories and Practices of Regional Employment Development', published by the ILO in *Bringing Jobs To People*, ILO Geneva, 1988.

Mayo, E. *The Human Problems of an Industrialised Civilisation*, Macmillan, 1933.

Meadows, D. H. with D. L. Meadows, J. Randers and W. W. Behrens. *The Limits to Growth*, London, Earth Island, 1972.

Meadows, and others. *Beyond the Limits*, Earthscan, 1992.

Meck S. (ed.). *Growing Smart: Legislative Guidebook* (Loose-leaf and CD-ROM), American Planning Association, 2002.

Medlik, S. *Dictionary of Travel Tourism and Hospitality*, Butterworth-Heinemann 2002.

Meeker-Lowry, S. *Economics as If the Earth Really Mattered*, New Society Publishers, 1988.

Meier, R. L. *Ecological Planning and Design: Paths to Sustainable Communities*, Centre for Environmental Design, Berkeley, 1993.

Memon, P. A., and H. C. Perkins, *Environmental Planning in New Zealand*, Dunmore Press, 1993.

Meltz, R. with D. H. Merriam, and R. M. Frank. *The Takings Issue*, Island Press, 1999.

Merwick, D. *Possessing Albany 1630–1710: The Dutch and English Experiences*, Cambridge University Press, 1990.

Meyer, A. 'The Evolution of Global Climate Change', in *All of Us: Environmental Education Dossiers* 2, Unesco, 1993.

Micklethwait, J. with Adrian Wooldridge. *A Future Perfect*, Heinemann, 2000.

Mill, J. S. (original 1840). Essay on 'Coleridge' quoted in *Collected Works of John Stuart Mill; Essays on Ethics, Religion and Society* (ed. J. M. Robson), University of Toronto Press, 1969.

Mill, J. S. (original 1859). *Utilitarianism* (ed. Mary Warnock), New American Library Press, 1974.

Milroy, B. M. 'Into Postmodern Weightlessness', *Journal of Planning Education and Research*, 10 (3), 1991.

Ministry for Planning and Environment (Victoria). *Planning Guide for Urban Open Space*, 1989.

Mintzberg, H. *The Rise and Fall of Strategic Planning*, Free Press, 1994.

Mishan, E. J. *The Economic Growth Debate*, London, Allen and Unwin, 1976.

Mishan, E. J. *Cost-Benefit Analysis*, George Allen and Unwin, 1971.

Mollison, B. *Permaculture: A Designers' Manual*, Tyalgum Press, Australia, 1988.

Moore, T. with Paul Thorsnes. *The Transportation Land-Use Connection*, 1994.

Moorhead, A. *Darwin and the Beagle*, Hamish Hamilton, 1969.

Moriarty, P. and C. Beed, 'Reducing Vehicular Travel Need Through Increasing Travel Efficiency', *Urban Policy and Research*, 7 (4), Melbourne, Oxford University Press, 1989.

Morris, M. *Incentive Zoning*, PAS, 2000.

Morton, J. with D. Thom and R. Locker. *Seacoast in the Seventies: The Future of the New Zealand Shoreline*, Hodder and Stoughton, 1973.

Moseley, M. *Growth Centres in Spatial Planning*, Pergamon, 1974.

Moskowitz, H. S. and C. G. Lindbloom. *Development Definitions* (Illustrated), Centre for Urban Policy Research, 1992.

Moughtin, C. with Rafael Cuesta, Chritine Sarris and Paola Signoretta. *Urban Design: Method and Techniques*, Oxford, Architectural Press 1999.

Mumford, L. *Technics and Civilization*, New York, Harcourt Brace 1934.

Mumford, L. *The Culture of Cities*, New York, Harcourt, 1938.

Mumford, L. *The City In History*, Secker and Warburg, 1961.

Myers, D. (Chairman) et al. 'Anchor Points for Planning's Identification', *Journal of Planning Education and Research*, Spring 1997.

Myerson, G. and Yvonne Rydin. *The Language of Environment: A New Rhetoric*, UCL Press, 1996.

National Trust Of Australia [NSW]. *The Conservation Plan*, The National Trust of Australia, 1985.

Nelson, A. C. and K. J. Dueker. 'The Exurbanisation of America and Its Planning Implications', *Journal of Planning Education and Research*, 9 (2), 1990.

Nelson, A. C. with J. B. Duncan, C. J. Mullin and K. R. Bishop. *Growth Management Principles and Practices*, APA Planners Press, 1995.

Nelson, N. and S. Wright. *Power and Participatory Development: Theory and Practice*, Intermediate Technology Publications, 1995.

Newman, O. *Defensible Space*, Macmillan, 1972.

Newman, P. W. G. and J. R. Kenworthy. *Cities and Automobile Dependence*, Gower, 1989.

Newman, P. W. G. and J. R. Kenworthy. *Winning Back the Cities*, Australian Consumers Association, 1992.

Newman, P. W. G. and J. R. Kenworthy. *Sustainability and Cities*, Island Press, 1999.

Nile, R. (ed.). *Australian Civilisation*, Oxford University Press, 1994.

Norgaard, R. B. *Development Betrayed; The End of Progress and a Coevolutionary Revisioning of the Future*, Routledge, 1994.

Nozick, R. *Anarchy, State and Utopia*, Basic Books, 1974.

Odum, E. *Fundamentals of Ecology*, Saunders Press (2nd edition), 1959.

Odum, H. T. and E. C. Odum. *Energy Basis for Man and Nature*, New York, McGraw-Hill, 1976.

OECD. *The Polluter Pays Principle*, Paris, OECD, 1975.

Oldenberg, R. *The Great Good Place*, Paragon Press, 1989.

Oliver, W. H. 'Social Policy in New Zealand: An Overview', Introductory essay in volume I of the *Royal Commission on Social Policy*, Government Printer, 1988.

Orloff, N. *The Environmental Impact Assessment Process*, Information Resources Press, Washington, 1988.

O'Riordan, T. *Environmentalism*, London, Pion, 1976.

O'Riordan, T. (ed.). *Environmental Science for Environmental Management*, Longman, 1995.

O'Riordan, T. and W. Sewell. *Project Appraisal and Policy Review*, Wiley 1991.

Osborn, A. *Applied Imagination*, Scribner, 1954.

Otway, H. J. and M. Fishbein. *The Determinants of Attitude Formation*, International Institute for Applied Systems Analysis, Austria, 1976.

Owens, S. *Energy, Planning and Urban Form*, Pion, 1986.

Owens, S. 'Viewpoint – The Good the Bad and the Ugly; Dilemmas in Planning For Sustainability', *Town Planning Review*, 64 (2), 1993.

Pearson, D. *The Natural House Book*, Conran-Octopus, 1989.

Peattie, L. 'Anthropology and Planning', *Journal of Planning Education and Research*, 9 (2), 1990.

Perraton, J. 'Evaluation as part of the Planning Process', *Land Use and Built Form Studies*, 33, Department of Architecture, University of Cambridge, 1972.

Perroux, F. 'Economic Space, Theory and Applications', *Quarterly Journal of Economics*, 64, 1950.

Perry, C. A. 'Neighbourhood and Community Planning' in *Regional Survey of New York and Environs*, vol. 7, New York, 1929.

Perry, R. B. *Realms of Value*, Harvard University Press, 1954.

Petts, J. *Environmental Impact Assessment for Waste Disposal Facilities*, Wiley, 1994.

Pirog, R. and S. Stamos. *Energy Economics: Theory Policy*, Prentice Hall, 1987.

Pliscke, E. A. *Design and Living*, NZ Government Printer, 1947.

Polanyi, K. *The Great Transformation*, Beacon Press, 1957.

Ponting, C. *A Green History of the World*, Sinclair-Stevenson, 1991.

Popper, Sir Karl. *Conjectures and Reputations: The Growth of Scientific Knowledge*, Routledge and Kegan Paul, 1963.

Popper, Sir Karl (original 1945). *The Open Society and Its Enemies*, 2 vols, Routledge and Kegan Paul, 1974.

Popper, Sir Karl. *Objective Knowledge: An Evolutionary Approach*, Clarendon Press, 1975.

Porritt, J. *Playing Safe: Science and the Environment*, Thames and Hudson, 2000.

Porter, B. *The Lion's Share: A Short History of British Imperialism*, Longman, 1996.

Porter, D. R. with Patrick Phillips and Terry Lassar. *Flexible Zoning: How It Works*, Urban Land Institute, 1991.

Porter, M. *The Competitive Advantage of Nations*, The Free Press, 1990.

Porterfield, G. A. and K. B. Hall. *A Concise Guide to Community Planning*, McGraw-Hill, 1994.

Pritchard, M. F. L. (ed.). *The Collected Works of Edward Gibbon Wakefield*, Collins, 1968.

Putnam, R. D. *Bowling Alone: The Collapse and Revival of American Community*, Simon and Schuster, 2000.

Queensland Regional Planning Advisory Group. *Creating our Future*, Local Government Planning Services, Brisbane, 1993.

Rabinovitz, F. F. *City Politics and Planning*, Atherton Press, New York, 1969.

Rader, C. 'A Primer on Permit Conditioning', in *Coastal Zone '87*, Report of the 5th Symposium on Coastal and Ocean Management, vol. 4, Published ASCE, 1987.

Rainbow, S. *Green Politics*, Oxford University Press, 1993.

Rapoport, A. *History and Precedent in Environmental Design*, Plenum Press, 1990.

Rawls, J. *Theory of Justice*, Cambridge, Mass., Harvard University Press, 1971.

Reade, E. 'An analysis of the use of the concept of rationality in the literature of planning', in *Rationality in Planning* ed. M. Breheny and A. Hooper, Pion, 1985.

Reade, E. *British Town and Country Planning*, Open University Press, 1987.

Redclift, M. *Sustainable Development; Exploring the Contradictions*, Methuen, London, 1987.

Redclift, M. *Strategies for Sustainable Development*, Wiley, 1994.

Register, R. *Ecocity Berkley*, North Atlantic Books, 1987.

Reilly, J. W. *The Language of Real Estate*, Real Estate Education Coy., 1982.

Reps, J. W. *The Making of Urban America*, Princeton University Press, 1965.

Rexroth, K. *Communalism: From Its Origins to the Twentieth Century*, New York, Seabury Press, 1974.

Richardson, H. W. *The Economics of Urban Size*, London, Saxon House, 1973.

Richardson, J. *Partnerships in Communities*, Island Press, 2000.

Richardson, N. H. 'The Rise and Fall of Provincial Planning in Ontario', *Canadian Public Administration*, Winter 1981.

Richter, L. 'Manpower and Employment Information Through Key Informants', in *Bringing Jobs To People*, ILO Geneva, 1988.

Riddell, R. B. *Ecodevelopment: Economics, Ecology and Development*, London, Gower Press, and New York, St Martins Press, 1981.

Riddell, R. B. *Regional Development Policy: The Struggle for Rural Progress in Low Income Nations*, London, Gower and St Martins, 1985.

Riddell, R. B. 'Development and Conservation: The Call for Regional Brokerage', *People and Planning*, 1987.

Riddell, R. B. 'Planning's Moral and Ethical Basis', *Planning Quarterly*, March 1994.

Rio Declaration. *Agenda 21*, United Nations Conference on Environment and Development, 1992.

Rittel, H. W. J. and M. W. Webber. 'Dilemmas in a General Theory of Planning', *Policy Sciences*, 4, 1973.

Ritzdorf, M. 'Feminist Thoughts on the Theory and Practice of Planning', in Campbell and Fainstein (eds), *Readings in Planning Theory*, Blackwell, 1996.

Robertson, J. *The Sane Alternative*, Villiers Publications, 1978.

Robinson, J. with G. Francis, R. Legge and S. Lerner. 'Defining a Sustainable Society', *Alternatives: Perspectives on Society Technology and Environment*, 17 (2), 1990.

Rogers, Lord. *Report of the Urban Task Force*, Department of the Environment-Spon, 1999.

Rogers, Lord. 'England sold out to Poundbury' *Observer*, 21 May 2000.

Rondinelli, D. A. *Development Projects as Policy Experiments*, Routledge, 1993.

Rondinelli, D. A. and K. Ruddle. *Urbanization and Rural Development: A Spatial Policy for Equitable Growth*, Praeger, 1978.

Roseland, M. with M. Cureton and H. Wornell. *Toward Sustainable Communities*, New Society Publishers, 1998.

Ross, H. with E. Young and L. Liddle. 'Mabo: An Inspiration For Australian Land Management', *Australian Journal of Environmental Management*, 1, 1994.

Rostow, W. W. *The Stages of Economic Growth: A Non-Communist Manifesto*, Cambridge University Press (first published 1960), 1973.

Rotenberg, R. and G. McDonogh (eds). *The Cultural Meaning of Urban Space*, Bergin and Garvey, 1993.

Rothblatt, D. N. 'Rational Planning Re-Examined', *Journal of the American Institute of Planners*, 37 (1), 1971.

Rousseau, J. J. (first published 1762). *The Social Contract*, Dent, 1973.

Rowe, P. G. *Making a Middle Landscape*, MIT Press, 1991.

Royal Commission on Social Policy. Vol. I: *New Zealand Today*, vols 2 and 3: *Future Directions*, vol. 4: *Social Perspectives*, Government Printer, Wellington, 1988.

Rutherford, A. *Popular Places: Australian Cities and Towns*, Dungaroo Press, 1992.

Rybczynski, W. *City Life: Urban Expectations in a New World*, Scribner, 1995.

Rydin, Y. 'Environmental Dimensions of Residential Development', *Journal of Environmental Planning and Management*, 35 (1), 1992.

Sale, K. *Rebels Against the Future*, Quartet Books, 1996.

Sale, K. 'The Democratic Essential', *Fourth World Review*, 88, 1998.

Sandel, M. J. *Liberalism and the Limits of Justice*, Cambridge University Press, 1982.

Sanders, W. 'The Cluster Subdivision – A Cost Effective Approach', *Journal of the American Planning Association*, 1950.

Santayana, G. *The Life of Reason: The Phases of Human Progress*, Collier, 1962.

Satterthwaite, D. *Sustainable Cities*, Earthscan 1999.

Saul, J. R. *The Unconscious Civilization*, Penguin, 1997.

Saul, J. R. *On Equilibrium*, Penguin, 2002.

Sauvré, L. 'Environmental Education', *Connect*, 27 (1), 2002.

Schaeffer, K. *Women and the Bush: Forces of Desire in the Australian Cultural Tradition*, Cambridge University Press, 1988.

Schama, S. *Landscape and Memory*, Knopf, New York, 1995.

Schon, D. *The Reflective Practitioner: How Professionals Think in Action*, Basic Books, 1983.

Schleuning, N. *The Meaning of Ownership in the United States*, Praeger, 1997.

Schneekloth, L. H. and Robert Shibley. *Placemaking: The Art and Practice of Building Communities*, Wiley, 1995.

Schumacher, E. G. *Small is Beautiful: A Study of Economics as if People Mattered*, Abacus, 1974.

Schumpeter, J. *History of Economic Analysis*, Oxford University Press, 1954.

Scott, M. F. G. with J. D. M. MacArthur and D. M. G. Newbery. *Project Appraisal in Practice*, Heinemann, 1976.

Scruton, R. *Thinkers of the New Left*, Longman, 1985.

Seager, J. *Earth Follies*, Routledge, 1993.

Seaton, A. V. and others (eds). *Tourism: The State of the Art*, Wiley, 1994.

Sen, A. *Poverty and Families*, London, Oxford University Press, 1981.

Sennett, R. 'Something in the City', *Times Literary Supplement*, 23 September 1995.

Sennett, R. *The Corrosion of Character: The Personal Consequences of Work in the New Capitalism*, Norton, 1998.

Service, E. R. *Origins of the State and Civilisation*, Norton, 1975.

Sewell, J. 'Between Heaven and Hell: Planning New Communities', *The Canadian Architect*, March 1995.

Sharp, M. *The State, The Enterprise and The Individual*, Weidenfeld and Nicolson, 1973.

Sheldrake, R. *The Presence of the Past*, Collins, 1988.

Shirley, I. *Planning for Community*, Dunmore Press, 1979.

Short, J. R. *The Humane City: Cities as if People Mattered*, Blackwell, 1989.

Silverstone, R. (ed.). *Visions of Suburbia*, Routledge, 1997.

Simmons, I. G. *The Ecology of Natural Resources*, London, Edward Arnold, 1981 (first published 1974).

Simpson, B. T. and M. T. Purdy. *Housing on Sloping Sites: A Design Guide*, Construction Press, 1984.

Simpson, S. R. *Land Law and Registration*, Cambridge University Press, 1976.

Sinclair, Sir Keith. *A History of New Zealand*, (first published 1959 by Penguin Books), Pelican Edition, 1988.

Slovic, P. 'Perception of Risk', *Science*, 236, April 1987.

Smart, B. *Postmodernity*, Routledge, 1993.

Smart, J. J. C. *A System of Utilitarian Ethics*, University of Melbourne Press, 1972.

Smith, A. *An Inquiry Into the Nature and Causes of the Wealth of Nations* (1776), Dent, 1910.

Smith, R. A. 'Beach Resort Evolution', *Annals of Tourism Research*, 1992.

So, F. S. *The Practice of State and Regional Planning*, American Planning Association, 1986.

Soja, E. W. *Postmetropolis: Critical Studies of Cities and Regions*, Blackwell, 2000.

Solnit, A. with C. Reed, P. Glassford and D. Erley. *The Job of the Practicing Planner*, Planners Press, Chicago, 1988.

Sorensen, A. D. and M. L. Auster. 'Fatal Remedies: The Source of Ineffectiveness in Planning', *Town Planning Review*, 60 (1), 1989.

Soros, G. 'The Capitalist Threat', *The Atlantic Monthly*, February 1997.

Spain, D. *Gendered Species*, University of Illinois Press, 1992.

Stanbek, T. and others. *Suburbanisation and the City*, Osmun Press, 1976.

Steele, F. *The Sense of Place*, CBI Publishing House, Boston, 1981.

Stein, C. S. *New Towns for America*, New York, 1951.

Stein, J. M. (ed.). *Growth Management: The Planning Challenge of the 1990s*, Sage Publications, 1993.

Steinhart, J. S. and others. *Pathway to Energy Efficiency: the 2050 Study*, Friends of the Earth Publishing, 1979.

Stern, R. with John Massengale. *The Anglo American Suburb*, Arch. Design Press, 1981.

Stewart, D. with L. Drew and M. Wexler. 'How Conservation Grew from a Whisper to a Roar' *National Wildlife*, Dec.–Jan. 1999.

Stewart, F. *Technology and Underdevelopment*, London, Macmillan, 1978.

Stewart, J. D. *The Dilemma of Central-Local Relations*, Denman Lecture, Land Economy, University of Cambridge, 1981.

Stohr, W. 'Regional Planning at the Crossroads: An Overview' in *Regional Planning at the Crossroads* (ed. L. Albrechts), Jessica Kingsley, 1989.

Stokes, S. and others. *Saving America's Countryside – A Guide to Rural Conservation*, John Hopkins University Press, 1989.

Stokowski, P. A. *Leisure in Society*, Mansell Press, 1994.

Strahler, A. M. and A. H. Strahler. *Environmental Geoscience*, Santa Barbara, Hamilton, 1973.

Strasser, S. *Waste and Want: A Social History of Trash*, Metropolitan, 1999.

Stretton, H. *Ideas for Australian Cities*, published by Transit Australia, Sydney 1989: first published 1973.

Stretton, H. *Urban Planning in Rich and Poor Countries*, Oxford University Press, 1978.

Sucher, D. *City Comforts*, City Comforts Press (4th Printing), 1995.

Sudjic, D. *The 100 Mile City*, Flamingo Press, 1992.

Susskind, L. and J. Cruikshank. *Breaking the Impasse: Consensual Approaches to Resolving Public Disputes*, Basic Books, 1987.

Susskind, L. and P. Field. *Dealing with an Angry Public*, Free Press, 1996.

Susskind, L. with P. F. Levy and J. Thomas-Larmer. *Negotiating Environmental Agreements: How to Avoid Escalating Confrontation*, Island Press, 2000.

Susskind, L. with S. McKearnan and J. Thomas-Larmer (eds). *The Consensus Building Handbook: A Comprehensive Guide to Reaching Agreement*, Sage, 1999.

Sutherland, K. *Inquiry into the Nature and Causes of the Wealth of Nations; A Selected Edition*, Oxford University Press, 1998.

Suzuki, D. with Amanda McConnell. *Sacred Balance: Discovering Our Place in Nature*, Allen and Unwin, 1997.

Suzuki, D. with Holly Dressel. *Good News for a Change*, Allen and Unwin, 2001.

Swinburne Centre for Urban and Social Research (Victoria: together with Sarkissan Associates). *Medium Density Housing*, 1990.

Tanghe, J. with S. Vlaeminck and J. Berghoef. *Living Cities: A Case for Urbanism and Guidelines for Re-Urbanisation*, Pergamon Press, Oxford, 1984.

Taylor, N. *The Village in the City*, Maurice Temple Smith, London, 1973.

Tett, A. and J. M. Wolfe. 'Discourse Analysis and City Plans', *Journal of Planning Education and Research*, 10 (3), 1991.

Thayer, R. L. *Grey World Green Heart: Technology Nature and Sustainable Landscape*, Wiley, 1994.

Therivel, R. and others. *Strategic Environmental Assessment*, Earthscan, 1995.

Thomas, A. and C. Logan. *Mondragon: an Economic Analysis*, Allen and Unwin, 1982.

Thomas, H. and P. Healey. *Dilemmas of Planning Practice: Ethics, Legitimacy, and the Validation of Knowledge*, Gower, 1991.

Thompson-Fawcett, M. 'The Urbanist Revision of Development', *Urban Design International*, 1 (4), 1996.

Thomson, D. *Selfish Generations: The Ageing of New Zealand's Welfare State*, Williams Books, 1991.

Thorns, D. C. *Suburbia*, Paladin, Great Britain, 1972.

Thurow, L. *The Zero Sum Solution*, Basic Books, 1980.

Tibbalds, F. *Making People-Friendly Towns*, Longman, 1992.

Toman, M. A. 'The Difficulty in Defining Sustainability', in *Resources for the Future*, 106, 1992.

Toynbee, A. *A Study of History*, New York, 1972.

Troy, P. N. (ed.). *Australian Cities*, Cambridge University Press, 1995.

Troy P. N. *Perils of Urban Consolidation: A Discussion of Australian Housing and Urban Development Policies*, Federation Press, 1996.

Troy, P. N. (ed.). *Equity Environment Efficiency* Melbourne University Press, 2000.

Udy, J. 'The Planner: A Comprehensive Typology', *Cities*, 11 (1), Butterworth-Heinemann, 1994.

Udy, J. *Typology of Urban and Regional Planners*, Edmund Mellon Press, 1991.

United Nations Conference on Environment and Development. *Agenda 21: The Rio Declaration*, 1992.

United Nations Environment Programme. *Environmental Codes of Conduct for Tourism* (Technical Report No. 29), 1995.

United Nations Environment Programme and United Nations Centre for Human Settlement. *Environmental Guidelines for Settlement Planning and Management*, Vols. 1, 2, and 3, UNEP and UNCHS 1987.

United States Real Estate Research Corporation. *The Costs of Sprawl*, HUD and EPA, 1974.

Unwin, R. 'High Building in Relation to Town Planning', *Journal of the American Institute of Architecture*, March 1924.

Urban Land Institute. *Mixed Use Development Handbook*, Urban Land Institute, Washington, 1987.

Urban Land Institute (D. R. Porter, P. L. Phillips, T. L. Lasser). *Flexible Zoning*, Urban Land Institute, 1991.

Urmson, J. O. and Jonathon Rée. *The Concise Encyclopedia of Western Philosophy*, London, Unwin Hyman, 1989.

Urry, J. *The Tourist Gaze: Leisure and Travel in Contemporary Societies*, Sage Publications, 1990.

Vale, B. contributor Robert Vale. *Green Architecture: Design for a Sustainable Future*, Thames and Hudson, 1991.

Victorian Government. *Shaping Melbourne's Future*, Government Printer, 1987.

Visser, M. *The Way We Are*, HarperCollins, 1994.

Voase, R. *Tourism: The Human Perspective*, Hodder and Stoughton, 1995.

Wachs, M. (ed.). *Ethics in Planning*, Rutgers University Press, 1985.

Wackernagel, M. and W. Rees. *Our Ecological Footprint: Reducing Human Impact on the Earth*, New Society Publishers, 1996.

Walter, B. with Lois Arkin and Richard Grenshaw (eds). *Sustainable Cities*, Eco-Home Media, 1992.

Ward, C. 'Editor's Introduction' to *Peter Kropotkin's: Fields, Factories and Workshops Tomorrow*, Freedom Press, 1985 (Kropotkin 1889).

Waterston, A. *Development Planning: Lessons of Experience*, Baltimore, Johns Hopkins Press, 1969.

Weaver, D. *Ecotourism*, Wiley Publishing, 2002.

Weber, M. *The Theory of Social and Economic Organization* (ed. T. Parsons), The Free Press, 1947.

Weisberg, R. *Creativity: Beyond the Myth of Genius*, 1993.

Weisman, L. K. *Descrimination By Design: A Feminist Critique of the Man-Made Environment*, University of Illinois Press, 1992.

Weitz, J. *Sprawl Busting*, APA Planners Press, 1999.

Weitz, J. and T. Moore. 'Development Inside Urban Growth Boundaries', *Journal of the American Planning Association*, Autumn 1998.

Wekerle, G. R. with C. Whitzman. *Safe Cities; Guidelines for Planning Design and Management*, Reinhold, 1995.

Welmer, A. *The Persistence of Modernity*, MIT Press, 1991.

Wentling, J. and L. Bookout. *Density by Design*, Urban Land Institute, USA 1988.

Weston, R. *Modernism*, Phaidon Press, 1996.

Williams, M. 'Parkland Towns of Australia and New Zealand', *Geographical Review*, 1966.

Williams, W. T. *District Scheme Planning*, New Zealand Planning Institute, 1985.

Wolf, P. M. *Hot Towns: The Future of the Fastest Growing Communities in America*, Rutgers University Press, 1999.

Womack, J. with D. Jones. *Lean Thinking*, Simon and Schuster, 1996.

Wood, C. *Environmental Impact Assessment: A Comprehensive Review*, Longman, 1995.

World Commission on the Environment and Development. *Our Common Future*, Oxford University Press, 1987 (the 'Brundtland Report').

World Tourism Organisation. *Policy and Activities for Tourism and the Environment*, Madrid, 1989.

Worpole, K. with Liz Greenhalgh. *The Richness of Cities: Urban Policy in a New Landscape*, Comedia-Demos, 1999.

Wright, B. *Expectations of a Better World: Planning Australian Communities*, RAPI, 2001.

Yaro, R. D. 'Regional Contexts for Growth Management', in *Rural by Design* (Randall Arendt) Planners Press, USA, 1994.

Yeang, K. *Designing with Nature*, McGraw-Hill, 1995.

Yoon, Hong-Key. *Maori Mind: Maori Land*, Berne, Peter Lang, 1986.

Zelinka, A. and Dean Brennan. *SafeScape*, APA Planners Press, 2001.

Zuchin, S. *Landscapes of Power: From Detroit to Diseney World*, University of California Press, 1991.

Index

Note: Numbered figures and text boxes are indicated by page references in **bold** type; *italic* page references indicate the smaller side-bars.

and growth pattern management 186–7
and land banking **258**
large/small scale 83–4, *84*, 272
minimal (Nozickian) 66
and planning failure 41–2
regional, *see* regions
and social value 31
and sustainability 3, *9*, 10, 276
and tourism policies **179**
see also democracy; local government;
  participation
greenfield development 217, 225–7,
  228–33
greenhouse gases **99**, 267, 287 n. 27
growth, economic:
  basic-export sector 122–4, 125, **126**, 133,
    134, 142, 146, 168–9, 181
  and conservation 1–3, 8, 89
  definition 12
  and democracy 9–10
  equitable 37, 100
  future effects 88
  and globalization 82
  and 'hidden hand' 75, 78–9
  limits 91–6
  management 26
  and project propagation 133–9
  and radical planning 65, 67
  regional 1, 118–50
  residentiary (consumer-model) theory
    122–4, 125, **126**, 134, 142, 146
  and Smith's *Wealth of Nations* 74–6, 78
  and social value 31
  and sustainability 9, 11, 12–16, 40, 272,
    274
  and tourism 170, 172
  unsustainable *73*, 74, 89, 96–7
growth pattern management 13, 117–87
  agriculture and forestry 166–9, 215–16
  coastal zone 163–6, *164*, 221
  and information needs 124–33
    data assembly and raw data analysis
      55, **56**, **62**, 125–9, 138–9, 143
    linkage and pattern analyses 129–32
    rural-urban understandings 132–3
  macro practice patterns 124–5, 150–86
  and ownership and rights 151–6
  policy directions 186–7
  policy markers 118–20
  and project implementation 148–50

and project propagation 133–9
and risk assessment and management
  139–48
and tourism 169–81
and unemployment alleviation 135,
  181–3
urban-rural 156–63, 194, 214–17, 225
waste disposal management 183–6
see also multiplier mechanisms; urban
  growth management
Guha, R. 78
Guidelines:
  Betterment 137, 181
  Buttress 136–7, 181
  Discovery 137, 181
guilt, landscape *19, 24*

Haar, Charles and Kayden, Jerold 191–2
Habermas, Jürgen **27–8**, 32, 54, 63
Hardin, Garrett *86*, 171, 177
harmony with nature 45, 67, 116
Harper, Thomas, and Stein, Stanley **27–8**,
  61
Harvey, David *28*, 31, 40–1, *44*, *80*, *87*,
  101, *198*
Hawken, P., et al. *8*, 116, *183*, 193, 239,
  291 n. 16
Hayek, F. 79
Healey, P. 20, **27**, 40, 61
Healey, P., et al. *40*, 52, 64, *65*
hedonism **27**, 114, 150, 159, 185
Heilbroner, Robert *9*, *273*
Hendler, Sue 35
herbicides 101, **103**, 105, 154, 185, 200
Heywood, Phil *159*, *162*
Hillier, J. 33, 58–9
Himmelfarb, G. 286 n. 8
Hoch, Charles 285 n. 15
Hodge, Gerald, and Robinson, Ira *64*,
  118, *162*
Hofstee, E. W. 155, *155*
home ownership, and suburbia 193, 195,
  236
household 25, 30, *115*, 183, 189
  single 83, *115*, 262
housing:
  affordable 162, 225, **232**, 233, 238, 278
  apartment 235, 247
  co-housing 191, *230*, 231, 244, 249
  detached/ranch-style 191, 235, 243

*Index compiled by Meg Davies (Registered
Indexer, Society of Indexers)*